CUT OFF

Colonel Jedediah Huntington's 17th Continental (Connecticut) Regiment at the Battle of Long Island August 27, 1776

Charles H. Lewis

HERITAGE BOOKS
2009

HERITAGE BOOKS
AN IMPRINT OF HERITAGE BOOKS, INC.

Books, CDs, and more—Worldwide

For our listing of thousands of titles see our website
at
www.HeritageBooks.com

Published 2009 by
HERITAGE BOOKS, INC.
Publishing Division
100 Railroad Ave. #104
Westminster, Maryland 21157

Other books by the author:

*John Lewis of Berkshire, Vermont, and Other Descendants of
William Lewis (Who Came to Boston on the Ship "The Lion" in 1632)
through His Grandson James Lewis of Jamaica, Long Island*

International Standard Book Numbers
Paperbound: 978-0-7884-4924-6
Clothbound: 978-0-7884-8175-8

Dedication

To my wife, Margo, for not only tolerating this obsession, but for being an enthusiastic fellow sufferer.

Table of Contents

List of Illustrations..vii

Introduction ix

Acknowledgements.. xiii

1. Candles in a Box..1
2. Figures in Peace and Figures in War...........................17
3. The Black Facings 55
4. A Great Smoke and Show 75
5. Isolated and Cut Off 85
6. The Conduct of Infernal Spirits...............................123
7. Very Indifferent Quarters 137
8. Mansions of Despair..155
9. Hardship, Ill Usage, Hunger and Cold 191
10. Artful, Mean and Pitiful Pretences 213
11. Devoted Wholly, Lord, to Thee..............................223

Appendix 263

Bibliography 271

Index 283

Illustrations

Jedediah Huntington, Colonel, 17th Continental (Connecticut) Regiment of Foot, 1776 (from A Genealogical Memoir of the Huntington Family, *courtesy CT State Library)* i
Connecticut Towns 6
A soldier of the 17th Continental Regiment 68
The home of Simon Bergen 83
Map and Plan of the Battle of Long Island 87
Map of the Battlefield at Gowanus 93
Blockje's Bergh 96
View to the west from Battle Hill about 1850 102
View to the west from Battle Hill today 119
Battle Hill in Green-Wood Cemetery 119
View from Battle Hill in Green-Wood Cemetery 120
Altar to Liberty on the summit of Battle Hill 121
The capture of Captain Joseph Jewett 136
The Middle Dutch Church and Sugar House 190

Introduction

The following story came to light while trying to find records relating to a particularly illusive great-great-great-great-grandfather. His name was John Lewis, and some evidence was found to indicate that he had lived in eastern Connecticut during most of the mid to late seventeen-hundreds. Both the French and Indian War and the Revolutionary War occurred during that time period, and published collections of enlistment records are readily available for both of those conflicts. As it turns out, those collections included the name "John Lewis" on quite a few muster rolls for military companies raised in eastern Connecticut while my ancestor was in residence there.

One Revolutionary War record was particularly interesting: a John Lewis was reported among the 185 men missing in action from Colonel Jedediah Huntington's 17th Continental (Connecticut) Regiment after the Battle of Long Island. This action took place for the most part within the boundaries of present day Brooklyn, New York, on August 27, 1776. The men in Huntington's Regiment had been recruited primarily from eastern Connecticut, and "my" John Lewis was probably one of them. But, as I began to research the background of this regiment's service at the battle, I found some very intriguing circumstances. So intriguing in fact, that it wasn't long before curiosity got the best of me, and I promptly relegated the strictly genealogical work to a back burner.

At first the roll of the missing from Huntington's Regiment seemed to lead to a dead end. This lone piece of information clearly showed that the regiment fought at the Battle of Long Island and sustained very heavy losses there, but beyond that, I just couldn't find out much about the regiment. There was plenty of information in the many written histories of the battle about virtually every other American unit that fought in the Battle of Long Island, just not Huntington's Regiment. The number of casualties that were reported certainly indicated some sort of remarkable circumstances, but no published material could be found to explain what happened.

A host of questions came to mind. Why was Huntington's Regiment on Long Island in the first place? What role did they play in the Battle? Where were they on the battlefield? Did the roll of the missing mean those men were all killed, or were they taken prisoner? Considering the massive losses, why has no one in the last two centuries written about what happened to the regiment? More and more, it was looking like the regiment had marched off into oblivion on August 27, 1776.

Battle reports contained little snippets of information like: "The Action [on Long Island] was chiefly with the Troops from Jersey, Pennsylvania, the lower counties, and Maryland, and Col. Huntingdon's [sic] Regt.; they suffered greatly, being attacked and overpowred [sic] by numbers of the Enemy greatly superior to them."; or, "Huntington's regiment sustained a high character in the action on Long Island, and suffered a heavy loss there..."; and, "the general damage fell upon the Regiments from Pennsylvania, Delaware, and Maryland, and Col. Huntindon's [sic] of Connecticut."; and finally, "The principal loss has fallen on First Pennsylvania Battalion, Atlee, Smallwood, Huntington, and Haslett's; all of whom behaved so as to command the admiration of all those who beheld the engagement."

But, even though these glowing compliments have great emotional value, they still did not provide any more real information than was given in the roll of the missing. Were Huntington's men really a "lost regiment," or had evidence been ignored or overlooked that could clear up the mystery? Because of the unanswered questions, it became the first purpose of this book to fill in the empty places in the record of service of Huntington's 17th Continental Regiment at the Battle of Long Island. Since none of the written histories of the battle had proved very illuminating, it was going to be necessary to dig deeper to find what scattered primary records might have endured the centuries since the battle.

The Revolutionary War pension applications later submitted by survivors from Huntington's Regiment were among such needed primary sources. To begin with, the very fact of their existence happily proved that there were survivors of the events of 1776. Although they were written decades after the fact, some of those applications contained important information about the regiment that did not appear anywhere else. Digging deeper still, diaries, state and national archives, town histories, vital records, old family genealogies, and later military records provided clues, not only to what happened to the regiment as a whole, but important information about the soldiers who made up the regiment. This biographical material helped to develop a second purpose to this work.

And that purpose was to create something like a biographic encyclopedia of as many of the soldiers from Huntington's Regiment as were clearly identified during the course of the research on the regiment as a whole. Brief biographical sketches of those men have been included with as much information as was relevant and could enhance the story. It is probably not possible to identify every man that fought with the regiment, but those that appear here are a substantial representation. The intent was to make as many of the soldiers as possible become more than just names on a muster roll: we find they were farmers, tinsmiths, shopkeepers, rum merchants, sailors, and shoe makers; they were also men of faith, citizen activists, schoolmasters, militiamen, fathers, sons, and husbands. In their stories they further reveal themselves to have been common men, with a common great dream for a new nation free from tyranny, and the willingness to risk their lives to bring that dream to fruition.

The biographical sketches appear primarily in two places: in Chapter 2, to introduce the men who have left records that give us information about their lives prior to the Revolutionary War; and in the final chapter to follow the later lives of the survivors. There is also some biographical information provided in a few places through the body of the work, when that information relates to the history of the moment. Unfortunately, in a few cases no information could be found about some of the men whose names are introduced during the record of the regiment. It will be left to others to find if any evidence has been missed that might lead to a clear identification of those men. Perhaps the methods used here will help guide others to find their ancestors among the men of the regiment who have not yet been clearly identified. Wherever biographical information is introduced, it will be indicated on the left margin by the following symbol:

 with the soldier's name appearing afterwards in **Bold Type**.

It should shortly become clear to the reader why the fate of Huntington's 17th Continental Regiment has so far laid buried by history. Hopefully, the story that finally surfaces here will bring long overdue credit, honor, and an appropriate measure of glory to the regiment. However, a regiment is no better or worse than the men who compose it, and more than anything else, this will be their story. Higher ranking officers usually receive the credit for success at arms, but those of lesser rank, the lieutenants, ensigns, sergeants, corporals, and privates usually make the greater sacrifice. The officers have not been neglected here, but because they are usually overlooked and their contributions unheralded, I wanted to shine just as bright a light on the lives of the common soldiers. These men suffered terribly, not only during the Battle of Long Island, but from its horrific aftermath. When they survived the ordeal, there were often health consequences that affected them for the rest of their lives. But considering the fate of the majority of their regimental comrades-in-arms, these men probably would have considered themselves to be the lucky ones.

Acknowledgements

It is probably safe to say that this work would not have been possible without the online resources provided by the Connecticut State Library in conjunction with the Connecticut Department of Higher Education. Their cooperative effort provides an extraordinary search engine known as iCONN.org free to every Connecticut State resident with a library card. iCONN can be accessed, not only from the local library, but from any home computer in the state with internet access. This database contains literally millions of digital images of historical documents, magazine articles, historical newspapers, and other primary source materials. Under contract to iCONN, the ProQuest Company and its HeritageQuest database makes thousands of additional volumes of local histories, genealogies, Revolutionary War Pension Applications, Census Records, and other historical records available to Connecticut researchers through the same website. The vast majority of the genealogies, town histories, historical newspapers, and pension applications that have been used as references for this work came from this source.

Two other online sites have also been important resources. The American Memory database of the Library of Congress provides access to the approximately 65,000 digitized documents of the *George Washington Papers*. Most of the general orders and letters penned by Washington that are referenced here came from that database. Also, the National Archives and Records Administration in partnership with Footnote.com now provides access to digitized images of all of the pages of the Revolutionary War Pension Applications, Revolutionary War Rolls, and the Pennsylvania Archives, all of which have been important references.

Although access to online digital documents, has saved hundreds of hours of travel time and associated expenses, it has still been necessary to do much of the research in the field. The more-than-helpful staff and the enormous archives of the Connecticut State Historical Library in Hartford have been invaluable. Every historical research project involving Connecticut almost inevitably begins there. Richard C. Roberts and the staff of the History and Genealogy section of the library provided considerable assistance finding relevant material and illustrations in their collections.

Acknowledgements

Both the library and archives of the Connecticut Historical Society and the historical collections of the Pittsfield Massachusetts Athenaeum have also provided important information. And the Digital Gallery of The New York Public Library has permitted the use of two important illustrations that have been reprinted here.

I also want to thank Richard Alan Stowe, Ed.D, whom I have come to depend on for his enthusiastic support, sage advice and creative ideas with this and other projects. He has devoted an enormous amount of time to meticulous, line-by-line editing of this work. As I review each page I can see his input and imprint, and am greatly indebted to him for it.

In addition to tolerating the amount of time it has taken for me to complete this book, my wife, Margo, has also devoted many, many hours to further proof-reading. Where others had read and reread the material, she was still able to find errors that would have proved an embarrassment if they had made it into the final draft. I am very grateful for her participation and hard work.

It may be a bit unusual, but someone who has been dead for nearly two-hundred years deserves to be recognized for his contribution as well. I think that Lieutenant Jabez Fitch would be pleased that his diary, which was never published during his lifetime, had contributed so significantly to the story of his regiment. Fitch's diary, and that of Ensign Anthony Bradford, which has still not been published, provided key, on-the-spot, eyewitness testimony about what happened to Jedediah Huntington's 17th Continental (Connecticut) Regiment on Long Island in 1776. Without those two diaries, many of the men of the regiment would still have had no one to tell their stories.

1. Candles In a Box

The American Revolution was just sixteen months old when, on a sweltering hot Tuesday, August 27, 1776, a newly organized and still inexperienced American Army took on the full might of an enormous British expeditionary force at the Battle of Long Island. The field of battle primarily fell within the confines of what is now known as the Borough of Brooklyn, New York. Sadly, however, 230 years of ever-expanding urban development have long since obliterated much of the original ground. Whereas so many other great Revolutionary War battles and battlegrounds have been honored and preserved in dedicated national or state parks, only a few old bronze plaques and eroding stone monuments are scattered around Brooklyn to mark the various points of interest of the Battle of Long Island. All of these monuments had to be retrofitted into the already cluttered urban environment by later generations of well-meaning historians and historically-minded citizens. Hundreds, if not thousands, of Brooklyn's busy residents pass by these inadequate memorials every day without taking notice of them. But it is not their fault: the great struggle that occurred on the ground that lies buried under their feet, not only deserves more impressive monuments, but a fuller appreciation by history to attract their attention.

For a variety of reasons, it is probably safe to say that most Americans have never heard of the Battle of Long Island. The obvious might be guessed, that it took place on Long Island, but, if pressed further most would likely admit that they don't know anything about the circumstances of the battle; perhaps not even which war was being fought.

If for no other reason than the sheer size of the Battle of Long Island, it deserves to be remembered. Based on the number of participants from both sides, it was arguably the largest battle of the Revolutionary War. Although estimates vary, the invading British Army on Long Island, planning for a quick and decisive victory, had amassed perhaps 24,000 men (an eighteenth century version of "Shock and Awe"). On the other side, the over-matched American forces on Long Island probably numbered about 7,500. By comparison, at the far better-known Battle of Saratoga one year later,

ınd British General John Burgoyne, marching
about 5,800 men under his command. His
tio Gates, commander of the American
⌐ about 16,000 Continental soldiers and New
⌐␣ stop them.

⌐ver, it wasn't just the size of the Battle of Long Island that
ıas so significant. The results were to have important consequences
that would play out during the entire Revolutionary War. Among
other lessons, perhaps the most significant legacy of the battle was
that it demonstrated that there would be no quick or easy victory for
either side, and the war was to become a protracted and bloody affair.
But, even though it was a pivotal event in the early stages of our
national birth struggle, this too has not made it particularly
memorable in American history.

We have already touched on one of the reasons for the recognition
problem: the loss of the original battleground under the streets and
high-rises of Brooklyn, but a second reason may be that historians
have never really agreed on what to call the battle. Since that brutal
August day 230 years ago, the battle has been known, not only as the
Battle of Long Island, but the Battle of Brooklyn, the Battle of
Brooklyn Heights, and the Battle of Flatbush, leading to endless
confusion. Some historians have persuasively argued that the most
appropriate name would be the Battle of Brooklyn, since it was fought
for the most part within the boundaries of today's Brooklyn, but the
Battle of Long Island has persisted in being the most common name
attributed to the conflict, and is therefore the name that will be used
here.

The Battle of Long Island may also have been deleted from the
collective memory of the American consciousness because at the time
it was considered to be a disaster to the cause of freedom and a
crushing, humiliating defeat. Later historians, however, have been
much more forgiving, taking into consideration that the defeat came at
the hands of a well-trained, well-equipped, and highly experienced,
professional British Army, with an overwhelming numerical
advantage. Nevertheless, whereas great victories, such as that at
Saratoga, are long celebrated by the victorious, the memories of
defeats are, in time, often conveniently misplaced by the defeated: No
one likes a loser.

It almost seems that subsequent generations of developers have
intentionally obliterated all traces of the American setback by burying

most of the area of the battlefield under multiple layers of asphalt, stone, concrete, and brick. The dramatic alteration of the battlefield has rendered it virtually impossible for the casual tourist (or the serious historian for that matter) to comprehend the strategies of the combatants or the scope of the battle.

This destructive process was begun by the occupiers immediately after the retreat of the American Army, when many of the fortifications built by the Americans prior to the battle were either leveled or significantly altered. To add to the problem, the Tory-leaning local population was largely happy to see the American rebels go, and was at least indifferent to the preservation of the sites and the relics of the battle. The British remained in possession of Long Island and the battlefield until the close of the War in 1783, and for those seven years the battleground was neglected. Particularly lamentable was the fact that most of the graves of those killed in action were untraceable when the United States regained possession of Long Island. Because of the precipitous nature of the American retreat, there had been no opportunity to retrieve their dead, and the British either left the bodies of those they considered "vile enemies to their King and country" lying where they fell, or buried them in unmarked graves.

The only part of the Long Island campaign that has been given a significant place in American history was General George Washington's nearly miraculous Dunkirk-style evacuation of the battle-weary remnants of his Long Island division across the East River to New York City. For two days after the battle, the surviving American soldiers were trapped; hunkered down in hastily constructed fortifications on Brooklyn Heights with their faces to an entrenching enemy and their backs to the East River. It was believed that an overwhelming assault could breach the American lines at any moment. The British, on the other hand, confident in their ability to crush the remnants of Washington's army, were biding their time. They could afford to wait for favorable winds to bring their fleet up the East River to pin down the Americans from the rear, while, their army laid slow, deliberate siege to Washington's fortifications.

Siege tactics were the classic European approach to taking strong, fortified positions, and involved digging a series of approaching trenches or "parallels." These interconnecting, zigzagging trenches would gradually be dug closer and closer until siege guns could be dragged through the cover of the trenches into virtually point-blank range. Normally these tactics would prevent incurring the casualties that might be expected by an attempt at taking a fortress by storm. The very threat of bombardment at close range would usually prompt defenders to surrender. It might take several days or weeks to complete the process, but in this case, the British were in no hurry and believed they had plenty of time.

However, contrary to the expectations of the enemy, and screened by heavy fog during the night of August 29-30, Washington silently evacuated several thousand soldiers from his surviving division on Long Island across the East River to relative safety on Manhattan Island. the British awoke on the morning of the 30th only to find the Brooklyn fortifications empty and abandoned, with hopes for an immediate and mortal blow to Washington's army vanishing in the fog. It is ironic that a brilliantly executed evacuation became more famous than the enormous battle which preceded it, but this should further amplify the point that victory (if a brilliantly executed evacuation can be considered such), will be remembered over defeat.

The successful evacuation of Long Island was one of the few bits of good news to come out of New York for the Americans that year. Although safer on Manhattan Island, at least for the moment, Washington still had to reorganize his decimated and demoralized army, and prepare for the inevitable British invasion of New York City. But because he had been able to preserve the greater part of his Long Island division, he at least still had an army to fight with.

In order to understand how the two armies came to blows on Long Island, it is necessary to go back a few months to the late winter of 1775-1776. At that point, the British had themselves been besieged in Boston for nearly a year since the beginning of the war. In the one major effort to break the siege, they had grossly miscalculated the American will and ability to fight, and suffered enormous casualties at the Battle of Bunker Hill. In March 1776, after the Americans had moved their big guns into a commanding position on Dorchester Heights, the British finally realized that their occupation of Boston was no longer tenable. After an abortive effort to dislodge the Americans, the "Ministerial Troops,"as Washington called them, evacuated and sailed off en masse for the friendlier and safer colony of Nova Scotia. Jubilation in the colonies over this early American victory quickly subsided when it became understood that the British exodus would not be permanent: Nova Scotia was only to be the temporary destination for their army in order to regroup, re-supply and await reinforcements. While Boston may not have been of lasting value to the British, New York was of much greater strategic importance, and could serve as an invaluable staging area for renewing the effort to subdue their rebellious colonies. If they could secure Manhattan Island under the protection of the largest and most powerful fleet in the world, the British could sail up the Hudson River at their leisure to divide the colonies and isolate the most troublesome region: New England. Early on, General Washington and the Continental Congress had anticipated that the British army would soon swoop south to take New York. Even prior to the evacuation of Boston, American troops had begun to fortify various strategic locations around New York Harbor. Placed in charge of the project, American General Charles Lee commenced designing and building these fortifications on February 3, 1776, using a force of 12,000 Connecticut Militia. As soon as it was no longer needed to contain the British in Boston, Washington marched his main army to New York to take over the job of preparing for, what was expected to be, an imminent attack. General Lee was then ordered south to Charleston, South Carolina to meet an anticipated secondary British invasion there.

Among the twenty-one regiments that marched from Boston to New York in Washington's army in the spring of 1776 was Colonel Jedediah Huntington's 17th Continental Regiment. For the most part, this regiment was composed of men recruited from eastern Connecticut. Originally organized as Huntington's 8th Connecticut Regiment by order of the Connecticut General Assembly in July 1775, the regiment had taken part in the siege of Boston as part of Gen. Joseph Spencer's brigade encamped at Roxbury. When General Washington formed his new national, or Continental Army at the end of 1775, the regiment was reorganized as the 17th Continental Regiment. The new regiment included not only many of the soldiers from the old 8th Connecticut, but also quite a few men whose enlistments had expired who had served in other Connecticut regiments which had disbanded or were reorganized under Washington's command.

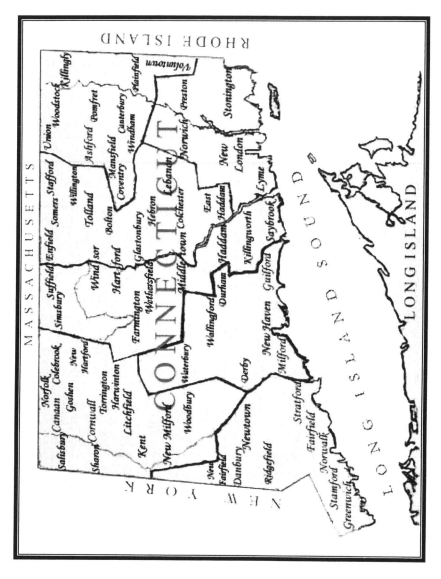

Connecticut Towns
(map by the author)

☞ The commanding officer of the 17th Continental Regiment was **Colonel Jedediah Huntington**, a member of one of the wealthier, most powerful, and accomplished families of Norwich, Connecticut. Huntington's ancestors had been among the founders of the town over 100 years before, and their descendants had since frequently occupied important positions in business and public service. Two of Jedediah's brothers, Ebenezer and Joshua, were also to serve with distinction during the Revolutionary War. Their father, Jabez Huntington, among other notable public positions, became major-general in overall command of the Connecticut state militia during the war. A cousin, Samuel Huntington, later became president of the Continental Congress and, following the Revolution, a governor of Connecticut.

Born at Norwich, Connecticut, in 1743, Jedediah Huntington graduated from Harvard College in 1763. Upon graduation, he joined the family trading business and later became a successful merchant in his own right. As conflict loomed with Great Britain, Jedediah joined the militia, was soon promoted to captain, and was one of the original Sons of Liberty in Norwich. According to the *History of Norwich,* "Gen. Huntington was a man of small stature and sedate temperament, but of great energy, steadiness, and dignity; very neat and precise in his personal appearance, and polished, though reserved, in his demeanor. He made a profession of religion at the age of twenty-three, and his conduct through life was that of a consistent Christian."[1]

Colonel Huntington married Faith Trumbull of Lebanon, Connecticut, on May 1, 1766.[2] She was the daughter of Connecticut Governor Jonathan Trumbull, the only colonial governor at the beginning of the war to take up the rebel cause against the mother country. By this marriage, two of the most powerful families in Connecticut at the time of the Revolutionary War were united. The marriage produced only one child, a son, Jabez, born September 17, 1767, but the alliance of the two families would have an important impact on the critical role that Connecticut would play during the war.

When Huntington's military career began in 1769, he was first made an ensign in the Norwich militia or "train-band." In 1771, he

---

[1] Francis Manwaring Caulkins, *History of Norwich* (Hartford: Case, Lockwood & Brainard, 1873), p. 418,
http://persi.heritagequestonline.com/hqoweb/library/do/books/
[2] CT State Library, *Barbour Collection of Connecticut Vital Records* (alphabetical statewide slip index).

was promoted to lieutenant, and in 1774, he was again promoted, this time to captain of his own company. In October of the same year, as war threatened, he was appointed colonel of the 20th Regiment of Connecticut Militia, consisting mostly of men from Norwich.[1]

When the shooting war began with the British on the morning of April 19, 1775, at Lexington and Concord, express riders were sent in all directions to warn the other colonies. One of those riders was Israel Bissell of Windsor, Connecticut, who was sent with a dispatch to Connecticut and other states to the south. His ride was of epoch proportions: after riding his first horse to its death at Worcester, he received a fresh mount and rode off through Pomfret and Brooklyn, Connecticut, to Norwich, arriving there at four o'clock on the afternoon of the 20th. At Norwich, his dispatch was addressed and personally delivered to Jedediah Huntington before Bissell continued on his way. Eventually Bissell ended his ride at Philadelphia four days later, on April 24th, having covered nearly 345 miles.[2]

With Norwich warned by Bissell, Jedediah Huntington immediately prepared his militia to march north to support Massachusetts. Five days later, on April 26, 1775, he arrived at Wrentham, Massachusetts, with between one and two hundred men from his militia regiment.[3] Within a few days, his men were setting up camp at Roxbury as part of the disparate colonial forces assembled in the area to contain the British in Boston; and the siege of Boston had begun.

Fortunately, Huntington was a prolific letter writer: many were written to his father, brothers, and father-in-law, Governor Trumbull, during the time period that Huntington's men were encamped at Roxbury. They have been preserved in the *Collections of the Massachusetts Historical Society*, Fifth Series, Vol. IX (The Trumbull Papers), and the *Collections of the Connecticut Historical Society*, Volume XX (The Huntington Papers). By May 5, 1775, the

---

[1] *The Public Records of the Colony of Connecticut, April 1636-October 1776* (Hartford: Brown & Parsons, 1850-1890), Vol. XIII, pp. 243, 524; Vol. XIV, pp. 267, 331, www.colonialct.uconn.edu

[2] David Weber, "No Glory for Israel Bissell," *Republican-American* (Waterbury, CT), April 19, 2007, p. 2A; Daniel Coit Gilman, *A Historical Discourse delivered in Norwich, Connecticut, September 7, 1859* (Boston: G. C. Rand and Avery, 1859), pp. 107-108, http://persi.heritagequestonline.com/...

[3] "Jedediah Huntington to Jonathan Trumbull, April 26 & 27, 1775," *Collections of the Massachusetts Historical Society* (5th Series, Boston: Published by the Society, 1885), Vol. IX, pp. 493-495.

immediate emergency of Lexington and Concord was over, and Huntington wrote that many of the militia units that had responded to the first alarm were now returning home, and that he too expected to be home soon.[1] It was a chaotic time in the American camps, with little organization and no effective overall command structure. Without proper logistical support, many of the men who had first responded to the battles at Lexington and Concord could not be provisioned, and were sent home.

It appears that his regiment remained at Roxbury, but by May 22, Huntington himself had returned to Norwich to put his family and business affairs in order before returning to his command. While he was there, Huntington devised a plan to escort his wife, and some of the other Connecticut officers' wives, back to Roxbury to be near their husbands in camp. In a letter to his father written from Providence on the journey back to Roxbury on June 13, Huntington told of the misfortune of having had one of their carriages wrecked by an inept innkeeper who lost control of the horses while they were being fed.[2] It was a bad omen: the lesser of two disasters resulting from this trip that were to personally affect Huntington.

The Huntington entourage arrived at Roxbury just in time to witness the horrible aftermath of the Battle of Bunker Hill. The awful reality of war was too much for Faith Huntington, who promptly had a mental breakdown. Her brother, John Trumbull, later wrote that, "Being a woman of deep and affectionate sensibility, the moment of her visit was most unfortunate. She saw too clearly the life of hardship and danger upon which her husband and a favorite brother [the writer] had entered, and it overcame her strong but too sensitive mind, and she became deranged."[3] She was sent back to Norwich, but Faith Huntington's mental and physical health declined in spite of the best efforts of local doctors and the family members who cared for her.

Over the next four months, Faith's condition continued to deteriorate. Jedediah, having tried everything else, asked his mother

[1] "Jedediah Huntington to Joshua Huntington, May 5, 1775," *Collections of the Connecticut Historical Society* (Hartford: Published by the Society, 1923), Vol. XX, pp. 220-221.
[2] "Jedediah Huntington to Jabez Huntington, June 13, 1775," *Collections of the Connecticut Historical Society*, XX, p. 224.
[3] *Collections of the Massachusetts Historical Society*, Vol. IX, footnotes pp. 505-506.

to bring Faith to Dedham, Massachusetts, to be close to her husband, so that he could personally minister to her, and monitor her treatment by the best doctors in the area. But even that effort failed, and on November 24, 1775, Faith Trumbull Huntington died. Jedediah later wrote his father-in-law, the governor:

> *I never knew what it was to sorrow till my best earthly friend was taken away from me. I devoutly wish that my improvements in goodness, love, and friendship to her parents and relations may bear some proportion to those qualities which shone in my lovely companion, that we may be prepared for the period of our continuance here, be matured for the enjoyment of our ascended Saviour* [sic], *and in the highest degree partake of the society of our departed dear ones.* [1]

The complex issues relating to the organization of his regiment must have been rendered infinitely more difficult considering the ongoing illness of his wife. In spite of what must have been an extremely emotional diversion, Jedediah Huntington's patriotism and sense of duty were preeminent in his character, and he retained his command. In July, shortly after his wife had been taken ill, the 8th Connecticut Regiment was raised under Huntington's orders. With hope still alive for a speedy end to the conflict with England, the term of enlistment was to be only eight months. Many of the men from Huntington's old militia regiment enlisted in the new organization, but that was not sufficient, and more men had to be raised. By August 10, however, all but three of the companies of the new regiment were in camp at Roxbury.

The other three companies were temporarily ordered to New London by the governor of Connecticut, to respond to an alarm there.[2] Private Solomon Ingham of Capt. Rowley's Company later wrote that his company's march for Roxbury was interrupted at Pomfret, in northeast Connecticut, where they received orders to reverse direction and proceed south to the coast at New London. Once at New London, Ingham's company and the others were employed building fortifications, guarding the coast, and training in the use of firearms.

---

[1] "Jedediah Huntington to Jonathan Trumbull, March 6, 1776," *Collections of the Massachusetts Historical Society*, Vol. IX, p. 515.
[2] "Jedediah Huntington to Jonathan Trumbull, Aug. 10 &14, 1775," *Collections of the Massachusetts Historical Society*, Vol. IX, pp. 496-498.

The only action that occurred in the area while Ingham was there was the shelling of Stonington Point by Captain James Wallace in command of the British man-of-war, *H.M.S. Rose* on August 30, 1775. Ingham reported that they marched for Stonington Point upon news of the cannonade and "saw the houses shot through and through by [Captain Wallace's] cannon balls." After that, Ingham's company was marched to Lyme where they were employed in guarding Lieutenant Governor Griswold. When the threat of British attack had diminished along the Connecticut coast, the three companies of Huntington's 8th Connecticut Regiment that had been stationed there marched to join the rest of the regiment at Roxbury.[1]

Private Daniel Barber, of Captain Elihu Humphreys' Company in Huntington's 8th Connecticut Regiment left us an eyewitness description of the camp conditions at Roxbury:

After about nine or ten days' marching [from Simsbury, Connecticut], *in company with our ox team, loaded with our salt pork, peas, and candlestick bottoms* [a reference to shape and consistency] *for bread, and the barrel of rum to cheer our spirits and wash our feet, which began to be very sore by traveling, we came to Roxbury, the place of our destination. There the place of our encampment was already marked out, and a part of our regiment on the spot. For every six soldiers there was a tent provided. The ground it covered was about six or seven feet square. This served for kitchen, parlor and hall. The green turf, covered with a blanket, was our bed and bedstead. When we turned in for the night, we had to lie perfectly straight, like candles in a box: this was not pleasant to our hip bones and knee joints, which often in the night would wake us, and beg to turn over. Our household utensils, altogether, were an iron pot, a canteen, or wooden bottle holding two quarts, a pail, and wooden bowl. Each had to do his own washing, and take his turn at the cookery.[2]*

---

[1] National Archives and Records Administration, Series M805, Roll 462, Revolutionary War Pension and Bounty-Land Warrant Application File, W13527, www.footnote.com/image/2414182

[2] John Warner Barber, *Connecticut Historical Collections* (New Haven: by the author, 1836), p. 104.

Although perhaps told with a local bias, the *History of Norwich* relates that Huntington's "regiment was the best equipped of any in the colony, and was distinguished by a British uniform, the Governor and Council having appropriated to them a quantity of English red-coats taken in a prize vessel."[1] That history does not go on to mention any confusion that may have resulted from having the regiment uniformed in the fashion of the enemy, but this was not a unique problem at the beginning of the War. There was a plethora of different styles and colors worn by the various American regiments, if they wore uniforms at all.   In ordering the provisioning of the 8th Regiment, the Connecticut General Assembly declared that each soldier who supplied his own firearm with bayonet and cartridge-box, would receive a bounty of ten shillings.[2] This order resulted in further confusion. Wherever soldiers had to provide their own arms, it resulted in a wide variety of weapons in use within the regiments. Inevitably, there were ammunition supply problems resulting from a lack of standard barrel size.

Just four months after the organization of an army based on state forces enlisted for eight months, the Continental Congress in Philadelphia, on November 4, 1775, ordered the formation of a new Continental Army. The new army was to replace the old one on January 1, 1776, after the eight-month enlistments had expired. This Continental Army would be the first army raised by the national government under the overall command of General George Washington.

Each one of the twenty-six new regiments was to have a total troop strength of 728 officers and men, broken down into eight companies: each consisting of a captain, two lieutenants, an ensign, four sergeants, four corporals, a fifer, a drummer, and 76 privates. The term of enlistment of the army was to be one year, or until January 1, 1777. Huntington's 17th Continental Regiment was organized along these lines, under the ultimate authority of the Continental Congress (as opposed to the Connecticut Assembly), and the old 8th Connecticut Regiment was disbanded.[3]   Connecticut retained the authority to organize local militia units, generally under

[1] Caulkins, *History of Norwich*, p. 417.
[2] *The Public Records of the Colony of Connecticut, 1636-1776*, Vol. XV, p. 97.
[3] www.uswars.net/1775-1783/units-american/1776.htm

shorter periods of enlistment, to respond to alarms within the state itself, and to augment the Continental forces as needed.

By the beginning of January 1776, the efforts made by recruiting officers had not been entirely successful, and only about 400 men had reported for duty in the 17th Regiment; well short of the goal.[1] By January 31, Colonel Huntington wrote that he only had two companies that were nearly full. The others still had a compliment of only about 60 men each. Most of the new Continental regiments were in the same predicament, each containing only about 500 men, on average.[2] Nevertheless, Washington and his new troops were clamoring for action, and it was time for the new army to test itself against the enemy who had too long been in possession of Boston.

As the spring offensive began in March 1776, Huntington's 17th Regiment was among the American units that were ordered by General Washington to seize and fortify Dorchester Heights overlooking Boston. Cannon captured from the British at Fort Ticonderoga the year before had been dragged across Massachusetts on frozen ground during the winter. These very welcome additions to what had been a small American arsenal were positioned on the Heights behind hastily, but ingeniously, prepared fortifications on the night of March 4-5. Waking up on the morning of the 5th, the British suddenly found themselves directly under the guns of the rebels. They responded with a cannonade of their own in an attempt to dislodge this new and very serious threat. Years later, one old soldier who had been on the Heights that day would recall "that going the rounds, or reconnoitering, the British opened fire upon them from Boston. While ever and anon the balls would scatter the earth over them, General [the rank to which he later attained] Huntington moved as unconcernedly as if at home in his own meadow."[3] In spite of this initial resistance by the British, within several days they had concluded that Boston was no longer defensible.

[1] "Jedediah Huntington to Jabez Huntington," *Collections of the Connecticut Historical Society*, Vol. XX, p. 260.
[2] Jedediah Huntington to Joshua Huntington," *Collections of the Connecticut Historical Society*, Vol. XX, p. 265.
[3] Benjamin Tinkham Marshall, (ed.), *A Modern History of New London County Connecticut* (New York: Lewis Historical Publishing Co., 1922), p. 141, http://persi.heritagequestonline.com/...

14   *Cut Off*

Before 10 o'clock on Sunday, March 17, 1776, the enemy had evacuated their troops plus all the Boston Tories aboard their fleet, and the first of the American soldiers entered Boston. The very next day, ignorant of the intended destination of the British fleet, and very anxious that it might be bound directly for New York, Washington began to move most of his army south. He left one brigade to garrison Boston in case the British returned, and sent his four other brigades south. By April 4, the last of those four brigades, that of General Joseph Spencer, which included Huntington's Regiment, had marched for New York. From Boston, the route of the army led through Providence, Rhode Island, to Norwich and then New London, Connecticut. Private Solomon Ingham wrote that the regiment marched "in the spring just as winter was breaking up and the traveling was very bad."[1] The bad roads were just what General Washington was trying to avoid when he ordered that the army was to spend the last leg of the journey by water from New London to New York aboard ship. It was his intention to get his troops there as fast as possible, and to have them well rested and in good condition for the ongoing work of building entrenchments and fortifications when they reached New York.[2]

At least two men deserted along the march, the evidence of which appeared in the following classified ad in the *Hartford Courant and Hartford Weekly Intelligencer* of April 29, 1776:

Deserted from Capt. Timothy Perceval's [sic] *Company, Col. Huntington's regiment, in the continental army on the night of the 7th inst. Corporal John Strong, about 36 years of age, a stout well built fellow, dark complexion, very black hair which he generally wears clubbed; had on a butternut coloured coat and scarlet waistcoat: Also Benjamin Tubbs, about 20 years of age, a middling size fellow, dark complexion, black hair, and wears blue cloaths: both the above deserters belong to Colchester in this colony. Whoever takes up and secures said persons in any of the continental gaols* [jails], *so that they may be returned to their*

[1] NARA, Series M805, Roll 462, Revolutionary War Pension Application, W13527.

[2] "George Washington to Continental Congress, March 13, 1776," *The George Washington Papers*, Series 3, Subseries A, Letterbook 1, pp. 165-166, http://memory.loc.gov/ammem/gwhtml/gwseries.html

regiment, shall have three dollars for Strong, and two for Tubbs, and all refundable charges paid by Timothy Perceval.[1]

As their regiment crossed into Connecticut, the temptation to return to their farms and families in nearby Colchester must have been too great for Strong and Tubbs.

Shortly after this incident, the 17th regiment crossed the Shetucket River, in southeast Connecticut, at the fording place below Greeneville, just northeast of Norwich. Having marched 93 miles in four days from Boston, the regiment arrived at Norwich on April 8. Colonel Huntington immediately dispatched a letter inviting Governor Trumbull to dine with General Washington at the Huntington home. It was only ten miles to Trumbulls' home in Lebanon, and he received the letter at 3:00 P.M. the same day.

Trumbull responded to the invitation to meet with his son-in-law and the commander-in-chief, and rode off to Norwich, where they all dined together.[2] Their meeting gave General Washington and Governor Trumbull the opportunity to deepen an already more than cordial and very constructive relationship. Throughout the war Governor Trumbull remained one of Washington's staunchest allies, responding favorably to nearly every request made by Washington for troops and supplies. The next day, General Washington resumed his journey and went on to New London to, "expedite the embarkation of the troops." Rather than boarding the ships with his men, he instead went overland to New York, arriving there on Saturday, April 13, 1776.[3]

By order of Commissary-General Thomas Mifflin, vessels from all over Connecticut had been gathering at New London since late March to ferry the approximately 10,000 men in Washington's army down Long Island Sound to New York.[4] Among the last to leave from New London, Spencer's Brigade set sail on April 21. Colonel

[1] Classified Ad 2, *The Connecticut Courant and Hartford Weekly Intelligencer*, Apr. 29, 1776, p. 4, http://proquest.umi.com/
[2] Caulkins, *History of Norwich*, p. 393; "Jedediah Huntington to Jonathan Trumbull, April 8, 1776," *Collections of the CT Historical Society*, Vol. IX, pp. 517-518.
[3] "George Washington to Congress April 15, 1776," *G. W. Papers*, Series 3, Sub. A, Letterbook 1, p. 185, http://memory.loc.gov/ammem/gwhtml/gwseries.html
[4] "Thomas Mifflin to Joshua Huntington, March 23, 1776," *Collections of the CT Historical Society*, Vol. XX, p. 276.

Huntington himself went overland to New York, stopping at Wethersfield and Milford, Connecticut, along the way.

By April 22, Huntington was in New York when he wrote that only six of his companies had arrived, and he had not yet received orders as to the ultimate destination of his regiment. At this point, there was the possibility that his men might be sent to Albany to support the Northern Army in its efforts to subdue Canada.[1] That potential did not develop, however, and the 17th Regiment would remain in New York as a part of General Washington's command to prepare a welcome for the reappearance of the Ministerial Troops.

---

[1] "Jedediah Huntington to Jabez Huntington, April 22, 1776," *Collections of the CT Historical Society*, Vol. XX, p. 279.

2. Figures In Peace and Figures In War

With morale high after the successful siege of Boston, Colonel Jedediah Huntington's 17th Continental Regiment was securely encamped in relative comfort at New York by the end of April 1776. During this lull in the action, it is perhaps timely to introduce some of the other men of the regiment and their background.

New England troops at the beginning of the Revolutionary War had the reputation of being an unruly and undisciplined lot. If the soldiers had had any military training at all, it had come from of a long tradition of participation in the musters of local militia companies. Under entirely local command, the quality of training and equipment provided the militia varied wildly from town to town, and company to company. But, however unruly and unmilitary-like they may have been, on various occasions during their colonial history it had been demonstrated that New England militia could be effective in combat. This was especially true when their passions were fueled by a great cause, or their homes, families, or property was threatened. Since very early on, New Englanders had proven themselves adept in unconventional guerrilla, or Indian-style fighting. This was a result of life on, or near a frontier with their belligerent neighbors, the French, and their Indian allies.

There were earlier examples of New England's fighting ability, but there were many old soldiers still active at the beginning of the Revolution who had participated in King George's War thirty years before. In 1745, a force of 4,000 colonial soldiers, recruited almost entirely from New England, laid siege to the French fortress of Louisbourg, on Cape Breton Island in Nova Scotia. To the great surprise of the world, the siege was successful, and the New Englanders took the place. There were several causes for the colonists' attack on Louisbourg, including the French seizure of New England fishing vessels, but more than that, they were inflamed with the protestant religious zeal of the Great Awakening: the Louisbourg expedition took on the aura of a great crusade. The Protestant Reformation was not that distant a memory, and New Englanders at the time were responding to what they considered to be the satanic forces of French catholic popery to their north. The nearly fanatical zeal of the soldiers, coupled with a desire for promised plunder, must have made up for the lack of training and experience.

A decade after the siege of Louisbourg, the Seven Years War, known as the French and Indian War in America, broke out. Settlements along the northern New England frontier were attacked by the French, as well as forts along the Lake Champlain-Lake George-Hudson River corridor just to the west. Again, the New England militia had a prominent fighting role, this time alongside British regular troops fighting against the French and their Indian allies. The combined effort of both colonial and regular British troops in seven years of warfare resulted in the final eviction of French colonial government from Canada.

Now, at the outset of the Revolution, the passions of the New Englanders were again awakened in a great cause: this time the cause of freedom from the tyranny of an overbearing motherland. Many of the New England militia units that had participated in the siege of Boston in 1775-1776, were a mixture of grizzled old veterans of the colonial wars, and younger untested men and boys. This was certainly true of Huntington's 17th Regiment, as can be seen from the biographies of some of the men that made up the regiment. The names of the officers that follow come from the list of officers and staff of the 17th, which is found in *The Record of Service of Connecticut Men in the War of the Revolution.*[1] Except for Captain Brewster's and Captain Ebenezer Fitch Bissell's Companies (see Appendix), there are no muster rolls for non-commissioned officers and privates of the 17th prior to the Battle of Long Island. We know who some of those men were from the returns of the missing and killed after the Battle of Long Island, from later pension records, from town or family records, or other records that will be noted with the individual soldiers.

☞   Second in command of the 17th was **Lieutenant-Colonel Joel Clark**, born in New Haven, Connecticut on July 28, 1728, the son of

---

[1] Adjutants-General, *Record of Service of Connecticut Men in the War of the Revolution* (Hartford: Case, Lockwood & Brainard Co., 1889).

Moses and Dinah (Bishop) Clark. Joel married Lois Clark of Southington, Connecticut, on May 12, 1748. She was a cousin, the daughter of Silas and Eunice (Cook) Clark. Between the years 1748, and 1759, Lois gave birth to six children.[1]

Joel and Lois Clark settled in the south end of Southington, where they eventually owned at least two farms. By occupation, Joel was both a farmer and a trader. We are given an indication of what kind of merchandise he dealt with, in a letter he wrote to Jedediah Huntington's brother, Captain Joshua Huntington on March 26, 1775, just before the regiment left Roxbury. The letter was addressed to Joshua at Norwich, and requested that he sell two hogsheads of rum and six barrels of rye flour that belonged to Joel, and send the money to his colonel, Jedediah Huntington.[2]

Joel Clark's military career began in 1745, when he was a private with the New England volunteers at the conquest of fortress Louisbourg. In 1755, he was appointed sergeant in the 4th Connecticut Regiment, and by 1759 had achieved the rank of captain in the 2nd Connecticut Regiment. He served in all the annual campaigns of the French and Indian War. On May 9, 1775, just after the outbreak of hostilities with Great Britain, he wrote the following letter to Governor Jonathan Trumbull to complain that, in spite of his extensive experience, he was being passed over for higher command:

May it please your Honour: I have been too long a soldier to feel my breast unmoved at the sound of my neighbours beating to arms. I feel too much for my distressed and injured Country to see the dangers which threaten it without wishing to share them with my countrymen; and I partake too much of the spirit of those ancestors we boast, not to offer my services at this crisis in any way inconsistent with honour and fidelity to my Country. I take the freedom to address your Honour as the Captain-General of this Colony, and tender therefore my services. I served in the ranks at the age of fifteen, in the reduction of Louisbourg, in '45. I served in every other station in the last war, until I was appointed

---

[1] Heman R. Timlow, *Ecclesiastical and other Sketches of Southington, Conn.* (Hartford: Case, Lockwood and Brainard Co., 1875), pp. 214, 235, li, lii, liv, http://persi.heritagequestonline.com/...

[2] "Joel Clark to Capt. Joshua Huntington, March 26, 1776," *Collections of the CT Historical Society*, Vol. XX, p. 277.

to the command of a Company in the three last years before the peace; in all which stations I appeal to those in the service for my conduct. Once I received the General's thanks for my services in a command of four hundred men, in 1760, and the additional pay of a Captain in the regular service. Now this don't argue either a want of skill or readiness in me of doing my duty. When I saw last winter the appointment of Field Officers by the honourable Assembly, of the Regiment I belong to, I had thoughts which I suppress. The gentlemen I have no objection to. They may make a figure in peace, and they may make a figure in war. They have never had experience. I now see the danger to which my Country is reduced; and my love to that, and duty to your Honour, demand this offer of my service. I do not apply for want of bread or business of my own. I have enough of both, and a property to defend. The present union of hearts and hands of all ranks of people in the cause renders it Needless for me to take up your Honour's time. When dangers were represented in the alarm in September last, I raised a Company at some expense of my own. I know not whether it is in your Honour's power to give me a proper appointment in the service, but I shall always be satisfied in having done my duty in this address to your Honour, and am, with much respect, your Honour's most obedient and most Humble servant,

Joel Clark

P.S.   If your Honour will condescend to enquire of Generals Wooster, Spencer, Putnam, and Colonels Ward, Wadsworth, Waterby, Champion, Etc., for my character, etc., I shall esteem it a favour: also Mr. Root, a Representative.[1]

Clark's letter must have had some impact, for when the 8th Connecticut Regiment was organized in July he was appointed major by the Connecticut Assembly, and upon reorganization as the 17th Continental Regiment in January 1776, to lieutenant-colonel.

---

[1] W. H. W. Sabine, (ed.), *The New-York Diary of Lieutenant Jabez Fitch*, (New York: pub. by the editor, 1954), p. 87.

☞   Next in rank in Huntington's regiment was **Major Elihu Humphreys** of Simsbury, Connecticut. He was born April 14, 1738, in Simsbury, the son of Esquire John Humphreys, and Lydia (Reed) Humphreys. Elihu married Asenath Humphreys, the daughter of Col. Jonathan and Desire (Owen) Humphreys, on April 7, 1763, at Simsbury. Asenath was born in April 1746.[1]

Major Humphreys experienced his first military service during the French and Indian War as a drummer and a clerk in Capt. Nathaniel Holcomb's Company of Col. Phineas Lyman's 1st Connecticut Regiment, during the campaign of 1758. In the same year he was promoted to sergeant in Capt. Noah Humphreys's Company in the same regiment.[2] He was an ensign in Colonel/Captain Phineas Lyman's Company (regimental commanders were also required to serve as company commanders in the Connecticut service) encamped at Montreal, in 1760. Later on in that year, he was promoted to lieutenant in the 10th Company of Lyman's 1st Regiment of Connecticut troops. In 1761, Humphreys had the same rank in the 1st Company of the same regiment.[3] He was also along on the ultimately successful, yet still disastrous expedition against the Spanish at Havana in 1762, which sustained a mortality rate of over 50% among the regular British and colonial troops.

In private life, Elihu Humphreys was a surveyor. His father, John H. Humphreys, was one of the Governor's Council, and a Justice of the Court of Common Pleas for the County of Hartford, Connecticut. It was said of the son that, "Captain Elihu was a well-bred gentleman; his friendly turn of mind, with a sweetness of disposition, secured him the love of all good men; his confidence and esteem, procured him the commission of major..."[4] Immediately after the Battle of Bunker Hill, Elihu raised a company of local men to join Colonel Huntington's 8th Connecticut Regiment. A grateful contemporary wrote, "On the eve of their march to Boston [Elihu] paraded them before this house,

---

[1] Frederick Humphreys, *The Humphreys Family in America* (New York: Humphreys Print., 1883), p. 136, http://persi.heritagequestonline.com/...
[2] *Rolls of Connecticut Men in the French and Indian War, 1755-1762*, (Hartford: Connecticut Historical Society, 1903; Electronic edition, Heritage Books, Inc. CD1360, Westminster, Maryland: 2005), Vol. II, pp. 21, 117.
[3] *The Public Records of the Colony of Connecticut,* Vol. XI, pp. 353, 485.
[4] *The Humphreys Family in America*, p. 137; Barber, *Connecticut Historical Collections*, p. 103.

where he then lived, for the purpose of giving them the opportunity of taking a tender leave of their wives and children and dearest friends."[1] When the 8th Regiment was reorganized as the 17th Continental Regiment, Humphreys was promoted from captain to major, the third ranking officer in the regiment.

Surgeon's Mate Silas Holmes was born June 5, 1755, the son of John and Hannah (Halsey) Holmes, of Stonington, Connecticut.[2] Silas was baptized in the North Stonington church on August 3, 1755. He was a resident of Stonington, Connecticut, when he received an appointment as surgeon's mate to the 8th Connecticut Regiment on July 6, 1775. Silas Holmes continued as surgeon's mate when the 8th became the 17th Continental Regiment in January 1776. He married Louisa, (Fox, possibly the daughter of Ezekiel and Mehitabel Fox) in October 1779.[3]

Reverend John Ellis was the chaplain of Huntington's 17th Continental Regiment. He was the son of Caleb Ellis of Cambridge, Mass., and was born in 1727. John Ellis graduated from Harvard College in 1750, and was called to be the pastor of the Franklin, Connecticut, Congregational Church, near Norwich, in 1752. He was ordained at that church on September 6, 1753.[4] In July 1775, he was appointed chaplain of Huntington's 8th Connecticut Regiment, and in January 1776, he remained a chaplain for the transition to Huntington's 17th Continental Regiment. Rev. Ellis married Bethiah Palmer October 24, 1750, in Cambridge, Massachusetts. They had two children in Cambridge, and eleven others were born after the family moved to Norwich, Connecticut.[5]

Adjutant Elisha Hopkins was baptized at the Hartford First Church on October 17, 1731, the son of Elisha and Martha

[1] J. Hammond Trumbull, (ed.), *Memorial History of Hartford County* (Boston: Edward Osgood Pub., 1886), Vol. I, p. 362, http://persi.heritagequestonline.com/...
[2] Jacob Lafayette Halsey and Edmund Drake Halsey, *Thomas Halsey of Hertfordshire, England, and Southampton, Long Island 1591-1679* (Morristown, NJ: by the authors, 1895), pp. 464-465, http://persi.heritagequestonline.com/...
[3] NARA, Series M805, Roll 438, Revolutionary War Pension Application, W8282.
[4] George Augustus Wheeler and Henry Warren Wheeler, *History of Brunswick, Topsham, and Harpswell, Maine* (Boston: Alfred Mudge & Son, 1878), p. 833, http://persi.heritagequestonline.com/...; CT State Library, *Church Records Slip Index*.
[5] CT State Library, *Barbour Collection*, and *Church Records Slip Index*.

(Buckingham) Hopkins. There is some confusion in the genealogy of this family related to the service record of Elisha, the father, and Elisha, the son. The pension file of Frederick Hopkins, the brother of Elisha, the younger, provides that his father entered the War of the Revolution at the beginning of the war and died of smallpox at White Plains on April 9, 1777.[1] But *The Record of Service of Connecticut Men* seems to provide only the record of the son, and does not reveal a service record for any Elisha who could have been at White Plains in 1777. Assuming that all the records from *The Record of Service*, pertain to Elisha, the son, he enlisted first in Captain John Ripley's 10th Company, Huntington's 8th Connecticut Regiment, on July 12, 1775, and was discharged December 18, 1775, at the end of his term of enlistment. When Huntington formed his 17th Continental Regiment in January 1776, Elisha was promoted to sergeant. Frederick Hopkins' pension file also reveals that his brother's middle initial was "B," which the Hopkins genealogy says stood for Buckingham, his mother's maiden name.[2]

The following are the eight captains/company commanders of Jedediah Huntington's 17th Continental Regiment in 1776 listed alphabetically by surname. All of them had previous military experience, most of them during the French and Indian War:

Captain Ebenezer Fitch Bissell was born in 1736, at Windsor, Connecticut. He was the son of Daniel Bissell, Jr., and Jerusha Fitch. E. F. Bissell married Esther Hayden, daughter of Daniel Hayden and Esther Moore, on June 24, 1756.[3] He was first a sergeant in the company commanded by Captain Nathaniel Holcomb in the 1st Connecticut Regiment in 1758, during the French and Indian War.[4] Next, Bissell was appointed ensign of Capt. Edward Barnard's 8th company in the 1st Regiment of Connecticut troops in 1759. In 1760,

---

[1] NARA, Series 805, Roll 441, Revolutionary War Pension Application, R5215/BLWT45961-160-55.
[2] Timothy Hopkins, *John Hopkins of Cambridge, Mass., 1634* (N.D.: N.D., 1932), pp. 202-203, http://persi.heritagequestonline.com/...
[3] Henry R. Stiles, *The History and Genealogies of Ancient Windsor, Connecticut* (Hartford: Case, Lockwood, & Brainard Co., 1892; Electronic edition, Family Tree Maker CD#515, Disc 2), Vol. II, pp. 37 & 83.
[4] *Connecticut Men in the French and Indian War*, Vol. II, p. 22.

he was made lieutenant in the 1st company of the 1st Connecticut Regiment. When Huntington's 8th Connecticut Regiment was formed in 1775, Bissell was appointed 1st lieutenant, and was appointed captain when the 17th was organized.[1] Rev. Daniel Barber, who served with Bissell in 1775, wrote that Bissell was "a gentleman, though not of the most easy and familiar turn; yet for his steady, correct attention to the duties of his station, was well respected."[2]

☞   **Captain Ozias Bissell**, a distant cousin of Ebenezer Fitch Bissell, was born May 13, 1731, at Bolton, Connecticut, the son of John and Hannah (Denslow) Bissell. He married Mabel Robarts, of Hartford, Connecticut, on December 31, 1751.[3]   They had 12 children, all born before the start of the Revolutionary War. Ozias served with the Connecticut troops throughout the French and Indian War. He first saw action at Lake George in 1755, in Lt.-Col. John Pitkin's Company in the 1st Connecticut Regiment. In 1756, he was a sergeant in Captain Noah Grant's Company. He was later made a lieutenant of a company from Hartford. He served with the colonial troops in Britain's war with Spain in the West Indies in 1762, and he was reportedly captured and held prisoner at Havana, Cuba, where he became acquainted with the famous Revolutionary War hero, Ethan Allen, who was also being held prisoner. Immediately after the Battle of Lexington and Concord in April 1775, Bissell was appointed a lieutenant in Captain Timothy Cheney's company of Hartford minutemen, and marched to Boston. He was appointed lieutenant in Captain George Pitkin's 2nd Company, Colonel Benjamin Hinman's 4th Connecticut Regiment on May 1, 1775, and promoted to captain on September 1. Although part of this regiment served at Ticonderoga and Crown Point, the 4th Company served at the Siege of Boston. His term of enlistment expired on December 10, 1775, and on January 1, 1776, he reenlisted and was appointed captain in Huntington's 17th Continental Regiment.[4]

---

[1] *The Public Records of the Colony of Connecticut*, Vol. XI, p. 227 & 353; Vol. XV, p. 95.
[2] Barber, *Connecticut Historical Collections*, p. 103.
[3] CT State Library, *Barbour Collection*.
[4] Edith Newbold Jessop, *General Daniel Bissell, His Ancestors and Descendants* (New York: N. D., 1927), pp. 31-34, http://persi.heritagequestonline.com/...; *Connecticut Men in the War of the Revolution*, pp. 15, 59, 101.

☞ **Captain Jonathan Brewster** of Preston, Connecticut, the son of Joseph and Dorothy (Witter) Brewster, was born September 13, 1735, at Norwich, Connecticut.[1] He married Mary, the daughter of Joseph Williams at Poquetanuck in 1771. Jonathan Brewster was a private soldier in Capt. John Baldwin's Company of militia in 1757, during the French and Indian War. He was a clerk in the 2nd Company, 2nd Regiment of Connecticut troops in the campaign of 1758. In 1761, Brewster was a sergeant in Capt. Hugh Ledlie's Company.[2] He was appointed 2nd lieutenant in 1st Company, Huntington's 8th Connecticut Regiment in July 1775, and was promoted to captain on September 5, 1775. He was discharged December 10, and reenlisted as a captain in Huntington's 17th Continental Regiment in January 1776.[3]

☞ The next captain was identified as **Captain "Elihu" Hubbard** of Middletown, Connecticut, in the *Record of Service of Connecticut Men in the War of the Revolution*. The place of residence (Middletown) associated with the entry of Hubbard's name was placed in brackets in *Connecticut Men* indicating the original roll does not contain the town name and is the opinion of the editor. It appears that both the given name of this man (Elihu) and his place of residence, Middletown, were in error. Unfortunately, subsequent histories that have relied on the published *Record of Service of Connecticut Men* have perpetuated this mistake. From the time of his appointment as 1st lieutenant of Huntington's 8th Connecticut Regiment in 1775, the *Public Records of the Colony of Connecticut* identified this man as "Elizur" Hubbard. There is a continuum of records that trace the appointment of rank, and service record, of Elizur Hubbard of Glastonbury, Connecticut, until the transition of the Connecticut 8th Regiment to the Continental 17th Regiment. There are no such records for any Elihu Hubbard of Middletown, although there was a Private Elihu Hubbard from Middletown, who had several periods of service during the Revolutionary War.[4]

---

[1] CT State Library, *Barbour Collection*.
[2] *Connecticut Men in the French and Indian War*, Vol. I. p. 214; Vol. II, p. 254.
[3] Emma C. Brewster Jones, *The Brewster Genealogy, 1566-1907* (New York: Grafton Press, 1908), p. 71 & 117, http://persi.heritagequestonline.com/...; *Public Records of the Colony of Connecticut*, Vol. XV, p. 95; *Connecticut Men in the War of the Revolution*, pp. 85, 101.
[4] NARA, Series M805, Roll 449, Revolutionary War Pension Application, W16610.

Further evidence that the correct given name for Capt. Hubbard was "Elizur" comes from two Revolutionary War pension files. Seth Turner was a private in Hubbard's Company in both the 8th Connecticut Regiment and the 17th Continental Regiment. He referred to his company commander during this entire time as Capt. Elizur Hubbard.[1] Private Solomon Ingham also identified his company commander in Huntington's 17th Continental Regiment in 1776 as Captain Elizur Hubbard, adding that he was from Glastonbury.[2]

The best evidence- and virtually certain proof- that the man was "Elizur" Hubbard, comes from the papers of George Washington in a list of "Names of Commissioned Officers of the 17th Regiment of Foot in the Service of the United Colonies," completed on January 1, 1776. Capt. Hubbard's first name can be clearly made out to be Elizur.[3] Since the Continental service, and not the Connecticut government, was responsible for determining the rolls of this regiment, the definitive source for the names of the men of the regiment would have to be the roll issued January 1, 1776, by the Continental Army, under the authority of George Washington himself. Also good evidence is provided in a letter from Colonel Huntington to his father, Jabez Huntington, on November 23, 1775, in which he lists the officers of the new 17th Regiment. Captain Hubbard's first name is given "Eleaz." Eleaz. was short for Eleazar, a spelling variant of the name Elizur.[4]

Now, our having determined his identity with a great degree of certainty, Captain Elizur Hubbard was born in Glastonbury, Connecticut, in 1736, the son of Prudence (Goodrich) and David Hubbard. He married Lois Wright, the daughter of Lois (Loomis) and James Wright, born in 1745.[5] The first record of service for Elizur

---

[1] NARA, Series M805, Roll 816, Revolutionary War Pension Application, S35365.
[2] NARA, Series M805, Roll 462, Revolutionary War Pension Application, W13527.

[3] "Names of the Commissioned Officers of the 17th Regiment of Foot, Jan. 1, 1776," *The George Washington Papers*, Series 6, Subseries A, http://memory.loc.gov/ammem/gwhtml/gwseries.html
[4] *Collections of the Connecticut Historical Society*, Vol. XX, p. 254.
[5] Lucy Abigail Brainard, *The Genealogy of the Brainerd-Brainard Family in America 1649-1908* (Hartford: Case, Lockwood & Brainard Co., 1908), Vol. II, Part VI, p. 60, http://persi.heritagequestonline.com/...; Eastbury Cemetery Records, http://rootsweb.com/pub/usgenweb/ct/hartford/towns/glastonbury/cemetery/eastbur

Hubbard was as a sergeant in Capt. David Hubbard, Jr.'s (his father) 12th Company, in Gen. Lyman's 1st Regiment in the campaign of 1760, during the French and Indian War.[1] In May 1769, he was made lieutenant of the 12th Company in the Colonial Militia, and in October 1770, he was made captain of the 11th Company by the Connecticut Colonial Assembly.[2] It is noted in the *History of Hartford County* that on the Monday following the battles at Lexington and Concord, "a large company assembled at the house of Captain Elizur Hubbard, in Eastbury [the eastern section of Glastonbury], and under his command started for Boston."[3] This fact is confirmed on the Lexington Alarm list for the Town of Glastonbury. He was appointed a 1st lieutenant in July 1775, in Lt.-Colonel Douglas' 2nd Company in Huntington's 8th Connecticut Regiment, being discharged on December 10, 1775. He regained his rank of captain when the 17th Continental Regiment was formed in January 1776.[4]

Captain Joseph Jewett was born December 13, 1732, in North Lyme, Connecticut, the son of Nathan and Deborah (Lord) Jewett. Joseph married Lucretia Rogers, his second cousin, the daughter of Theophilus and Elizabeth (Hyde) Rogers, on May 18, 1758. By the beginning of the Revolutionary War, they had had ten children.[5] Joseph was made an ensign in the Lyme, Connecticut, train-band in 1768, and a lieutenant in 1772. In October 1774, he was promoted to captain in the Lyme train-band.[6] He was on the Lexington Alarm list in April 1775, and served 31 days. He was made a captain in Huntington's 8th Connecticut Regiment in July 1775, and when

y.txt; Nathaniel Goodwin, *Genealogical Notes or Contributions to the Family History of some of the First Settlers of Connecticut and Massachusetts* (Hartford: 1856; Electronic edition, Family Tree Maker, CD515), p. 78.
[1] *Connecticut Men in the French and Indian War*, Vol. II, p. 189.
[2] *The Public Records of the Colony of Connecticut*, Vol. XIII, pp. 178, 377
[3] Trumbull, *The Memorial History of Hartford County*, Vol. II, p. 223.
[4] *Connecticut Men In the War of the Revolution*, pp. 11, 86, 101.
[5] Frederic Clarke Jewett, *History and Genealogy of the Jewetts of America* (Rowley, Mass: The Jewett Family in America, 1908), Vol. I, pp. 104, 105, 193, 194, http://persi.heritagequestonline.com/...; *The New York Diary of Lt. Jabez Fitch*, p. 33; CT State Library, *Barbour Collection*.
[6] *The Public Records of the Colony of Connecticut*, Vol. XIII, pp. 10 & 256; Vol. XIV, p. 341.

Huntington's 8th Connecticut Regiment became the 17th Continental Regiment in January 1776, Joseph Jewett continued as captain.[1]

☞   **Captain Timothy Percival**, the son of John Percival of East Haddam, Connecticut, and Hannah (Whitmore) Percival, was born February 4, 1733/34, in East Haddam, Connecticut.[2] He married Mary Fuller of Mansfield, Connecticut in 1753.[3] He was a corporal in Capt. Samuel Dimock's Company, in the pay of New York during the campaign of 1755, in the French and Indian War. In 1756, he was a sergeant in Capt. Wells' Company in the 4th Connecticut Regiment, and served again as a sergeant in Capt. Cone's Company in 1757. He was an ensign in the 3rd Company, 2nd Regiment of Connecticut troops in the campaign of 1758. In March 1760, he was appointed 2nd lieutenant of the 2nd Company, 2nd Regiment of Connecticut troops, and served again at the same rank in the 7th Company of the 2nd Regiment during the campaign of 1761. He was a lieutenant on the Lexington Alarm List for the Town of Chatham in April 1775, and was 1st lieutenant in Captain Abraham Filer [sic]'s 9th Company of Huntington's 8th Connecticut Regiment in July 1775. Percival was appointed captain upon the formation of Huntington's 17th Continental Regiment in January 1776.[4]

☞   **Captain Caleb Trowbridge**, the son of Joseph and Mary (Woodward) Trowbridge, was born August 7, 1747, in New Haven, Connecticut. He married Anna Sherman, the daughter of James Sherman of Stratford, on November 29, 1769. According to the Trowbridge family history, he was a sea captain prior to the war. Upon the commencement of hostilities with Great Britain, he aided Benedict Arnold in raising a company of soldiers and marched to

[1] *The Jewett Family of America Yearbook of 1912-1913* (Rowley, Mass: The Jewett Family of America, 1913), p. 46, http://persi.heritagequestonline.com/...; *Connecticut Men in the War of the Revolution*, pp. 16, 89, 101.
[2] CT State Library, *Barbour Collection*.
[3] William Hyslop Fuller, *Some of the Descendants of Matthew Fuller* (Palmer, Mass: by the author, 1914), Vol. III, p. 72, http://persi.heritagequestonline.com/...
[4] *Rolls of Connecticut Men in the French and Indian War,* Vol. I, pp. 72, 73, 147, 148, 202; Vol. II, p. 34; *The Public Records of the Colony of Connecticut*, Vol. XI, pp. 354, 486; *Connecticut Men in the War of the Revolution,* pp. 6, 89, 101.

Boston as a lieutenant.[1] The *Connecticut Men in the War of the Revolution* confirms that Caleb Trowbridge was in the New Haven Company under Benedict Arnold when it was organized March 2, 1775. He was appointed captain in Benedict Arnold's 5th Company in the 1st Regiment, commanded by Colonel David Wooster, on May 1, 1775, and although the majority of this regiment was posted on Long Island, and later in the Northern Department, Trowbridge's Company served at the Seige of Boston. He was discharged on December 10, 1775, and when the 17th Regiment was formed, he was appointed captain.[2] Apparently Trowbridge had been acquainted with Benedict Arnold for some time, as the Trowbridge history relates an incident prior to the war when a business dispute between the two nearly led to a duel. Trowbridge would not be the only one to have problems with Benedict Arnold as time went on, but at this point those issues did not prevent Trowbridge from serving with him.

☞ **Captain Abraham Tyler** was born November 12, 1733, the son of Col. Abraham and Eunice (Arnold) Tyler of Haddam, Connecticut.[3] Abraham, Jr., first saw service in the French and Indian War, and was an ensign in the 5th Company, 2nd Regiment of Connecticut troops during the campaign of 1758. He was appointed 2nd lieutenant of the 8th Company, 1st Regiment of Connecticut troops in March 1759. The next year he was made 1st lieutenant of the 5th Company, 2nd Regiment. In March, he served again at that rank in the 9th Company of the 2nd Regiment.[4] Tyler married Jedidah Thomas April 9, 1761, in Haddam, Connecticut.[5] In April 1775, Tyler was the captain of the company of minutemen on the Lexington Alarm List for the Town of Haddam, Connecticut. In July 1775, he was appointed captain of the 9th Company in Huntington's 8th Connecticut Regiment (his surname is misspelled "Filer" in *Connecticut Men in the War of the Revolution*), and in January 1776, he retained the rank

---

[1] F. W. Chapman, *The Trowbridge Family* (New Haven: Punderson, Crisand & Co., 1872), pp. 53-56, http://persi.heritagequestonline.com/... ; CT State Library, *Barbour Collection* and *Church Records Slip Index*.
[2] *Connecticut Men in the War of the Revolution*, pp. 18, 41, 101.
[3] CT State Library, *Barbour Collection*; *A Roster of Revolutionary Ancestors of the Indiana Daughters of the American Revolution* (Evansville, IN : Unigraphic, 1976), p. 322, http://persi.heritagequestonline.com/...
[4] *The Public Records of the Colony of Connecticut*, Vol. XI, pp. 96, 227, 354, 486.
[5] CT State Library, *Barbour Collection*.

of captain with the transition to Huntington's 17th Continental Regiment.[1]

Descending in rank, the following are some of the other officers of the 17th, presented in alphabetical order according to that rank. For a complete list of the officers, see the Appendix for *Connecticut Men in the War of the Revolution*, page 101, "Colonel Huntington's Regiment-1776."

☞ **First Lieutenant Jabez Fitch, Jr.**, was born February 15 (Old Syle), or February 26 (New Style), 1737, in Norwich, Connecticut. He was the son of Jabez and Ann (Knowlton) Fitch. He was a deeply religious man whose puritan ancestors no doubt helped to shape his faith. Although he does not seem to have had any formal education outside the local public school, he took his studies seriously, and developed a love of reading, and especially writing. It is because of the latter interest that we have the most detailed history of the 17th Regiment that exists today. Beginning in 1756, Jabez Fitch kept a diary that he maintained for the next 56 years until he died in 1812. Although there are a few months missing, much of his diary has been preserved in various parts, and is one of the most important references for this work. In his diary he detailed his service in 1756 on the Crown Point expedition during the French and Indian War, which is verified in the *Rolls of Connecticut Men in the French and Indian War*. He was made a sergeant in Captain Adonijah Fitch's Company in Phineas Lyman's Regiment for the campaign of 1757-58. At the taking of Fort William Henry by the French, he was stationed nearby at Fort Edward. He was married June 3, 1760, to Hannah, the daughter of Jabez Perkins of Norwich, Connecticut. He remained active in the local militia after the French and Indian War, and recorded his attendance in his diary at a meeting of The Sons of Liberty in February 1766.[2] He was on the Lexington Alarm List for the Town of Norwich in April 1775, and on July 6, 1775, Jabez Fitch

---

[1] *Connecticut Men in the War of the Revolution*, pp. 12, 89, 101.
[2] Sabine, *The New York Diary of Lieutenant Jabez Fitch*, pp. 9-11; Emma C. Brewster Jones, *The Brewster Genealogy, 1566-1907* (New York: Grafton Press, 1908), p. 112, http://persi.heritagequestonline.com/...; *Public Records of the Colony of Connecticut*, Vol. XV, p. 95; *Connecticut Men in the War of the Revolution*, pp. 85, 101.

was appointed 1ˢᵗ lieutenant in Captain Joseph Jewett's 8ᵗʰ Company, Huntington's 8ᵗʰ Connecticut Regiment. He was discharged December 17, 1775, and reenlisted as a lieutenant in Huntington's 17ᵗʰ Continental Regiment in January 1776.[1]

☞   **First Lieutenant Jonathan Gillet** (or Gillett, or Gillette, seemingly interchangeably) was born in West Hartford, Connecticut, February 4, 1738. He was a farmer and married Elizabeth Steele in 1758. She was born January 2, 1741.[2]   Jonathan Gillet served throughout the French and Indian War, working his way through the ranks from private soldier, to corporal, to sergeant, and then, in the campaign of 1759, as an ensign in the 2ⁿᵈ Company of Colonel Nathan Payson's 1ˢᵗ Regiment of Connecticut troops. The next year he was promoted to 2ⁿᵈ lieutenant in the 2ⁿᵈ Company of Colonel Phineas Lyman's 1ˢᵗ Regiment of Connecticut troops.[3] When Huntington's 8ᵗʰ Connecticut Regiment was formed in July 1775, Gillet was made 2ⁿᵈ lieutenant in Captain Abijah Rowley's 6ᵗʰ Company. In January 1776, Gillet was promoted to 1ˢᵗ lieutenant in Capt. Elizur Hubbard's Company in Huntington's 17ᵗʰ Continental Regiment.[4]

☞   **First Lieutenant Nathaniel Gove** was born in Lebanon, Connecticut, in 1737, and baptized there May 18, 1743. He was the son of Nathaniel Gove and Elizabeth (no last name determined by the author of the *Gove Book*). Lt. Nathaniel Gove married Esther, the daughter of Capt. Moses Tyler of Preston on November 1, 1759.[5] At the start of the Revolutionary War, Gove was a sergeant on the Lexington Alarm List for the Town of Preston. He was commissioned 2ⁿᵈ lieutenant in July 1775, in Joseph Jewett's 8ᵗʰ Company of Huntington's 8ᵗʰ Connecticut Regiment. When Huntington's Regiment became the 17ᵗʰ Continental Regiment, Gove was promoted to 1ˢᵗ lieutenant in Captain Timothy Percival's company.[6]

---

[1] *Connecticut Men in the War of the Revolution*, pp. 19, 89, 101.
[2] Stiles, *The History and Genealogies of Ancient Windsor, Connecticut*, Vol. II, pp. 298, 299.
[3] *The Public Records of the Colony of Connecticut*, Vol. I, pp. 38, 134, 173; Vol. XI, pp. 8, 226, 353.
[4] *Connecticut Men in the War of the Revolution*, pp. 88, 101.
[5] William Henry Gove, *The Gove Book* (Salem, Mass: Sidney Perley, 1922), pp. 59, 68, http://persi.heritagequestonline.com/...; CT State Library, *Barbour Collection*.
[6] *Connecticut Men in the War of the Revolution*, pp. 20, 89, 101.

☞ **First Lieutenant Simeon Huntington** was born April 2, 1740, in Norwich, Connecticut, the son of Peter and Ruth (Edgerton) Huntington. Simeon was a blacksmith, and was still unmarried at the commencement of the Revolution. According to the Huntington Genealogy, he was a powerful and athletic man whose patriotism was evident even before the start of the war.[1] On July 4, (a date which at that time had no special significance) 1774, Mr. Francis Green, a Boston merchant, and noted Tory, came through Connecticut on business and to collect debts in the area. Word of his mission came to Norwich from patriots who had refused to allow Green to stay at a tavern when he was passing through Windham. Preparing a reception at Norwich:

> *The Sons of Liberty were greatly excited at the news, and it was arranged that the moment Mr. Green appeared, Diah Manning should ring the church bell. In the morning, when Mr. Green's carriage arrived at Lathrop's tavern, a large crowd was ready to receive him, and he was allowed his choice, to depart at once or be sent out on a cart. Mr. Green pleaded for delay, attempted to address the people, but Simeon Huntington, calling him rascal, grasped him by the collar with no gentle hand, and a cart with a high scaffolding appearing in sight, Mr. Green thought it wise to get at once into his carriage, and with all possible speed leave the town, followed by "drums beating and horns blowing." On his arrival in Boston, he offered $100 reward for anyone who would give information that would lead to the conviction of "those villains and ruffians," particularly mentioning "one Simeon Huntington." The advertisement was republished in a handbill, which was sold about the town, and created considerable merriment.[2]*

In March 1775, Simeon Huntington was made an ensign by the Connecticut Colonial Assembly in the 20th Regiment of militia.[3] He

---

[1] *The Huntington Family in America*, (Hartford: The Huntington Family Association, 1915), pp. 986; CT State Library, *Barbour Collection.*

[2] Mary E. Perkins, *Old Houses of the Antient [sic] Town of Norwich 1660-1800* (Norwich, CT: The Bulletin Co., 1895), p. 249, http://persi.heritagequestonline.com/....

[3] *The Public Records of the Colony of Connecticut*, Vol. XIV, p. 396.

was on the Lexington Alarm List for Norwich as an ensign in April 1775. No doubt impressed with Simeon Huntington's martial and patriotic spirit demonstrated on the occasion mentioned above, Col. Jedediah Huntington (a distant cousin) in July of this year, petitioned Governor Trumbull to make Simeon Huntington a 2nd lieutenant upon the formation of the 8th Connecticut Regiment. When the regiment was reorganized in January 1776, Simeon Huntington was made 1st lieutenant in Captain Jonathan Brewster's Company of the 17th Continental Regiment.[1]

☞ **First Lieutenant Solomon Orcutt** was born May 4, 1730, in Tolland, Connecticut, the son of William and Sarah Orcutt. The date was confirmed in his Revolutionary War pension application, in which he reports his age as 90 in 1820. He married Mary Rockwell, the daughter of Samuel and Margaret Rockwell of Willington, Connecticut, on November 18, 1756. The couple was living at Stafford, Connecticut, when a daughter was born there in 1758.[2] In July 1775, the family was living at Willington, Connecticut, when Orcutt was made a 2nd lieutenant in Captain Abraham Tyler's 9th Company of Huntington's 8th Connecticut Regiment. In January 1776, Orcutt was promoted to 1st lieutenant in Tyler's Company in Huntington's 17th Continental Regiment.[3]

☞ **First Lieutenant Abraham Wright**, of Berlin, Connecticut, was born about 1738, and married Rebeckah Norton March 6, 1777.[4] He was both a tavern keeper and a tinsmith during his life.[5] He enlisted first during the Revolutionary War as an ensign in Major/Captain Joel Clark's 9th Company in the 8th Connecticut Regiment, in July 1775. Colonel Huntington recommended him for promotion to 2nd lieutenant on October 19, 1775. Upon organization of the 17th Continental Regiment in January 1776, Wright was made a lieutenant in Ozias Bissell's Company.[6]

---

[1] *Connecticut Men in the War of the Revolution*, pp. 19, 101
[2] CT State Library, *Barbour Collection*; NARA, Series M805, Roll 623, Revolutionary War Pension Application, S41037.
[3] *Connecticut Men in the War of the Revolution*, pp. 89, 101.
[4] NARA, Series M805, Roll 891, Revolutionary War Pension Application, W22699; CT State Library, *Barbour Collection*.
[5] Catharine Melinda North, *History of Berlin, Connecticut* (New Haven: Tuttle, Morehouse & Taylor Co.), p. 231, http://persi.heritagequestonline.com/....
[6] *Connecticut Men in the War of the Revolution*, pp. 86, 90, 101.

☞ **Second Lieutenant Thomas Fanning** was the quartermaster of Huntington's 17th Continental Regiment. He was born July 18, 1750, at Norwich, Connecticut the son of Thomas and Anne (Reynolds) Fanning.[1] He enlisted first in Huntington's 8th Connecticut Regiment on July 10, 1775 as the quartermaster. Upon the formation of the 17th Continental Regiment, he continued in that capacity.[2]

☞ **Second Lieutenant Thomas Hayden** of Windsor, Connecticut, was the son of Daniel and Esther (Moore) Hayden. Thomas was born June 14, 1745, and married Abigail Parsons of Durham, Connecticut, November 19, 1767. By trade Thomas was a carpenter. At the outbreak of hostilities at Lexington and Concord, he was the express rider who carried the news to the town of Suffield, Connecticut. He was a sergeant in the Lexington Alarm party that rode to Boston under the command of his cousin, Captain Nathaniel Hayden. Thomas left his wife and five children at home. He enlisted next in the company of his brother-in-law, Ebenezer Fitch Bissell, in Huntington's 8th Connecticut Regiment, and participated in the construction of the fortifications at Roxbury during the siege of Boston. On August 11, 1775, he was promoted to sergeant-major in the same regiment. In January 1776, he was promoted to 2nd lieutenant in Capt. Elizur Hubbard's company in Huntington's 17th Continental Regiment.[3]

☞ **Second Lieutenant Solomon Makepeace** from Warren, Massachusetts, was born September 24, 1753, the son of Gershom and Jane (Elyot) Makepeace.[4] Warren, Massachusetts, was a town about half way between Springfield and Worcester, and although that was his place of birth, he had no Massachusetts service record during the Revolutionary War. By 1775, Makepeace was employed as a schoolmaster at Stafford, Connecticut, a town just south of the Massachusetts state line.[5] In July 1775, he was made a sergeant in

[1] *Vital Records of Norwich, 1659-1848*, (Hartford: Society of Colonial Wars in the State of Connecticut, 1913), Vol. I, p. 263.
[2] *Connecticut Men in the War of the Revolution*, pp. 85, 101.
[3] CT State Library, *Barbour Collection*; Stiles, *History and Genealogies of Ancient Windsor*, Vol. II, pp. 372-373; *Connecticut Men in the War of the Revolution*, pp. 27, 85, 101.
[4] Warren, MA, Vital Records, (Family Tree Maker CD#220).
[5] NARA, Series M805, Roll 603, Testimony of Benjamin Moulton in Salmon Moulton's Revolutionary War Pension Application, S23810.

Captain Charles Ellsworth's Company in Huntington's 8th Connecticut Regiment, and on October 19, was promoted to ensign. In January 1776, he was appointed a 2nd lieutenant in Captain Ozias Bissell's Company in Huntington's 17th Continental Regiment.[1]

☞ **Ensign Anthony Bradford** was born Sept. 6, 1749, the son of James and Jerusha (Thomas) Bradford of Plainfield, Connecticut.[2] His name is found on the Lexington Alarm List for the town of Plainfield for April 1775. He enlisted next as a sergeant in the 2nd Company of Colonel Jedediah Huntington's 8th Regiment on July 9, 1775, and then was promoted to ensign in Captain Caleb Trowbridge's Company when the 17th Regiment was organized in January 1776.[3]

Although not as extensive as Lt. Fitch's, or for the most part as detailed, Anthony Bradford kept a diary that has contributed important details to the history of the 17th Regiment. The first part of his diary dealt with his company's march to Boston in April 1775 through November 1775. He may have been orderly sergeant to his company during this time, for the bulk of his entries consist of daily general orders, the assignment of the daily watch for the regiment, the courts martial, and a few daily happenings. The second part of his diary begins on August 21, 1776, just before the Battle of Long Island through January 1778. This second part of the diary is in a very different style without the routine daily orders, but has far more detail concerning the everyday life of the soldiers.[4]

☞ **Ensign Elisha Brewster**, according to the Brewster Genealogy, was born July 8, 1751, the son of Elisha and Lucy (Yeomans) Brewster of Middletown, Connecticut. However, *Connecticut Men in the War of the Revolution* provides Brewster's residence at the time of enlistment as Preston, Connecticut, where he is on the Lexington Alarm List in April 1775. An Elisha Brewster was a private in Captain Rowley's 6th Company of Huntington's 8th Connecticut Regiment in July 1775. An Elisha Brewster was next enlisted as an

---

[1] *Connecticut Men in the War of the Revolution*, pp. 87, 90, 101.
[2] Charles Henry James Douglas, *Douglas or Allied Families of that Name* (Providence: E. L. Freeman & Co., 1879), p. 204, http://persi.heritagequestonline.com/...
[3] *Connecticut Men in the War of the Revolution*, pp. 19, 86, 101.
[4] Anthony Bradford, *Diary, 1775-1778* (Connecticut Historical Society Manuscripts Collection: Unpublished manuscript, transcribed by S.F. Bradford, 1886).

ensign in Huntington's 17th Continental Regiment, when it was organized in January 1776; however, these may be two different men, taking into account the considerable disparity in rank, and the confusion over the place of residence.

The *Brewster Genealogy* provides the source for the identity of Ensign Elisha Brewster in Brewster's written commission as a 2nd lieutenant on January 1, 1777, in Huntington's 1st Connecticut Regiment. In that commission he is identified as "Elisha Brewster, Jr., Gent." This record is in direct conflict with the record of the Elisha Brewster, private, of Preston, Connecticut, who enlisted for the war from December 27, 1776, until 1783, in Colonel Sheldon's Light Dragoons. That Elisha Brewster applied for a pension in 1818, and claimed no service record prior to the enlistment record in Sheldon's Light Dragoons, nor any rank higher than sergeant. As a result of the 2nd lieutenant's commission quoted by the Brewster Genealogy, this writer believes the author of that work has correctly identified Ensign Elisha Brewster as the man from Middletown, Connecticut.[1]

Ensign Joseph Chapman, unfortunately, had a name that was fairly common at the time, and published genealogies don't provide convincing evidence of his lineage or date of birth.[2] In his pension application of April 1818, he stated he was 70 years old, but provided no other family information, except that he had children with whom he had lived.[3] His stated age at the time of his pension application would have indicated a date of birth about 1748. The closest date of birth for any one by that name listed in Connecticut vital records was at Ashford, where Joseph Chapman, son of Thomas and Mary Chapman was born May 9, 1747. But this is probably not our man, as all enlistment records for Ensign Joseph Chapman that provide a place of residence point to Norwich, Connecticut. For now, his parents and place of birth are not known. According to the *Hyde Genealogy*, Joseph Chapman of Norwich, Connecticut, married Lois Birchard (or Burchard), the daughter of John and Jane (Hyde)

---

[1] *The Brewster Genealogy*, pp. 89 & 151; *Connecticut Men in the War of the Revolution*, pp. 20, 88, 101, 146, 273; NARA Series M805, Roll 118, Rev. War Pension Application, W14394.

[2] F. W. Chapman, *The Chapman Family* (Hartford: Case, Tiffany and Co., 1854), pp. 272, 273, 279, http://persi.heritagequestonline.com/...

[3] NARA, Series M805, Roll 177, Revolutionary War Pension Application, S40821/BLWT377-200.

Birchard, on May 23, 1767. Lois gave birth to one child, a son, born October 31, 1768, but Lois died less than a year later, in March 1769. Later the same year, Joseph married second, Elizabeth Abel, born Dec. 5, 1749, the daughter of Capt. Joshua Abel and his second wife Anne Bachus. By March 1776, Elizabeth had borne four children.[1]

In his pension application, Ensign Joseph Chapman stated that he first enlisted in 1775 in the company commanded by Capt. (Jonathan) Brewster, in the regiment commanded by Col. Jedediah Huntington (the 8th Connecticut), a fact confirmed by *Connecticut Men in the War of the Revolution*, which provides his rank as sergeant during that period of service. Chapman went on to say that on the first day of January 1776 he was made an ensign in Capt. Ozias Bissell's Company. This was at the time when the 8th Connecticut became the 17th Continental Regiment.[2]

Ensign Joel Gillet, at the time of his pension application, stated that he was 72 years of age.[3] This would have made his date of birth about 1746. Farmington vital records provide the date of birth of a Joel Jealet (sic) in 1745, the son of Zachariah. Southington church records give the date of baptism of Joel Gillet, son of Zachariah, on October 27, 1745. The *Record of Service of Connecticut Men in the War of the Revolution* guesses that his place of residence was Lyme, Connecticut at the time of his enlistment, but that is probably incorrect. He was living at Harwinton, Connecticut, when he later applied for his pension. A soldier from Southington writing to his wife in 1776 identified Joel Gillet as a fellow resident of that town.[4] He first enlisted in July 1775 as an orderly sergeant in Captain Joel Clark's 3rd Company, in the 8th Connecticut Regiment, and when that regiment became the 17th Continental Regiment, he was promoted to ensign.[5]

Ensign Cornelius Higgins was born August 2, 1744, the son of Cornelius and Sarah (Hawes) Higgins of Haddam, Connecticut. Ensign Higgins married Eleanor Hazelton on November 8, 1767. She

---

[1] Reuben H. Walworth, *The Hyde Genealogy* (Albany, NY: J. Munsell, 1864), p. 148, http://persi.heritagequestonline.com/...; CT State Library, *Church Records Slip Index*; *Vital Records of Norwich*, Vol. I, p. 521.

[2] *Connecticut Men in the War of the Revolution*, pp. 85, 101.

[3] NARA, Series M805, Roll 358, Revolutionary War Pension Application, S36540.

[4] Timlow, *Ecclesiastical and Other Sketches of Southington*, p. 539.

[5] *Connecticut Men in the War of the Revolution*, pp. 86, 101.

died at the age of 32 on March 17, 1775. He first enlisted as a sergeant in Captain Abraham Tyler's Company, Col. Jedediah Huntington's 8th Regiment in July 1775. In December 1775, when the transition was being made to Huntington's 17th Continental Regiment, Higgins was promoted to ensign.[1] After the death of his first wife, Eleanor, Ensign Higgins married 2nd, Esther Kelsey on September 24, 1777.[2]

☞ **Ensign John Kinsman** was born May 7, 1753, the son of Jeremiah and Sarah (Thomas) Kinsman. John's mother, Sarah, was the sister of General John Thomas who served in the Revolutionary War.[3] John Kinsman enlisted first during the Revolutionary War in the 2nd Company in Colonel Jedediah Huntington's 8th Regiment on July 12, 1775, as a sergeant. He was promoted to ensign in the same company on October 19, 1775. When the 17th Regiment was formed in January 1776, Kinsman continued as an ensign in Captain Joseph Jewett's Company.[4]

☞ **Ensign Elihu Lyman** was probably the Elihu Lyman, born about 1751, the son of John and Hope (Hawley) Lyman of the towns of Durham and Middlefield, near Middletown, Connecticut. Elihu's only known period of service was in Captain Elizur Hubbard's Company, in Huntington's 17th Continental Regiment during 1776. He enlisted at Middletown, Connecticut.[5]

☞ **Ensign Joshua Tracy** was born August 13, 1745, at Norwich, Connecticut, the son of John and Margaret (Hyde) Tracy. He married Naomi Bingham, the daughter of Jonathan and Mary (Abbey) Bingham of Windham, Connecticut, on May 2, 1771. By 1776, they

---

[1] NARA, Series M855, Roll 425, Revolutionary War Pension Application, W21325; CT State Library, *Barbour Collection*; Old Cemetery, Haddam, Middlesex Co., CT, http://freepages.genealogy.rootsweb.com/~jdevlin/source_files/haddam_cem.htm

[2] This date is from his pension application, but the *Barbour Collection* has the date as September 23.
[3] CT State Library, *Barbour Collection*; *History of Trumbull and Mahoning Counties* (Cleveland: H. Z. Williams & Bro., 1882), Vol. II, p. 296, http://persi.heritagequestonline.com/...
[4] *Connecticut Men in the War of the Revolution*, pp. 86, 90, 101.
[5] Lyman Coleman, *Genealogy of the Lyman Family* (Albany: J. Munsell, 1872), pp. 203, 204, 210, http://persi.heritagequestonline.com/...; *Connecticut Men in the War of the Revolution*, p. 101.

had had three sons.[1] Joshua Tracy is first on the Lexington Alarm List for the Town of Norwich, and he next enlisted in Jedediah Huntington's 8th Connecticut Regiment, in Captain Jonathan Brewster's Company on July 13, 1775, as a sergeant. He was discharged on December 10, 1775, and was later promoted to ensign in the same company upon the formation of Huntington's 17th Continental Regiment in January 1776.[2]

Now follows a sampling of some of the non-commissioned officers and privates of the 17th, taken from *Connecticut Men In the War of the Revolution* (See the Appendix), and other sources, as provided. Again, the listing is alphabetical within rank:

☞ **Sergeant Elisha Benton** of Captain Abraham Tyler's Company, son of Daniel and Mary (Wheeler) Benton, was born August 9, 1748, at Tolland Connecticut. According to family tradition, just prior to the Revolutionary War, Elisha fell in love with a local girl named Jemima Barrows. She returned his love, and the two vowed to marry. Unfortunately, Jemima was only about fifteen years old; nearly twelve years younger than Elisha. Perhaps for that reason, the family strongly disapproved of the relationship. Perhaps Elisha was fleeing the conflict with his family when he decided to enlist in the army. Elisha Benton's name appears first at the outbreak of the Revolution on the Lexington Alarm List for the Town of Tolland in April 1775. He is next a corporal in Captain Abraham Tyler's 9th Company, in Huntington's 8th Connecticut Regiment, organized in July of the same year. Upon the formation of Huntington's 17th Continental Regiment in January 1776, Elisha was made a sergeant in Tyler's Company. His brother, Private Azariah Benton, also served in the same company in Huntington's 17th Continental Regiment.[3]

☞ **Sergeant Roger Coit** was born March 28, 1755, in Preston, Connecticut, the son of Benjamin and Abigail (Billings) Coit.[4] He

---

[1] Reuben H. Walworth, *Genealogy of the Family of Lt. Thomas Tracy of Norwich, Connecticut* (Milwaukee: D. S. Harkness Co., 1889), pp. 10-11, http://persi.heritagequestonline.com/...; CT State Library, *Barbour Collection*.

[2] *Connecticut Men in the War of the Revolution*, pp. 19, 85,101.

[3] CT State Library, *Barbour Collection*; *Connecticut Men in the War of the Revolution*, pp. 23, 90, 102.

[4] CT State Library *Barbour Collection*.

was a private on the Lexington Alarm List in 1775 from Preston, and enlisted again as a private in Captain John Tyler's 2nd Company, Col. Parsons' Regiment from May 6, to December 10, 1775, first stationed at New London, Connecticut, and later at Roxbury. Coit was promoted to sergeant in Captain Timothy Percival's Company upon the formation of Huntington's 17th Continental Regiment in January 1776.[1]

☞   **Sergeant Roswell Graves** was born about 1740 in East Haddam, Connecticut, the son of Benjamin and Mary (Jones) Graves. He married Elizabeth Driggs, the daughter of Daniel and Elizabeth (Strickland) Driggs of East Haddam on November 15, 1763. By the time of the Revolutionary War, the couple had five children. Roswell first entered the service during the Revolutionary War upon the Lexington Alarm as a corporal in April 1775. He next was made a sergeant in Captain Joseph Jewett's Company in Huntington's 17th Continental Regiment, and was stationed with his regiment at Roxbury, Massachusetts, until the British evacuated Boston. He was on Dorchester Heights when the army fortified that position, and witnessed four men killed there during a bombardment by the British on March 9.[2]

☞   **Sergeant Hezekiah Hayden** of Windsor, Connecticut, the son of Nathaniel and Naomi (Gaylord) Hayden, was born April 24, 1741. He married about 1770, Elizabeth, the daughter of Nathaniel Mather. He was a skilled harness maker who enlisted in the Revolutionary War in 1775, and was stationed at Roxbury during the siege of Boston. The Hayden family was one of the distinguished old families of Windsor, and his brother, Nathaniel Hayden, was the captain of the Windsor militia, who at the outbreak of hostilities in April 1775, led 23 Windsor men to Boston. Hezekiah was also the cousin of Lt. Thomas Hayden, mentioned earlier. Hezekiah continued in service with the formation of Huntington's 17th Continental Regiment in

---

[1] *Connecticut Men in the War of the Revolution*, pp. 20, 73, 102; *The Brewster Genealogy*, p. 91.
[2] Kenneth Vance Graves, *John Graves 1635 Settler of Concord, MA* (Wrentham, MA: pub. by the author, 2002); CT State Library *Barbour Collection*; *Record of Service of Connecticut Men in the War of the Revolution*, pp. 8, 102.

January 1776, and was appointed sergeant in Capt. Ebenezer Fitch Bissell's Company.[1]

☞ **Sergeant Theophilus Huntington** was born November 23, 1753, in Bozrah, Connecticut, at that time a section of Norwich. He was the son of Theophilus and Lois (Hyde) Huntington. Sergeant Huntington was unmarried at the time of the outbreak of war, but married Ruth Talcott of Bolton, Connecticut, on November 1, 1777.[2] He was on the Lexington Alarm List for the Town of Norwich, and in July 1775 he enlisted in the 8th Connecticut Regiment of his cousin, Colonel Jedediah Huntington in Capt. Jonathan Brewster's Company and was made a corporal. When the 8th was reorganized as the 17th Continental Regiment in January 1776, Theophilus was made a sergeant with the same company commander.[3]

☞ **Sergeant Stephen Otis** (or Ottis) was born at Montville, Connecticut, September 30, 1738, the son of James and Sarah (Tudor) Otis. Stephen served in every annual campaign of the French and Indian War from 1757 to 1762: Capt. Adonijah Fitch's Company in 1757; Capt. Joshua Barker's Company and then Capt. Timothy Mather's Company in 1758; Major John Durkee's Company in 1759; Lt.-Col. Joseph Spencer's Company in 1760; Captain Zebulon Butler's Company in 1761; and Capt. Samuel Elmore's Company in 1762. He married Lucy Chandler of Duxbury, Massachusetts, on February 9, 1762. They lived at Colchester, Connecticut, for most of their lives. Before the start of the Revolutionary War they had already had eight children.[4] Stephen Otis' name appears on the Lexington Alarm List as a corporal from the Town of Lyme. When Huntington's 17th Continental Regiment was formed in January 1776, Otis was made a sergeant in Captain Joseph Jewett's Company.[5]

[1] CT State Library, *Barbour Collection*; Trumbull, *Memorial History of Hartford County*, p. 512; Stiles, *History and Genealogies of Ancient Windsor*, Vol. II, *p. 371; Record of Service of Connecticut Men in the War of the Revolution*, p. 102.
[2] *The Huntington Family in America*, pp. 98-99; CT State Library, *Barbour Collection*.
[3] *Record of Service of Connecticut Men in the War of the Revolution*, pp. 19, 85, 102.
[4] William A. Otis, *The Otis Family in America* (Chicago: pub. by the author, 1924), pp. 86, 111-119, http://persi.heritagequestonline.com/...; *Connecticut Men in the French and Indian War*, Vol. 1, p. 182; Vol. 2, pp. 48, 69, 164, 194, 250, 336.
[5] *Record of Service of Connecticut Men in the War of the Revolution*, pp. 16, 102.

☞ **Sergeant Cornelius Russell** was born in Windsor, Connecticut,
April 18, 1750, the son of Samuel and Mareitje (or Mary) (Hoff)
Russell.[1] He enlisted first during the Revolutionary War in April
1775, for five days as a corporal in Captain Hayden's Windsor
Company during the Lexington Alarm. Next, he enlisted as a private
in Captain Elijah Robinson's Company in Colonel Spencer's 2nd
Connecticut Regiment in May 1775. He served for seven months, and
then enlisted in Captain Ebenezer Fitch Bissell's Company of
Huntington's 17th Continental Regiment, and was made a sergeant.
He marched with the 17th to New York in the spring of 1776, and was
promoted to sergeant-major on August 12, 1776.[2]

☞ **Sergeant William Talmage** (as spelled in *Connecticut Men in
the War of the Revolution*, but properly spelled Tallmadge, or
sometimes Talmadge), was born at Setauket (Brookhaven), Long
Island, on October 17, 1752, the oldest of five sons of Rev. Benjamin
and Susannah (Smith) Tallmadge. His name appears first in the
Revolution on the Lexington Alarm List for the Town of Glastonbury,
Connecticut. On July 11, 1775, he enlisted as a corporal in Capt. John
Douglas' 2nd Company, Col. Huntington's 8th Connecticut Regiment,
and was stationed with his regiment at Roxbury. When the regiment
was reorganized in January 1776, he was promoted to sergeant in
Captain Elizur Hubbard's Company, Huntington's 17th Continental
Regiment. He had three other brothers who served in the Revolution,
two of whom served with particular distinction. Next in age was
Benjamin Tallmadge, a Yale graduate and school principal before the
war at Wethersfield, Connecticut, who eventually attained the rank of
colonel. At the time of the Battle of Long Island, Benjamin was the
lieutenant/adjutant of Colonel John Chester's Connecticut Regiment.
Benjamin made many significant contributions during the war, among
them the supervision of George Washington's confidential
correspondence from 1778 until the close of the war. Another brother,
Samuel, was the adjutant of the 4th New York Regiment for much of

[1] George Ely Russell, *The Descendants of William Russell of Salem, Mass., 1674*
(Middletown, MD: Catoctin Press, 1989), family numbers 6375 & 6439.
[2] NARA, Series M805, Roll 710, Revolutionary War Pension Application,,
S41112/BLWT248-200; *Record of Service of Connecticut Men in the War of the
Revolution*, pp. 27, 47, 102.

the war, keeping orderly books which have been published, and a diary of his experiences.[1]

👉 **Corporal George Gordon** was probably the George Gordon, born May 10, 1755, the son of George and Jennet (Gibson) Gordon, of Voluntown, Connecticut. His name appears as George Gordon, Jr., on the Lexington Alarm List for the Town of Voluntown, He next enlisted on July 10, 1775, in Captain John Douglas' Company, Colonel Huntington's 8th Connecticut Regiment, and was stationed at Roxbury during the siege of Boston. Upon the formation of Huntington's 17th Continental Regiment in January 1776, Gordon was appointed corporal in Captain Caleb Trowbridge's Company.[2]

👉 **Corporal Oliver Jennings** (*Connecticut Men* misspells the name "Olive" Jennings), was born July 15, 1749, the son of David and Sarah (Turner) Jennings, of Willington, Connecticut. Oliver married Joanne Clerk (or Clark), January 21 or 31, 1771. By the time of the outbreak of war with Great Britain, they had three children. He enlisted in Captain Abraham Tyler's Company, upon the formation of Huntington's 17th Continental Regiment in January 1776. In a letter to his wife from camp in Roxbury, dated February 13, 1776, Oliver wrote (the spelling corrected, but not the grammar or punctuation):

Loving wife after my love and good wishes and to my children hoping these few lines find you all well as they leave me, we live at a great distance from each other yet I hope we shall not forget one another yet I hope if it is God's will we shall see each other and live to gather in joy and peace. I have nothing strange to write to you but I would inform you that we got all the camps the fourth of February and my duty is not hard for I have not been on duty but one time, we expect to have a battle with the regulars in a few days. Yesterday one of our men run away to Boston. I would have you take good care of my children and see that they don't suffer. I have 30 shillings and I will send it home as soon as I can and you

---

[1] Almon W. Lauber, (ed.), *Orderly Books of the Fourth New York Regiment, 1778-1780, the Second New York Regiment, 1780-1783* (Albany: University of the State of New York, 1932), pp. 5-8, http://persi.heritagequestonline.com/...; *Record of Service of Connecticut Men in the War of the Revolution*, pp. 11, 86, 102.

[2] CT State Library, *Barbour Collection*; *Record of Service of Connecticut Men in the War of the Revolution*, pp. 24, 86, 102.

must buy 20 pounds of flax as soon as you can and you must buy it with the money that I send home if you can't sell no tallow. I would have you write me as often as you can and let me know how you all do and if you are sick I will try to get a furlough and go home and see you. So I remain your kind and loving husband till death.

Oliver Jennings

When you write to me you must write to Mr. Oliver Jennings at Roxbury Camp in Colonel Huntington's Regiment and Capt. Tyler's Company.

A second letter written by Corporal Jennings survives, written March 9, 1776, just after the Americans had seized and fortified Dorchester Heights, and reads as follows:

Loving wife and children: I gladly take this opportunity to write to you hoping these lines will find you all well as I am at this time and through Divine Goodness of God, I have been well ever since I left home. All our soldiers are well that come from Willington that are with me and it's a time of health in Roxbury, but it is very sickly at Cambridge, but not very dying time. Loving wife I would have you remember me while I am absent from you and pray for me. Now I am fighting for you. I should be glad to see you and my children but I can't see you at present so I am contented and like well as yet. I would let you know that I intend if I live to come home in about a month. I wrote you in a letter dated the 5th instant that we had got Dorchester Point and that we had very hot firing and that I expected a bloody week but the regulars left firing the 2 days and we have got strong on Dorchester and it seems to be very still times. I would have you buy some flax if you can sell some tallow and if you can't sell no tallow I will send you some money as soon as I can for I have got 5 dollars and have four pounds due now if I don't have no opportunity to send money before I come home, I shall fetch it home then. So I remember with love and am your loving husband til death.
Oliver Jennings

Such participant testimonies are rare. Corporal Jennings letters are touching and priceless relics. They give us a glimpse of what life was like for a common soldier, husband, and father, at the beginning of the Revolutionary War.[1]

☞ **Corporal Nathan Raymond** was born about 1754, the son of Joshua and Lucy (Jewett) Raymond of the North Parish of New London, now Montville, Connecticut. Nathan was the nephew of Captain Joseph Jewett. Upon the formation of Huntington's 17th Continental Regiment in January 1776, he was made a corporal in his uncle's company.[2]

☞ **Private Azariah Benton**, was born March 29, 1754, in Tolland, Connecticut. He was the son of Daniel and Mary (Wheeler) Benton, and the brother of Sergeant Elisha Benton. Azariah Benton's name appears first on the Lexington Alarm List for the Town of Tolland, and then in Captain Solomon Willes' 5th Company, of Colonel Spencer's 2nd Connecticut Regiment, which was organized in May 1775. This regiment also served at Roxbury during the siege of Boston. He was discharged December 17, 1775, and when Huntington's 17th Continental Regiment was organized in January 1776, he enlisted in that regiment.[3] At least two other men, Private Jeremiah Sparks, of Tyler's Company, and Private John Lewis of Captain Jonathan Brewster's Company, had also previously served in the 5th Company of Spencer's 2nd Connecticut regiment before reenlisting in the 17th when their first term of enlistment had expired.

☞ **Private Rufus Cone** was born October 10, 1737, the son of James and Grace Cone in East Haddam, Connecticut. Rufus married Esther Stewart, the daughter of James and Keziah Stewart, on December 18, 1761, in East Haddam, Connecticut. By the time of the outbreak of the Revolutionary War, the couple had seven children. His name appears first during the War in Captain William C. Hubbell's 8th Company of Colonel Charles Webb's 7th Connecticut

---

[1] Frank Lamont Jennings, *A Genealogy of a Jennings Family and Allied Families of Lamont-Aldrich and Germond* (Greenwood, IN: by the author, 1972), p. 8-16, http://persi.heritagequestonline.com/...; *Record of Service of Connecticut Men in the War of the Revolution*, p. 102.

[2] *History and Genealogy of the Jewetts in America*, pp. 192, 193; *Record of Service of Connecticut Men in the War of the Revolution*, p. 102.

[3] CT State Library, *Barbour Collection*; *Record of Service of Connecticut Men in the War of the Revolution*, pp. 23, 48, 102.

Regiment, in July 1775. This regiment was posted at various places along Long Island Sound until September 14, when it was ordered to the Boston camps at Winter Hill as part of General Sullivan's Brigade. In January 1776, Rufus enlisted in Captain Joseph Jewett's Company of Colonel Jedediah Huntington's 17th Continental Regiment.[1]

☞ **Private Roger Filer** (misspelled Tyler in *Connecticut Men*) was born in Bloomfield, Connecticut, May 3, 1743, the son of Jeremiah and Jerusha (Kelsey) Filer.   He married the widow Tryphena (Wolcott) Allyn, the daughter of Henry and Abigail (Colley) Wolcott on April 7, 1760.[2] By the time of the Revolution they had five children, Asa, Allyn, Roxy, Roger, Jr., and Jerusha. Roger Filer served during the French and Indian War in the campaigns of 1761 and 1762. In both of those years he served in the 4th Company of Major-General Phineas Lyman's 1st Connecticut Regiment. In 1762 he served with that Regiment during the campaign at Havana, Cuba. The only enlistment record that has been found for Roger Filer during the Revolution was in Captain Ebenezer Fitch Bissell's Company in Huntington's 17th Continental Regiment in 1776.[3]

☞ **Private Lemuel Fuller** was born in Norwich, Connecticut, July 14, 1757, the son of Judah and Abigail (Wentworth) Fuller.[4] The name Lemuel Fuller appears for the first time after the start of the Revolution on the Lexington Alarm List for the Town of Norwich. The *Record of Service of Connecticut Men in the War of the Revolution* lists a Lemuel Fuller in Captain Ebenezer Fitch Bissell's Company of Huntington's 17th Continental Regiment, but "our" Lemuel Fuller provided in his pension application that he enlisted in

---

[1] CT State Library, *Barbour Collection*; F. Phelps Leach, *Additions and Corrections for Thomas Hungerford* (East Highgate, VT: pub. by the author, 1932), pp. 15-16, http://persi.heritagequestonline.com/...; *Record of Service of Connecticut Men in the War of the Revolution*, p. 83, 102.
[2] Stiles, *History and Genealogies of Ancient Windsor*, Vol. II, p. 276; CT State Library, *Barbour Collection*, and Church Records slip index.
[3] *Connecticut Men in the French and Indian War*, Vol. II, pp. 244 , 305; *Record of Service of Connecticut Men in the War of the Revolution*, p. 102.
[4] *Some of the Descendants of Captain Matthew Fuller*, pp. 72-73; CT State Library, *Barbour Collection*.

Captain Joseph Jewett's Company, not Capt. Bissell's Company, on November 28, 1775, for one year.[1]

☞ **Private Carmi Higley** was born in Canton, Connecticut, May 16, 1749, the son of John and Apphia (Humphreys) Higley. Carmi married his cousin, Hester, the widow of Thomas Case, and the daughter of Captain Josiah Case and his wife, Hester Higley. She was born May 10, 1745. Carmi and Hester had one child, a son that was born during the year 1775. Carmi Higley enlisted in January 1776, in Captain Ebenezer Fitch Bissell's Company, in Huntington's 17th Continental Regiment.[2]

☞ **Private Alexander Ingham** was born February 18, 1738, in Hebron, Connecticut, the son of Dr. Samuel and Ruth Ingham. The Ingham genealogy that provided this information does not contain the name of his mother, which comes from his baptismal record in Bolton, Connecticut, church records for August 26, 1739.[3] Alexander first enlisted as a soldier in the French and Indian War in the campaign of 1757, in Capt. Edmund Wells' 11th Company in Col. Phineas Lyman's 1st Regiment. He enlisted next in 1759, in Capt. Ichabod Phelps' 5th Company in Col. Nathan Whiting's 2nd Regiment. In 1760 he again enlisted, but Capt. Ichabod Phelps' Company that year was designated the 8th Company in the same regiment. Alexander's brother, Thomas, lost his life in the campaign of 1762, in Cuba. When Huntington's 17th Continental Regiment was organized in 1776, Alexander enlisted as a private in Capt. Elizur Hubbard's Company.[4] Alexander Ingham married Catherine Noble (or Trumbull according to the Ingham genealogy) at Hebron on May 1, 1759.[5] By 1764, they had had three children.

---

[1] *Record of Service of Connecticut Men in the War of the Revolution*, pp. 19, 102; NARA, Series M805, Roll 343, Revolutionary War Pension Application, W648/BLWT26490-160-55.

[2] Mary Coffin Johnson, *The Higleys and Their Ancestry* (New York: D. Appleton & Co., 1896), p. 409-410, http://persi.heritagequestonline.com/...; *Record of Service of Connecticut Men in the War of the Revolution*, p. 102.

[3] Arthur B. Ingham, *The Ingham Family* (Pebble Beach, CA: pub. by the author, 1968) family #'s 12 & 21; CT State Library, *Church Records Slip Index*.

[4] *Connecticut Men in the French and Indian War*, Vol. I, p. 188; Vol. II, pp. 135, 202; *Record of Service of Connecticut Men in the War of the Revolution*, p. 102.

[5] CT State Library, *Church Records Slip Index*.

☞ **Private Solomon Ingham**, cousin of the above, was born November 1, 1751, in Hebron, Connecticut. He was the son of Daniel and Mahitabel (Phelps) Ingham.[1] He enlisted first during the Revolutionary War in Captain Abijah Rowley's Company, Colonel Jedediah Huntington's 8th Connecticut Regiment on July 1, 1775. He served with his company at New London and then marched with his company to Roxbury to join the rest of the regiment. When the 8th Connecticut was reorganized into the 17th Continental Regiment, Ingham enlisted for one year in Captain Elizur Hubbard's Company.[2]

☞ **Private John Kingsbury** was born in Plainfield, Connecticut, July 3, 1757, the son of Stephen and Sarah (Spalding) Kingsbury. John was the first child born to the couple. He was eighteen years of age when he enlisted in Captain Caleb Trowbridge's Company, Huntington's 17th Continental Regiment in January 1776.[3]

☞ **Private John Lewis** was born in Reading, Massachusetts, January 4, 1723, the son of another John Lewis, and the widow Martha (Mills) Denton of Jamaica, Long Island. Shortly after 1730, the family moved from Reading to Ashford, Connecticut. John Lewis married Sarah Cross, the daughter of John and Patience (Fuller) Cross, of Mansfield, on April 23, 1746. The marriage was recorded in the Bozrah, Connecticut, First Church Records.[4] Before becoming a separate town, Bozrah was known as the New Concord section of the town of Norwich. One year later, John Lewis fathered a son. The birth record, which did not include the mother, came from Tolland, Connecticut, a town about twenty miles north of Bozrah.

Considering his name was somewhat common (there were other Connecticut men named John Lewis, four of whom have been identified and appear on the muster rolls of other military units during the Revolution), the following records can only be considered probable enlistment records for John Lewis. That assumption is based

[1] NARA, Series M805, Roll 462, Revolutionary War Pension Application, W13527; *The Ingham Family*, family #96.
[2] *Record of Service of Connecticut Men in the War of the Revolution*, pp. 88 & 103.
[3] Frederick John Kingsbury, *The Genealogy of the Descendants of Henry Kingsbury* (Hartford: Case, Lockwood & Brainard Co., 1905), pp. 122, 123, 571, http://persi.heritagequestonline.com/...; CT State Library, *Barbour Collection*; *Record of Service of Connecticut Men in the War of the Revolution*, p. 102.
[4] Charles H. Lewis, *John Lewis of Berkshire, Vermont* (Westminster, MD: Heritage Books, Inc., 2004), p. 46.

on the proximity of his towns of residence (Bozrah/Norwich and Tolland) to the enlistment locations in Connecticut of the various military units. John Lewis was first a private in Lt.-Col. Samuel Coit's, 2nd Company, 2nd Regiment, during the campaign of 1758;[1] private, Major/Captain John Durkee's 3rd Company, in Col. Eleazer Fitch's 4th Regiment, during the Campaign of 1759;[2] and private, Major/Captain John Durkee's 3rd Company, Major-General Phineas Lyman's 1st Regiment, during the Campaign of 1762 in the expedition against Havana.[3] Company commanders at that time generally recruited from their own towns or the surrounding areas. Samuel Coit was from Preston, a town adjacent to Norwich, and John Durkee was from Norwich, so that the men in their companies were most likely from that immediate area.

At the commencement of the Revolutionary War, John Lewis (spelled Luis) was on a payroll dated May 10, 1775, for men given credit for three half-day's training between October 1774, and May 1775, in the South Tolland Military Company.[4] Many of those men then enlisted in Captain Solomon Willes 5th Company, in Colonel Joseph Spencer's 2nd Connecticut Regiment. John Lewis was given credit for service in that regiment from May 3 to December 17, 1775. This regiment was stationed, along with Huntington's 8th Connecticut Regiment, at Roxbury during the siege of Boston. When the 2nd Connecticut Regiment was disbanded in December 1775, the name John Lewis appeared in Captain Jonathan Brewster's Company in Jedediah Huntington's 17th Continental Regiment.[5] Other men from the Fifth Company of the 2nd Regiment also enlisted in the new 17th Continental Regiment.

Private Levi Loveland was born in Glastonbury, Connecticut, November 19, 1749, the son of Elisha and Hannah (Hills) Loveland. He married April 20, 1775, his first cousin, Esther Hills, who was born about 1754, the daughter of Ebenezer Hills of East Hartford. The

---

[1] Jonathan Brewster, later his captain in Huntington's 17th Regiment, was clerk of this company.

[2] His brother, Reuben Lewis, of Capt. Timothy Hierlihey's Company, died during this campaign.

[3] *Rolls of Connecticut Men in the French and Indian War*, Vol. II, pp. 34, 164, 302.

[4] CT State Library, *Connecticut Archives/ Revolutionary War, 1763-1789*, Series. I, Vol. IIa, Document 38d.

[5] *Connecticut Men in the War of the Revolution*, pp. 48 & 102.

first of ten children was born to them in August 1775.[1] According to his Revolutionary War pension file, he enlisted first in Colonel Wolcott's Regiment of Connecticut State militia from January 1, 1776, until April 1, 1776. By the time of the Battle of Long Island, he was in Captain Elizur Hubbard's Company, Huntington's 17th Continental Regiment.[2]

👉 **Private Daniel Moses** was born June 22, 1729, the son of Caleb and Hannah (Beaman) Moses of Simsbury, Connecticut. Daniel married Mary Wilcox, born 1732, the daughter of Azariah Wilcox.[3] They settled at West Simsbury, and had eight children prior to the Revolutionary War. Daniel enlisted in Captain Ebenezer Fitch Bissell's Company, Huntington's 17th Continental Regiment in 1776. His name is found only on the ammunition return of Capt. Bissell's Company, completed in New York on May 15, 1776.[4]

👉 **Private Salmon (Samuel in *Connecticut Men*) Moulton** was born September 6, 1759 (according to the family Bible), in Stafford, Connecticut, the son of Stephen and Eleanor (Converse) Moulton.[5] Shortly after the Battle of Bunker Hill, in the latter part of June or early July 1775, he went as a substitute for his brother, Howard Moulton, and enlisted as a private in Lt. Elijah Robinson's Company in Colonel Enos' Connecticut State militia regiment. The regiment marched to Roxbury where he served until discharged in December when he returned to Stafford. He shortly reenlisted in Captain Ozias Bissell's Company in Huntington's 17th Continental Regiment, in

---

[1] J. B. Loveland and George Loveland, *Genealogy of the Loveland Family* (Fremont, Ohio: I. M. Keeler & Son, 1892), p. 198, http://persi.heritagequestonline.com/...; CT State Library, *Barbour Collection*.
[2] NARA, Series M805, Roll 539, Revolutionary War Pension Application, W9145; *Record of Service of Connecticut Men in the War of the Revolution*, p. 102.
[3] Zebina Moses, *Historical Sketches of John Moses, of Plymouth* (Hartford: Case, Lockwood & Brainard, 1890), pp. 53, 55, 56, 57, http://persi.heritagequestonline.com/...; CT State Library, *Barbour Collection*.
[4] *Rolls and Lists of Connecticut Men in the Revolution 1775-1783* (Hartford: CT Historical Society, 1901; Electronic edition, Heritage Books, Inc., CD #1360), p. 27.
[5] NARA, Series M805, Roll 603, Revolutionary War Pension Application, S23810; Barbour File gives date of birth as Sept. 8, 1758; Eleanor Johnson Baker, *A Genealogy of the Descendants of William Johnson of Charlestown, MA* (Newburyport, MA: Newburyport Press, Inc., 1969), p. 133, http://persi.heritagequestonline.com/...

January 1776. He mentioned in his pension application enlisting with 2nd Lt. Solomon Makepeace: Joseph Chapman was the ensign, and Ozias Bissell, Jr., was the orderly sergeant. His company marched from Stafford back to Roxbury, and Moulton remained there with the rest of the regiment until the evacuation of Boston by the British the following March.

☞ **Private Robert Newcomb** may have been the Robert Newcomb, born September 25, 1759, the son of Robert and Mary (Young) Newcomb of Truro, Massachusetts.[1] The genealogy of the Newcomb family, unfortunately, claims two conflicting records of service during the same period: one in Huntington's Regiment, and the other for service on Cape Ann. The service on Cape Ann was probably attributable to another Robert Newcomb from Gloucester, Massachusetts (son of Henry and Mary, born Feb. 11, 1757). If the individual in the Newcomb genealogy from Truro is "our" Robert Newcomb, it is not stated how he happened to enlist in a Connecticut regiment. However, there were members of a related Newcomb family living in, and around Norwich, Connecticut at the time, and he might have been in residence with them. If so, he first enlisted as a private in Captain Jonathan Brewster's Company, in Huntington's 8th Connecticut Regiment, on July 25, 1775. He would have been 15 years of age. He served until December 10, 1775, and then reenlisted as a drummer in Captain Ebenezer Fitch Bissell's Company, in Huntington's 17th Continental Regiment in January 1776.[2]

☞ **Private Zadock (or Zadoc) Pratt** was born January 15, 1755, in Hartford, Connecticut, the son of Zephaniah and Abigail Pratt.[3] By occupation, Zadock was a tanner. According to his pension file, Zadock first enlisted at Lyme, Connecticut, in December 1755, and served for about one month in Captain Christopher Ely's Company, in Colonel Parsons' Connecticut Regiment. He then enlisted in

---

[1] Bethuel Merritt Newcomb, *Andrew Newcomb, 1618-1686, and His Descendants* (New Haven: The Tuttle, Morehouse & Taylor Co., 1923) , p. 58, http://persi.heritagequestonline.com/...

[2] *Record of Service of Connecticut Men in the War of the Revolution*, pp. 85, 102, 103.

[3] Chapman, *The Chapman Family* , pp. 257, 258, 262.

Huntington's 17th Continental Regiment in 1776, and served in Captain Joseph Jewett's Company.[1]

☞ **Private Elijah Stanton** was born in Preston, Connecticut, on November 25, 1754, the son of Daniel and Dinah Stanton.[2] According to his pension file, he first volunteered in Captain Ebenezer Brewster's Company in 1775, and marched to Roxbury during the siege of Boston, arriving there about May 1. Ebenezer Brewster's Company was the 2nd Company in Colonel Parsons' 6th Regiment. Once at Roxbury, the company was employed building fortifications in and around Roxbury. After his initial term of enlistment expired, Stanton reenlisted, this time in Huntington's 17th Continental Regiment upon its formation in January 1776, in Captain Timothy Percival's Company. In March his company took part in building the fortifications on Dorchester Heights, overlooking Boston.[3]

☞ **Private Jacob Sterling** (or Starling) was born in Lyme, Connecticut, on March 3, 1744, the son of John and Jane (Ransom) Sterling. Jacob married Edey Tucker on October 14, 1765. They had four daughters born before the start of the Revolution. Jacob enlisted first, after the start of the Revolution, in Captain David Fithian Sill's Company in Colonel Samuel Parsons' 6th Connecticut Regiment, on May 8, 1775. This company remained in New London until June 17, after which time they were ordered to Roxbury as part of General Joseph Spencer's Brigade. Jacob Sterling served until the end of his enlistment on December 18, 1775. While he was gone, his first daughter, Abigail, died in August 1775. On December 16 his wife gave birth to another daughter whom they named Abigail as well. Upon the formation of Huntington's 17th Continental Regiment in January 1776, Jacob reenlisted in Joseph Jewett's Company.[4]

---

[1] NARA, Series M805, Roll 665, Revolutionary War Pension Application, S44263; *Record of Service of Connecticut Men in the War of the Revolution*, p. 102.
[2] CT State Library, *Barbour Collection*.
[3] NARA, Series M805, Roll 766, Revolutionary War Pension Application, S14623; *Record of Service of Connecticut Men in the War of the Revolution*, pp. 73, 102.
[4] CT State Library, *Barbour Collection*; NARA, Series M805, Roll 767, Revolutionary War Pension Application S36797; Albert Mack Sterling, *The Sterling Genealogy* (New York: The Grafton Press, 1909), pp. 324-325, http://persi.heritagequestonline.com/...; *Record of Service of Connecticut Men in the War of the Revolution*, pp. 73, 102.

☞ **Private Peter Way** of Lyme, Connecticut, deposed in his Revolutionary War Pension application that he first enlisted on or about April 1, 1776, in Captain Joseph Jewett's Company in Huntington's 17th Continental Regiment. This date coincides with the march of the regiment to New London, before embarking for New York. He enlisted for the term of eight months. His parents are not known, but at the time of his pension application in 1818, he was 64 years of age, which would make his date of birth about 1754.[1]

☞ **Private Duroy (or Duren, or Duran, etc.) Whittlesey** was the son of Joseph and Abigail (Chapman) Whittlesey of Saybrook, Connecticut. No date of birth has been found, but his parents were married January 28, 1719, with the known dates of birth of the children occurring during the 1720's. The spelling of his first name is given as "Duren," in the Whittlesey genealogy, which seems to be the most common spelling of the name. His wife is unknown, but Duren lived at Haddam, Connecticut, and had five sons, one of whom, also named Duren, was born October 24, 1775, and later settled in Butler County, Ohio.[2] On May 11, 1775, Duren enlisted in the 1st Company in Colonel Joseph Spencer's 2nd Connecticut Regiment, which was also posted at Roxbury during the siege of Boston. His name is on the list of men from East Haddam who were exempt from certain taxes for serving during the campaign of 1775. He served in Spencer's 2nd Connecticut Regiment until December 17, 1775, and then in January 1776, he enlisted in Captain Joseph Jewett's Company, Colonel Huntington's 17th Continental Regiment.[3]

[1] NARA, Series M805, Roll 844, Revolutionary War Pension Application, W18228; *Record of Service of Connecticut Men in the War of the Revolution*, p. 102.
[2] Charles Barney Whittelsey, *Genealogy of the Whittlesey-Whittelsey Family* (2nd edition, New York: McGraw-Hill Book Co., 1941), pp. 63 & 79, http://persi.heritagequestonline.com/....
[3] *Lists and Returns of Connecticut Men in the Revolution, 1775-1783* (Hartford: CT Historical Society, 1909; Electronic edition, Heritage Books, Inc., CD1360), p. 3; *Record of Service of Connecticut Men in the War of the Revolution*, pp. 46, 102.

3. The Black Facings

Between April and August of 1776, Washington cobbled together an army using regular Continental regiments plus state militia units from all over the newly declared United States. He used them first to complete the defenses around New York harbor. Without a navy, yet surrounded by one of the best deepwater anchorages in the world, the General understood that his position on Manhattan Island was extremely vulnerable to attack from all sides by the enormous firepower and mobility of the British fleet. Nevertheless, New York was considered by many, including the Continental Congress, to be the key to the continent and was not to be surrendered without a fight.

Now that Washington's army had arrived in New York, the extensive infrastructure needed for the support of the army had to be reproduced a second time since the start of the war. Just as during the siege of Boston, housing for officers and soldiers alike had to be found among the current residences in the city or built from scratch. Lt. Fitch, in his diary, noted the position of the encampment of Huntington's Regiment near Jones' Hill, in what is now known as the Lower East Side. This was on the north side of present-day Grand Street, and in the line of Ridge St.[1] This would have been a vast tent encampment in that area, designated by Washington's General Orders of April 29, 1776. The 1st Brigade, under General Heath, was to camp on the right; the 2nd Brigade, under General Spencer, of which Huntington's Regiment was still a part, was on the left; and the 4th Brigade, under General Lord Stirling, was to camp in the center. A regiment of artillery set up their camp in the rear.[2] Eventually a small fort, known as Spencer's redoubt, was built on a hill overlooking the encampment, probably the Jones' Hill referred to by Fitch.

In order to protect New York, Washington had to build extensive and widespread fortifications at key points around New York harbor. Multiple fortifications were built on Manhattan Island, across the East

---

[1] Sabine, *The New York Diary of Lt. Jabez Fitch*, p. 98.
[2] "General Orders, April 29, 1776," *The George Washington Papers*, Series 3, Subseries G, pp. 231-232, http://memory.loc.gov/ammem/gwhtml/gwseries.html

River in Brooklyn, on Governor's Island, at Paulus Hook (now Jersey City) on the New Jersey side of the harbor, and on Staten Island. Men who had signed on to fight, now had to contribute other skills, as well as considerable unskilled labor, in the construction of these fortifications. Each morning the various regiments would muster on their camp parade grounds and then separate into work parties to contribute to the construction of the many fortifications.

From Huntington's Regiment, Lt. Jabez Fitch of Capt. Joseph Jewett's Company supervised a crew helping to construct Fort Independence at King's Bridge on the northern tip of Manhattan.[1] Jacob Hazen, a private in Jonathan Brewster's Company stated in his pension application that he was employed part of the time in building chevaux-de-frise (in this case, obstructions to navigation made from a variety of sunken ships and other obstacles connected by chains) on the "North River" (Hudson's River) prior to the Battle of Long Island. The General Orders of May 25 sent at least some of the men from Huntington's Regiment over to Red Hook on Long Island to work on the fortification there.

☞ Private Solomon Ingham of Capt. Hubbard's Company wrote that Huntington's Regiment was employed building forts around the City of New York and "preparing places to store water, etc." Ingham also recorded the first death in his company, that of **Sergeant Samuel Skinner**, the company steward, who died of dysentery, "before the arrival of the British."[2] This information is at odds with the *Record of Service of Connecticut Men in the War of the Revolution*, that reports Skinner as missing after the Battle of Long Island. In this case Solomon Ingham is probably correct, since he would have had direct knowledge of, or perhaps actually witnessed, his fellow soldier's death. Samuel Skinner was probably the Samuel Skinner born at Colchester, Connecticut, on September 11, 1735, the son of Nathaniel Skinner, Jr.[3]

Private Ingham was also a witness to one of the more troubling episodes of the summer: the execution of Thomas Hickey, one of General Washington's Life Guards, who was found guilty of sedition and mutiny. The execution took place on the parade ground between

---

[1] Sabine, *The New York Diary of Lt. Jabez Fitch*, p. 12.
[2] NARA, Series M805, Roll 462, Revolutionary War Pension Application, W13527.
[3] CT State Library, *Barbour Collection*.

Spencer's and Stirling's encampment at 11 A.M. on June 28. All of the men in camp at the time were ordered to march in formation to bear witness to the spectacle.[1]

Although the trial of Thomas Hickey was the most serious disciplinary incident that occurred in Washington's army in New York, there were nearly daily courts-martial convened to try men for desertion and a variety of lesser offenses. During the spring and summer, four men from Huntington's Regiment were brought up on charges: on May 2, Samuel Londers and Abner Fuller of Capt. E. F. Bissell's Company were convicted of desertion and received 30 lashes on their bare backs; the next day John Maxfield of Capt. Tyler's Company was tried for desertion and received 39 lashes; on August 13, John Gardner of Capt. Trowbridge's Company was convicted of desertion and received 39 lashes. The men of Huntington's Regiment were not singled out, however, and there were many from other regiments who were on the receiving end of courts-martial while the army was in New York.[2]

Washington now commanded an army of occupation in New York, and was confronted with many of the same problems the British had experienced the year before when they held Boston. He not only had to deal with the logistical support of his troops, but with the even more complex issue of the army's interaction with a civilian population that was not entirely amenable to the situation. Where the towns surrounding Boston had been overwhelmingly friendly to the rebel cause, New York was deeply divided in its allegiance. Unlike much of New England, New York had a powerful and active Loyalist community, which in a number of instances proved openly hostile to the rebel cause. Colonel Huntington wrote on June 13, that there had been two violent clashes recently between Whig and Tory mobs in the city, in which "some of the Army had imprudently meddled." In the future, soldiers were ordered not to take part in such confrontations unless directed to do so.[3]

[1] "General Orders, June 27, 1776," *The George Washington Papers*, Series 3, Subseries G, p. 292, http://memory.loc.gov/ammem/gwhtml/gwseries.html
[2] "General Orders, May 2 & 3, and August 13, 1776," *The George Washington Papers*, Series 3, Subseries G, pp. 231-232, http://memory.loc.gov/ammem/gwhtml/gwseries.html
[3] "Jedediah Huntington to Jabez Huntington, June 13, 1776," *Collections of the CT Historical Society,* Vol. XX, p. 298,

To further complicate matters, the New Englanders among the American troops had inherited a long-standing bias against the "Yorkers." For years there had been nearly open conflict between the New England colonies and New York over land claimed by both sides along the shared border. Even prior to that, there were inherent differences in values, lifestyle, and governance, and particularly the system of land ownership and management. The government of the colony of New York was deeply influenced by extremely wealthy land barons, who owned vast tracts of land up and down the Hudson corridor. Too large to manage themselves, these huge estates were divided by their owners into smaller parcels, which were leased to farmers who actually did the work farming the land. These tenant farmers paid the land barons according to the terms of their leases, usually in crops or other products. The tenants rarely had the opportunity to own their own land in fee simple. Although the system varied in the details from one large land grant to another- and one land baron to another- New Englanders, used to the freedom of owning their own land, viewed the system as akin to medieval serfdom, if not actual slavery.

Colonel Huntington in a letter written from New York to Governor Trumbull of Connecticut on July 22, 1776, expressed his concerns regarding this issue:

Since the Declaration of Independence, I have often thought how anxious you would be that the leaders of the present day, though they themselves may not reap the fruits of their labours, should not spare any pains to have the foundations of the great Continental government well laid, and as well that of particular States, that publick virtue and liberty, which make the publick happiness, may be secured and perpetuated. It is plain to see, from a small acquaintance with the manners of this people [the New Yorkers], the pernicious influence of some overgrown estates. The Landlords, though few in number, have the power of disobliging their numerous dependants, and therefore assume the right of dictating to them in their most interesting and tenderest concerns. Ought not or cannot a timely remedy be provided against the limitation of the descent of large tracts of land that carry such evil power with them?[1]

General orders issued from Washington's headquarters in New York during this time are replete with concerns over the discipline and welfare of the troops. Although General Washington now had a national army drawn from the various colonies, it had not yet coalesced, and order and discipline varied from regiment to regiment. Unfortunately, some of those regiments fit the description provided by many of their own officers of an unruly and undisciplined lot. It was a struggle to prevent soldiers from preying on the civilian population. Officers also worried that the hoard of local prostitutes would infect the soldiers with a variety of diseases that would sideline them and keep them from performing their duties. The puritan sensibilities of some of the New Englanders were offended by the situation, as Colonel Loammi Baldwin of Massachusetts confided in a letter to his wife, Mary, at Woburn dated June 12, 1776:

...The inhabitants of the holy ground [a euphemism for the red light district which had established itself on church owned property in southern Manhattan] *has brought some of the officers and a number of the soldiers into difficulty. The whores (by information) continue their imploy which is become very lucrative. Their unparalleled conduct is a sufficient antidote against any desires that a person can have that has one spark of modesty or virtue left in him and the last attum* [atom] *must certainly be lost before he can associate himself with these bitchfoxly jades, jills, haggs, strums, prostitutes and all these multiplied into one another and then their full character not displayed.*

Perhaps You will call me censorious and exclaim too much upon bare reports when I say that I was never within the doors of nor 'changed a word with any of them except in the execution of my duty as officer of the day in going the grand round with my guard of escort, have broke up the knots of men and women fighting, pulling caps, swearing, crying "Murder" etc-hurried them off to the Provost dungeon by half dozens, there let them lay mixed till

---

[1] Peter Force, *American Archives* (5th Series, published under authority of an act of Congress passed on March 2, 1833, and March 3, 1843: 1848-1853), Vol. I, p. 510.

next day.   Then some are punished and sum get off clear-Hell's work.[1]

It wasn't just "Yorkers" and New Englanders that had their differences.   None of the colonies prior to the Revolution had had much interaction, and regional biases thrived throughout the colonies.   This became a serious threat to military order that had to be addressed. Fighting between soldiers of the various colonies prompted Washington via general orders from headquarters on August 1st to lecture the troops that there was no better way to assist the enemy than through divisions amongst themselves.   Although the following description is tainted by the very same regional biases that Washington was working so hard to eliminate, it still paints a vivid picture of the challenges that had to be faced in creating a new, unified American Army.   It was written by Captain Alexander Graydon, an articulate but cynical officer from Pennsylvania:

> *A considerable portion of our motley army had already assembled in New York and its vicinity.   The troops were chiefly from the eastern provinces; those from the southern, with the exception of Hand's, Magaw's and our regiment, had not yet come on.   The appearance of things was not much calculated to excite sanguine expectations in the mind of a sober observer.   Great numbers of people were indeed to be seen, and those who are not accustomed to the sight of bodies under arms are always prone to exaggerate them.   But this propensity to swell the mass had not an equal tendency to convert it into soldiery; and the irregularity, want of discipline, bad arms and defective equipment in all respects of this multitudinous assemblage gave no favourable impression of its prowess.*
>
> *The materials of which the eastern battalions were composed were apparently the same as those of which I had seen so unpromising a specimen at Lake George.   I speak particularly of the officers, who were in no single respect distinguishable from their men, other than in the coloured cockades, which, for this very purpose, had been prescribed in general orders; a different*

---

[1] Henry Steele Commager and Richard B Morris, (eds.), *The Spirit of 'Seventy-Six* (New York: Harper Collins, Pub., 1958, 1967; reprint, Castle Books, 2002), pp. 420-421.

colour being assigned to the officers of each grade. So far from aiming at a deportment which might raise them above their privates, and thence prompt them to due respect and obedience to their commands, the object was, by humility, to preserve the existing blessing of equality: an illustrious instance of which was given by Colonel Putnam, the chief engineer of the army, and no less a personage than the nephew of the major-general of that name.

"What," says a person meeting him one day with a piece of meat in his hand, "carrying home your rations yourself, Colonel?"

"Yes," says he, "and I do it to set the officers a good example."

But if any aristocratic tendencies had been really discovered by the colonel among his countrymen, requiring this wholesome example, they must have been of recent origin, and the effects of southern contamination, since I have been credibly informed that it was no unusual thing in the army before Boston for a colonel to make drummers and fifers of his sons, thereby not only being enabled to form a very snug, economical mess, but to aid also considerably the revenue of the family chest. In short, it appeared that the sordid spirit of gain was the vital principle of this greater part of the army.[1]

As in nearly all military encampments during the Revolutionary War, the troops suffered more from disease than wounds in battle. Washington struggled to keep them healthy, despite close quarters, prostitution, bad food, bad sanitation, and bad water. The returns of the troops submitted for Huntington's regiment are typical for the time, and provide graphic evidence of the extent of the problem.

When they were originally organized at the end of 1775, all Continental regiments were to consist of 728 men, but on July 20, 1776, Colonel Huntington had 264 soldiers fit for duty and in camp; 146 sick, but present; and 5 sick and absent in the hospital. One week later, on July 27, there were now 226 present and fit for duty; 134 sick; and 25 now sick and absent in the hospital. By August 3, Huntington's Regiment had been reduced to 214 present and fit for duty; 184 sick, but only one was in the hospital. On each of the three

---

[1] "Memoirs of Captain Alexander Graydon," *The Spirit of 'Seventy-Six*, p. 419.

returns, about 130 other soldiers, presumed to be fit for duty, were listed as "on command (assigned to duties outside the camp)." Most of these men would probably have been called in to camp as the time for action approached. Therefore, by August 3, just three weeks prior to the Battle of Long Island, Huntington had more than a third of his already undermanned regiment unavailable for duty due to illness, out of a total complement of about 540 men at the time.[1]

To defend New York, Washington divided his forces into five divisions under Generals Nathanael Greene, Israel Putnam, William Heath, Joseph Spencer, and John Sullivan. Not knowing where the British might attack, one division was deployed to the northern end of Manhattan, at King's Bridge; three were deployed to the southern end of the island around the City of New York itself; and General Greene was placed in charge of the forces on Long Island. Because the Americans had no effective deterrent to the inherent mobility of the British fleet, it remained a guessing game right up until the day of the attack just where the British army might make its primary push. As a result, Washington could not concentrate all his forces in any one place.

In May, General Greene took over the construction of the Brooklyn defenses, begun by General Lee in February. It is hard to visualize now, but in 1776, underlying the modern city of Brooklyn, there was a sparsely populated, rural, agricultural community. In the immediate area of the Long Island terminus of the East River ferry, there were about fifty scattered homes, surrounded by pastures, wood lots, orchards and gardens. Brooklyn itself was a small village located about a mile east of the ferry along the road to the still smaller villages of Bedford and Jamaica.

The shoreline in the area has changed significantly as well. In 1776, Brooklyn was situated on a peninsula, or lobe of land, roughly shaped like a human ear, at the western end of Long Island. Bordering on three sides were the East River on the west, Wallabout Cove on the north, and Gowanus Bay on the south. Landfill has now obliterated much of the expanse of both Wallabout Cove and the Gowanus Bay, which in earlier times more clearly intruded into the topography of Long Island. Gowanus Bay terminated a mile or so into the Island in a long, wide salt-marsh that flooded at high tide, in turn ending in a small creek that was dammed for a mill pond. On the southwest

---

[1] Force, *American Archives*, 5th Series, Vol. I, pp. 508, 640, 764.

corner of our "earlobe," bordering Gowanus Bay and its expansive tidal marsh, a small peninsula jutted out towards Governor's Island known as Red Hook. A fortification constructed at Red Hook guarded the channel between Governor's Island and Brooklyn.

Near the extreme inland terminus of Gowanus Creek, just to the east of Red Hook, began a connected chain of fortifications constructed outside Brooklyn Village and built to protect New York City from any invasion by the enemy landed on Long Island. The fortified line extended three miles northeast to Wallabout Cove, in effect creating one extended fortified position with the other three sides protected (or sealed off, depending on your perspective) by water. It was impossible in the time allotted to build a solid fortification on that long a line, so three separate self-contained forts and two smaller redoubts were constructed, connected by breastworks, chevaux-de-frise (in this case sharpened poles anchored in the ground to face the enemy), and abattis (another type of hastily constructed fortification using felled trees with sharpened branches facing a potential enemy).

On the right (or southwest) end of the American line of fortifications overlooking the Gowanus Marsh was Fort Box, a diamond-shaped fort named for Daniel Box, General Nathanael Greene's brigade major. Three hundred yards farther left (or northeast) was a star-shaped fort called Fort Greene for General Nathanael Greene. It was garrisoned by a full regiment and guarded the road east to Jamaica. On the other side of the road was a smaller, round redoubt, and this together with Fort Greene commanded the center of the American lines. Farther to the left, and up rising ground, was another star-shaped fort named Fort Putnam after the chief engineer, and son of the general, Colonel Rufus Putnam. On the other side of the same hill, a small fortification, simply called The Redoubt, anchored the left end of the line overlooking Wallabout Cove.[1]

Other fortifications inside the main line of defense, such as the one at Red Hook, were strategically placed to prevent the enemy gaining the rear of the American lines by water. Although we are focused here on the works at Brooklyn, it should be remembered that across the East River on Manhattan Island, another series of

---

[1] Henry R. Stiles, *The Civil, Political, Professional and Ecclesiastical History and Commercial and Industrial Record of the County of Kings and the City of Brooklyn, NY* (New York: W. W. Munsell & Co., 1884), p. 51, http://persi.heritagequestonline.com/...

fortifications from the southern tip of the Island north to King's Bridge were being completed at the same time. By the middle of June the fortifications at Brooklyn, though not entirely complete, were substantially manned and armed.

On June 29, true to expectations, a vast sea of masts, delineating a British fleet over one hundred vessels strong, appeared in the Lower Bay of New York harbor, and proceeded to anchor off Sandy Hook, New Jersey. On July 1, the fleet weighed anchor and moved over to Long Island, where they set anchor once again about a half a mile off shore. Reinforcements were immediately sent to General Greene on Long Island in the belief that the landing was about to occur in that place, but after discovering the strength of the rebels on Long Island the British did not disembark. Among Gen. Greene's reinforcements was Private Solomon Ingham of Hubbard's Company, who wrote that, "While the British lay at the Hook, and were slowly moving up their fleet some of our men fired at a Long boat which was returned by cannon balls from the ship by which a man near me had his thigh broke."[1] Several days later, the fleet moved again, finally unloading the British Army on Staten Island with no opposition from the largely Tory population there.

The Ministerial Army was commanded by General William Howe, who had the year before been in command of the attacking forces on Bunker Hill. His older brother, Admiral Lord Richard Howe, was in command of the British fleet. Slowly, over the next month and a half, the British gathered their forces, both from Halifax, Nova Scotia, and from England. At various times they probed the American defenses with heavily armed ships and gunboats, but gave no real indication where their army might ultimately land and attack the Americans.

The British on Staten Island, protected by a massive fleet, and camped in the midst of a very sympathetic Tory population, were virtually invulnerable to attack. Washington mulled over the possibility, but did not have a navy capable of delivering his forces or protecting an amphibious landing. As a result, Washington had to sit and await General Howe's next move, staying in a constant state of tension and readiness. The August 8 general orders instructed Washington's troops that:

---

[1] NARA, Series M805, Roll 462, Revolutionary War Pension Application, W13527.

As the movements of the enemy, and intelligence by deserters, give the utmost reason to believe that the great struggle in which we are contending for everything dear to us, and our posterity, is near at hand, the General most earnestly recommends the closest attention to the state of the men's arms, ammunition, and flints; that if we should be suddenly called to action, nothing of this kind may be to provide; and he does most anxiously exhort both officers and soldiers, not to be out of their quarters or encampments.[1]

Both state militias and new Continental Army units were still pouring into New York at this late date. Some were outfitted with uniforms by their respective states, but many came with nothing but their own clothes. Washington did not have the resources to outfit all the troops in common uniforms, but did order that the new troops at least be provided with frilled hunting shirts and long pants made "gaiter-fashion about the legs." Such clothing was cheap, and by wearing almost anything underneath, the soldiers could stay warm in cool weather. A bonus to outfitting troops this way was the fear it ostensibly instilled in the British soldiers. This was the type of dress chosen by back-woods sharpshooters who had been found capable of picking off British officers at long distance with deadly accurate hunting rifles; shooting from behind the cover of trees or rocks, Indian fashion.[2] A general belief among the British troops was that anyone dressed this way was a consummate marksman.

Although the new troops coming into New York were clothed in a variety of different ways, the Continental Congress and General Washington had originally intended that the new regiments making up the Continental Army would be provided with common uniforms. A delegation from the Continental Congress meeting with General Washington at Cambridge the previous fall agreed "that as much as possible of the Cloth for this purpose be dyed brown and the Distinctions of the Regiments be in the Facings."[3] It was ordered that the new troops should spend:

---

[1] Force, *American Archives*, 5th Series, Vol. I, pp. 912-913.

[2] Force, *American Archives*, 5th Series, Vol. I, pp. 676-677.

[3] "Minutes of the Continental Congress Conference Committee, Oct. 20, 1775," *The George Washington Papers*, Series 4, p. 485, http://memory.loc.gov/ammem/gwhtml/gwseries.html

their money in Shirts, Shoes, Stockings and a good pair of leather Breeches and not in Coats and Waistcoats, as it is intended that the new army shall be cloathed in uniform. To effect which The Congress will lay in Goods upon the best terms they can be bought anywhere for ready Money, and will sell them to the Soldiers without any profit, by which means a Uniform Coat and Waistcoat will come cheaper to them than any other Cloathing of like kind can be bought. A number of Tailors will be immediately set to work to make Regimentals for those brave men who are willing at all hazards to defend their invaluable rights and privileges[1].

Ten shillings out of the forty shillings a month a private received were to be withheld from their wages until their clothing was paid for.[2] Further, the officers were not to go to great expense for their coats and waistcoats "until they are arranged into proper corps and the uniforms of the regiment they belong to ascertained..."[3] Upon the General Orders of November 12, 1775, the colonels of the new regiments were to decide as soon as possible what the uniforms of their regiments would be so that buttons with the proper regimental number on them could be made. By December 27, the colonels of the new regiments were already purchasing clothing for their men from the quartermaster's store. By January 5, 1776, the regimental coats were being furnished to the colonels for their men.

The General Orders are silent as to what the decision was regarding the individual regimental colors, but there is some evidence indicating what Huntington's 17th Continentals colors were. The Connecticut Courant on April 22, 1776, published an ad for the return of a deserter from Captain Percival's Company who was wearing a butternut colored coat and scarlet waistcoat. According to the Connecticut Gazette on April 19, 1776, Captain Tyler's Company wore a light colored coat and leather breeches. Regimental coats with

---

[1] "General Orders, Oct. 28, 1775," *The George Washington Papers*, Series 3, Subseries G, pp. 101-102, http://memory.loc.gov/ammem/gwhtml/gwseries.html
[2] "General Orders, Oct. 31, 1775," *The George Washington Papers*, Series 3, Subseries, G, pp. 103-105, http://memory.loc.gov/ammem/gwhtml/gwseries.html
[3] "General Orders, November 1, 1775," *The George Washington Papers*, Series 3, Subseries G, p. 105, http://memory.loc.gov/ammem/gwhtml/gwseries.html

black lapels were made for Lt. Fitch on February 14, 1776.[1] Taken collectively, this all sounds like something of a hodge-podge, but the different pieces of information probably describe the various components of the same uniform.

Private Solomon Ingham wrote that the regiment was known in New York as the "Black facings."[2] What was referred to as "facing" by both the orders of Congress and Private Ingham, was the lining of uniform coats which would have been turned out to form black lapels, collars and cuffs. This is consistent with the description of the coats made for Lt. Fitch. Since the other Continental Regiments at Boston had the same brown (or buff, or butternut) colored coats, the regimental distinction was in the color of the facing. For a regiment to have been nicknamed the "Black facings," the men would have been attired in regimental coats with black trim.

On April 22, 1776, Colonel Huntington now in New York wrote to his father in Norwich, "to order Benjamin Backus to send me all the Black Ribbonds he has on Hand by first safe Conveyance and direct them to Mr. Vandervoort for me."[3] What Huntington referred to as "Black Ribbonds" could have been used for trim for uniforms. Since Huntington's previous regiment, the 8th Connecticut, was known for being well-equipped and uniformed one year before, it is likely that Huntington's 17th Continental Regiment was similarly equipped just one year later. By the time the regiment reached New York they were probably uniformed with light brown, or butternut colored regimental coats with black lapels, cuffs and collars. They also probably wore a scarlet waist coat and leather breeches. Typically, the privates would have worn a round-crowned, wide-brim felt hat as well.

---

[1] Marko Zlatich and Peter F. Copeland, *General Washington's Army 1: 1775-1778* (Men-At-Arms Series 273, Oxford, UK: Osprey Pub., 1994), p. 13-14.
[2] NARA, Series M805, Roll 462, Revolutionary War Pension Application, W13527.
[3] *Collections of the Connecticut Historical Society*, Vol. XX, p. 280.

A soldier of the 17th Continental Regiment (by the author)
Brown coat w/ black facings(cuffs, lapels, collar, lining)

Each regiment was to have its own individual flag, or "standard," that was to bear the colors of the uniform. The number of the regiment was to appear in the same color as the facings of the regimental uniform. A brief slogan to be determined by the commanding colonel of the regiment was to be sown into the flag.[1] The slogan that would have appeared on the standard of Huntington's regiment has not been discovered, but the background color would most likely have been light brown and the lettering in black like their facings.

Despite the general perception of the unmilitary-like appearance of Washington's army, the following newspaper article written by a reporter from New York on July 11, 1776, demonstrates that at least some of the units (in this case also from Connecticut) made a suitably "martial" impression:

Since our last [report], *several of the new-raised Regiments of Connecticut troops have arrived in town, and appear to be as fine a body of men as any engaged in the present grand struggle for Liberty and Independence. Among them the Light Dragoons, between 4 and 600, who came to town yesterday, and paraded on horseback, through the city, made a noble and martial appearance: and as this corps are composed of the substantial Yeomanry of a virtuous Sister State, nothing could be more agreeably animating to all the friends of their country. Some of these worthy soldiers attired in their present uniforms at the first reduction of Louisbourg, and their "lank lean cheeks, and war worn coats," are viewed with more veneration by their* [illegible] *countrymen than if they were glimmering Nabobs from India, or Bashaws with* [nine] *Tails.*[2]

The reference above to the "first reduction" of Louisbourg was the siege of the French fortified city on Cape Breton Island, in Canada, on June 17, 1745, by New England volunteers. This would have made some of these Connecticut soldiers to be at least in their fifties, and although the 17th Regiment would not have been among the group

---

[1] "General Orders, February 20, 1776," *The George Washington Papers*, Series 3, Subseries G, pp. 185-186, http://memory.loc.gov/ammem/gwhtml/gwseries.html
[2] "Article 3-No Title," *The Connecticut Courant and Hartford Weekly Intelligencer*, July 15, 1776, p. 2, http://proquest.umi.com/

that was marching, this fact was born out in the ranks of the 17th as well.

General orders provided that each regiment was to have one ammunition cart and horse with spare cartridges kept in readiness near each regiment. One-half pint of rum was rationed out for each man and kept in the care "of a very discreet officer" to be delivered only in battle. As there were still some regiments not fully outfitted with arms, it was ordered that weapons should be taken from those who were sick and unfit for duty and given to those who needed them.[1]

Illness did not strike just the rank-and-file. General Nathanael Greene was taken down by malaria and replaced by General John Sullivan to command on Long Island. Colonel Huntington also became ill, and wrote on August 19 that his fever had reduced his "strength and flesh considerably."[2] It is likely that he too had malaria, but John Waldo, the regimental surgeon, reported only that Huntington was "abed with a slow fever" when he also was replaced by his second in command, Lieutenant-Colonel Joel Clark.[3] By August 26th, Huntington's condition had not improved, and if Washington had not been disinclined to approve furloughs he would have requested one. Colonel Huntington was very ill and totally unable to perform his duties.[4]

Colonel Samuel Holden Parsons was promoted to brigadier-general by Congress on August 9, and took over command of what had been General Spencer's 2nd Brigade, to which the 17th was attached. Parsons was formerly colonel of the 6th Connecticut Regiment in 1775. Like Huntington's, his regiment had been posted at Roxbury during the siege of Boston, and marched to New York after the siege was lifted in March. Besides Huntington's 17th, the continental regiments commanded by Colonels Wyllys, Deane,

---

[1] Force, *American Archives*, 5th Series, Vol. I, p. 913.
[2] "Jedediah Huntington to Jabez Huntington, August 19, 1776," *Collections of the CT Historical Society*, Vol. XX, p. 321.
[3] Sabine, *The New York Diary of Lt. Jabez Fitch*, p. 12; "Col. Joseph Trumbull to his brother, Aug. 27, 1776," quoted by Henry P. Johnston, *The Campaign of 1776 Around New York and Brooklyn* (1878: reprint Scholar's Bookshelf, Cranbury, NJ, 2005), Part II, p. 40.
[4] "Jedediah Huntington to Jabez Huntington, August 26, 1776," *Collections of the CT Historical Society*, Vol. XX, p. 322.

Durkee and Tyler of Connecticut, and Ward of Massachusetts, were also assigned to Parsons' brigade; in all about 2,500 men- at least on paper.[1]

Washington's general orders and letters during this painful time of waiting took on a more and more anxious tone as the inevitable, yet unpredictable, landing of the enemy approached. Fortifications were hastily completed, and regiments were supplied and made ready to march at a moment's notice. But still the American divisions could not be concentrated in any one place, and had to remain widely dispersed, without any certainty where the British attack would come. On August 8, Washington wrote his brother, John Augustine Washington in Virginia that:

> ...*We have a powerful fleet* [British] *within full view of us, distant about eight miles. We have General How's* [sic] *present Army, consisting, by good report, of about eight or nine thousand men upon Staten Island, covered by their ships. We have Lord Howe just arrived, and we have ships now coming in, which we suppose, but do not know, to be part of the fleet with the expected reinforcement. When this arrives, if the reports of deserters, prisoners, and Tories, are to be depended upon, the enemy's numbers will amount at least to twenty-five thousand men; ours to about fifteen thousand. More, indeed, are expected; but there is no certainty of their arrival, as harvest and a thousand other excuses are urged as the reasons of delay. What kind of opposition we shall be able to make, time only can show. I can only say, that the men appear to be in good spirits; and, if they will stand with me, the place shall not be carried without some loss, notwithstanding we are not yet in such a posture of defense as I could wish.*[2]

That same day, general orders warned that the "great struggle" was about to commence and recommended that close attention be given to the condition of every soldier's arms, ammunition and flints. On August 12, Washington wrote to congratulate General Charles Lee on his recent victory over the British on Sullivan's Island, Charlestown, South Carolina, and shared his worries that:

---

[1] Charles S. Hall, *Hall Ancestry* (New York: G. P. Putnam's, 1896), p. 315.
[2] Force, *American Archives*, 5th Series, Vol. I, p. 509.

At present, the enemy can bring more men to a point than we can, and, when reinforced by the Hessians (unless the Militia, faster than heretofore, come to our aid) their numbers, when the Hessians arrive, cannot, by the best intelligence we can get, fall short of twenty-five thousand men; ours are under twenty, very sickly, and posted on Governour's Island, Long Island, at Powles Hook [or Paulus Hook on the New Jersey side of the Hudson River opposite New York City], *Horn's Hook* [here Washington may mean Corlear's Hook, today on the lower east side of Manhattan just below the Williamsburg Bridge], *and at the pass near King's Bridge. More Militia are expected; but whether they will be in time, time only can tell, as also where the point of attack will be. An opinion prevails, countenanced by hints from some of the principal Tories, and corroborated by intelligence from Staten Island, that part of the enemy's fleet and army will go into the Sound, whilst another part of it runs up the North River, thereby cutting off all communication by water with this place, whilst their troops form a chain across the Neck, and stop an intercourse with Connecticut by land. Others think they will not leave an army in their rear, whilst they have the country in their front, getting, by that means, between two fires, unless it is intended as a feint to withdraw our troops from the city, that they may slip in and possess themselves of it. All this is but a field of conjecture.*[1]

Washington reported to Congress that because of increased ship traffic back and forth through the Narrows at the southern end of New York harbor, he concluded that Long Island was about to be attacked, but still had no firm intelligence to confirm it.[2] Time was running short now, and in a glorious, final exhortation Washington tried to fan the fires of patriotism in hopes that he could meld his disparate forces into a unified American Army with a common and great purpose:

The General therefore again repeats his earnest request that every officer and soldier will have his arms and ammunition in good order; keep within their quarters and encampment, as much as possible; be ready for action at a moment's call; and when called

---

[1] Force, *American Archives*, 5th Series, Vol. I, p. 916.
[2] Force, *American Archives*, 5th Series, Vol. I, p. 963.

to it, remember that liberty, property, life, and honour, are all at stake; that upon their courage and conduct rest the hopes of their bleeding and insulted country; that their wives, children, and parents, expect safety from them only; and that we have every reason to expect Heaven will crown with success so just a cause. The enemy will endeavour to intimidate by show and appearance, but remember how they have been repulsed on various occasions by a few brave Americans. Their cause is bad; their men are conscious of it; and if opposed with firmness and coolness at their first onset, with our advantage of works and knowledge of the ground, victory is most assuredly ours. Every good soldier will be silent and attentive, wait for orders, and reserve his fire till he is sure of doing execution. The officers to be particularly careful of this. The Colonels, or Commanding Officers of Regiments, are to see their supernumerary officers so posted as to keep the men to their duty; and it may not be amiss for the troops to know that if any infamous rascal, in time of action, shall attempt to skulk, hide himself, or retreat from the enemy without orders of his Commanding Officer, he will instantly be shot down as an example of cowardice. On the other hand the General promises that he will reward those who shall distinguish themselves by brave and noble actions; and he desires every officer to be attentive to this particular, that such men may afterwards be suitably noticed.[1]

Such sentiments and eloquence were not confined to the general officers. The following letter, written by our own Sgt. Hezekiah Hayden of Huntington's Regiment, mirrors the comments of his commander in chief:

Honored Father and Mother,

The time is now near at hand which must probably determine whether Americans are to be freemen or slaves. Whether they are to have any property they can call their own. Whether their houses and farms are to be pillaged and destroyed, and they confined to a state of wretchedness from which no human effort will deliver them. The fate of unborn millions will now depend

---

[1] Force, *American Archives*, 5th Series, Vol. I, p. 965.

under God on the courage and conduct of this army. Our cruel and unrelenting enemy leaves us no choice but a brave resistance or the most abject submission: this is all we can expect. We have therefore to resolve to conquer or die. Our own and our country's honour all calls upon us for a vigorous and manly exertion, and if we now shamefully fail we shall become infamous to the whole world. Let us therefore rely upon the goodness of our cause, and the aid of the Supreme Being, in whose hand the decree is, to animate and incourage [sic] us to great and noble actions. The eyes of all our countrymen are upon us, and we shall have their blessings and praises, if happily we are the means of saving them. Let us therefore animate and incourage each other, and show the whole world that freemen contending for liberty on their own ground are superiour to any slavish mercenary on earth. The General recommends to the officers great coolness in time of action, and to the soldiers strict attention and obedience, with a becoming firmness of spirit.

I would proceed to write more, but the drum beats. I must turn out the fatigue men, and main guard. 'Tis, thanks be to God, pretty healthy [?] in the army.

I remain your healthy and dutiful son, Hezekiah Hayden.[1]

A little more than a week after Washington's final exhortation, the British made their long anticipated move. The time had come to see how thorough and effective all of the commander-in-chief's efforts had been to prepare his untested army for battle.

---

[1] "Hezekiah Hayden, to his parents, camp New York, July 4, 1776," *Hartford Daily Courant*, Dec. 21, 1841, p. 2, http://proquest.umi.com/

4. A Great Smoke and Show

On the morning of the 22nd of August 1776, the British began to ferry their troops across the Narrows from Staten Island. They landed at a spot near the little community of New Utrecht, at the southwest corner of Long Island, about eight miles south of the American fortifications at Brooklyn.[1] The British fleet anchored in Gravesend Bay, in front of New Utrecht. By noon 15,000 men and 40 artillery pieces had been landed with virtually no opposition from the lone, hopelessly outnumbered American regiment that was stationed outside the Brooklyn works that day: a small picket force of about 550 Pennsylvania riflemen under the command of Colonel Edward Hand. As they retreated, the American pickets set fire to corn stacks and barns, making, according to one American soldier, "a great smoke and show."[2]

The British troops then proceeded to encamp upon a broad plain that stretched north from four to six miles, and included the villages of New Utrecht, Gravesend, Flatlands, and Flatbush. The northern edge of the plain ended abruptly at a range of low, but steep, heavily wooded hills, known as the Mount Prospect Range. These hills ran from Gowanus Bay on the southwest for a considerable distance into the heart of the island to the northeast. Representing the terminal moraine of the last retreating glacier, these hills formed a natural barricade separating the British on the plain to the south from the fortified American lines at Brooklyn.

The highest elevations in the Mount Prospect Range were little more than 200 feet, but the slope of the ridge facing the British was steep. With a heavy cover of woods and brush, the southern slope of the Prospect Hills presented an impassible barrier to artillery and wagons, except for a few natural saddles, through which primitive,

---

[1] Although the 22nd is the generally accepted date for the landing, interestingly, Ensign Anthony Bradford reported in his diary that the British landing actually took place on the 21st.

[2] "Benjamin Trumbull's Journal," *Collections of the Connecticut Historical Society*, Vol. VII, p. 184.

rough roads passed. The slope of the hills to the northwest, that facing the American works at Brooklyn, was more gradual. This allowed the Americans easy access to the hills from their side for use as a formidable, natural, defensive barrier between them and the British.

Over the next three days, General Howe spread his troops out over the plain, from New Utrecht and Gravesend, east to Flatlands, and northeast to Flatbush, immediately in front of the Mount Prospect Range. Washington countered by pouring reinforcements onto Long Island. Several regiments were ordered out of the Brooklyn lines and into position in the hills, intending to do as much damage as possible before any British advance could reach the primary American fortifications at Brooklyn.

Within a distance of six miles from the western terminus of the hills near Gowanus Bay, there were four passes through natural saddles or depressions in the hills. For obvious reasons, the roads through these passes became the focus of attention of both armies. On the extreme right (West) of the American position, the Gowanus Road headed south from Brooklyn skirting the western portion of the Mount Prospect Range known as the Greenwood Hills. Meandering back and forth a bit, the road proceeded close by Gowanus Bay to a three-way junction with the road to the Narrows and Martense Lane.

Somewhat less than three miles south of Brooklyn, at the Red Lion Tavern, Martense Lane branched off from its junction with the Gowanus Road, to pass through a hollow in the ridge and then proceed southeast to the roads on the plain. On a map of today, Martense Lane would roughly form the southwest border of Green-Wood Cemetery in Brooklyn. Using either the Narrows Road or Martense Lane to approach the Gowanus Road, the British would find the first and most direct pass from New Utrecht to Brooklyn.

The Jamaica Road ran east from Brooklyn through Bedford towards Jamaica, paralleling the hills on the north, until it dipped down through the farthest pass, known as Jamaica Pass, about four miles from Brooklyn. Between the Gowanus Road and the Jamaica Pass, two other primary roads branched off the Jamaica Road and headed roughly south through two other passes in the hills onto the plain. The first of these two was the road that turned off about a mile east of Brooklyn and headed through a narrow defile, known as Flatbush Pass. This pass was no more than a hundred yards across and was flanked by two surprisingly steep hills. After going through the pass the road continued onto the plain at Flatbush. The topography of this pass has been preserved in the northeast corner of Brooklyn's Prospect Park, and is now known as Battle Pass. About a mile still farther east along the Jamaica Road at Bedford, a second road ran south through Bedford Pass, eventually joining the road to Flatbush just below Flatbush Pass.

Huntington's Regiment, now under the command of Lt.-Col. Clark, along with several other regiments, responded to the first alarm of the British landing. At about twelve noon on August 22nd, the regiment received orders to cross the East River from their camp in New York to Brooklyn to reinforce General Sullivan in command on Long Island. By three in the afternoon, the regiment had been ferried across to the Island.[1]

At sunset, according to Lt. Fitch, while other regiments were sent south to guard the Gowanus Road south of Red Hook, the men of Huntington's, and Colonel John Tyler's 10th Continental Regiment loaded their weapons and marched through the American lines at Brooklyn, proceeding to a point just past the 3-mile marker along the Jamaica Road. There they turned to the right, or south, and marched another mile into the woods, where they took up position and bivouacked in the hills for the night. No man was allowed to sleep, and had to keep his musket in hand ready for a fight should it come. They had hauled field-pieces out with them, but none were fired in the night. There was only scattered small arms fire until morning, likely from nervous sentries.[2]

Based on Fitch's note that they had marched out past the 3-mile marker along the road the night before, Huntington's regiment must have been camped in the area of the Bedford Pass. As they advanced farther south through the pass early the next morning, August 23rd, Huntington's and Tyler's Regiments received a reinforcement of two regiments of Pennsylvania riflemen under Colonels Miles and Lutz. This enlarged American force encountered an advance guard of Hessian soldiers where the hills met the plain just in front of the village of Flatbush, and there began to exchange both small arms and artillery fire. Colonel Hand's Pennsylvania Rifle Regiment eventually joined the fray, and the combined American force succeeded in

---

[1] Bradford, *Diary 1775-1778*, p. 41.
[2] Sabine, *New York Diary of Lt. Jabez Fitch*, p. 25.

driving the advanced units of the Hessian troops back about half a mile onto their main lines.

Sporadic and scattered fire from both small arms and artillery continued throughout the rest of the day of the 23rd. Huntington's Regiment remained for the most part under cover of the woods on the lower slope of the hills; sometimes advancing onto the edge of the plain to observe the movements of the enemy and exchange volleys of small arms fire. By the end of the day, the Americans had driven the Hessians south of the village church in Flatbush, and burned several houses, stacks of grain, and barns to keep them out of the hands of the enemy. In his journal, Benjamin Trumbull reported that "A number of officers' hangers [short swords] were taken and one dead body."[1] One of the houses burned was that of Judge Lefferts, just south of Flatbush Pass, which the Hessians had been occupying. A reconstruction of that historic house now stands at the Willink entrance to Prospect Park in Brooklyn, incongruously located next to the children's carousel.

At sunset on the 23rd, a battalion of New York troops relieved Col. Tyler's Regiment, which returned to the American lines. Huntington's Regiment then bivouacked in the woods for the second night, and, still without tents, made primitive shelters of tree branches and brush.[2] Lieutenant Fitch wrote that his company commander, Captain Jewett, due to illness, was forced to return to the American lines that evening, taking with him fifteen dollars in Continental currency that Lt. Fitch had entrusted to him for safekeeping. This left Fitch in command of the company, and a man was promptly sent off to a neighboring farm to "procure" a bottle of rum, no doubt to fortify the sentries posted through the night. Fitch also reported that they hadn't lost a single man during the day's engagement, but that several of the riflemen (probably Colonel Hand's) were wounded and one perhaps mortally.[3]

General Sullivan, overly pleased at the day's events, immediately issued a congratulatory order, stating that "The General returns his thanks to the brave officers and soldiers who with so much spirit and intrepidity, repulsed the enemy and defeated their designs of taking

---

[1] *Collections of the Connecticut Historical Society*, Vol. VII, p. 185.
[2] *Fitch*, pp. 26-27.
[3] *Fitch*, p. 27.

possession of the woods near our lines."[1] General Washington was appalled that Sullivan would take credit for a general engagement when he well knew the action of the 23rd to be nothing more than a preliminary skirmish. He promptly replaced Sullivan with General Putnam the next day. Sullivan retained second in command. "Old Put," as General Putnam was lovingly known by his troops, was an old Indian fighter from the French and Indian War, but, unfortunately had no senior command experience, and no knowledge of the lay of the land on Long Island.

At dawn on the morning of the 24th, Huntington's Regiment was relieved and returned to the American lines at Brooklyn, driving a small herd of cattle they had seized before them. Once inside their lines, they drew provisions, including a number of locally grown watermelons, and set about preparing a meal. They ate and rested while listening to the continuing boom of cannon fire coming from the area of their previous position near Flatbush. Only a few wounded were brought into camp during the day. Late in the afternoon, the regiment was ordered into the meetinghouse and a nearby barn for the night; accommodations they gratefully received, considering the previous two nights out in the open, and the fact that rain was threatening. Separate, more comfortable rooms were provided for the officers.[2]

In his diary for that day, Lt. Fitch noted, "At about 6 o'clock, the Revd: Mr: Ellis, who set off with us from Camp [on the 22nd] with great Zeal, but when we pass'd the Lines of Genll: Greens Encampment, he somehow seem'd to Disappear, & had not been hear'd of again in the Regt: until now; but he now Attend' with Regt: in the Church." Carefully deciphering Fitch's shorthand, we discover only thinly veiled contempt for what he perceived to be Ellis' cowardice.

During that evening, Col. Ephraim Martin of the 4th New Jersey Regiment was brought in wounded with a musket ball in his chest, and was not expected to live. Two other wounded soldiers were brought in later: one private whose leg had been shattered by a cannon ball, and could not be saved; and another who had been shot

---

[1] Henry Whittemore, *The Heroes of the American Revolution and their Descendants, Battle of Long Island* (Brooklyn: Heroes of the Revolution Pub. Co., 1897), p. 10, http://persi.heritagequestonline.com/...
[2] *Fitch*, p. 27.

in the groin.[1] In spite of these somewhat disturbing events, Fitch reported that he rested comfortably on the floor during what had become a very rainy night.

By the end of the day on the 25th, two more Hessian brigades had been landed on Long Island and advanced towards Flatbush. There was again some exchange of artillery fire during the day between the Hessians at Flatbush and the Americans, but no significant action. By now, the total British strength on the Island was about 21,000 men. On the same day, General Washington ordered General Putnam, now in overall command on Long Island, to form a proper line of advance defenses outside the works at Brooklyn to "harass and annoy" any British advance through the passes in the hills.[2] A brigadier-general of the day was to be constantly on duty out upon the advance defenses, and was to take immediate command in the eventuality of attack. General Stirling was to take the first watch on the night of the 25th-26th.[3]

Unfortunately, the outer defensive line now established was strung out more than four miles in length, and was not parallel, but set out in an oblique angle to the main Brooklyn lines. At its closest point this advance line was about two miles from Brooklyn along the Gowanus Road, but at its farthest point, it was more than four miles away, at the Jamaica Pass. Because of a scarcity of available troops, Putnam placed most of his men in fixed positions at the points of most probable attack: along the Gowanus Road, at the Flatbush Pass, and at the Bedford Pass. Considering the Jamaica Pass too far to the east to be a serious threat, the Americans posted only a small mounted guard to patrol there.

At about 10 o'clock on the morning of Sunday, the 25th, Huntington's Regiment was ordered out of the Brooklyn lines again; this time to the right end of the American outposts along the Gowanus Road, south of Red Hook. Two hours' march later they arrived at

---

[1] *Fitch*, pp. 27-28; "George Washington to Congress, August 26, 1776," *The George Washington Papers*, Series 3, Subseries A, p. 388, http://memory.loc.gov/ammem/gwhtml/gwseries.html
[2] "R. H. Harrison [secretary to General Washington] to Congress, August 27, 1776," *The George Washington Papers*, Series 3, Subseries A, p. 390, http://memory.loc.gov/ammem/gwhtml/gwseries.html
[3] Brigadier General William Alexander was commonly known as Lord Stirling for his claim to a Scottish earldom. His claim was not recognized by the House of Commons, but he used the title nevertheless.

their position, and Lieutenant Fitch and Ensign Chapman were assigned to take charge of the guard posted along the bay. The officers were assigned very comfortable evening quarters in the house of a Dutch farmer, Simon Bergen. The house was a typical, low, Dutch style, one-story stone home, built before 1690 by one of the ancestors of Bergen's wife. The Bergen farm was located on the shore of Gowanus Cove, near the junction of today's Thirty-seventh Street and Third Avenue. By the time of the Revolution, the house already had a long and colorful history, having served as a guest home for travelers, fur-traders and missionaries.

Congress had allowed seven shillings a week to families that provided room and board for American officers.[1] This must have been sufficient, because the officers, according to Fitch, were treated with "great generosity" by Bergen's family. They were fed dinner and watermelons in abundance; this, in spite of the fact that most of the local crops had been destroyed by American troops to prevent the produce from falling into the hands of the enemy.

Fitch wrote that Colonel Clark and Major Humphreys also dined with the gracious Bergens, and later the group was joined by Lord Stirling, the general-officer-of-the-day, just returned from reviewing the advanced defenses and the disposition of the enemy. Since the Gowanus Road was the closest and easiest approach for the British to march on Brooklyn, it was considered by the Americans to be the most likely route of attack. Located near the junction of Martense Lane with the Gowanus Road, the Bergen house was perfectly situated for billeting the officers in charge of the outposts.

It rained heavily in the night, soaking the weapons of the soldiers posted outside on picket duty, so that the guns had to be test fired periodically to ensure they were still operable. From their position on the right, Huntington's men heard little shooting compared to what they had experienced two days before, and received no reports of any casualties for the day.[2]

At two A.M. on the 26th, American picket forces at the center of the outposts on the Flatbush and Bedford Roads attacked the Hessians in their camp at Flatbush, and then again in the afternoon. Lord Cornwallis, now in command of the advance British guard at

---

[1] Henry Onderdonk, Jr., *Revolutionary Incidents of Suffolk and Kings Counties, With an Account of the Battle of Long Island* (New York: Leavitt & Co., 1849; reprint by Higginson Book Co., Salem, MA, 2007), Sec. 775, p. 116.
[2] *Fitch*, p. 28.

Flatbush, withdrew from that position to Flatlands, and later that evening moved farther eastward on the road to New Lots.

Also early in the morning of the 26th, Lt. Fitch received orders from Lt.-Col. Clark to drive off their host's cattle to keep them out of the hands of the enemy. Having already had his grain burned and many of his cattle confiscated, Simon Bergen, was, needless to say, rather upset.   Lt. Fitch reported these facts in his diary and also mentioned that Bergen's family was in fear of their lives "on account of some foolish words spoken by some of our Men." Fitch did not elaborate on the "foolish words," but as a result, he and Ensign Chapman had to assure the Bergens that there was nothing to fear from their men.

In spite of what they must have considered harsh treatment at the hands of the Americans, the Bergens continued to offer their hospitality, and at 3 P.M. provided the men with dinner. Shortly after this, the regiment was relieved and returned to the Brooklyn lines. There, Lt. Fitch, Lt. Gillet, and Ensign Lyman found lodging on the floor of another house that was being used for billeting the troops. It would be the last relatively comfortable lodging they were to receive for quite some time to come.[1]

---

[1] *Fitch*, p.30.

*The home of Simon Bergen in the left foreground
As it appeared about 1867
(Courtesy New York Public Library)*

5. Isolated and Cut Off

General Washington had an army of nearly 19,000 men in and around New York on the night of August 26, 1776. However, many of those were not fit for duty, and only about 7,000 men had been sent over to Long Island. Although General Howe had landed large numbers of troops on Long Island, the exact number was not known to Washington, and he could still not fully anticipate where Howe's attack might come. Under the circumstances, Washington could not commit more troops to Long Island and leave New York City exposed. Of the 7,000 men on Long Island, probably no more than 2,800 were manning the advanced positions at the outposts in the various passes through the hills, and the rest were within the fortified lines at Brooklyn.

If the main British attack came on Long Island, the troops stationed in the hills were expected to blunt the impact of the initial blow of the British onslaught before it reached the Brooklyn fortifications. At each major pass through the hills on the night of the 26th, about 800 men- really no more than a picket force- were posted. On the American right (west), near the Red Lion Tavern and the trifurcation of Martense Lane, the Gowanus Road, and the Road to the Narrows, there was an advance guard drawn from various regiments of Pennsylvania, Maryland, and New York troops. Huntington's Regiment had been included in the picket there but had been relieved the night before to return to Brooklyn. They, and the majority of the other men assigned to guard the right were close by, or behind, the lines at Brooklyn, ready to respond to any alarm by the pickets near the Red Lion.

At the Flatbush Pass, in the center of the American outpost defenses, General Sullivan's brigade was posted. This brigade now included the continental regiments of Cols. Daniel Hitchcock of Rhode Island, Moses Little of Massachusetts, and a battalion of New Jersey militia under the command of Col. Philip Johnston. Farther left (east), at the Bedford Pass, were Col. Samuel Wyllys's 22nd Connecticut Continentals, and Col. John Chester's Connecticut troops, then under the command of Lt.-Col. Solomon Willes. Slightly farther to the left, on the other side of the road through the Bedford Pass, Col. Samuel Miles' Pennsylvania rifle regiment was bivouacked with about 500 of his men who were fit for duty. Only a small, mounted patrol of five militia officers was left to watch the Jamaica Road and Jamaica Pass to the east of Miles' position. Although General Nathaniel Woodhull, commander of the Long Island militia, was stationed still farther out on Long Island, he had few men in his command and had been ordered to drive all the cattle he could find to the east end of the island to keep them away from the British. Those were his only orders, and he would not play an active role in the coming fight.

In contrast to the small American force stationed in the hills along the advanced front, Gen. Howe commanded upwards of 21,000 well-trained veteran British troops on Long Island by the night of the 26th. Having learned his lesson about frontal assaults on fortified American positions at the Battle of Bunker Hill the year before, Howe now devised a more devious, and far more intricate plan of attack. Instead of pushing directly north along the Gowanus Bay, or at the center of the American position at either the Flatbush or Bedford Passes, he planned a flanking maneuver several miles to the east around the American left through the relatively unguarded Jamaica Pass. If executed successfully, the flanking march would bring the British column into position between all the American outposts and their main lines at Brooklyn.

At the commencement of major hostilities on Tuesday, August 27, British Gen. Grant, with two full brigades, was ordered to advance along the Gowanus Road in a feint intended to deceive the Americans into believing this was the main point of attack. To enhance the deception, Howe then sent his warships north to threaten New York City, and the troops and forts within range on the American right wing at Brooklyn. This part of the British plan was thwarted by a northerly wind and ebb tide: After tacking for a considerable period of time in an unsuccessful attempt to make progress upriver, the British squadron was forced to fall back down and anchor in Gowanus Bay. Only one ship was able to reach as far north as Red Hook, where it exchanged a few shots with the American battery there, before drifting back down river as well. In the British center, General DeHeister's Hessian forces were to commence an artillery barrage

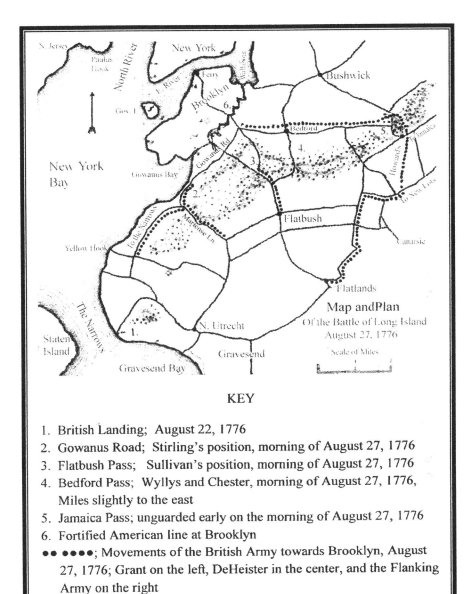

KEY

1. British Landing; August 22, 1776
2. Gowanus Road; Stirling's position, morning of August 27, 1776
3. Flatbush Pass; Sullivan's position, morning of August 27, 1776
4. Bedford Pass; Wyllys and Chester, morning of August 27, 1776, Miles slightly to the east
5. Jamaica Pass; unguarded early on the morning of August 27, 1776
6. Fortified American line at Brooklyn

•• ••••; Movements of the British Army towards Brooklyn, August 27, 1776; Grant on the left, DeHeister in the center, and the Flanking Army on the right

Map and Plan of the Battle of Long Island
(adapted by the author from a map by Henry Onderdonk, Jr.)

early in the morning on the American redoubt in Flatbush Pass to pin down Sullivan's regiments stationed there.

Early on the evening of the 26th, the British plan began to unfold as Sir Henry Clinton pulled out of Flatbush and withdrew slightly to the south, and then east to Flatlands to form the vanguard of the flanking army. He was closely followed by Generals Cornwallis and Percy's brigades with General William Howe himself; a force perhaps 10,000 strong. The British brigades engaging the American center and right were ordered to refrain from all-out assault until a prescribed cannon signal that would announce that the flanking army had successfully gained the American rear.

Howe's massive flanking corps began to move east from Flatlands under the cover of darkness. They left their former camps intact with fires burning at Flatbush to deceive the Americans into believing that the British remained in position in their front. The success of the British plan required absolute secrecy and stealth along the route of the march. With local Tories acting as guides, by two o'clock on the morning of the 27th, the flanking army had turned north and gained the base of the hills near the Jamaica Pass. To this point, they had not been observed by the American left wing under Col. Miles, or the mounted patrol sent out to guard the Jamaica Pass. Undiscovered, the British advance guards were able to enter the pass where they captured the lone mounted patrol of five American officers before they could sound an alarm. British apprehensions were now dispelled as the captured officers informed them upon "interrogation" that, except for their patrol, the pass was unguarded.

At William Howard's Tavern near the pass, the British took the innkeeper and his son prisoner and forced them to guide them along a little used carriage path through the hills to the Jamaica Road. Once on the Jamaica Road, the British advance continued west towards Brooklyn. By dawn of the 27th, Howe's flanking maneuver had been completed without opposition, and his army was in position in the American rear near Bedford without having been discovered. Although all the fighting had yet to be done, the inevitable outcome of the battle had already been determined. By dawn, all the Americans in the outposts were trapped between the closing jaws of the flanking army in their rear and Grant's and DeHeister's brigades in their front.

While the main force was marching to flank the American outposts during the night, the British left wing under General Grant began the diversion against the American right. At the time, a picket force of about 120 Americans was stationed by the Red Lion Tavern at the junction of the Gowanus Road with Martense Lane and the Road to the Narrows. This tiny force consisted of a portion of Colonel Atlee's First Regiment of Pennsylvania Musketry, a part of Lt.-Col. Kichlein's Pennsylvania Rifle Battalion, some of Colonel Hand's Continental's (Pennsylvania), some of Colonel Lutz's Berks County, Pennsylvania, Militia, under Major Edward Burd, and a few New York State troops. About midnight, two British scouts were discovered approaching through a melon patch near the Red Lion. They were immediately fired on and dispersed by the American pickets. Meeting this resistance, the British scouts, and the main body to which they were attached, temporarily withdrew. This preliminary action took place near, or at, the modern-day intersection of Thirty-Ninth Street and Fifth Avenue.

Between one and two o'clock on the morning of the 27th, the enemy reappeared in the area, this time with a force of between two and three hundred, along the Road to the Narrows, where Major Burd's pickets were stationed. Stiles' *History of the City of Brooklyn* places the location of this action slightly west of the first skirmish, in the vicinity of today's intersection of 39th Street and 2nd or 3rd Avenues.[1] According to one of Col. Atlee's officers, after firing two or three volleys, the American pickets perceived they were hopelessly outnumbered and retreated precipitously.[2] Major Burd and several of his men were taken prisoner; the first of many. General Parsons was general officer of the day and later wrote:

> *On the day of the surprise I was on duty, and at the first dawn of day the guards from the West road near the Narrows, came to my quarters & informed me the enemy were advancing in great numbers by that road. I soon found it true & that the whole guard had fled without firing a gun;[3] these (by way of retaliation I must tell you) were all New Yorkers & Pennsylvanians; I found by fair daylight the enemy were through the wood & descending the hill on the North side, on which with 20 of my fugitive guard being all I could collect, I took post on a height in their front at about half a*

---

[1] Henry Reed Stiles, *A History of the City of Brooklyn* (Brooklyn: published by subscription, 1867), Vol. I, p. 269.
[2] Onderdonk, *Revolutionary Incidents*, p. 148.
[3] Other testimony stated that the pickets had put up a brief resistance.

*mile's distance, which halted their column & gave time for Lord
Stirling with his forces to come up.*[1]

As Parsons made a rather strong statement regarding the performance
of the picket guard along the Gowanus Road, it is perhaps necessary
to understand Parsons' own circumstances at the time. As duty-
officer-of-the-day, Parsons was required by his general orders to
"remain constantly upon the lines, that he may be upon the spot to
command, and see that orders are executed."[2] The duty officer of the
previous day, Lord Stirling, had been billeted at the home of Simon
Bergen near 37th Street and 3rd Avenue, as testified to by Lt. Fitch. It
is therefore reasonable to believe that General Parsons would have
been billeted at the same place, as he was now in command of the
same guard just one day later. The home of Simon Bergen was in the
immediate vicinity of the pickets on the night of the 26-27th. At the
Bergen place, General Parsons would have been very close to the
scene of the action that had just taken place, and eminently qualified
to bear witness to the actions of his pickets. His anger at the fleeing
pickets would have been quite understandable, since his own position
would have then been exposed and, except for his personal
bodyguard, entirely unprotected from the advancing British troops.
One can only imagine the scene, as Parsons and his guard, abandoned
to fend for themselves, fled Bergen's house by horseback in the dark
early morning hours to run down the wayward pickets.

At the first contact by the picket guard with the British at the Red
Lion Tavern, a messenger had been sent to General Putnam, in overall
command behind the Brooklyn lines. Putnam gave orders at 3 A.M. to
Lord Stirling to head south along the Gowanus Road to meet the
British threat. Stirling took with him the only available units of his
brigade, Col. William Smallwood's Maryland Regiment, and Col.
John Haslet's Delaware Regiment. Neither Colonel Smallwood nor
Colonel Haslet were with their regiments at the time, as both were
participating in the court-martial of Lt.-Col. Zedwitz in New York
City, and did not reach Long Island until later in the day.[3] The two

---

[1] "Samuel Parsons to John Adams, Oct. 8, 1776," Johnston, *The Campaign of 1776*,
Part II, p. 35.
[2] "George Washington to General Putnam, August 25, 1776," *The George
Washington Papers*, Series 3, Subseries B, p. 34,
http://memory.loc.gov/ammem/gwhtml/gwseries.html
[3] Force, *American Archives*, 5th Series, Vol. I, p. 1194.

regiments were temporarily under the command of Major Mordecai Gist and Major Thomas MacDonough, repectively.

Shortly, if not immediately, after Stirling marched, Colonel Huntington's Regiment, under the experienced command of Lieutenant-Colonel Joel Clark, and another part of Lt.-Col. Peter Kichlein's Pennsylvania Battalion were also sent south along the Gowanus Road to be placed under the command of General Parsons, who had been holding off the British with his tiny force of corralled pickets.

Lord Stirling reached the scene of the action with Haslet and Smallwood's regiments just before dawn, meeting General Parsons with Colonel Atlee along the Gowanus Road near present-day Third Avenue and Twenty-Third Street. When Huntington's and Kichlein's men arrived, Parsons gathered his little brigade, now consisting for the most part of Huntington's undermanned regiment, and placed himself at the disposal of Lord Stirling to provide support. Finding a good defensive position, Stirling then fell back slightly to between Eighteenth and Twentieth Streets to form his brigade for battle. He proceeded to deploy his regiments in a "V" formation, pointed south towards the advancing enemy. The British had by now marched to a point about a half a mile north of the Red Lion, or about 2 ½ miles south of the Brooklyn lines. Stirling was fortunate to find a piece of rising ground that commanded a narrow defile just to his south, across which the British were now attempting to advance.

A small stream or tidal inlet ran through the defile, terminating perhaps two hundred yards inland from the bay in a small shallow marsh at the foot of the Greenwood Hills. The Gowanus Road crossed this stream on a small wooden bridge at the western end of the marsh. As the British approached the bridge and stream from the south, the road wound over a hill which presented a steep bluff down to the bay, known by the Dutch as "Blockje's Bergh" (or Bluckie's Barracks, or a variety of other spellings). Although it no longer exists, this hill was located by Stiles at the western terminus of present-day 23rd Street. In order to continue north, Grant's forces would have to expose themselves on the open north slope of Blockje's Bergh while narrowing to a small column in order to pass over the little bridge.

The steep slope of Blockje's Bergh next to the water prevented any flanking maneuver by the British on the bay side. Grant's men could pass, however, over the less precipitous eastern flank of Blockje's Bergh and slog through the swamp now commanded by

Stirling's forces on the higher hill immediately to the north and above
the swamp. Failing that, the British could attempt to flank the
Americans through the heavily wooded Greenwood Hills, yet farther
inland and east of the little swamp. The heavy forest in this direction,
however, would prevent the passing of Grant's artillery.[1]

To allow time for Stirling to form his brigade, Colonel Atlee's
regiment was sent forward on the east side of the road to the base of
the hill (identified by Onderdonk as Wykoff's Hill) upon which
Stirling's brigade was now forming. This position placed Atlee with
his regiment in an orchard on the farm of the Dutchman, Wynant
Bennett, located on the north side of the tidal creek.   Other than
Bennett's barn, there was no significant cover, and Atlee, more or less
in the open, sustained the enemy's small arms and cannon fire coming
from the other side of the marsh until Stirling's brigade was formed.
When his small force could no longer prevent the British from
crossing the shallow morass, Atlee fell back, and was ordered to move
off to the left and extend the left wing of Stirling's line into the
Greenwood Hills to the east.

With the steep bluff of Blockje's Bergh preventing the British
from advancing on the Bay side of the road, Stirling formed his
brigade primarily on the east, or left side, of the road on the open
ground of Wykoff's Hill. His right wing consisted for the most part of
Smallwood's Maryland Regiment. The other arm of the "V" was
formed from Haslet's Delawares, and extended from a point just north
of today's main entrance to Green-Wood Cemetery northeast towards
the Port Road on Stirling's left. This placed the rear of Haslet's
formation only about a mile from the Brooklyn lines. Some of those
men in the rear were kept in reserve until late in the morning when
they were ordered forward to the front of the line where they were
mistaken by a unit of British soldiers for Hessians because of their
similar uniforms. Twenty-three British prisoners were taken by this
unit of Haslet's men before the British realized their mistake.

To take the place of Atlee's men, some of Kichlein's riflemen
were sent forward to the foot of Wykoff's Hill, and placed along
hedges there to retard the advance of the enemy crossing the stream
and swamp. The advancing British forced at least two local residents

---

[1] Johnston, *Campaign of 1776*, p. 164-167; Whittemore, *The Heroes of the
American Revolution*, p. xv; Stiles, *History of the City of Brooklyn*, Vol. I, pp. 58-
59.

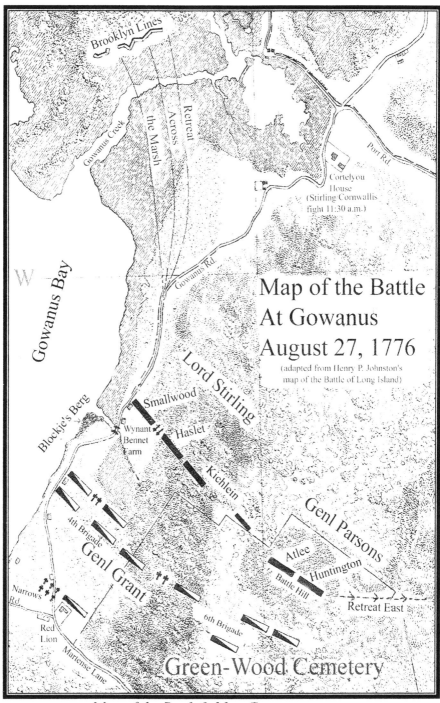

Map of the Battlefield at Gowanus
(adapted by the author from a map by Henry P. Johnston)

to guide them into the area of the swamp where the group was confronted by the Pennsylvania riflemen. The guides later reported that the riflemen mowed down the British soldiers around them and left them standing almost alone. What few British soldiers were left alive after this encounter fled back to their lines.[1] It was said that many British bodies were later buried next to the marsh.

As he took up position, Lord Stirling undoubtedly perceived that his left wing was vulnerable and could be flanked on the east through the forests in the Greenwood Hills. If they succeeded in such a maneuver, the British would come into position in the woods on higher elevations above Stirling's main battle line. To intercept any British advance in this quarter, Stirling ordered Parsons with Huntington's Regiment, and Atlee, and some of Kichlein's men to extend the line into the woods and hills to protect his left flank.

It is possible that the reassignment of Atlee's force from General Stirling's Brigade to General Parsons' Brigade in the heat of battle produced some confusion in the command structure. Col. Atlee's battle report made little mention of the presence of Huntington's men on the left. Indeed, he gave the impression that if he had not actually been operating as an independent command, he was still looking for orders only from Stirling, not Parsons.[2] Lord Stirling, in his report to General Washington two days later, did little to clarify the situation, making no mention whatsoever of the arrival of Huntington's regiment, or for that matter of Col. Atlee after he had been sent off to the left.[3]

General Parsons left little doubt about his understanding of the structure of his command in a letter to John Adams at Philadelphia dated two days after the battle on August 29, 1776.[4] Lord Stirling had ordered him "…with Col. Atlee & part of his Reg't & Lt.-Col. Clark with Huntington's Reg't to cover the left flank of our main body." Lt. Jabez Fitch also wrote that Huntington's Regiment was ordered very early in the morning to the post they had occupied while on picket the day before (on the Gowanus Road). At first, the regiment marched up to the woods on the left for a flank guard and then moved back some

[1] Stiles, *History of the City of Brooklyn*, Vol. I, note p. 271.
[2] "Journal of Samuel J. Atlee," Force, *American Archives*, 5th Series, Vol. I, pp. 1251-1255.
[3] Force, *American Archives*, 5th Series, Vol.I, p. 1246.
[4] Charles S. Hall, *Life and Letters of Samuel Holden Parsons* (Binghamton, NY: Otseningo Pub. Co., 1905), pp. 54-55.

distance reconnoitering the woods.[1]   Clearly, Stirling intended that Parsons with the 17th Continental Regiment and Atlee's Regiment were to operate together as one unit under Parsons' command to protect the left flank of Stirling's main battle line. Atlee, in less than battalion strength, would have been sent off to the left after he had been withdrawn from the foot of Wykoff's Hill to reinforce General Parsons with Huntington's Regiment already on the left wing.

By now, Lord Stirling had drawn up his little brigade, formed in the field from two undermanned regiments, in battle formation. Two full British brigades under Major-General Grant, each consisting of four regiments, formed their main battle line a few hundred yards in front of the Americans on the other side of the little stream and swamp, on and behind the crest of Blockje's Bergh. Stirling probably had no more than sixteen hundred men along the American line, including Parsons' Brigade, to face Grant's force of about seven thousand. Stirling placed his two artillery pieces on a hill on his left to command the Gowanus Road and the obvious approach to his position, while Grant moved his two artillery units into an opposing position a few hundred yards away. Grant placed one of his brigades to face the western arm of Stirling's brigade, and his other brigade to face the regiment forming the eastern arm of Stirling's brigade.

In this position, the opposing armies traded small arms and cannon fire for the next several hours. Grant tested the American position with a few sorties across the swamp from his light infantry, but, finding that they were met with stubborn resistance from the American riflemen, he allowed them to fall back to his main line. The principal action along this part of the outer defenses was a cannonade by both sides that lasted until about 11 A.M. This was the first time during the Revolution that an American Army faced the British in the open field, outside fortified positions, and the Americans resolutely stood their ground.

Between ten and eleven in the morning, Grant received a reinforcement of between two and three thousand men and ammunition from a British naval squadron that anchored in what was known as either Gowanus or Bennet's Cove, just west of the junction of Martense Lane and the Gowanus Road.[2] This anchorage was

---

[1] *Fitch*, p. 30.
[2] Stiles, *History of the City of Brooklyn*, Vol. I, notes, p. 278; Vol. II, notes, p. 187.

Looking south from the area of Wykoff's Hill over the narrow defile to Blockje's Bergh (from Heroes of the American Revolution, *courtesy CT State Library)*

adjacent to the home of Simon Bergen between what is now Thirty-second and Thirty-seventh Streets, where the American officers in charge of the Gowanus Road picket had been posted the previous few nights. Although now reinforced and resupplied, the British infantry still made no large-scale assault against Stirling's center. This was consistent with Grant's orders to delay a general engagement on the Gowanus Road until the flanking column had gained the American rear. The British deception was successful, and Stirling's men, still unaware of the flanking column, continued to believe through the morning that they were holding off the full brunt of the main British assault force.

The disposition of Parsons' depleted brigade- which consisted mostly of Huntington's and part of Atlee's Regiment- on Stirling's left, made them the only American force in an extended, hilly, heavily wooded, roadless gap between Sullivan's brigade at Flatbush Pass, and Stirling's Brigade. The men of Parsons' Brigade probably did not know it at the time, but they were now the most isolated American unit on the battlefield, without the numerical strength to sustain a major assault on their position. Although General Grant did not press his advantage at the strength of Stirling's center, he did probe the left in force in an attempt to flank Stirling, precisely where Parsons' men were positioned. General Parsons, in his letter of August 29, went on to say:

> *...I was ordered with Col. Atlee & part of his Reg't & Lt. Col. Clark with Col. Huntington's Reg't. to cover the left flank of our main body. This we executed though our number did at no time exceed 300 men, and we were attacked several times by two regiments, the 44th and 23rd, and repulsed them in every attack with considerable loss. The number of dead we had collected together & the heap the enemy had made we supposed amounted to about 60. We had 12 or 14 wounded prisoners who we caused to be dress'd & their wounds put in the best state our situation would admit.[1]*

Among the men of Huntington's Regiment that later mentioned their involvement in the battle, Lt. Jabez Fitch wrote in his diary, "...we

---

[1] Hall, *Life and Letters of Samuel Holden Parsons*, pp. 54-55.

again advanced and extended a line on the left of Lord Stirling's party, where we had two or three severe attacks in which a Lt.-Col. of ours [Parry] was killed, and also Col. Grant."[1] Lt.-Col. Parry was second in command of Colonel Atlee's regiment. Col. Grant was British Lt.-Col. James Grant of the Fortieth Regiment. His death led to a case of mistaken identity; the Americans at first believing they had killed Major-General Grant.

Lt. Solomon Orcutt of Huntington's Regiment also spoke of the battle in his pension application, writing that he was in four actions in one day during the Battle of Long Island.[2] The discrepancy in the number of actions between his and Fitch's account is likely because Orcutt was adding a fight that occurred somewhat later in the day, which will be described further on.

It is to Colonel Atlee, however, that we are indebted for the most lengthy and detailed description of what happened during this part of the battle. Because it was widely published, it is also the best known and most frequently referenced account of what transpired in that area of the battle:

> *Upon filing off to the left according to the orders received, I espied, at the distance of about 300 yards, a hill of clear ground, which I judged to be a proper situation to oppose the troops ordered to flank us, and which, I determined, if possible, to gain before them. At the foot of this hill a few of Huntington's Connecticut Regiment, that had been upon the picket, joined me. In order to gain and secure the hill, I ordered the troops to wheel to the right and march up the hill abreast. When within about forty yards of the summit, we very unexpectedly received a very heavy fire from the enemy taken post there before us, notwithstanding the forced march I made. The enemy's situation was so very advantageous, the back of the hill where they had taken post being formed by nature into a breastwork, that had they directed their fire properly or been marksmen, they must have cut off the greatest part of my detachment. I having, before I advanced the hill, posted a part of my small number along the skirt of a wood upon my right, and left a guard at the foot of the hill, to prevent my being surrounded, and my retreat to the*

---

[1] *Fitch*, p. 30.
[2] NARA, Series M805, Roll 623, Revolutionary War Pension Application, S41037.

brigade in case of necessity, being cut off, the enemy being vastly superior in numbers, their detachment consisting of the Twenty-Third and Forty-Fourth Regiment, and part of the Seventeenth. Upon receiving the above heavy fire, which continued very warm and they secure behind the hill, a small halt was made, and the detachment fell back a few paces. Here Captain Stedman, with all the Delawares, except the Lieutenants Stewart and Harney [both Stewart and Harney were later reported missing by Colonel Haslet from his Delaware Regiment[1]], *with about sixteen privates, left me, and drew after them some of my own. The remainder, after recovering a little from this, their first shock, I ordered to advance, at the same time desiring them to preserve their fire and aim aright. They immediately, with the resolution of veteran soldiers, obeyed the order. The enemy, finding their opponents fast advancing, and determined to dispute the ground with them, fled with precipitation, leaving behind them twelve killed upon the spot, and a Lieutenant and four privates wounded. In this engagement I lost my worthy friend and Lieutenant-Colonel (Parry) shot through the head, who fell without a groan, fighting in defence of his much injured country. In the midst of the action I ordered four soldiers to carry him as speedily as possible within the lines at Brookline.*

My brave fellows, flushed with this advantage, were for pushing forward after the flying enemy; but perceiving at about 60 yards from the hill we had gained across a hollow way, a stone fence lined with wood, from behind which we might be greatly annoyed, and fearing an ambuscade might there be placed, I ordered not to advance farther, but to maintain possession of the hill, where kind nature had formed a breastwork nearly semicircular. They halted, and found, by a heavy fire from the fence, it was lined as I suspected. The fire was as briskly returned; but the enemy finding it too hot, and losing a number of men, retreated to and joined the right of this wing of their Army.

After this first attack, which continued from the first fire about half an hour, we brought from the field six wounded soldiers and about twenty muskets. The wounded I placed in my rear, under the shade of some bushes; the arms I distributed to such of the

---

[1] Onderdonk, *Revolutionary Incidents*, section 809, p. 142.

soldiers as were most indifferently armed. The wounded Lieutenant I sent, with two soldiers, to Lord Stirling.

After placing some sentinels to observe the further movements of the enemy, if any should be made, I ordered my men, greatly fatigued, to rest themselves. In about twenty minutes the enemy was observed marching down to make a second attempt for the hill. The sentinels gave the alarm. Officers and men immediately flew to arms, and with remarkable coolness and resolution sustained and returned their fire for about 15 minutes, when the enemy were obliged once more to a precipitate flight, leaving behind them, killed, Lieutenant-Colonel Grant (a person, as I afterwards understood, much valued in the British Army) besides a number of privates, and some wounded. Such of the wounded as I thought might be assisted I had brought in and placed with the rest in my rear; one slightly through the leg I sent with a soldier to Lord Stirling. I had in this attack but one private wounded, with two balls through his body.

I now sent my adjutant, Mr. Mentgis[1], to his lordship [Stirling], with an account of the successive advantages I had gained, and to request a reinforcement, and such further orders as his Lordship should judge necessary. Two companies of Riflemen, from Keichlien's Flying-Camp, soon after joined me, but were very soon ordered to rejoin their regiment, the reason for which I could not imagine, as I stood in such need of them. Very luckily, after our second engagement, our ammunition cart belonging to Col. Huntington's regiment arrived at my post, of which we stood in great need, having entirely emptied our cartridge-boxes, and had used several rounds of the enemy's ammunition, of which I stripped the dead and wounded every time we had the good fortune to beat them off the field. The officers were extremely alert, and from the ammunition so opportunely arrived, soon supplied their men with sufficient stock to sustain another attack, if the enemy should think proper to make it.

They did not suffer us to wait long, for in about half an hour we were alarmed by our sentinels of their approach the third time.

---

[1] Lieutenant Francis Mentges, subsequently promoted to lieutenant-colonel, 5th Pennsylvania Regiment. He was not listed among the missing after the Battle of Long Island.

The eagerness of the officers and soldiers to receive them deserves my warmest acknowledgements. They were received as usual, and as usual fled, after another conflict of about a quarter of an hour. I then was determined to pursue; but observing a regiment making down to sustain them, which proved to be the Forty-Second, or Royal Highlanders, I thought best to halt and prepare to receive them, should they advance upon me; but the drubbing their friends had so repeatedly received, I believe, prevented them, and they seemed fully satisfied to have protected the fugitives, and of conducting what was left, which such of the wounded as could crawl to them, to the Army. [1]

Without Colonel Atlee's description of the battle location, we might not have known exactly where the fighting took place. He described the scene of the fighting as a cleared summit 300 yards from Stirling's position, on the left, or southeast, side of the Gowanus Road. As it happens, the tallest prominence in the area is almost exactly 300 yards from the spot established by historians as the position of Stirling's main battle line, and at a very early date after the action was given the name Battle Hill. Battle Hill is today located in the northwest part of Green-Wood Cemetery, about 300 yards from the main entrance. At 220 feet, this hill is the highest elevation in Brooklyn, and possession of it by the British would have allowed them a commanding position above Stirling's battle line.

As good as Atlee's description was of the fighting on Battle Hill, it is likely because of him that the role that Huntington's Regiment played in the battle has largely been overlooked by history. In his story, Atlee took nearly all the credit for the command and execution of the successful work in which he was engaged on Stirling's left wing. There is only brief mention that a "few" of Huntington's men joined him, and that he received Huntington's ammunition cart at a very opportune moment. But, since only one ammunition cart was assigned per regiment, either the 17th exhibited what would have been a nearly suicidal act of generosity, or they were fully present for the same battles in which Atlee was engaged, and quite understandably shared the contents of their cart during the heat of a common battle. Atlee also used the word "our" ammunition cart when referring to the cart

---

[1] Force, *American Archives*, 5th Series, Vol. I, 1252-1253.

*View from Battle Hill towards the west about 1850
(from* Green-Wood *by N. Cleaveland,
courtesy CT State Library)*

belonging to Huntington's Regiment, and therefore inadvertently admitted that Huntington's men were under the same command.

It was not unusual for an officer to embellish his role during a battle, and Colonel Atlee must have been still smarting from Parsons' criticism of his men for having fled precipitously after the first shots on the early morning picket. When Atlee wrote his journal, he was perhaps reluctant to give General Parsons any credit for command decisions, or to even fully acknowledge the presence and involvement of other than his own men in the fight on Battle Hill.

The substance of Colonel Atlee's journal regarding the Battle of Long Island may have also been influenced by a personal need for recognition by the Pennsylvania state government. When, by its passage of an "An Act for the more effectual supply and honorable reward of the Pennsylvania Troops in the service of the United States of North America," in 1779, the General Assembly overlooked the service of officers from Pennsylvania, including Atlee, who had served at the beginning of the war, Atlee took umbrage and submitted a detailed defense of his actions and service. His journal, as it related to the Battle of Long Island was submitted as a part of the petition.[1]

For further evidence that Huntington's Regiment played a significant role in the fight, we need only to return to Parsons' letter to John Adams, which shares some of the same facts that Atlee reported in his journal. In his letter, Parsons made no distinction between Huntington's and Atlee's men during these engagements, and the strong implication was that they functioned as one unit under his command. Later on in that same letter Parsons stated that, "In my party, a Lt.-Col. Parry was killed..." As mentioned before, Lt.-Col. Parry was Colonel Atlee's second in command. Parsons could hardly have stated more clearly that he considered Atlee's men to be under his command. Lt. Fitch made mention of the same fact in his diary when he stated that, "a Lt.-Col. of ours (Parry) was killed." Parsons also wrote that the opposing British regiments were the 44th and 23rd regiments, the same regiments that Atlee says he was engaged with in his battle description. In addition, Lt. Fitch noted the death of British Lt.-Col. Grant during the battle, an incident also referred to by Atlee.

---

[1] *Pennsylvania Archives*, Series 2, Vol. I, (Harrisburg: Lane S. Hart, 1879-), pp. 511-512, www.footnote.com/image/290685

Certainly, Atlee deserves great credit for the part he and his men played in the fight on Battle Hill, but the men of Huntington's 17th Continental Regiment deserve the same recognition. And, belatedly, General Parsons must receive credit for overall command during the time his brigade, of which Atlee's men were just a part, fought on Battle Hill. If the reader would substitute "we" for the majority of the "I's" in Atlee's story, we would likely have an accurate and complete description of one of the most successful American engagements of the day.

This writer recently listened to a talk presented by a tour guide on Battle Hill. In his presentation the hill was described only as a place where a skirmish occurred between the British and about 30 unknown American riflemen. This oral history derives from some of the written histories, such as Stiles' history of Brooklyn that did not fully comprehend the scope of the fighting on Stirling's left wing. Battle Hill would surely not have come to be known by that name soon after the battle if it was merely the scene of a minor skirmish. Colonel Atlee testified that the summit of Battle Hill was clear at the time, and as the highest of the hills, its possession would have been critical to the American position on the Gowanus Road, and just as critical for the British to try to take it. For that reason, all of Parsons' brigade, not just 30 lone riflemen, fought like men possessed for most of the morning of the 27th of August 1776. Their heroic efforts, in all likelihood, prevented the complete encirclement and annihilation of Stirling's command.

There may be some truth to the story about the riflemen on Battle Hill, though. If we return to Colonel Atlee's memoirs, there is the implication that Atlee's men deserved the credit for the killing of British Lieutenant-Colonel Grant. General Parsons made no mention of the death of Grant in his letter of August 29, but the next day witnesses reported that Parsons brought into the Brooklyn lines "a hat, with two bullet holes, marked Colonel Grant, and Grant's watch."[1] But neither Parsons nor Atlee gave credit to any specific person or unit for Grant's demise. Responsibility for that act might have to be assigned to Kichlein's Pennsylvania riflemen, a portion of whom, perhaps 50 or so, apparently fell under Parsons' command, and fought on Battle Hill.

---

[1] Force, *American Archives*, 5th Series, Vol. I, 1195.

Riflemen of that era were so called because of their use of the Pennsylvania long-rifle, instead of the commonly issued, smooth-bored musket. With its grooved barrel, the long-rifle was a much more accurate weapon, with a far greater range than the musket. The British feared the colonials who were armed with such weapons, knowing their ability and propensity for picking off their officers at long range. Today, riflemen would be known as snipers.

The drawback of the rifle in the heat of battle was its difficulty, and length of time in loading. Muskets could be fired at a rate of three rounds a minute, but rifles often took a minute or more to load. The rifleman had to brace his weapon against a tree or rock to be able to ram the tight fitting load home. Rifles also could not be fitted with bayonets, so for these reasons, riflemen were at a distinct disadvantage in close-in fighting.

Lieutenant-Colonel Kichlein's rifle battalion, consisting of four companies, had been divided among the various areas of the battleground in the vicinity of the Gowanus Road. Some had been upon the picket during the night, and sustained the first fire of the British troops before dawn. These were part of the guard that had retreated at the British advance along the Gowanus Road in the pre-dawn hours.

Another part of Kichlein's battalion-perhaps the same part- was later sent by Stirling into the trees and hedges in front, and at the foot of Wykoff's Hill, upon which Stirling made his stand. Their position placed these riflemen next to the swamp and bridge in front of Blockje's Bergh where we have already noted that they did significant damage to the advance parties of the British. Still more of Kichlein's men were sent south from the Brooklyn lines with Huntington's Regiment. It was probably this portion of Kichlein's battalion that took part in the fight on Battle Hill, and may have been responsible for the death of Lieutenant-Colonel Grant, a casualty of the long distance marksmanship of these Pennsylvania riflemen. This fact was said to have been testified to by William Howe himself in a dispatch after the battle, but that dispatch apparently no longer exists.[1] However, in 1867, Dr. Henry Stiles wrote in his *History of the City of Brooklyn* that:

---

[1] Randall Wert, *Samuel Wirth: Historical Information* (unpublished research, n. d. www.user.fast.net/~rtwert/nti00108.htm), Section II, D, 4.

Traditions current among the old inhabitants of the Gowanus neighborhood, and worthy of credit, especially mark "Battle Hill" as a place of historic interest.   Here it is said a small body of riflemen had been stationed among the trees which then crowned that eminence; and when the right wing of the British army (under Cornwallis), unconscious of their presence, had approached within range, these unerring marksmen commenced their fire, each ball bringing down an officer. Unfortunately for them, the hill was surrounded before they could escape, and they were all shot down.[1]

Although Stiles did not state specifically that these riflemen were Kichlein's, it is likely that they were, since the other Americans on the field near the Gowanus Road, the Delaware, Maryland, and Connecticut men, were all equipped with muskets. If this oral tradition is accurate, then Kichlein's riflemen lingered too long on Battle Hill and were trapped and killed when Cornwallis' troops came up in their rear. A still earlier version of events was written in 1824, and was based on stories told by people still living in the area who had been witnesses to the battle of a half century before:

...part of the British army marched down a lane or road leading from the Brush tavern to Gowanos [This was the Port Road, which ran from Sullivan's position in Flatbush Pass to the Gowanus Road just north of Battle Hill], *pursuing the Americans. Several of the American riflemen, in order to be more secure, and at the same time more effectually to succeed in their designs, had posted themselves in the high trees near the road. One of them, whose name is now partially forgotten, shot the English Major* [sic] *Grant: in this he passed unobserved. Again he loaded his deadly rifle, and fired- another English officer fell. He was then marked, and a platoon ordered to advance, and fire into the tree; which order was immediately carried into execution, and the rifleman fell to the ground, dead. After the battle was over, the two British officers were buried in a field, near where they fell, and their graves fenced in with some posts and rails, where their remains still rest. But for "an example to the rebels," they refused to the American rifleman the rites of sepulture; and his*

---

[1] Stiles, *History of the City of Brooklyn*, p. 270.

remains were exposed on the ground till the flesh was rotted, and torn off his bones by the fowls of the air. After a considerable length of time, in a heavy gale of wind, a large tree was uprooted; in the cavity formed by which some friends to the Americans, notwithstanding the prohibition of the English, placed the brave soldier's bones to mingle in peace with their kindred earth.[1]

Several other versions of the above story survive, with credit for the shooting of Grant given to either a man of Atlee's regiment, or a Maryland soldier. Both of these, however, would have been equipped with muskets. The anecdotal evidence is reinforced by information regarding Kichlein's riflemen from the Pennsylvania Archives. Lt.-Col. Kichlein himself was taken prisoner, but in particular, Captain John Arndt's company seems to have suffered far more than any other company in the regiment. That company alone lost 19 privates and two sergeants on August 27.[2] It is most likely that this company of Pennsylvania riflemen fought with the rest of Parsons' Brigade on Battle Hill and was responsible for the death of British Colonel Grant.

It may seem morbid to dwell on this specific incident of battlefield violence, but if the snipers were Kichlein's men, their heroism would go a long way towards redeeming their reputations. Some of their men had been among the Pennsylvania troops that had been harshly accused by General Parsons of fleeing without firing their weapons at the first sight of Grant's troops near the Red Lion in the pre-dawn hours.

With the men on Battle Hill still fully engaged in the morning fight, the British sprang their trap. That portion of the flanking column under General Cornwallis reached Bedford behind the Americans in the outposts at about 8:30 in the morning, after passing through the Jamaica Pass in the dead of night. Colonel Miles, stationed on the far left of the American lines in the hills just west of the Bedford Road, claimed that he had suspected all along that the British would try to attack along the Jamaica Road, but had been unable to convince his superiors of that probability. When the Hessians began firing in the Flatbush Pass on Sullivan's position, Miles tried to march west to

---

[1] Gabriel Furman, *Notes, Geographical and Historical Relating to the Town of Brooklyn* (Brooklyn: A. Spooner, 1824), p. 51, http://persi.heritagequestonline.com/...
[2] *Pennsylvania Archives*, 5th Series, Vol. VIII, p. 24.

assist, but was almost immediately stopped by Colonel Wyllys who told him to stay and help guard the Bedford Road. Miles then hastily explained his belief that the majority of Howe's army was trying to flank them and get in their rear along the Jamaica Road. After some discussion, Colonel Wyllys agreed that Miles should reverse his march to investigate his suspicions.

Miles immediately wheeled around with his regiment and marched two miles northeast through the woods before emerging on the Jamaica Road at about 8:00 A.M. He was too late. The massive British column was already advancing west towards Brooklyn past Miles' position, and was now in the rear of every American regiment stationed in the passes. Only the baggage train at the rear of the British column was left in the road in front of Miles, but even that was a full brigade strong. Miles had arrived on the Jamaica Road with only the first battalion of his regiment, and after assessing the vast numerical superiority of the enemy in the road, sent word to his second battalion under Lt.-Col. Brodhead, who was some distance behind him, to try to escape through the hills with his command to the Brooklyn lines. Brodhead had, however, lost touch with his colonel, and on his own had discovered the hopelessness of the situation and ordered his battalion to retreat to Brooklyn. As they fled, they came into contact with scattered units of the enemy and had one brief skirmish, but Brodhead with most of his battalion were able to reach safety relatively unscathed.[1]

After considering his options with the other officers of his battalion, Miles determined to follow Brodhead and fight his way through the British flanking guards that were beginning to fan out through the hills. But by now the way had been cut off, and after two skirmishes, Miles' regiment disintegrated, breaking up into small parties or individual soldiers that were left to fend for themselves. Miles and most of his battalion were eventually rounded up and made prisoners.[2]

Wyllys and Chester's regiments, guarding the Bedford pass just to the west of Miles, were alerted to the danger in their rear by the fleeing soldiers from Miles' regiment and were able to withdraw in good order. They reached the American lines with little loss. The line of retreat for most of the men at the eastern end of the line was likely

---

[1] Johnston, *Campaign of 1776*, Part II, p. 63-66, Document 21.
[2] Johnston, *Campaign of 1776*, Part II, p. 60-63, Document 20.

through the woods and hills, crossing the Flatbush Road near Sullivan's position before picking up the Port Road that ran from there to Brooklyn.

General Sullivan's position at the Flatbush pass was the last to come under attack as the British moved west down the Jamaica Road behind him. Early in the morning the Hessians at Flatbush had begun to shell the American redoubt there but did not press an attack. According to historian Henry P. Johnston, Sullivan himself had spent the previous night behind the lines at Brooklyn, and upon the commencement of hostilities, rode out to the Flatbush Pass at about 8:30 in the morning to reconnoiter. At that time, he still had no idea of the enemy's intentions and was not aware of the advancing flanking force. Upon arriving at Flatbush Pass, Sullivan was informed- erroneously as it turned out- that the main body of the enemy was in front of Stirling, to Sullivan's right. Reacting to this intelligence, according to his report after the battle, Sullivan sent another battalion off to assist Stirling. But, he did not identify the battalion, and it is not known if it ever reached Stirling.[1]

It was probably only a few minutes after arriving on the Flatbush Road before Sullivan became aware of the extreme danger of his position. At about 9:00 A.M. he heard artillery and small arms fire behind him as the Americans fleeing the eastern outposts were fired on by the British flanking guards. It was reported that Sullivan sent word to Stirling to retreat, knowing that the British advance along the Jamaica Road would soon cut Stirling off as well. Leaving the pickets from Colonels Little and Hitchcock's regiments close by the redoubt at the junction of the Port and Flatbush Roads to hold off the Hessians in his front, Sullivan reversed direction to face the threat in his rear, taking with him the approximately 400 men of Colonel Philip Johnston's New Jersey Militia.

Sullivan and Johnston met the enemy on the flats just north of the junction of the Port Road with the Flatbush Road, where, "By the well-directed fire from his battalion the enemy were several times repulsed, and lanes were made through them, until he [Johnston] received a ball in his breast, which put an end to the life of as brave an officer as ever commanded a battalion. General Sullivan, who was close to him when he fell, says, that no man could behave with more

---

[1] Onderdonk, *Revolutionary Incidents*, p. 140, Document 807.

firmness during the whole action."[1] Sullivan reported that he held off the British from 9:30 until noon when his men broke up into small parties and fled. In spite of the death of their colonel, losses among the New Jersey men were light, and the majority of them were able to safely reach the Brooklyn lines. Sullivan himself, however, was not so lucky, and was captured by the British sometime after noon.

Almost simultaneously with the advance of the flanking column in Sullivan's rear, the Hessians began their attack on the redoubt and pickets in the Flatbush Pass. Faced with an overwhelming force, and without Sullivan present to give them orders, the two regiments left to guard the pass (those of Colonel Little, under Lt.-Col Henshaw, and Colonel Hitchcock, under Lt.-Col. Cornell), escaped the trap and withdrew in good order with little loss. Henshaw later deposed that as they retreated they came upon the vanguard of the British flanking army just as their officers were holding a council of war. With the British so diverted, Henshaw and Cornell were able to get by before they were detected and belatedly fired on.[2]

While the British light infantry and dragoons were engaged with Sullivan and the fleeing Americans in the eastern hills, the main British column under Cornwallis continued along the Jamaica Road before coming to a halt in front of the Brooklyn lines near the junction of the Port Road and the northern end of the Gowanus Road. Lord Stirling had now been engaged in a cannonade with the enemy under General Grant for several hours, when, late in the morning, Stirling discovered that Cornwallis' troops were in his rear. This fact effectively eliminated Stirling's line of retreat back along the Gowanus Road to the Brooklyn lines.

Realizing he was trapped between Cornwallis and Grant, Stirling immediately reversed direction and marched north to attack Cornwallis. Some of those British troops had already occupied a stone farmhouse that the Americans had previously fortified near the mouth of Gowanus Creek. This farmhouse was known as the Vechte or Cortelyou House, for either of the two families who had historically occupied it. It was one of several old Dutch farmhouses strung out along the Gowanus Road, and was built of thick stone walls resistant to musket and cannon fire.

---

[1] Force, *American Archives*, 5th Series, Vol. 1, p. 1251.
[2] Johnston, *The Campaign of 1776*, Part II, p. 47, Document 11.

Stirling took with him about half of Smallwood's Maryland Regiment to engage Cornwallis, hoping that the remainder of his brigade could make its escape through the only avenue left open to them: the Gowanus Marsh and Creek. Three times Stirling's Marylanders attacked Cornwallis and very nearly succeeded in taking the old stone house. Behind the nearby Brooklyn lines, General Washington could observe the Stirling/Cornwallis fight in the distance, and immortalized the moment exclaiming, "Good God, what brave fellows I must this day lose."[1]

While Stirling kept Cornwallis in check, the rest of his brigade- mostly Haslet's Delawares- made good their escape through the marsh before Grant's men could overtake them from the south. Of necessity, the fleeing Americans abandoned most of their arms and equipment in order to keep their heads above water in the rising tide. Meanwhile, the pursuing British, who had now filled the Gowanus Road behind them, tried to pick them off one by one.

Incredibly, Haslet's men were able to force their twenty-three recalcitrant British prisoners, just recently captured, through the swamp ahead of them. The area of escape through the marsh was between today's 23rd and 3rd streets, then a distance of about a mile with no ford or bridge. In more peaceful times, the Gowanus Swamp had been dammed at its head to form a tidal millpond that powered two mills. Colonel Smallwood, in his report, said that where the men forded the swamp the pond was about 80 yards across.[2]

Behind the safety of the Brooklyn lines, brothers-in-arms watched as their comrades struggled through the marsh just in front of them. Colonel Smallwood, having now returned from New York, was sent in command of an available regiment of Connecticut state troops with two field-pieces down the slope to the marsh to provide covering fire. Without that help the men in the water would have been completely defenseless and fully exposed to a withering British fire. General Washington watched in frustration from Brooklyn Heights as his desperate soldiers tried to reach him, knowing he could not risk sending out any more men in an effort to save them. Remarkably, despite British reports to the contrary, losses in the marsh were small.

---

[1] Stiles, *History of the City of Brooklyn*, p. 279.
[2] Onderdonk, *Revolutionary Incidents*, Sec. 811, p. 144.

Perhaps as few as seven men were drowned or shot, and two of these may have been Hessian prisoners.[1]

Stirling had accomplished an heroic diversion, but, succumbing to overwhelming numbers, he was captured with virtually all that remained of Smallwood's Marylanders. After Stirling's surrender, the Gowanus Road filled with British troops marching from both the north and south, effectively isolating all the Americans in the hills who had not yet made it across the Gowanus Marsh.

Because of Stirling's heroism, much of the American Army was now relatively safe behind the Brooklyn lines. For some unexplained reason, however, Stirling had failed to notify Parsons when he was abandoning his position to move north to attack Cornwallis. As a result, the men of Huntington's, Atlee's, and Kichlein's regiments were oblivious to events occurring behind them, and now effectively isolated and cut off in the forests and swamps of the Greenwood Hills. Because of their isolation and the cover of the forest, their struggle was not observed by General Washington or the men behind the Brooklyn lines. There were no famous witnesses to immortalize the heroism of the men on Battle Hill. General Parsons wrote in his report:

> *About 10 o'clock we found a large body of the enemy had advanced on the other roads near our lines, but a constant fire was kept up on the enemy till about 12, when we found them fast advancing on our rear to cut off our retreat. Our little main body advanced boldly up to the enemy in the rear & broke through their lines and secured the retreat of most of the party* [here Parsons is referring to Stirling's attack on Cornwallis]*; but it fared still harder with my little party who had three times repulsed the enemy in front and once in the rear; we had no notice of the retreat of the main body* [Stirling] *till it was too late for us to join them, the enemy having cut off our retreat on three sides & the main body having broke through the enemy's lines on the other side and left them between us.*[2]

Lt. Jabez Fitch of Huntington's Regiment provided more detail for the time period subsequent to the three fights on Battle Hill:

[1] Stiles, *History of the City of Brooklyn*, p. 279.
[2] Hall, *Life and Letters of Samuel Holden Parsons*, p. 55.

While we were thus engaged here [on Battle Hill], *we heard a smart fire toward our left wing, which gave us to apprehend that we were in danger of having our retreat cut off, on which our regiment were ordered to march toward the fire* [This is likely the skirmish that Parsons described with the enemy in his rear; the fourth battle of the day for his regiment, confirming Lt. Orcutt's numbers], *and on our approaching in sight of the enemy (to our surprise) we found our apprehensions but too well grounded. After this we met with several small attacks, in which we generally fought on retreat, without much loss, until we found ourselves surrounded by the enemy, when we attempted to join Lord Sterlings* [sic] *party, but found ourselves likewise cut off from them.[1]*

Colonel Atlee also wrote about what happened after the third fight on Battle Hill, but described his movements in terms that seem to indicate that he now separated himself from General Parsons and Huntington's Regiment:

I fully expected, as did most of my officers, that the strength of the British Army was advancing in this quarter to our lines [Grant's attack along the Gowanus Road]. *But how greatly were we deceived when intelligence was received by some scattering soldiers that the right wing and center of the Army, amongst whom were the Hessians, were advancing to surround us. This we were soon convinced of by an exceeding heavy fire in our rear...I once more sent my Adjutant to Lord Stirling, to acquaint him with the last success obtained by my party, and to request his further orders; but receiving no answer, the Adjutant not returning, and waiting near three-quarters of an hour for the enemy, they not approaching in front, but those in the rear drawing near, I thought it most prudent to join the* [Stirling's] *Brigade, where I might be of more advantage than in my present situation. I therefore ordered a march...How great was my surprise I leave any one to judge, when, upon coming to the ground occupied by our troops, to find it evacuated and the troops gone off, without my receiving the least intelligence of the movement, or order what*

---

[1] *Fitch*, p. 30.

*to do, although I had so shortly before sent my Adjutant to the
General for that purpose. The General must have known, that by
my continuing in my post at the hill, I must, with all my party,
inevitably fall a sacrifice to the enemy. An opportunity yet
afforded, with risking the lives of some of us, of getting off. But
perceiving a body of the enemy advancing, which proved to be the
English Grenadiers, under Lieutenant-Colonel Monckton, to fall
upon the rear of our brigade, which I could see at a distance, I
ordered my party once more to advance and support a few brave
fellows, endeavouring to prevent, but without success, the
destruction of their countrymen. The timely assistance of a
number often tried, and as often victorious, encouraged those
already engaged, and obliged the enemy to quit the ground they
had gained and retire to a fence line with trees. Here we kept up
a close fire, until the brigade had retreated out of our sight, when,
not being able, through the weakness of my party, already greatly
fatigued, and once more destitute of ammunition, to break through
the enemy, and finding my retreat after the brigade cut off, I filed
off to the right, to endeavour, if possible, to escape through that
quarter...*[1]

Atlee made it clear by this statement that he felt he was still under
Stirling's command, and looking for orders from him. Both Parsons
and Fitch described a fight with the enemy in their rear, but Atlee
retreated from Battle Hill upon the approach of the enemy in his rear
and attempted to rejoin Stirling. Until this point in time, Atlee still
had mentioned no contact with Parsons of any kind. Atlee returned to
the area along the Gowanus Road previously occupied by Stirling,
and found himself cut off by the British grenadiers, with the remains
of Stirling's brigade retreating out of sight.

Atlee turned and scrimmaged with the enemy now filling the
Gowanus Road, but finding escape in that direction impossible, he
marched back east towards Battle Hill (which in his description he
says was then to his right), hoping to escape in that direction. Atlee
went on to say, "After marching about half a mile to the right, fell in
with General Parsons and a small number by him collected. In
consultation with the general it was determined to break through the
enemy, who were here within a little way of us, and endeavour to

---

[1] Force, *American Archives*, 5th Series, Vol. I, pp. 1253-1254.

make up the Island." By this statement Atlee established that he had regained his former position on Battle Hill and united with General Parsons. For the first time, he referred to any consultation with Parsons. They agreed that together they should try to force their way through the British blocking their way to the east end of the Island, and away from Brooklyn. Parsons said of this moment:

> *We had no alternative left but force through one line into a thick wood, which we attempted & effected with part of our men, the part with Col. Clark being before sent into the wood. When we had made our way into the wood, I was accidentally parted from Col. Atlee & most of the men, whom I have never seen since.*[1]

Based on Parsons' statement, it appears that Col. Clark, with Huntington's Regiment, had already been sent ahead into the woods to the east, and separated once and for all from their brigade commander, General Parsons. Fortunately for our history, we have Lt. Fitch to fill us in on what happened to Huntington's men next:

> *We then collected our scattered force in the best manner possible, and took our march over eastward, with intention to break through the enemy and secure a retreat that way, but after crossing a thick swamp, we came onto a plain partly covered with wood, where we soon found ourselves between two severe fires from the Hessian troops, on which we again retreated into the swamp, and repaired to the ground that we had occupied before [Battle Hill], where we were again attacked by a small party who soon retreated. We had now lost Colonel Clark and General Parsons, on which a number of our officers assembled and concluded it best, as we were entirely surrounded by the enemy, to resign ourselves up to them in small parties, and each one take care for himself, accordingly, I went alone down to the northward where I lit of Sergeant Wright, who had his leg broke, I carried him some way down the hill, and laid him in a shade where I left him. I then went up the hill to the eastward, where I see at a small distance a party of regulars, on which I immediately advanced to them, and gave up my arms. They treated me with humanity, etc.*

---

[1] Hall, *Life and Letters of Samuel Holden Parsons*, p. 55.

Colonel Atlee also described what happened to the remnants of his command as they followed in the same general direction as Huntington's men who had moved off to the east ahead of them:

> *I then pushed off with such of the officers and soldiers that were willing to run this hazard. What became of General Parsons I know not, never having seen him since. I had not gone above two hundred yards when a Highlander made his appearance in the edge of a wood. I instantly presented, as did some of those with me. The fellow clubbed his firelock and begged for quarter. I had hardly time to assure him of it, when I found him to be a decoy sent from a party of Highlanders within fifty yards of our right. I immediately jumped forward, ordering the party to follow, taking with me the Highlander's musket, which I had, fortunately for me, deprived him of. We received in our flight the fire of this party, and sundry others through which we were obliged to run for near two miles. What of my party, or if any, in this flight were killed, wounded, or taken, I cannot tell, as it is uncertain how many, or who they were, that followed me. I imagined that if I could cross the Flatbush road, I could then make my escape by Hell-Gate, but coming to the road found it everywhere strictly guarded. After trying the road in several places, both to the right and left, and finding no passage, we retired to an eminence about sixty perches from the road, to consult whether best to conceal ourselves in the adjacent swamps or divide into small parties, when we espied a party of Hessians, who had discovered and were endeavouring to surround us. The opinion we had formed of these troops determined us to run any risk rather than fall into their hands; and finding after all our struggles no prospect of escaping, we determined to throw ourselves into the mercy of a battalion of Highlanders posted upon an eminence near the Flatbush road, not far from where we had last sat. This we did about five o'clock in the afternoon to the number of twenty-three, thereby escaping the pursuit of a party of Hessians, who came to the Highlanders immediately after our surrender.*[1]

Based on the previous accounts, from the same spot on or near Battle Hill, although apparently moving separately, both those still under

---

[1] Force, *American Archives*, 5th Series, Vol. I, p. 1254.

Atlee's command, and the remnants of Huntington's Regiment tried to escape to the east through the Greenwood Hills. Lt. Fitch described emerging from the hills, probably in the vicinity of Flatbush, into a swamp. This should not be confused with the Gowanus Marsh which was then more than two miles to the west of their position, and through which many of Stirling's command had found their way to safety. The swamp mentioned by both Fitch and Atlee must have been located at the foot of the hills at the edge of the southern plains, a position directly east of Battle Hill. This was probably the southern portion of what is known today as Prospect Park. That area is now filled with a man-made lake, but in 1776 was nothing but a swamp.[1]

Lt. Fitch did not say how many men were still with him as he emerged from the swamp near Flatbush. At any rate, it was not a large enough force to fight their way through the Hessian troops that fired on them there. Therefore, finding any possible escape route to the east cut off, Fitch and the men with him reversed direction and retraced their steps back to the area of Battle Hill. Colonel Atlee and the remains of his command continued their march east through the swamp, probably emerging a little to the north of where Fitch had been, along the Flatbush Road. From his location, Atlee found the situation hopeless. To avoid the thoroughly unattractive prospect of becoming prisoners of the Hessians, the best that Atlee could do was to seek out a regiment of Highlanders to surrender to.

General Parsons had now become separated from the rest. With seven others, whom he did not identify, he spent the night out in the open. Miraculously, Parsons evaded capture and was able to make his way back to the Brooklyn lines the next morning, reporting that he had fought his way through the enemy six or seven times.[2]

Lt. Fitch's retreat to Battle Hill only postponed the inevitable for him and the last organized remnants of Huntington's Regiment. British troops filled all the roads, and were now scouring the hills and woods for American stragglers. After one final skirmish, Huntington's exhausted men found further resistance useless. It now became every man for himself. Lt. Fitch's last effort as a free man was to selflessly attend to the wounded Sgt. Wright. This would have been Sgt. Ebenezer Wright of Capt. Ozias Bissell's Company. After

---

[1] Samuel White Patterson, *Famous Men and Places in the History of New York City* (New York: Noble and Noble, 1923), p. 162, http://persi.heritagequestonline.com/...
[2] "Benjamin Trumbull's Journal," *Collections of the Connecticut Historical Society*, Vol. VII, p. 187.

making sure that the sergeant was as comfortable as possible, Fitch surrendered his arms to the victorious British who once and for all took possession of Battle Hill.

View from Battle Hill towards the west (photo by the author)

Battle Hill in Green-Wood Cemetery (photo by the author)

Wide View to the west from Battle Hill in Green-Wood Cemetery
(photo by the author)

Altar to Liberty on the summit of Battle Hill in Green-Wood Cemetery, waving towards the Statue of Liberty in the distance across New York harbor (photo by the author)

6. The Conduct of Infernal Spirits

By shortly after noon on the 27th of August, effective, organized resistance by the Americans had ceased outside the Brooklyn defenses. Alone, or in small broken bands, the exhausted soldiers that were now trapped in the hills either surrendered, or desperately tried to find breaks in the encircling British ranks through which they might make their way back to the safety of their own lines.

As bad as the situation in the Gowanus Marsh had been for Stirling's troops, the men of Jedediah Huntington's 17th Continental Regiment had it far worse. They had lingered on Battle Hill too long, and were now surrounded by the enemy that had occupied all the roads through the hills. Scattered in small groups or traveling alone, the men of the 17th were among those forced to wander in all directions, trying to find escape routes. All afternoon, into the night, and through the next morning the British rounded up the exhausted rebels. Scattered resistance from the larger bands of Americans broke out here and there during the afternoon of the 27th, but the vast majority was forced to surrender in the face of overwhelming odds, hoping that mercy would be granted them.

Mercy, unfortunately, was at a premium. Many sought to surrender to British soldiers, rather than to the Hessians, who had a reputation among the Americans for the brutal treatment of prisoners. The Hessians had been indoctrinated by their British overlords into believing that the American rebels were savages, commonly taking to the Indian practice of scalping their enemies. One British officer later wrote:

We took care to tell the Hessians that the Rebels had resolved to give no quarters to them in particular, which made them fight desperately and put all to death that fell into their hands. You know all stratagems are lawful in war, especially against such vile enemies to their King and country.[1]

The consequences of the Hessians' indoctrination were soon born out in their treatment of some of the men of Huntington's Regiment. Lt. Jonathan Gillet of Capt. Ozias Bissell's Company was a case in point:

My Friends; No doubt my misfortunes have reached your ears. Sad as it is, it is true as sad. I was made prisoner the 27th day of August past by a people called heshens, and by a party called Yagers the most Inhuman of all Mortals. I can't give Room to picture them here but thus much--I at first Resolved not to be taken, but by the Impertunity of the Seven taken with me, and being surrounded on all sides I unhappily surrendered; would to God I never had--then I should never [have] known there unmerciful cruelties; they first disarmed me, then plundered me of all I had, watch, Buckles, money, and sum Clothing, after which they abused me by bruising my flesh with the butts of there [guns]. They knocked me down; I got up and they [kept on] beating me almost all the way to there [camp] where I got shot of them--the next thing was I was allmost starved to death by them.[2]

Also from Capt. Ozias Bissell's Co., Private Daniel Thomas stated in his pension application that, "he was in the battle of Flat Bush, and was surrounded in a swamp by the Hessians and made a prisoner of war."[3] This is likely the same swamp to the east of Battle Hill that Lt. Fitch and Col. Atlee mention. Since Thomas was from the same company, it is also possible that he was one of the seven men that Lt. Gillet said were present with him when he was captured.

The most brutal story of the day involving any of Huntington's men, was the capture of Captain Joseph Jewett. Several versions of the story of his capture have been passed down, two of which are told in the genealogy, *The Jewett Family of America*: One version relates that he was murdered by the British officer to whom he surrendered his sword; another that he was killed by his own sword after he had

---

[1] "Extract of a letter from an officer in General Frazier's battalion," *The Spirit of '76*, p. 443.
[2] "Lt. Jonathan Gillet, to his wife Elizabeth, Dec. 2, 1776," Stiles, *The History and Genealogies of Ancient Windsor*, Vol. II, p. 298.
[3] NARA, Series M805, Roll 797, Revolutionary War Pension Application, S11536.

surrendered it to the British officer. But, the only contemporary written testimony comes again from Lt. Fitch, who wrote in his diary:

> *Having surrendered myself to the 57th Regt., I was kept under the care of a guard for some time, while some others likewise came in and surrendered, and at about 5 o'clock, I was guarded by said Regt. over on to the edge of Flat Bush Plain, where I see a large body of Hessian troops on a hill at our left. We then took a turn to the right, and was marched by the front of several battalions of the Hessians, where I received many insults from those formidable Europeans. We then marched through a considerable wood, and came onto the hill, where I first discovered the enemy in the morning. Here we found the greater part of two brigades under arms and General Agnue* [Brigadier-General James Agnew of the 6th British Brigade] *at their head. I was then conducted down to a barn near the* [Gowanus] *road where I marched homeward the night before and confined with a great number of prisoners of different regiments. Here I found Captain Trowbridge, Captain Percival, Lt. Fanning, and Ensign Gillet, and soon after Captain Jewett was brought in who was wounded with the stab of a bayonet in the breast, and also another in the belly...[1]*

Several months later, Lt. Fitch wrote a narrative of his adventures as a captive of the British, in which he provided further details about his own, and Capt. Jewett's capture:

> *It would be impossible to rehearse the many instances of insult, with which we have been treated, especially in the forepart of our captivity, when those unthinking mercenaries vainly supposed they had little more to do, than ravage a rich and plentiful country, deserted by its inhabitants, and also to treat us (who were so unfortunate as to fall into their hands) with as much insolence as their narrow, though savage capacities were capable of. Yet it ought to be mentioned, to the honor of some (both of the Army and inhabitants) who treated us with humanity, and endeavored to protect us from the insults of others. I myself was so happy, as to fall at first into the hands of a party of this kind when taken prisoner. It was part of the 57th Regt. who used me*

---

[1] *Fitch*, p. 31.

with some degree of civility, although some particular officers were very liberal of their favorite term (Rebel) and now and then did not forget to remind me of a halter [hangman's noose]*, etc. They did not rob or strip me of any of my clothing but took only my arms and ammunition, and after keeping me in the field some time, in confinement with several others, under a strong guard, was sent off to General Grant's headquarters at Gowanus.*

In this march we passed through the front of several brigades of Hessians, who were paraded on several eminences in order of battle. They indeed made a very warlike appearance, and as no power appeared at that time to oppose them, their whole attention seemed to be fixed on us, nor were they by any means sparing of their insults. But, their officers especially, represented to the life (as far as their capacities would admit) the conduct of Infernal Spirits, under certain restrictions. Having passed through those savage insults, we at length came onto a hill nigh to the place where we at first engaged the enemy in the morning [by this Fitch probably means the exact ground between Eighteenth and Twentieth Streets, where Stirling had set up his battle line that morning]. *We were here met by a number of insolent soldiers, among whom was one woman who appeared remarkably malicious and attempted several times, to throw stones at us, when one of our guard informed me that her husband had been killed in this day's action. We were then conducted down to a barn* [likely the barn in Wynant Bennett's orchard where Colonel Atlee had held the British in check at the commencement of the day's actions]*, near the water side, where we were drove into a yard among a great number of officers and men who had been taken before us. Soon after we came here, Captain Jewett with a number of others, were brought in, and confined with us. Capt. Jewett had received two wounds with a bayonet after he was taken, and stripped of his arms and part of his clothes, one in the breast and the other in the belly...Sgt. Graves was also stabbed in the thigh with a bayonet, after he was taken with Capt. Jewett...* [1]

Lt. Fitch did not claim to have been a witness to the capture of Capt. Jewett, only to his treatment afterwards. However, Fitch must have been told Jewett's version of the story of his capture, which was the

[1] *Fitch*, pp. 137-138.

next best thing to his own eyewitness account. Sgt. Roswell Graves, also of Jewett's Company, captured with his captain, reportedly received similar treatment.

Some time later, when Fitch had had the opportunity to meet and share stories with other men of the 17th, he concluded that:

> *...it seems that most of the Officers and men, who were first confined at Flatbush, fell into the hands of the Hessian Troops, and were generally treated in a more Savage manner (if possible) than we who were first confined at Gowanus, and had been most of us taken by the British Troops, and although many had been both robbed and murdered by them, in a most scandalous manner, yet it is said that the Hessians generally treated those who fell into their hands, with more cruelty and insolence than the Britains, for it seems that the Hessian officers (though of never so high rank*) were not inactive in this ridiculous practice of stripping, robbing, insulting and murdering the unfortunate Americans who fell within the limits of their power. The present appearance of our officers and men, are an incontestable proof of those facts, for many of them yet remain almost destitute of clothes, several having neither britches, stockings, or shoes. Many of them when first taken were stripped entirely naked although some others present, who had some small degree of humanity in their composition, were so good as to favour them with some old dirty worn out garments, just sufficient to cover their nakedness, and in this situation we were made object of ridicule for the diversion of those foreign butchers.*
>
> *One Sam Talman (an Indian fellow belonging to the 17th Regt.)* [of Brewster's Company[1]] *after he was taken and stripped by the barbarians, was set up at a small distance as a mark for them to shoot at for diversion or practice, by which he received two severe wounds, one in the neck and the other in the arm, but although it appeared that their skill in the use of fire arms was not sufficient to dispatch him in that way...*

---

[1] Probably the Samuel Talman baptized at the New London 1st Church on May 12, 1745, the son of Samuel and Hannah (Manwaring) Talman: CT State Library, *Church Records Slip Index.*

Corporal [Nathan] *Raymond of the 17ᵗʰ Regiment* [Captain Jewett's nephew], *after being taken and stripped, was shamefully insulted and abused by General de Heister (in his own person), who was so lowlived as to seize Raymond by the hair of his head, throw him on the ground, etc.*[1]

One might wish that Ensign Anthony Bradford gave more information regarding his capture in his diary. Unfortunately, he only briefly mentioned that he was made a prisoner at about 9 o'clock in the morning the day after the Battle, and was then taken to the Dutch Church at Flatbush, where he remained a prisoner until September 3.[2]

The pension applications of the few ancient survivors of Huntington's Regiment by 1818, do not provide extensive testimony regarding their capture, but several men did note certain personal details regarding the aftermath of the battle. Some of them simply made mention that they were in the Battle of Long Island and taken prisoner. Others had a bit more to say, such as the previously mentioned Private Daniel Thomas, who was captured in the swamp by the Hessians.[3] Private Elijah Stanton of Capt. Percival's Company stated he was wounded in the hip during the battle, and taken prisoner.[4] Private Seth Turner of Capt. Hubbard's Company also said he was wounded during the Battle of Long Island and taken prisoner.[5] Lt. Solomon Orcutt managed to evade capture until the next morning, but did not say how, or if, anyone else was with him.[6] Sgt. Theophilus Huntington of Capt. Brewster's Company provided more detail stating, "That he furnished his own arms, accoutrements and clothing from the commencement of his services. That when he was taken prisoner…, he was deprived of every article of clothing except what he had on at the time, also of a valuable silver watch."[7]

Ensign Cornelius Higgins, seeking compensation from a compassionate government, testified in a petition to the Connecticut General Assembly in 1778, that he had had an unfortunate encounter

---

[1] *Fitch*, pp. 142-143.
[2] Bradford, *Diary*, pp. 41 & 50.
[3] NARA, Series M805, Roll 797, Revolutionary War Pension Application, S11536.
[4] NARA, Series M805, Roll 766, Revolutionary War Pension Application, S14623.
[5] NARA, Series M805, Roll 816, Revolutionary War Pension Application, S35365.
[6] NARA, Series M805, Roll 623, Revolutionary War Pension Application, S41037.
[7] NARA, Series M805, Roll 457, Revolutionary War Pension Application, S44960.

with the Hessians, who robbed him of "twenty dollars in cash and a silver watch... worth twenty dollars and sundry other things."[1]

Colonel Jedediah Huntington, who had been ill and absent during the Battle of Long Island, later resumed command of the remnants of his regiment. On November 8, 1776, he submitted a complete return to General Washington of all of his men that were killed or missing during the Battle of Long Island: 208 officers, non-commissioned officers, and privates were listed.[2] Considering that General Parsons claimed to have had no more than 300 in his brigade during the Battle, about one third of which may have been part of Colonel Atlee's regiment and some of Kichlein's Pennsylvania riflemen, then the vast majority of Huntington's Regiment that took part in the battle were captured or killed. But just how many out of the entire regiment were present that day? Most historians have been silent on the issue, however, Henry Stiles writing three-quarters of a century later said that General Parsons took "Colonel Huntington's Connecticut regiment of two hundred and fifty men" into battle. Unfortunately he did not state his source for that figure.[3]

In the return of Huntington's men dated at New York, August 3, before the battle, the colonel had 214 men in camp fit for duty. Considering the numbers of sick, and those assigned to other duties at the time, this may have been the minimum number of men who took the field on August 27. No doubt some of the 133 listed as "on command" on the return of August 3, would have been called to duty for the battle, therefore adding to the low estimate of 214. Private Obed Higley of Capt Ebenezer Fitch Bissell's Company, who was sick in New York during the battle, said in his pension application, "a great part of Col. Huntington's Regiment was cut off on Long Island."[4] It is probably safe to conclude that the "great part" to which Higley refers, means the vast majority of those that fought in the battle. Private Salmon Moulton of Capt. Ozias Bissell's Company said that "nearly all the regiment to which he belonged were killed or taken prisoners."[5] One Amos Hitchcock, a survivor of the battle from

---

[1] "Petition to the General Assembly, Jan. 12, 1778," CT State Library, *Connecticut Archives/ Revolutionary War, 1763-1789,* Series I, Vol. X, 144.
[2] *Record of Service of Connecticut Men in the War of the Revolution,* pp. 101-102.
[3] Stiles, *History of the City of Brooklyn,* p. 269.
[4] NARA, Series M805, Roll 425, Revolutionary War Pension Application, S17481.
[5] NARA, Series M805, Roll 603, Revolutionary War Pension Application, S23810.

another regiment, wrote in a letter to his wife on August 30, that "there is not but about seventy men left in Colonel Hunting's [sic] Regiment, six out of our place [Southington, Connecticut], Namely Colonel Clark, Ensign [Joel] Gillet, Sergeant [Uriah] Hungerford, Gad Fuller, John Dutton, Isaac Potter, killed or took [prisoner]..."[1] All these men were reported missing from Captain Percival's Company.

The total listed strength of Huntington's Regiment on August 3, was 540, so the figure of 208 casualties in the battle may have been somewhat less than one-half the total strength of the regiment. One of only two existing rolls of a complete company in Huntington's regiment is that of Capt. Brewster's Company, of an uncertain date prior to August 27. That roll lists 81 men, including officers.[2] Of those, 23 were listed as missing in the Battle or, a little less than one third of the men. The other existing full roll was that of Ebenezer Fitch Bissell taken on May 15, 1776, and a similar ratio of casualties to the complete roll exists there as well.[3]

We have another clue as to the possible size of Huntington's Regiment on Battle Hill that day. Private Lemuel Fuller, of Captain Joseph Jewett's Company was not captured during the battle. He stated in his pension application, that "Capt. Jewett's Company suffered the most of any-losing all his men but 14-as I recollect."[4] Including officers, there were 29 men listed as missing from Captain Jewett's company. If fourteen, including him, were present but escaped capture, as Fuller implies, then the total number of men of Jewett's Company in the battle was 43. Multiplying this number by the number of companies (8) in the regiment provides a total of about 344 men in the regiment that took part in the battle. Of course the numbers in each company would have varied somewhat that day. The actual number of Huntington's men who were in the battle is probably somewhere between the two figures of 214 fit for duty and present on August 3, and the figure of 344, projected from Lemuel Fuller's estimate. Therefore, Stiles' unsupported figure of 250 may be as close as we can come to the real number of those from Huntington's Regiment that were in battle on August 27.

---

[1] Timlow, *Ecclesiastical and Other Sketches of Southington, CT*, p. 539.
[2] *Record of Service of Connecticut Men in the War of the Rvolution*, pp. 102-103
[3] *Rolls and Lists of Connecticut Men in the Revolution*, p. 27.
[4] NARA, Series M805, Roll 343, Revolutionary War Pension Application, W648/BLWT26490-160-55.

Perhaps we cannot know the precise number of men from Huntington's Regiment that fought on Battle Hill, but we know with certainty the enormous impact that the casualties had on the regiment. Graphic evidence of the demise of the regiment is provided in the return submitted on September 27. On that return, there were only 97 men present and fit for duty in the entire regiment: Capt. Tyler's Company had 24 men, Capt. Jewett's Company had 5 men, Capt. Trowbridge's Company had 6 men, Capt. O. Bissell's Company had 11 men, Capt. Brewster's Company had 7 men, Capt. Percival's Company had 16 men, Capt. E. F. Bissell's Company had 15 men, and Capt. Hubbard's Company had 5 men left.[1] The entire regiment fit for duty would have consisted of just enough men to normally fill one fully completed company. At this strength, Huntington's 17th Continental Regiment would have ceased to exist as a functioning regiment. Indeed, Private Solomon Ingham wrote, "After the battle on Long Island our regiment was much scattered and torn to pieces…and so many of them were killed and captivated there it was not again organized to my knowledge during my enlistment."[2]

Checking the Revolutionary War Pension applications of the few men of Bissell's and Brewster's Companies who were not listed as casualties, we find some of the reasons why they weren't captured with the rest of their regiment. Privates Phineas Kellogg and Obed Higley of Bissell's Company both said they were sick in New York at the time.[3] Private Joel Humphreys, of the same company, said he was working in the New York shipyards along with another, unnamed man of his company at the time.[4] Private Jacob Hazen of Brewster's Company was occupied building chevaux-de-fris along the Hudson River, and was not in the battle.[5] Private Thomas Huntington of Brewster's Company said he was sent out of New York a few days

---

[1] NARA, Series M246, *Rev. War Rolls, 1775-1783*, "Continental Troops: 17th Regt.-Col. Jedediah Huntington, 1776," Folder 93, www.footnote.com/image/18395507
[2] NARA, Series M805, Roll 462, Revolutionary War Pension Application, W13527.
[3] NARA, Series M805, Roll 22, Revolutionary War Pension Application, S42774; NARA, Series M805, Roll 425, Revolutionary War Pension Application, S17481.
[4] NARA, Series M805, Roll 454, Revolutionary War Pension Application, W4246/BLWT13413-160-55.
[5] NARA, Series M805, Roll 414, Revolutionary War Pension Application, S17459.

before the battle, but did not indicate why.[1] Solomon Ingham simply wrote that he was "in the city" when the battle was fought.[2]

Privates John Whiting and William Andrus, both of Ebenezer Fitch Bissell's Company, do not take credit for being in the Battle of Long Island, and provide no details about where they were on that day.[3] Six other privates- four from Ebenezer Fitch Bissell's Company and two from Brewster's Company- claimed in their pension applications that they were in the battle, but they were not listed among the missing: Dudley Tracy, and Elisha Murdock of Brewster's Company; and James Lawrence, Increase Mather, Daniel Olmstead, and James Powers of Bissell's Company.[4]

☞   Only two of the men listed as casualties on Washington's November return were listed as killed during the Battle; Capt. Joseph Jewett, and **Sergeant Rous Bly** of Captain Percival's Company. But, some of the missing may have been unknown deaths in combat at the time of the November return. Rous Bly was a soldier from Preston, Connecticut, however, there is no birth record for him in the Connecticut Barbour Collection of vital records. He may have been born in Rhode Island, where other members of a family by that name lived at the time.

☞   DAR records provide the name of another man they claim was killed during the Battle of Long Island: **Private Alexander Ingham** of Captain Elizur Hubbard's Company.[5] The veteran of three campaigns in the French and Indian War left a wife, Ruth, and four children in Hebron, CT. He was a cousin of Private Solomon Ingham, also of Hebron.[6]

Estimates of the total number of casualties sustained by all of Washington's forces on August 27, 1776, vary wildly. American and British estimates place the number anywhere from one to three

---

[1] NARA, Series M805, Roll 457, Revolutionary War Pension Application, S44961.
[2] NARA, Series M805, Roll 462, Revolutionary War Pension Application, W13527.
[3] NARA, Series M805, Roll 862, Revolutionary War Pension Application, W19618; NARA, Series M805, Roll 22, Revolutionary War Pension Application, W23450.
[4] NARA, Series M805, Revolutionary War Pension Applications, Roll 810, R10667; Roll 606, R7506; Roll 516, S40921; Roll 558, S31831; Roll 622, W19936; Roll 664, S35570.
[5] *Index of the Rolls of honor (ancestor's index) in the Lineage Books of the National Society of the Daughters of the American Revolution,* (volumes 1-160, Press of Pierpont, Siviter, 1916-40), Vol. XL, p. 127.
[6] *The Ingham Family,* Family #21.

thousand killed, wounded, or missing. The majority of that number were those that were taken prisoner. Probably only a small minority were actually killed during the battle. In 1878, highly respected historian, Henry P. Johnston, conducted the most critical and exhaustive analysis of the numbers of casualties reported by both sides, and concluded that General Howe's figures were wildly exaggerated, but that General Washington's were the more accurate and the best documented. Washington concluded that about 1,000 Americans were killed, wounded, or taken prisoner, with about ¾ of the total in the latter category.[1]

The final determination of the number of British casualties has not been as widely disputed. Howe reported 63 killed and 337 wounded or missing. Relatively few of those were taken prisoner. If General Parsons' estimate that 60 British soldiers were killed on Battle Hill[2] is even close to the correct number, then the vast majority of the battle deaths sustained by the British would have been the result of that engagement. Parsons' observation was reinforced by the actual casualties reported by the four British regiments that faced Parsons' men during the day, the 17th, 23rd, 42nd, and 44th. Those regiments lost a total of 86 men killed or wounded. If the number of prisoners of war were subtracted from the casualty figures of both sides, then the number of British killed and wounded actually exceeded the number of Americans killed and wounded, again with the majority of those as a result of the fight on Battle Hill.

The published histories of the Battle of Long Island provide scant credit for the role that Huntington's Regiment played, but Colonel Joseph Reed, in a letter to General William Livingston, dated August 30, 1776, gave understated praise when he said, "The principal loss has fallen on First Pennsylvania Battalion, Atlee, Smallwood, Huntington, and Haslett's; all of whom behaved so as to command the admiration of all those who beheld the engagement."[3]

Author, Royal R. Hinman, in his *Historical Collection of the Part Sustained by Connecticut During the War of the Revolution*, also recognized the bravery and sacrifice of Huntington's 17th Continental Regiment, saying:

---

[1] Johnston, *The Campaign of 1776*, pp. 202-206.
[2] Hall, *Life and Letters of Samuel Holden Parsons*, p. 55.
[3] Force, *American Archives*, 5th Series, Vol. I, p. 1231.

The Connecticut forces constituted the nucleus of the army of Washington at this eventful period, and signalized themselves in all the achievements, and suffered more severely than any other portion of the army in this disastrous campaign. Huntington's regiment sustained a high character in the action on Long Island, and suffered a heavy loss there...[1]

None other than the Commander-In-Chief, George Washington, said "...the general damage fell upon the Regiments from Pennsylvania, Delaware, and Maryland, and Col. Huntindon's [sic] of Connecticut."[2] And again, "The Action [on Long Island] was chiefly with the Troops from Jersey, Pennsylvania, the lower counties, and Maryland, and Col. Huntingdon's [sic] Regt.; they suffered greatly, being attacked and overpowred [sic] by numbers of the Enemy greatly superior to them."[3]

Samuel Holden Parsons' little brigade on Battle Hill- mostly Huntington's men- should be credited with the greatest success on the field of battle for the Americans that day. Both Parsons and Atlee reported only one man killed (Lt.-Col. Parry) and perhaps two or three wounded, while inflicting far heavier casualties than were reported by the British for any other part of the conflict. Three times they chased the British off Battle Hill, and in the process prevented the enemy from completely destroying Stirling's command. But, because Parsons' Brigade was the most isolated unit on the field of battle, its actions went unobserved, and nearly unreported. Because of Atlee's widely published memoirs, his men received the recognition they deserved. But, because Atlee failed to give adequate credit to the other units engaged with him, and no comparable account to Colonel Atlee's was ever published for Huntington's Regiment, the full story of the role the 17th played in the battle was never told. These brave,

---

[1] Royal R. Hinman, *Historical Collection from Official Records, Files, etc., of the Part Sustained by Connecticut During the War of the Revolution* (Hartford: E. Gleason, 1842), p. 110.
[2] "George Washington to Massachusetts Assembly, Sept. 19, 1776," *The George Washington Papers*, Series 2, Letterbook 10,
http://memory.loc.gov/ammem/gwhtml/gwseries.html
[3] "George Washington to Jonathan Trumbull, Sept. 6, 1776," *The George Washington Papers*, Series 2, Letterbook 10,
http://memory.loc.gov/ammem/gwhtml/gwseries.html

determined, Connecticut soldiers have still not received a share of the glory long since granted to others.

But thanks to Fitch, Parsons, Gillet, Orcutt, and a few others, we have finally been able to piece together the story of their historically neglected regiment. In effect, Colonel Jedediah Huntington's 17th Continental (Connecticut) Regiment had a primary role in what was the most prolonged, and the most sanguinary action that took place during the Battle of Long Island. But, in spite of the rigors of the morning's forced march, and extended, close combat for much of the day, for the men of the 17th, most of whom were now prisoners of war, their ordeal had just begun.

Although intended to depict the capture of John Callender, a Massachusetts soldier at the Battle of Long Island, the above could also very well portray the capture of Captain Joseph Jewett (from Harper's New Monthly Magazine, *Vol. LIII, Aug. 1876. Courtesy D. M. Hunt Library, Falls Village, CT)*

7. Very Indifferent Quarters

Still committed to the defense of Long Island, in spite of the setbacks of the day, General Washington brought three more regiments over from New York during the night of the 27th to replace those that he had lost. This brought his total troop strength within the defenses at Brooklyn to about 9,500 men to oppose an inevitable assault by the British now encamped before them. Anticipating that the assault would come by storm, Washington was delighted to discover the next morning that the British were instead beginning the slow process of digging parallels in order to take the works by siege. The trenches were begun about 600 yards in front of Fort Putnam on the left side of the American line, part of a long process of gradual approaches to provide cover for Howe's mortars, and artillery. Without good intelligence about Washington's strength, Howe felt he could not risk an immediate and all out assault on a heavily fortified position with troops that were exhausted from the previous day's conflict.

In spite of rainy conditions on the 28th, some skirmishing took place between the two armies in front of the American lines. These small probing fights allowed Washington to discover the intentions and strength of the enemy. By the rate at which the parallels were being dug, the overwhelming numbers of British troops opposing him, and the condition of his troops exposed without shelter or adequate provisions, Washington determined that it would only be a day or two at most before his fortifications were overwhelmed. Late on the afternoon of the 29th, Washington held a council of war with his general officers. Because of the hopelessness of their position, it was voted unanimously to attempt an evacuation of the troops back across the East River to New York. So commenced the nearly miraculous event referred to at the beginning of this story that prevented the total destruction of the remains of Washington's army.

Boats were gathered from up and down the East River for the evacuation, which commenced at dark. At first, driving rain and a northeast gale prevented all but rowboats from being used, but after 11:00 P.M. the wind changed to a southwest breeze that calmed the water and allowed the entire fleet of little boats to be brought into play. The militia and levies (draftees) were the first to be evacuated, while the experienced continental regiments filled in the empty places in the American lines that were then created. All was done in virtually total silence, preventing the British sentries from discovering the movement of the Americans. Washington spent the entire night on horseback, nervously pacing back and forth along the ferry landing to personally ensure that all proceeded according to plan. In his report, Washington wrote, for the previous 48 hours "I had hardly been off my horse and had never closed my eyes…"[1]

As dawn approached, the last of the American units had still not been taken off, but a pea-soup fog settled in so thick that the evacuation was entirely obscured from British observation. The last of the Americans still remaining on the lines could not see the British close in front of them through the fog, but could hear the sounds of the picks and shovels as the enemy resumed the construction of the approaching entrenchments, now no more than a musket shot away. By 7:00 A.M. the evacuation was complete; Washington himself was in the last boat to leave Brooklyn. He had brought off his entire force and managed to save nearly all his equipment, stores and ordinance. By his brilliant maneuver, and the Providential intervention of the rain, wind and fog, his army was saved to fight another day.

While the remains of Washington's army was disappearing in the fog, so was any hope for rescue for the 1,000 or so American prisoners of war taken by the British two days before. Where there may have been some hope before, it would have now become very clear to the men of Huntington's Regiment that they were once and for all cut off from their comrades. After the British first gathered all the prisoners from the area of the Gowanus Road into a barn at sunset on the evening of the 27th, Lt. Fitch and about 20 other officers were taken out, and provided separate quarters in the adjoining farmhouse. The badly wounded Capt. Jewett and other wounded prisoners were taken elsewhere to have their wounds tended to by a British surgeon.

Although subjected to verbal assaults and attempts to recruit them into the British Army, Fitch and his companions were given adequate food, and otherwise treated well for the next two days and nights.

---

[1] "George Washington to Congress, August 30, 1776," *The George Washington Papers*, Series 3, Sub. A, http://memory.loc.gov/ammem/gwhtml/gwseries.html

Fitch wrote on Wednesday that General Grant himself provided, with his compliments, "two quarters of mutton well cooked, and several loaves of bread, which were very acceptable to us, as most of us had eat nothing since the Monday before."[1] Also that day, Capt. Jewett was brought back to the farmhouse having had his wounds dressed, but in extreme pain. A British doctor by the name of Horn was sent in to dress the wounds of the other prisoners, and continued to provide compassionate care for Captain Jewett who declined steadily throughout the day. Lt. Fitch wrote:

I sat with him most of the night, and slept but very little. The Capt. had his senses, while about 2 in the morning, and was sensible of his being near his end, often repeating that it was hard work to die, he also desired me to see him buried with deacence [sic] as far as our present circumstances would admit, and write the circumstances of his death to his wife. For 2 or 3 hours before he died, he was somewhat delirious, and talked somewhat irrational, he was also speechless for some short time before he expired.

THURSDAY THE 29th: About sunrise Major Brown waited on us to see how we were, etc., when I acquainted him with the death of Capt. Jewett, and desired preparation made for his being buried, he accordingly made report to General Grant, and at about 8 o'clock again came to us and acquainted us that there was a grave prepared and a number of men ready to assist in burying the Captain. I also desired liberty to attend the Captain's corpse to the grave, which on his application to the General for that purpose, was readily granted, and I accordingly attended. The Captain was buried in an orchard about an hundred yards distance from the house where he died.[2]

Historian Henry P. Johnston stated with certainty that Jewett "was buried in the Bennett orchard, near 22nd St. and Third Avenue."[3] This was quite probably the same orchard that Colonel Atlee had defended on the morning of the 27th. After the funeral, Fitch made note that the rain continued throughout the day of the 29th, completely unaware

---

[1] *Fitch*, p. 138

[2] *Fitch*, pp. 34-35.

[3] Johnston, *The Campaign of 1776*, p. 197.

that the evacuation of his army was about to take place just a few miles north of the farmhouse that was now his prison. Had he known of it, the fact would likely not have brought him any consolation. He was allowed to go out to the barn, and visit the soldiers that remained there, which included a number who were wounded and injured, including Sergeant Graves, badly wounded in the thigh by a bayonet during his capture.

During the afternoon, the officers, about 24 or 25 in number, with three or four hundred soldiers from the barn, were marched south to Gravesend Bay. There they were waded out through the mud flats, and loaded onto flat-bottomed boats to be ferried out to the *Pacific,* a British merchant ship of about 900 tons. Along the way, their boats passed a number of ships-of-the-line, and the prisoners endured a gauntlet of verbal abuse from "great numbers of women on deck, who were very liberal of their curses and execrations. They were also not a little noisy in their insults, but clapped their hands and used other peculiar gestures in so extraordinary a manner that they were in some danger of leaping overboard in this surprising ecstasy."[1]

Dragging themselves aboard the *Pacific,* all 400 men, regardless of rank, were stuffed below decks to find accommodations among the guns and rigging. Fitch's ongoing diary did not express complaint regarding their treatment aboard the *Pacific,* but several months later, free to express his feelings without fear of his daily writing being discovered, he wrote the following about those first few days in his *Narrative*:

> *Accordingly, at about sunset we were all drove down the hatches, with as many vile curses and execrations, as that Son of perdition, with his Infernal Understrappers could express. When we came down into this dungeon, we found but very indifferent quarters, for both the lower decks were very full of dirt, and the excessive rains that had fell of late, had drove in so plentifully as to quite cover them, so that a great number of men treading the dirt and water together, soon made the mortar or mud near half over our shoes. Besides all those inconveniences, there was no kind of platform, or places prepared for our lodging, but what was so cluttered with artillery, carriages, rough pieces of timber, rigging, etc., that there was not a sufficiency of room for a man to lay*

---

[1] *Fitch,* p. 139.

between them, nor was there sufficiency of room in the whole assigned us, for but little more than one half of our number, any how to lay down at one time. To add yet more (if possible) to our calamity, some time in the evening a number of the infernal savages came down with a lantern, and loaded two small pieces of cannon with grape shot, which were placed aft of a bulkhead and pointed through two ports for that purpose, in such a manner as to rake the deck where our people lay, telling us at the same time with many curses that in case of any disturbance or the least noise in the night, they were to be immediately fired on the damned rebels.[1]

In this unhappy situation the men spent the next three days and nights. Although a few men were allowed to come up on deck at any one time during the day, scant provisions were provided the prisoners, and no water fit to drink. Fitch noted, however, that the sailors had plenty of good water. Up until now, Fitch had been able to safeguard Captain Jewett's "Regimental Coat & Hat", as well as his own, but despite his care, those items now disappeared. A Lt. Dowdswell, in command of a party of marines placed on board to guard the prisoners, searched the ship, and found the missing items in the cabin of the ship's mate, a Mr. Spence. This reference to Jewett's regimental coat and hat provides further evidence that the men of the 17th had worn uniforms into battle, in contrast to many of the other American units in New York.

On Saturday, the 31st, the British commissary of prisoners, Joshua Loring, a Boston Loyalist, came aboard to take the names of the prisoners, and brought news that Lt.-Col. Clark and several other officers of the 17th had been held at Flatbush, and were now to be taken aboard one of the other ships in the fleet. Although Loring's treatment of American prisoners later received mixed reviews from various sources, one fact of his service was beyond any doubt: that upon receiving his commission from General Sir William Howe, Loring allowed Howe the services of his wife as mistress. Howe and the British government were so grateful for Loring's generosity that they provided him with the lucrative job of Commissary of Prisoners. Upon the death of her husband after the war, Mrs. Loring, was given a Loyalist pension that she received until her death in England in 1831.

---

[1] *Fitch*, p. 140.

The information that Mr. Loring gave about Lt.- Col. Clark's detention at Flatbush, is evidence that some of the men of the 17th, in their frantic scramble to evade capture, had persisted in their flight to the east of Battle Hill, and made it to the vicinity of Flatbush, before they were rounded up. Ensign Bradford, as we have already mentioned, was captured in the vicinity of Flatbush the morning after the Battle and taken there. Private Salmon Moulton confirmed in his pension application that "Col. Clark commanded the regiment & was also taken prisoner & that this deponent was taken prisoner & was taken to Flatbush Village & kept there about three days."[1] Besides the Dutch Church and a school-house, three private houses were used to keep American prisoners. The wounded officers were taken to the home of Mr. Rem Vanderbilt for treatment. It was reported by a resident of Flatbush who was absent during the battle that there were twenty-eight new graves in the Dutch Church cemetery when she returned. Many of those graves likely contained more than one body.[2]

The *Pacific* was at first anchored with its cargo of prisoners off Staten Island, but moved several times up and down New York harbor. On September 1st all the prisoners were transferred to the ship the *Lord Rochford*, about half the size of the *Pacific*. The commander of this vessel was Capt. Lambert, who, although Fitch described him as "sovereign and tyrannical," was not nearly so devoid of humanity as Captain Dunn, the commander of their first floating prison. More prisoners were added to their company during the day, including Private Libeus Wheeler, of Jewett's Company. Because the *Lord Rochford* was smaller than the *Pacific*, many of the officers were lodged on the quarterdeck. Fitch considered that a privilege after the dark hold of the *Pacific*, although they were exposed to rain through several of the upcoming nights.

The *Lord Rochford*, with its new compliment of prisoners, set anchor among the fleet still in Gravesend Bay, opposite New Utrecht. The next day, the prisoners were provided with paper, pen and ink, and allowed to write to family and friends, subject to the censorship of the British. Fitch made note that he wrote letters to his wife, Col. Wyllys of the 22nd Continental (Connecticut) Regiment, Col.

[1] NARA, Series M805, Roll 603, Revolutionary War Pension Application, S23810.
[2] Thomas M. Strong, *The History of the Town of Flatbush in Kings County on Long Island* (Brooklyn: Loeser & Co., 1908), p. 155, http://persi.heritagequestonline.com/...

Huntington, and to 2nd-Lt. John Harris, also of Jewett's Company. Harris was not present during the Battle of Long Island, and not taken prisoner. Knowing that his diary was subject to confiscation, Fitch seems to have been very careful not to portray the conditions of their confinement in very negative terms.

On September 3, the officers who had been held prisoner at Flatbush were taken aboard a still smaller sailing vessel known as a "snow," anchored next to the *Lord Rochford* in Gravesend Bay. The same day Fitch noted that there was a great movement north towards New York City among the ships that had been at anchor. On the following day, Lt. Fitch, and Lt. Thomas Fanning, the quartermaster of the 17th, were allowed on board the snow, named somewhat ironically the *Mentor*, to visit with some of the other officers who had been brought there. Fitch found Lt.-Col. Clark of the 17th, Col. Samuel Miles of the Pennsylvania Rifle Regiment, and most of the other officers of his own regiment there. He received news from the others that Sergeants Stephen Otis, and Rufus Tracy, also of Jewett's Company, were still being held on shore. Although Fitch did not mention him, Ensign Bradford wrote that he was also brought aboard the *Mentor* on the 3rd.

It is indicative of the liberal treatment that the American officers were receiving, that Cols. Clark and Miles were allowed to return aboard the *Lord Rochford* and share a bottle or two of porter- a kind of dark beer- with Fitch and company. Fitch noted that it was the first drink of any kind, other than water, that he had had since being taken captive eight days before. Such benefits may have been afforded in order to induce the American officers to desert and join the British Army, which, Fitch reported, quite a few of them did. Fitch did not mention that any of the officers of Huntington's Regiment defected, and they all seem to have been able to resist that temptation.

The next day, Thursday, the 5th of September, Fitch wrote that after making a tour of the deck of the *Lord Rochford*, he found many men sick or wounded, including Private Timothy Percival, Capt. Timothy Percival's son. In the afternoon a doctor came on board to tend to the sick and injured men, which had not been done in some time. Around sunset, all of the officers on the *Lord Rochford* belonging to the 17th were transferred to the *Mentor*. The rest of the officers of the 17th were already on board, and they all shared a "drink of Grog," a very great treat. To the northward, a considerable cannonade was heard by those aboard the *Mentor*, which continued through much of the night. Although in his daily diary Fitch did not describe the commander of the snow, he provided ample evidence of the character of the man in his later *Narrative*:

> *This snow was commanded by one Davis, (a very worthless lowlived fellow,) yet happy for us, his capacity was not sufficient to do any one much hurt yet we were now and then under an necessity of holding a severe wrangle with him on many occasions. We had also a guard of marines constantly on board, by whom we were sometimes highly insulted.*[1]

On Friday, the 6th, Brigadier-General Nathaniel Woodhull of the Suffolk and Queens County militia was transferred from the *Mentor* to a hospital on shore at New Utrecht. He had been wounded and captured the day after the Battle of Long Island while driving cattle away from the British. In another of the more infamous incidents of ill treatment of prisoners, Woodhull had been cruelly and horrifically wounded by a British officer, reportedly after he had surrendered on the 28th of August. His wounds were allowed to fester for ten days until his transfer to the hospital at New Utrecht. Dr. Silas Holmes, the surgeon's mate from Huntington's Regiment, had by then been pressed into service by the British to care for the wounded American prisoners in the church at New Utrecht, and later reported on the Woodhull incident:

> *The wounded prisoners taken at the battle of Brooklyn were put in the churches of Flatbush and New Utrecht, but being neglected and unattended, were wallowing in their own filth, and breathed an infected and putrid air. Ten days after the battle, Dr. Richard Bailey was appointed to superintend the sick. He was humane, and dressed the wounded daily, got a sack-bed, sheet, and blanket for each prisoner, and distributed the patients into the adjacent barns. When Mrs. Woodhull offered to pay Dr. Bailey for his care and attention to her husband, he replied, he had done no more than his duty, and if there was any thing due it was to me.*
>
> *What a pity Woodhull had not fallen into the hands of this good Samaritan in the earlier stages of his illness! His wounds, neglected for nine days in the hot months of August and*

---

[1] *Fitch*, p. 142.

September, had assumed such a malignant form, that not even the medical skill of Dr. Bailey could avail to save his valuable life.[1]

By the time Woodhull was transferred to New Utrecht, his wounds were infected beyond hope, and he died on September 20 with his wife by his side.

Fitch's diary reported that Captain Percival of Huntington's Regiment, allowed to attend his seriously ill son, had also been transferred from the *Mentor* to New Utrecht with Woodhull on September 6. The next day, Saturday, Captain Ozias Bissell was brought on board the *Mentor*, though Fitch did not say why he had been brought on board separately from the other officers of the regiment. On Sunday, the 8th of September, the Americans celebrated the anniversary of the great victory over the French at the Battle of Lake George in 1755. Fitch was also able to borrow a Bible from one of the sailors, and to honor the Sabbath, he spent time in study.

On Monday, Fitch arose before dawn to walk the decks, after which he spent the day studying the Bible he had borrowed. The next afternoon, word was brought that Private Timothy Percival had died. Captain Caleb Trowbridge was also ill, but Fitch noted that Ensign Joseph Chapman was recovering from an unspecified sickness. In the evening, Captain Percival returned on board after the death of his son. He brought news that General Parsons had avoided capture after the Battle of Long Island, and had safely returned to the American lines at Brooklyn, possibly with another-unnamed-officer of the 17th. Percival also gave them the news that Washington had received considerable reinforcements and moved the Army to the northern end of Manhattan Island near Kings Bridge.

That same evening, Ensign Elihu Lyman was sent aboard another ship nearby, what would soon be the infamous *Whitby*, to take the names of fifteen other men of Jewett's Company who were being kept there. Unfortunately, Fitch did not record the names of those men in his diary. However, in his pension application, Private Zadock Pratt of Jewett's Company said he was held on board the *Whitby*.[2] Also in their pension applications, Private Salmon Moulton[3], of Ozias Bissell's Company, and Private Daniel Thomas[4], of Ozias Bissell's

---

[1] Onderdonk, *Revolutionary Incidents*, p. 40
[2] NARA, Series M805, Roll 665, Revolutionary War Pension Application, S44263.
[3] NARA, Series M805, Roll 603, Revolutionary War Pension Application, S23810.
[4] NARA, Series M805, Roll 797, Revolutionary War Pension Application, S11536.

Company noted that they were confined on the *Whitby*. Quite possibly, Captain Ozias Bissell himself had first been confined aboard the *Whitby* with his men, which would explain why he was transferred to the *Mentor* some time after the other officers of his regiment.

The quartermaster of the 17th, Lt. Thomas Fanning, was allowed by his captors to go "up toward New York." On Wednesday, the 11th, he returned bringing with him a gallon of rum, about six or seven pounds of cheese, and six bottles of wine for the sixteen officers aboard the *Mentor*. He was also able to procure one shirt for each of them. Fitch considered these very meager supplies at best. Fortunately, Colonel Atlee, also on board the *Mentor*, was able to procure some provisions, including a cask of porter, much to the delight of the prisoners. According to Fitch, during "This night we were very much disturbed, after we turned in, by some scandalous behavior of particular officers, who are too much inclined that way." The "scandalous behavior" was no doubt fueled by the recently acquired porter.[1] Throughout his diary, Fitch made brief, cryptic references to behavior that he did not approve of, but we are left with nothing but our imagination for the further details of many of those incidents.

On September 4, 1776, a list of names of officers who were prisoners with the enemy and who had sent for their baggage and money under a flag of truce was published in the Connecticut Courant: from Huntington's Regiment were named Lt. Makepeace, Capt. Brewster, Ensign Lyman, Ensign Chapman, Ensign Kinsman, Ensign Bradford, Lt. Orcutt, Ensign Higgins, Capt. Bissell, Lt. Gillet, Lt. Gay (There was no officer by this name in Huntington's Regiment. This may have been Lt. Gove, who was a prisoner.), Adjutant Hopkins, Doctor Holmes, and Lt.-Col. Clark.[2]

On the 11th their baggage was received, according to Ensign Bradford. However, Lt. Fitch on Thursday, the 12th, complained that considerable baggage was received for many of the officers on board the *Mentor*, but nothing for any of the officers who had first been confined on the *Pacific*. Since Fitch and the other officers with him had not been transferred to the *Mentor* until September 5, it is likely that the published list of officers was gathered from those who had been confined at Flatbush before being transferred on board the

---

[1] *Fitch*, p. 42.
[2] Hinman, *Historical Collection*, p. 89.

Mentor. Fitch concluded that his family, and the families of those captured with him, still had no knowledge of their circumstances.

On Friday the 13th, a Col. Piper and Col. Kichlein of the Pennsylvania Rifle Battalion were transferred to the *Mentor* from the *Lord Rochford*. Also on that day, Fitch profited from the demise of Captain Jewett, by selling Jewett's coat to Col. Clark, and Jewett's hat to Ensign Chapman. Since Fitch had not received any of his property or money up to this point, his actions probably should not be judged too harshly. He was bereft of support of any kind and needed the money badly. Capt. Trowbridge was transferred to the hospital on shore this day, as his condition continued to worsen.

The next morning, Fitch made note that supplies were extremely short, and the officers were only able to partake of a breakfast of 1 ½ biscuits to a man, a small piece of cheese and a small drink of porter. In the evening "We borrowed a bottle of rum of Mr. Throop[1] (one of the New York gentlemen) of which we took a moderate drink of grog, remembering liberty, our country, and families."[2]

On Sunday, September 15, the British invaded Manhattan Island at Kips Bay. Those aboard the *Mentor* could clearly hear the cannonade taking place there, and later in the day, at Harlem. As a result, the American Army was forced to evacuate New York City and retreat to the northern end of the Island. Of course, the men on the Mentor did not know those details at the time. Supplies for the week were given out to the prisoners on the *Mentor* but weren't sufficient to provide more than one meal a day. Fortunately, the British allowed a fishing boat to come alongside and sell the prisoners a quantity of quahogs (large clams) that provided "the most agreeable meal." The prisoners were told the next day that the cannon fire they had heard the day before had been the result of the British invasion of New York and the American retreat to the north.

For the next several days, the officers aboard the *Mentor* continued to struggle with inadequate supplies of food, while listening to the sound of cannon fire continuing to the north. Their prolonged idleness was beginning to wear on them. Fitch was able to break the monotony with the study of his Bible.

---

[1] Lt. Robert Troop, one of the group of New York militia scouts who had been captured by the British flanking column in Jamaica pass on the night of August 27.
[2] *Fitch*, p. 43.

A notable mention in Fitch's diary during this time was the "considerable light up toward the northward," which later proved to be the fire that burned a quarter of the City of New York on September 21st. Ensign Bradford wrote that the fire burned from one in the afternoon until six. The American command had some time before applied to the Continental Congress for permission to burn the city upon retreat to prevent the enemy from using the city to house the British army, but the plan had been denied. Even so, the fire may have been set by rebel incendiaries with, or without, the sanction of their command.

At about noon on the next day, all of the ships that held prisoners of war, which, according to Ensign Bradford, were the *Mentor*, *Lord Rochford*, *Whitby*, and *Argo*, sailed under the escort of two men-of-war north to join much of the British fleet now anchored in the various waterways around Manhattan Island. At this point, the immense fleet included between four and five hundred ships, and appeared to one observer to be a forest of masts from one shore to the other; a sight never before seen in any port in America. The *Mentor* must have anchored in Gowanus Bay, for three days later, Fitch remarked that they lay within sight of the "ground where the action was on the 27th of August, the fatal day in which we were made prisoners, & of the house where I was first confined, and attended Captain Jewett at the time of his death."

The *Mentor* sailed up the west side of Manhattan on Tuesday, October 1, and anchored near the end of Murray St. The prisoners were told that they would be disembarking the next day, but it was a false alarm; it wouldn't be for another week before they were landed. In the meantime, rations were short, and the prisoners had to sleep where they could among the coils of rope and other gear on the deck of the *Mentor*. Although no cases of physical abuse of the prisoners by their captors were noted by Lt. Fitch during this time, verbal abuse was frequent, and there was little to eat. On October 2, Ensign Bradford wrote that, "A number of old countrymen were carried ashore from on board the *Whitby*, who had engaged in the King's service." Bradford's reference to "old countrymen," must have meant recent immigrants to the colonies who had been in the American Army and also taken prisoners at the Battle of Long Island. They had been pressured to defect and enlist on the side of the British and had therefore been released from close confinement.

On Thursday, a cold and cloudy morning, Fitch reported that Captain Jonathan Brewster of the 17th was ill (with a "pleuratic disorder," according to Bradford), and that there was no breakfast for anyone. By 10 o'clock, they were finally given a dish of chocolate to eat. Fitch continued to deal with the monotony by studying his Bible, and noting in his diary the activities of the fleet.

Finally, on Monday, October 7th, Loring, the Commissary of Prisoners, came aboard with the conditions of parole for the officers to sign. It would bind them by their honor to their next place of confinement. The field officers went ashore first, and at 4 o'clock the other officers disembarked with what baggage they had. During their time on the *Mentor*, many of the officers had been able to obtain personal property they had left in New York City before the Battle of Long Island, but Fitch and some of the others never retrieved any of their former possessions.

The prisoners were landed on a ferry wharf at what was then called The Bear Market, near the west end of Vesey St. About sunset they were directed to a large house with a small yard on the west side of Broadway, south of Warren St., known as Hampden House or Hampden Hall. Before the abandonment of the City by the Americans, it had been the headquarters of the New York Sons of Liberty. Here the prisoners were met by other New England officers who had been captured during the retreat from New York. Their new accommodations were considered by Fitch to be an improvement: less crowded and noisy. In his diary, Fitch summarized the provisioning aboard the three prison vessels where he had been held prisoner:

During the 39 days which I was confined on board the ships, I never tasted any kind of sauce [vegetables]*, except a very few peas, nor did I taste any kind of fresh meat or fish except four meals of quahogs while we lay down below the narrows, nor any butter, or other kind of provision except a very scanty allowance of salt, meat and bread, with a small matter of cheese and chocolate, which we have purchased. We have also lived about as scant on account of drink as victuals also.*[1]

Fitch found adequate sleeping quarters in Hampden Hall in the narrow gallery of a large room that he shared with several others, and

---

[1] *Fitch*, p. 54.

slept comfortably for the first time in weeks. In the morning, Fitch took a walk in the yard, and was then provided with a dish of chocolate for breakfast. Later, a visit was paid to him by Mr. Ebenezer Punderson and his wife, former friends from Norwich, who had gone over to the enemy and moved to New York. They informed him that Fitch's fifteen year-old son, Cordilla, who had accompanied Jabez to New York, but who had remained there during the battle, had escaped New York with the American troops. However, all Fitch's belongings had been lost. For dinner that night the prisoners received turnips, the first root crop they had eaten since they were captured. In the evening, the soldier that had captured Fitch, Sergeant Day of the 57th Regiment, called on him to pay his respects, and, remarkably, they seem to have had a very friendly conversation.

Ensign Bradford left us the names of the officers from his regiment now at Hampden Hall, by dutifully noting on the 8th, that the officers of Huntington's regiment had formed "into messes as follows:"

1st Mess- Captain Brewster, Capt. Percival, Capt. F. Bissell, Capt. O. Bissell, Capt. Trowbridge, and Lt. Gove.

2nd Mess- Lt. Fitch, Lt. Gillet, Lt. Orcutt, Ens. Higgins, Ens. Lyman.

3nd Mess- Lt. Fanning, Ens. Kinsman, Ens. Bradford, Ens. Gillet, Ens. Chapman.

The conditions of confinement of the officers in Hampden Hall were, in general, a great improvement over their previous quarters. Fitch reported over the next several days that more food of all kinds was provided. On the 8th, Ensign Kinsman received $76 in a letter from his father to be shared with Lt. Gove, and Ensign Bradford, which helped to purchase much needed food items in addition to what was provided by the British Commissary.[1]

On the 10th, all of the field officers that had been held at Hampden Hall were moved to new quarters, allowing the other officers considerably more room. W. H. W. Sabine, the editor of Fitch's diary, believed that the house the field officers were sent to was the home of a Mrs. S. Lasley, a shopkeeper who lived at 41 Broadway. Her name appeared in the *New York Directory* after the War. However, Ensign Bradford wrote in his account of the day's events,

---

[1] Bradford, *Diary*, p. 44; *Fitch*, p. 55.

that it was the home of a Mrs. Doughty. According to Fitch, fifty more prisoners marched past the house that day on the way to the hospital that had been established at the brick Presbyterian Church, across the Common from Hampden Hall. That night Captain Jonathan Brewster gave Fitch an extra blanket that had been sent to him. Until then, Fitch had had no cover at night.

Although it appears from Fitch's diary that Hampden Hall was strictly officers' quarters, in his entry of Saturday, October 12th he mentioned that Corporal George Gordon of Captain Caleb Trowbridge's Company was given a pass to go perform errands for the officers. The same day, Sergeant Roger Coit of Captain Percival's Company, and Sergeant Ebenezer Coe of Captain Elizur Hubbard's Company were allowed to move in with the officers. Although Fitch did not specifically say so, the presence of non-commissioned officers must have been allowed by request of the officers, to help with housekeeping, and to run errands. Colonel Clark was also allowed to visit his officers in Hampden House during the afternoon.

Also on the 12th, Captain Caleb Trowbridge moved into Hampden Hall "from the hospital."[1] He had probably been in the hospital at New Utrecht ever since he had been taken there sick on September 13. He brought the unfortunate news that Lt. Solomon Makepeace, of Captain Ozias Bissell's Company, who had been wounded in the Battle of Long Island, had died the previous Sunday (October 6). The young schoolmaster from Stafford, Connecticut, was dead at the age of 23.

The hospital where Capt. Trowbridge had been a patient was described in several letters written by Dr. Silas Holmes, Surgeon's Mate of the 17th, shortly after the War. Holmes had been transferred from the prison ships on or about September 6 to assist the British doctor, Richard Bailey (or Bayley), in caring for wounded and sick American prisoners of war in the makeshift hospital set up in the Dutch Church at New Utrecht. It was the same hospital where General Woodhull had been treated for his wounds. What precipitated Holmes' letters was a later investigation by American authorities into the conduct of Dr. Bailey towards the prisoners under his care. The following is an excerpt from one of those letters:

---

[1] Bradford, *Diary*, p. 44.

It was bad in every sense of the word, a dirty place, the prisoners wallowing in their own filth... It was eight or ten days before I saw Doctor Bailey, which was after I had been aboard the shipping. When I first saw Doctor Bailey, he expressed sorrow, that the wounded had been so long neglected- he declared that nothing in his power, should be wanting to make them as comfortable as their situation would admit of. We accordingly had an alteration in provision for the better, and medicines, such as I made a bill of, together with a quantity of wine, sugar, etc. He also furnished every man with a bedsack, sheet and blanket; and assisted in dressing once a day, exercising judgment and skill in his profession, and the humanity of a generous enemy. Thus, Sir, I have given the outlines of the Doctor's conduct towards the wounded. But, shall not do justice to him, if I do not declare to you, that his conduct was not only such as we have a right to expect from a generous enemy, but such as would meet with approbation, from a friend.[1]

From Fitch's diary, it is apparent that, as the wounded and sick survivors of the Battle of Long Island recovered, they were moved to the City of New York, as evidenced by Capt. Trowbridge's transfer. Lt. Makepeace had not survived to make that move.

The next day, Sunday, October 13, Fitch received word that Sergeant Roswell Graves, who had been wounded when Capt. Jewett was taken, was recovering from his wound. Sergeant Ebenezer Wright, whom Fitch had aided during the aftermath of the fight on Battle Hill, had lost his shattered leg, but was also expected to recover.

On Wednesday, October 16, Fitch wrote, "Ensn. Lyman had this Day (at our door) an Interview with young Hierlihy, Son to Majr. Hierlihy, with whom I was acquainted in the last War, he Informs, that his Father is now in Town, & in Expectation of a Place in the Kings Army." The visitor was Timothy Hierlihy the son of Major Timothy Hierlihy, both of Middletown, Connecticut. Fitch and other officers of Huntington's Regiment had served with the elder Hierlihy during the French and Indian War, when they were members of the same Connecticut colonial regiment. There is probably much more to

---

[1] *Fitch,* note, p. 64.

Ensign Lyman's "Interview" than Fitch felt comfortable writing about at the time.

Major Timothy Hierlihy had been offered a command in the American Army at the outbreak of the Revolution, but had sided with the British. He was in the process of organizing a Loyalist regiment to fight against his former comrades. Back in Middletown, he had renewed an old acquaintance with Governor Montfort Browne, the colonial governor of New Providence, in the Bahamas, who had been taken prisoner in a raid by the crew of an American privateer, and brought to Connecticut. Hierlihy was able to visit Browne, and the two secretly conspired to recruit other local Tories into what became known as the Prince of Wales American Regiment to fight for the British. The younger Timothy Hierlihy was sent to Lord Howe in New York to negotiate an exchange for Browne, so that the regiment could be organized under Browne's command as brigadier-general. The man that Howe decided to exchange for Browne was Lord Stirling, captured at the Battle of Long Island. General Washington agreed to the exchange.[1]

At the time of younger Hierlihy's visit to Hampden Hall, his father, Major Hierlihy, had just survived a harrowing escape from Connecticut across Long Island Sound in the dead of night in a leaky open boat. He made his escape in the hope of receiving a commission as colonel in the new Loyalist regiment. Unfortunately for him, he had to leave all his property, his wife and nine children behind.[2] Although the visit by Hierlihy's son appears to have been benign from Fitch's description of the incident, if we read between the abbreviated lines of the diary, the younger Hierlihy must have been trying to talk his father's former comrades-in-arms into deserting and joining His Majesty's forces. If so, he was not successful, and even after a subsequent visit on the 10th of November by "Mr. Hierlihy, and two other Gentn…who generously gave us a Drink &c," none of the officers of the 17th deserted.

A few months later, when Major Hierlihy's personal ambitions were disappointed, and he was passed over for a promotion to colonel in the Prince of Wales American Regiment, he formed a separate,

---

[1] Todd W. Braisted, "Prince of Wales' American Regiment," (lecture by the author, April, 1998), www.rootsweb.com/~canmil/uel/pwar.htm
[2] "Timothy Hierlihy to Lord George Germaine, August 27, 1779," Great Britain, Public Record Office, Colonial Office, Class 226, Vol. 7, folios 42-44, www.royalprovincial.com/military/rhist/indp_co_hierlihy/ichmen1.htm

independent corps, which was sent to off to serve, first at St. Johns, Newfoundland, and then at Nova Scotia. Father and son ended up settling in Nova Scotia permanently, where they served without seeing further action for the remainder of the war. But, the recruiting efforts on behalf of Governor/General Montfort Browne had done their damage, and the Prince of Wales' American Regiment fought with General Tryon on the Danbury Raid, and later on in the war, down south.

Lt. Solomon Orcutt, of Captain Abraham Tyler's Company, also a resident of Hampden Hall, on October 19, helped an ailing Lt. Fitch by providing him with some broth made from a small piece of beef. It is known that Lt. Jonathan Gillet was housed at Hampden hall as well because Fitch mentioned that the wife of a Masonic brother of Gillet's, John Archer, brought Gillet an apple pie that night which was shared with the other prisoners.

It had now been about three weeks since the enlisted men of the 17th Regiment had been disgorged from the floating prisons which had housed them for the first month after they were taken prisoner. However, the new conditions in which they were living were no improvement and were starting to take a terrible toll. Up until now, Fitch had made no mention of those men, or their current situation. However, on October 23, word was received, probably from Mrs. Archer, that Corporal Joseph White, of Capt. Abraham Tyler's Company, and several other unnamed men had died. The officers were informed that the privates were growing remarkably sick and were dying very fast; living in circumstances that were a stark and terrifying contrast to those under which the officers of the 17th were living at Hampden House.

8. *Mansions of Despair*

It was some months after the events of August 27, 1776, that word began to leak out of New York City that American prisoners of war were being kept in sub-human conditions and were dying by the hundreds. By then, the British had developed the thoroughly reprehensible habit of housing prisoners without adequate food, sanitation, bedding, or medical attention in what had previously been houses of worship. The first churches used for this purpose were the Dutch churches at Flatbush and New Utrecht, Long Island, which were also used as hospitals for wounded prisoners after the Battle of Long Island. We have already been introduced to the conditions in the New Utrecht Dutch Church by Surgeon's Mate Silas Holmes of Huntington's Regiment.

The only pre-existing jails in New York were too small to contain the unanticipated numbers of prisoners that the British had taken, so they seized more churches, gutted them of their altars and pews, and proceeded to pack them full of the prisoners from the Battle of Long Island. They then crowded more men in as the American Army suffered defeat after defeat on the retreat north into Westchester County.

The Presbyterian Church on Beekman Street, known as the Brick Church, the Quaker Church on Pearl Street, and the Presbyterian Church on Wall Street, were used to house the sick and wounded, and were called hospitals, though the use of the term was a travesty. The prisoners actually received very little attention for their wounds and diseases in these places, and were primarily sent there to die.

Two of the first houses of worship to be transformed into houses of horror, were the North Dutch Church at the corner of William and Fulton Streets, and the Middle Dutch Church on Nassau Street. All of the churches commandeered by the British were considered "dissenting" churches; churches that were considered in rebellion against the Church of England or had Whig pastors. But churches belonging to the Church of England were spared confiscation, as well as the Old Dutch Church on Garden Street, whose pastor was a noted Tory.

The British authorities also resorted to warehousing their prisoners in several other large buildings that had survived the great fire, including three factories built for processing sugar, appropriately called "sugar houses." Eventually, even these structures were not sufficient to house the numbers of prisoners the British were taking, and they began to house them in prison ships permanently anchored in Wallabout Bay, on the Brooklyn side of the East River. About October 20, the *Whitby* was anchored in the Wallabout near Remsen's Mill, still crowded with prisoners, and from that time on, continued to serve as the first full-time prison ship in New York Harbor. Some of the pension applications of the men from Huntington's Regiment seem to confirm that not all the prisoners from the Battle of Long Island were disembarked from the *Whitby* in the beginning of October.

Daniel Thomas of Ozias Bissell's Company, one of those who had been captured in the swamp by the Hessians after the Battle of Long Island, said in his pension application that he was "kept a prisoner sometime on Long Island, then removed on board of a transport ship of the British called the *Whitby*, and confined a prisoner in the whole for the period of five months." He does not mention being transferred to any of the prisons in New York; this was not likely an oversight or lapse of memory.

The abominable conditions on the *Whitby* and subsequent prison ships such as the *Jersey* are infamous. It was said that over 11,000 men died in these floating coffins before the end of the war. Many of the corpses were simply thrown overboard and allowed to wash up on the Brooklyn shore. Others were buried in shallow, mass graves in the sandy beach of The Wallabout. After the *Whitby* was anchored there, "the sand beach, between a ravine in the hill and Mr. Remsen's dock, [became] filled with graves in the course of two months." The *Whitby* was "the most sickly of all the prison ships. Bad provisions, bad water, and scanty rations, were dealt to the prisoners. No medical men attended the sick. Diseases reigned unrelieved, and hundreds died from pestilence or were starved on board this floating prison."[1]

After the war, the graves of the Wallabout were excavated and the remains of the soldiers found there were reburied in a hill by what

---

[1] John F. Watson, *Annals and Occurrences of New York City and State in the Olden Times* (Philadelphia: Henry F. Anners Co., 1846), p. 336, http://persi.heritagequestonline.com/...

became the Brooklyn Naval Yards. In 1808, the remains were removed and placed in a vault erected for that purpose.[1] After several early attempts to provide a permanent memorial for those who became known as the Prison Ship Martyrs, in 1908 a large monument was erected as the centerpiece of Fort Greene Park. This was the former site of Fort Putnam, part of the line of fortifications at Brooklyn constructed in the spring of 1776. What was left of the remains of the martyrs found their final rest in a crypt at the monument.

Although Thomas and perhaps a few others continued aboard the *Whitby*, it is likely that the vast majority of the men of the 17th were housed in either the North Dutch Church or the Middle Dutch Church. Significant evidence seems to point to the Middle Dutch Church being the primary repository for most of the privates of the 17th, as we shall see.

The North Dutch Church was the newest of the Dutch Churches in New York at the time of the Revolution, built only six years before, in 1769. This fact apparently had no influence on the British, who promptly gutted the place, including its pews, which were used for firewood. It was said that the mahogany pulpit of the North Dutch Church was taken down and sent to England to be used in a church there. What was left of the building was then divided into two levels by spanning the galleries with timber and flooring, so as to handle twice as many inmates.[2] It was said that the North Dutch Church alone housed as many as 850 American prisoners, but which prisoners were they?

Danske Dandridge, the author of the *American Prisoners of the Revolution*, quoted one William Slade, who said that 800 prisoners taken at the fall of Fort Washington on November 16, were put into the North Dutch Church.[3] Dandridge followed with another statement by one Henry Franklin, who affirmed, "that about two days after the taking of Fort Washington he was in New York, and went to the

---

[1] Furman, *Notes Geographical and Historical Relating to the Town of Brooklyn*, 53.
[2] Henry Onderdonk, Jr., (ed.), "Desecration of the Dutch Churches in New York During the Revolutionary War," *Long Island and New York in Olden Times* (Jamaica, LI: unpublished collection of newspaper extracts and historical sketches, 1851), http://persi.heritagequestonline.com/...
[3] Danske Dandridge, *American Prisoners of the Revolution*, (Charlottesville, Virginia: 1911), p. 44, www.gutenberg.org/ebooks/7829

North Church, in which were about 800 prisoners taken in said Fort."
Fort Washington did not fall until November 16, providing the British
with yet another bounty of 3,000 prisoners to house in New York
prisons. Since the capacity of the North Dutch church was stated to be
about 850 prisoners, it is likely that it was not used for significant
numbers of prisoners until the fall of Fort Washington, when it was
then filled to capacity with the prisoners taken there.

Evidence pointing to the Middle Dutch Church's use as housing
for the men of the 17th comes again from Lt. Jabez Fitch. Under the
conditions of their parole, the officers of Hampden House were
granted permission on November 20th to walk the streets of New York
during the day. Their concern turned almost immediately to the
condition of their soldiers, and Fitch began to visit the men of his own
regiment. The next day, November 21st, Fitch went to visit "our men
at the churches, who I found in a very miserable situation, especially
those at the Quakers Meeting House, which is now improved for a
hospital." He does not say what other church or churches he visited,
but in his diary entry of November 27th, Fitch said that he carried food
"to our poor men at the Church. I went accordingly down to the Dutch
Church."

On many later occasions, Fitch documented his visits to the men
of the 17th at "the" Dutch Church. The fact that he mentioned only
one Dutch Church is significant, as probably only one Dutch Church
was being used to house the prisoners of the 17th Regiment, since the
North Church had just been filled with the prisoners from Fort
Washington. He does not say which Dutch Church he visited, but his
speaking of going "down" to the Dutch Church provides another clue
as to its identity. The Middle Dutch Church would have been a few
blocks directly south of Hampden Hall, whereas the North Dutch
Church was across the Common, to the southeast. It is likely that
"down" would have meant south for Fitch, therefore the men were
most likely at the Middle Dutch Church. The Middle Dutch Church is
also mentioned in various histories to have contained about 800
prisoners. This would have been the vast majority of the prisoners
taken at the Battle of Long Island.

None of the pension applications of the men of the 17th
specifically mentions the Middle Dutch Church, but a brief biography
of Private Zadock Pratt of Jewett's Company written in *New England
Families*, stated that he "was confined in the Middle Dutch Church,

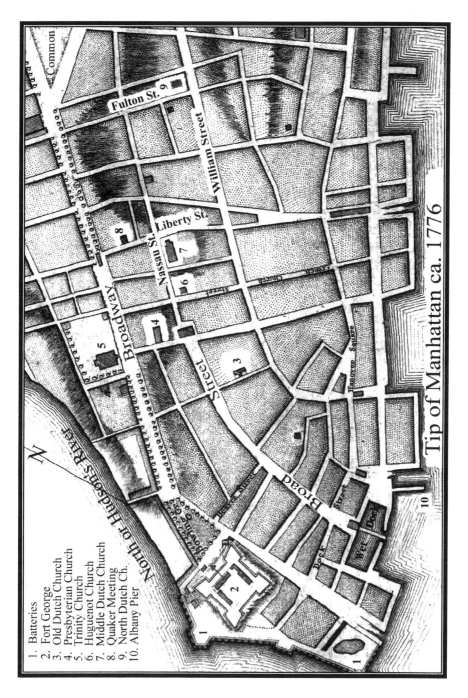

Key:
1. Batteries
2. Fort George
3. Old Dutch Church
4. Presbyterian Church
5. Trinity Church
6. Huguenot Church
7. Middle Dutch Church
8. Quaker Meeting
9. North Dutch Ch.
10. Albany Pier

Southern tip of Manhattan Island ca. 1776
(map adapted by the author)

New York, in the old sugar house and the *Whitby* Prison Ship."[1] Since Pratt's pension file does say he had been aboard the *Whitby*, this biography has credibility. If so, the order of his confinement is more likely, the *Whitby* first, then the Middle Dutch Church, and the adjacent sugar house probably towards the end of his confinement.

So, to conclude, we know that the prison ship, *Whitby*, continued to house at least a few of the men of the 17th, and some of the sicker men were taken to the Quaker Meeting House, which was being used as a hospital. The Brick Church was probably also used as a hospital for some of the men of the 17th, but the Middle Dutch Church was most likely the repository for the majority of the men of the 17th, as well as for most of the other 1,000 prisoners taken at the Battle of Long Island.

The horrific conditions that prevailed in all of the makeshift prisons and prison ships used by the British are infamous in the annals of American history, and we won't try to compare one location to another for the evil done in them. When eyewitness testimonies of the conditions in the various facilities are reviewed as a whole, the conclusion should probably be that they were all hell-holes, from which it was nearly miraculous that any of their inmates could have emerged alive. But, as it relates to our story, we do want to specifically address what it was like for the inmates of the Middle Dutch Church, among whom were most of the men of Huntington's 17th Continental Regiment.

The Middle Dutch Church was dedicated in 1729. When it was first built, it was known as the New Dutch Church, while the original Dutch church some blocks away became the Old Dutch Church. When the North Dutch Church was built, the New Dutch Church became the Middle Dutch Church, due to its location between the Old and North Dutch Churches. In 1764, English preaching in the church was inaugurated by the Rev. Archibald Laidlie. Unfortunately, Laidlie was a Whig and a chaplain in the Provincial Congress, and was forced to flee for his life upon the arrival of the British. He died in exile at

---

[1] William Richard Cutter, *New England Families, Genealogical and Memorial* (New York: Lewis Historical Publishing Co., 1913; Electronic edition, Family Tree Maker, CD515), p. 1280.

Red Hook, New York, in 1778.[1] It was no coincidence that upon his exodus from New York, the Middle Dutch Church was immediately commandeered for use as a prison. As with the North Church later, the pulpit was removed and the pews torn out and used for fuel.

Perhaps the only detailed account by a prisoner of the conditions within the Middle Dutch Church during the fall and early winter of 1776, came from Adolph Myer. He was from Colonel Lasher's battalion and was taken by the British upon the invasion of Montresor's Island (located at the confluence of the Harlem and East Rivers) on September 10. After various trials and tribulations, he was thrown into what he referred to as the "New Dutch Church," the old name for the Middle Dutch Church. Myer managed to escape on January 4, 1777, but prior to that:

> *He was treated with great inhumanity, and would have died had he not been supported by his friends...Many prisoners died from want, and others were reduced to such wretchedness as to attract the attention of the loose women of the town* [prostitutes], *from whom they received considerable assistance. No care was taken of the sick, and if any died they were thrown at the door of the prison and lay there until the next day, when they were put in a cart and drawn out to the intrenchments* [sic] *beyond the Jew's burial ground, when they were interred by their fellow prisoners, conducted thither for that purpose. The dead were thrown into a hole promiscuously, without the usual rites of sepulcher. Myer was frequently enticed to enlist.*"[2]

The entrenchments referred to in the story of Myer's captivity were those that were dug by the Americans as part of the fortifications constructed prior to the British invasion of New York. Thus, it is possible that some of the prisoners of the Middle Dutch Church had unwittingly dug their own graves during the previous summer.

Although not a prisoner, Mr. John Pintard, the nephew of the American Commissary of Prisoners, Lewis Pintard, wrote another graphic description of the conditions inside the Middle Dutch Church:

---

[1] Onderdonk, "Desecration of the Dutch Churches," *Long Island and New York in Olden Times.*

[2] Dandridge, *American Prisoners of the Revolution*, p. 43.

In the Middle Dutch Church, the prisoners taken on Long Island and at Fort Washington, sick, wounded, and well, were all indiscriminately huddled together, by hundreds and thousands, large numbers of whom died by disease, and many undoubtedly poisoned by inhuman attendants for the sake of their watches, or silver buckles.[1]

In another quote attributed to one Dunlap, in the *History of New York City*, "The beds of the prisoners were straw, intermixed with vermin. For many weeks, the dead-cart visited the prison every morning, into which from eight to twelve corpses were flung and piled up, then dumped into ditches in the outskirts of the city."[2] John Watson, the author of *Annals and Occurrences of New York City and State in the Olden Time*, interviewed a Mr. Andrew Mercein, a baker's apprentice who made bread for the British soldiers. Mercein said he used to see the dead-cart come every morning to the Middle Church and bear off six or eight of the dead.[3] The numbers of dead between the two accounts vary somewhat, but both present the chilling consequences of the ghastly living conditions inside the church. If even the lowest of the daily death tolls stated above was accurate, then the prisoners were dying at the rate of 180 a month.

Lt. Jonathan Gillet of Huntington's Regiment provided a general description of the conditions under which the prisoners of the Battle of Long Island were living, as the letter to his wife on December 2, 1776, continued:

I was kept here [probably Flatbush] *8 days and then sent on board a ship, where I continued 39 days and by* [them was treated] *much worse than when on shore- after I was set on* [shore] *at New York* [I was] *confined* [under] *a strong guard till the 20th day of November, after which I have had my liberty to walk part over the City between sun and sun, notwithstanding there generous allowance of food I must inevitably have perished with hunger had not sum friends* [the Archers] *in the* [city] *relieved my extreme necessity, but I cant expect they can always do it- what I*

[1] Dandridge, *American Prisoners of the Revolution*, p. 42.
[2] William L. Stone, *History of New York City* (New York: Virtue & Yorston, 1872), p. 255, http://persi.heritagequestonline.com/...
[3] Watson, *Annals and Occurrences of New York City and State in the Olden Times*, pp. 326-327.

shall do next I know not, being naked for clothes and void of money, and winter present, and provisions very skerce; fresh meat one shilling per pound, butter three shillings per pound, cheese two shillings, turnips and potatoes at a shilling a half peck, milk 15 Coppers per quart, bread equally as dear; and the General [Howe] *says he cant find us fuel thro' the winter, tho' at present we receive sum cole.*

I was after put on board seized violently with the disentarry- it followed me hard upwards of six weeks- after that a slow fever, but now am vastly better- my sincere love to you and my children. May God keep and preserve you at all times from sin, sickness, and death- I will Endeavor to faintly lead you into the poor cituation the soldiers are in, espechally those taken at Long Island where I was; in fact these cases are deplorable and they are Real objects of pitty- they are still confined and in houses where there is no fire- poor mortals, with little or no clothes- perishing with hunger, offering eight dollars in paper for one in silver to Relieve there distressing hunger; occasioned for want of food- there natures are broke and gone, some almost loose there voices and some there hearing- they are crouded into churches & there guarded night and day. I cant paint the horable appearance they make- it is shocking to human nature to behold them. Could I draw the curtain from before you; there expose to your view a lean Jawd mortal, hunger laid his Rotten Rags, close beset with unwelcome vermin. Could I do this, I say, possible I might in some [small] *manner fix your idea with what appearance sum hundreds of these poor creatures make in houses where once people attempted to Implore God's Blessings, &c, but I must say no more of there calamities. God be merciful to them- I cant afford them no Relief. If I had money I soon would do it, but I have none for myself.- I wrote to you by Mr. Wells to see if some one would help me to hard money under my present necessity I write no more, if I had the General would not allow it to go out, & if ever you write to me write very short or else I will never see it- what the heshens robbed me of that day amounted to the value of seventy two dollars at least.- I will give you as near an exact account of how many prisoners the enemy have taken as I can. They took on Long Island of the Huntington Regiment 64, and of officers 40, of other Regiments about 60. On Moulogin* [perhaps Manhattan] *Island 14, Stratton Island (Staten) 7, at Fort*

Washington 2,200 officers and men. On the Jersey side about 28 officers and men. In all 3135 and how many killed I do not know. Many died of there wounds. Of those that went out with me of sickness occasioned by hunger eight and more lie at the point of death. Roger Filer hath lost one of his legs and part of a Thigh, it was his left. John Moody died here a prisoner.

So now to conclude my little Ragged History- I as you know did ever impress on your mind to look to God, for so still I continue to do the same- think less of me but more of your Creator,- So in this I wish you well and bid you farewell and subscribe myself your nearest friend and well wisher for Ever

John'a Gillett
New York, Dec. 2nd, 1776. To Eliza Gillett at West Harford.[1]

☞   Lt. Gillet's estimates of the number of prisoners were not accurate, but his eyewitness testimony is invaluable, especially regarding the two soldiers he mentioned: Roger Filer, who was a private in Capt. Ebenezer Fitch Bissell's Company of Huntington's Regiment, and **John Moody**, who was a private in Capt. Timothy Percival's Company. John Moody was just twenty years old when he died. He was born in West Hartford, Connecticut, the son of Samuel Moody, in 1756. He was a descendant of one of the original settlers of Hartford.[2] Gillet does not specifically say where Filer or Moody were housed, but his graphic description of the conditions in "houses where once people attempted to implore God's blessing" is an obvious reference to the churches and to scenes he must have personally witnessed.

The "Mr. Wells" referred to in Lt. Gillet's letter was Major Levi Wells of Colonel Wyllys' 22nd Continental (Connecticut) Regiment. He was also taken prisoner at the Battle of Long Island, but was allowed by the British to travel home on parole on November 30 to raise money for the relief of the prisoners in New York.[3] It is perhaps by way of Major Wells, and the letters that he conveyed, that the public first became aware of the dire circumstances of the prisoners

---

[1] Dandridge, *American Prisoners of the Revolution*, p. 15; Stiles, *The History and Genealogies of Ancient Windsor*, Vol. II, p. 298.
[2] Herbert A. Moody, *Historical Notes Concerning the Moody Family* (Turners Falls, MA: 1947), p. 15, http://persi.heritagequestonline.com/...
[3] Bradford, *Diary*, p. 46.

held in New York. From a Connecticut newspaper on December 6, 1776, came the following press release:

> *This may inform those who have friends in New York, prisoners of war, that Major Wells, a prisoner, has come thence to Connecticut on parole, to collect money for the much distressed officers and soldiers there, and desires the money may be left at Landlord Betts, Norwalk; Captain Benjamin's, Stratford; Landlord Beers, New Haven; Hezekiah Wylly's, Hartford; and at said Well's Colchester, with proper accounts from whom received, and to whom to be delivered. N. B. The letters must not be sealed, or contain anything of a political nature.[1]*

The state formally weighed in for the support of the prisoners at a meeting of the Governor of Connecticut and the Council of Safety held on December 13, 1776. It was voted at that meeting that a letter of credit to merchants in New York for 500 pounds be issued to Major Wells for relief of the prisoners in New York. The letter of credit was issued the same day.[2]

Somehow the following letter was probably smuggled out of the prison ship, *Whitby*, and was dated Dec. 9, 1776, giving the public its first glimpse into what the prisoners were enduring there. The author is unknown; no doubt to protect his identity had the letter been intercepted by the British:

> *Our present situation is most wretched; more than 250 prisoners, some sick and without the least assistance from physician, drug, or medicine, and fed on two-thirds allowance of salt provisions, and crowded promiscuously together without regard, to color, person or office, in the small room of a ship's between decks, allowed to walk the main deck only between sunrise and sunset. Only two at a time allowed to come on deck to do what nature requires, and sometimes denied even that, and use tubs and buckets between decks, to the great offence of every delicate, cleanly person, and prejudice of all our healths. Lord Howe has*

---

[1] Dandridge, *American Prisoners of the Revolution*, p.39.
[2] Charles H. Hoadly, *The Public Records of the State of Connecticut, Oct., 1776-Feb., 1778* (Hartford: Case, Lockwood & Brainard Co., 1894), p. 86.

liberated all in the merchant service, but refuses to exchange
those taken in arms but for like prisoners.[1]

Returning to the subject of the churches, none other than the noted
Colonel Ethan Allen, of Fort Ticonderoga fame, also wrote of the
condition of the American prisoners in New York. Allen had been
taken prisoner the previous September in a failed attack on the British
at Montreal, and after a long odyssey, had been transferred to New
York at the end of November. He too, with the other American
officers, was granted parole and allowed to walk the streets of New
York during the day. Allen was a flamboyant, exuberant, and profane
officer, yet surprisingly expressive and literate; never one to mince
words as so often suited him. Capt. Alexander Graydon, also a
prisoner in New York, wrote of Allen, "I have seldom met with a
man, possessing, in my opinion, a stronger mind, or whose mode of
expression was more vehement and oratorical. His style was a
singular compound of local barbarisms, scriptural phrases, and
oriental wildness. And though unclassic and sometimes
ungrammatical, it was highly animated and forcible."[2] But, having
already heard from various other sources of the condition of
American prisoners, we will leave it to the reader to evaluate whether
or not Allen's testimony is exaggerated or credible, and therefore
consistent with the other testimonies:

The private soldiers, who were brought to New York, were
crowded into churches, and environed with slavish Hessian
guards, a people of a strange language, who were sent to America
for no other design but cruelty and desolation; and at others, by
merciless Britons whose mode of communicating ideas being
intelligible in this country, served only to tantalize and insult the
helpless and perishing; but above all, the hellish delight and
triumph of the tories over them, as they were dying by hundreds.
This was too much for me to bear as a spectator; for I saw the
tories exulting over the dead bodies of their murdered
countrymen. I have gone into the churches, and seen sundry of
the prisoners in the agonies of death, in consequence of very
hunger, and others speechless, and very near death, biting pieces

---

[1] Dandridge, *American Prisoners of the Revolution*, p. 39.
[2] *Fitch*, note, p. 76.

of chips; others pleading for God's sake, for something to eat, and at the same time, shivering with the cold. Hollow groans saluted my ears, and despair seemed to be imprinted on every [one] of their countenances. The filth in these churches, in consequence of the fluxes, was almost beyond description. The floors were covered with excrement. I have carefully sought to direct my steps so as to avoid it, but could not. They would beg for God's sake for one copper, or morsel of bread. I have seen in one of these churches seven dead, at the same time, lying among the excrements of their bodies.

It was a common practice with the enemy, to convey the dead from these filthy places, in carts, to be slightly buried, and I have seen whole gangs of tories making derision, and exulting over the dead, saying, there goes another load of damned rebels. I have observed the British soldiers to be full of their blackguard jokes, and vaunting on those occasions, but they appeared to me less malignant than tories.

The provision dealt out to the prisoners was by no means sufficient for the support of life. It was deficient in quantity, and much more so in quality. The prisoners often presented me with a sample of their bread, which I certify was damaged to that degree, that it was loathsome and unfit to be eaten, and I am bold to aver it, as my opinion, that it had been condemned, and was of the very worst sort. I have seen and been fed upon damaged bread, in the course of my captivity, and observed the quality of such bread as has been condemned by the enemy, among which was very little so effectually spoiled as what was dealt out to these prisoners. Their allowance of meat (as they told me) was quite trifling, and of the basest sort. I never saw any of it, but was informed, that bad as it was, it was swallowed almost as quick as they got hold of it. I saw some of them sucking bones after they were speechless; others, who could yet speak, and had the use of their reason, urged me in the strongest and most pathetic manner, to use my interest in their behalf; for you plainly see, said they, that we are devoted to death and destruction; and after I had examined more particularly into their truly deplorable condition, and had become more fully apprized of the essential facts, I was persuaded that it was a premeditated and systematical plan of the British council, to destroy the youths of our land, with a view thereby to deter the country, and make it submit to their despotism; but that I could not do them any material service, and that, by any public attempt for that purpose, I might endanger myself by frequenting places the most nauseous and contagious that could be conceived of. I refrained going into churches, but frequently conversed with such of the prisoners as were admitted to come out into the yard, and found that the systematical usage still continued. The guard would often drive me away with their fixed bayonets. A Hessian one day followed me five or six rods, but by making use of my legs, I got rid of the lubber. Sometimes I could obtain a little conversation, notwithstanding their severities.

I was in one of the church yards, and it was rumored among those in the church, and sundry of the prisoners came with their usual complaints to me, and among the rest a large boned, tall young man, as he told me, from Pennsylvania, who was reduced to a mere skeleton; he said he was glad to see me before he died, which he expected to have done last night, but was a little revived; he furthermore informed me, that he and his brother had been urged to enlist into the British Army, but both had resolved to die first; that his brother had died last night, in consequence of that resolution, and that he expected shortly to follow him; but I made the other prisoners stand a little off, and told him with a low voice to enlist; he then asked, whether it was right in the sight of God! I assured him that it was, and that duty to himself obliged him to deceive the British by enlisting and deserting the first opportunity; upon which he answered with transport that he would enlist. I charged him not to mention my name as his adviser, lest it should get air, and I should be closely confined, in consequence of it. The integrity of these suffering prisoners is hardly credible. Many hundreds, I am confident, submitted to death, rather than to enlist in the British service, which I am informed, they most generally were pressed to do. I was astonished at the resolution of the two brothers particularly; it seems that they could not be stimulated to such exertions of heroism from ambition, as they were but obscure soldiers; strong indeed *must the internal principle of virtue be, which supported them to brave death, and one of them went through the operation, as did many hundred others.*[1]

---

[1] Henry W. Depuy, *Ethan Allen and the Green-Mountain Heroes of '76* (New York: Phinney, Blakeman, & Mason, 1861; Facsimile reprint, Heritage Books, 1994), pp. 253-256.

Ethan Allen was speaking of the churches in general, so that the reader must assume that this was a collective impression from conditions that Allen witnessed within all of the churches. If we had not already heard several similar descriptions of the conditions of confinement of the American prisoners, it might be easy to dismiss Allen's account based on his reputation for exaggeration, but much of what he says he personally witnessed and cannot be easily dismissed. There is more to Allen's account, but we will leave his remarks here and return to them when he again becomes personally involved in the events with which we are concerned.

If the British kept records of the sick and dead in their prisons early in the war, they have not survived. We are dependent upon the scattered letters and testimonies that were written by those such as Gillet and Fitch to tell us what happened to friends who suffered in the prisons in New York. Fitch's diary is perhaps the best source for determining the casualties in the prisons from Huntington's Regiment, so every death and sickness he noted among those men will be provided here. In Gillet's case, and most often in Fitch's case as well, they mentioned the names of those they knew who came from their own towns or were in their own companies. We could wish they had written down all the names of those who died from their regiment, but they did not. When Fitch wrote in his diary entry for the 23rd of October, that Joseph White had died, he mentioned "several others" without naming them. History cries out to know who those "several others" were, but Fitch left no answer.

Also on October 23, Ensign Bradford wrote that **Caleb Green** of Capt. Trowbridge's Company had died. However, neither Bradford nor Fitch recorded the death of **Private Elijah Rose,** of Captain Timothy Percival's Company, who died on November 24th. Somehow word of his death, as well as that of Caleb Green, was conveyed to the Town of Griswold, Connecticut, where both names, with their dates of death, were noted in the parish church records.[1] Caleb Green was born in Griswold October 28, 1757, the son of Winter and Borrodil

---

[1] Daniel L. Phillips, *Griswold- A History* (New Haven: Tuttle, Morehouse & Taylor Co., 1929), p. 68, http://persi.heritagequestonline.com/...

(Bennet) Green. Elijah Rose was born July 26, 1757, the son of Thomas and Sarah (Harris) Rose of Griswold.[1]

Fitch continued in his diary on the 24th of October, writing that, "One Beebe (a tender in the Hospital) came to see us, and gave us some account of some wounded, etc., who were under his care." Again, Fitch did not say who these wounded were. Besides complaining that the officers had not received any bread for several days, he went on to write that, "the customers at the Holy Ground, were remarkably noisy, in consequence of which (it is said that) one of the matrons was found dead in the morning."

The "Holy Ground" surrounded Hampden House, an area of the city between Fulton Street on the south, and Duane Street on the north, and to the west of Broadway. Although Fitch's Puritan principles might not have allowed him to indulge the favors of the ladies of the night, doubtless some of the other officers enjoyed their company. Puritan principles not withstanding, many of the prostitutes had pity on the starving American soldiers in the prisons, and were among the few who brought them food as they were able. On Sunday, the 27th, Fitch mentioned that "In the afternoon, several women came to see us," without identifying who they were. The lack of specific identification perhaps implied they were local prostitutes.

☞ Also on the 27th, Ensign Bradford briefly noted in his diary that, "Died very suddenly this day **Ishmael Moffatt** of Capt. Trowbridge's Company." Unfortunately, Bradford did not record any of the circumstances of this soldier's death. Ishmael Moffatt was a private who was listed among the missing after the Battle of Long Island. He was born June 28, 1753, in Killingly, Connecticut, the son of John and Elizabeth (Bennit) Moffatt.[2]

The following Wednesday, Fitch made note that Lieutenant George Wert of Col. Miles' Pennsylvania Regiment and Major Wells paid a visit to Hampden Hall, bringing word that Colonel Clark had been sick for several days. On Thursday the 31st, Lt. Nathaniel Gove made Ensign Cornelius Higgins a pair of shoes. We might not have otherwise known that Gove had probably been a shoemaker in civilian life. On Friday, Private Nathan Barney of Capt. Ozias

---

[1] Larry Beam, "Moments in Time," *The Steeple-News and Current Events of the First Congregational Church of Griswold,* Vol. VIII, No. 5, May 2005, p. 21, www.firstchurchgriswold.org/steeples%20PDF/May%20steeples%202005.pdf
[2] CT State Library, *Barbour Collection.*

Bissell's Company, one of Dr. Silas Holmes' assistants, came from the hospital at New Utrecht to tend to some of the wounded men in New York. On November 2, Fitch received word that Sergeant Uriah Hungerford of Capt. Timothy Percival's Company, and Sergeant Bartlett Lewis of Captain Abraham Tyler's Company had both perished "in the Church this day."

That same day, Fitch wrote that the British Commissary of Prisoners, Joshua Loring, paid them a visit to inform the officers that one of their company was to be allowed to run errands and procure supplies. This arrangement was made prior to the officers being granted parole to walk the city during the day. The next day, Sunday, Loring sent the officers some bedding, which was found to be filthy and full of lice. A junior officer, Ensign Higgins was assigned the unpleasant and laborious task of washing the bedding to try to make it fit for use. On Tuesday, November 5, Fitch received word that two more soldiers had died since they were landed in New York, probably in the Middle Dutch Church: Private Rufus Cone and Private Theophilus Emerson, both of Capt. Jewett's Company. Private Cone left a wife and seven children, who subsequently never learned the circumstances of his death.[1] Certainly, the officers of the 17th must have been alarmed at the rising death toll in the churches, but could do nothing about it.

Dr. Silas Holmes was allowed to visit Hampden Hall from the hospital at New Utrecht on Thursday. Holmes informed them of the death of Private Adam Mitchel of Jewett's Company, who had been wounded during the Battle of Long Island, and had been confined at New Utrecht since August 27. Without identifying which hospital, Fitch said in the same daily entry that private Duran (see Duroy Whittlesey in the second chapter) Whittlesey, also of Jewett's Company died "in the hospital" the previous night, Wednesday, November 6, 1776. We can only assume it was one of the hospitals in the city. Whittlesey's family also never learned his fate. The same afternoon, Mrs. Archer paid a visit to Lt. Gillet who had been unwell for several days. By this entry in his diary, Fitch confirmed Lt. Gillet's own account of the illness described in his letter of December 2.

On Friday, November 8, Lt. Fitch recorded, "Sergeant Huntington and Sergeant Avery of our regiment were also here, they having for

---

[1] Leach, *Additions and Corrections for Thomas Hungerford*, pp. 15-16.

some time been sick in the hospital, where sickness and mortality greatly prevails among the prisoners, seven of whom having died the last 24 hours, among whom was Sergeant Talmage of Capt. Hubbard's Company." Fitch did not say which hospital, but it would have been either the one at the Quaker Church, or the Brick Church, both of which were nearby. Sergeant Huntington was Theophilus Huntington of Captain Jonathan Brewster's Company and Sergeant Avery was listed as Corporal Jabez Avery, also of Brewster's Company in the *Record of Service of Connecticut Men in the War of the Revolution*. Sergeant Talmage was Sergeant William Talmage of Captain Elizur Hubbard's Company. Given the distinctive service of his brothers, Colonel Benjamin Talmage and Adjutant Samuel Talmage, throughout the war, it is likely that Sergeant William Talmage would have also had a significant career in the service of his country had he been allowed to live.

The very next day, Saturday, Fitch reported two more deaths, without indicating where they occurred. The first was Sergeant Hezekiah Hayden of Captain Ebenezer Fitch Bissell's Company, and the second was "one Lewis of our regiment." Fitch had already reported the death of **Bartlett Lewis**, and there were only two other men with the surname "Lewis" reported missing from Huntington's Regiment. This one was likely **Private Lemuel Lewis** of Captain Abraham Tyler's Company. The town history of Clinton, Connecticut, lists both Bartlett Lewis and Lemuel Lewis, former residents of that town, as having died from either sickness or imprisonment during the war.[1] Bartlett Lewis was the son of George and Bathsheba (Swift) Lewis who was born July 30, 1745, in Middletown, Connecticut.[2] Lemuel Lewis was Bartlett's brother, baptized July 30, 1753, in Portland, Connecticut, across the river from Middletown.[3] Private John Lewis of Brewster's Company was the only other Lewis listed from the regiment as missing, and he likely survived the captivity as will be discussed later.

Hezekiah Hayden died of starvation after "having disposed of everything in his possession, even to his sleeve buttons, to purchase of his keeper food enough to sustain life."[4] He was highly respected and

---

[1] http://freepages.genealogy.rootsweb.com/~jdevlin/town_hist/clinton_history.htm
[2] CT State Library, *Barbour Collection*.
[3] CT State Library, *Church Records Slip Index*.
[4] Trumbull, *Memorial History of Hartford County*, Vol. II, p. 513.

esteemed by his family and friends in Windsor, Connecticut, and will be remembered as the author of the eloquent, emotional and highly patriotic letter he wrote to his parents from New York just prior to the Battle of Long Island.

In his diary entry of November 10th, Fitch wrote that "Our people who had been confined at Long Island were this day brought into the City." This probably refers to the wounded, who had remained at New Utrecht since the Battle of Long Island under the care of Dr. Bailey, and Dr. Silas Holmes. Fitch did not state where they were imprisoned next. The next day, Ensign Bradford tersely recorded that, "Our men that are prisoners die very fast," without noting if he had personally witnessed this fact or learned it from others.

Between November 10th and November 20th, Fitch's daily entries were filled with worries over adequate food and other provisions for the officers at Hampden Hall. No other news arrived from outside about the private soldiers during this time, but on the 16th and for the next three days, Fitch made note of the news of the fall of Fort Washington, and the arrival of nearly 3,000 more American prisoners of war in the city. Details of the capture of Fort Washington were related to Fitch by officers who were captured and brought to be housed with the officers captured on Long Island. Fitch did not elaborate on the specific intelligence he had received, however. He must have still feared that his diary might be found and read by the British, so he was very careful not to provide any information the British could use, or to complain too much of conditions. It is very apparent, though, that the sufferings of the officers were in no way comparable to what was happening to the privates. In his "Narrative," smuggled out later, Fitch's only complaint about the treatment of the officers was that they were subject to verbal abuse at the hands of their captors and the Tory citizenry. This treatment stood in stark contrast to his graphic account of the horrid abuse of the men in the churches:

November 20th: Most of the officers who were now prisoners, were indulged with liberty to walk the streets, etc., within the bounds of the city, from sunrise to sunset; which indulgence was continued as long as we remained in the city. Nor was this enlargement at all disagreeable, as we had suffered almost three months in close imprisonment, great part of which time, we had been in the most disagreeable situation. But yet we frequently met with insults in the streets, and when we visited those friendly people who had used us with humanity, and visited us in our close confinement, they were often insulted on our account. Having obtained the aforesaid indulgence, the first objects of our attention, were the poor men who had been unhappily captivated with us. They had been landed about the same time that we were, and confined in several churches and other large buildings. And although we had often received intelligence from them, with the most deplorable representation of their miserable situation, yet when we came to visit them, we found their sufferings vastly superior to what we had been able to conceive, nor are words sufficient to convey an adequate idea of their unparalleled calamity. Well might the prophet say, "They that be slain with the sword are better than they that be slain with hunger for these pine away, etc." (Lamentations 4: 9) Their appearance in general rather resembled dead corpses than living men. Indeed, great numbers had already arrived at their long home, and the remainder appeared far advanced on the same journey. Their accommodations were, in all respects, vastly inferior to what a New England farmer would have provided for his cattle, and although the commissary pretended to furnish them with two thirds of the allowance of the Kings Troops, yet it was often observed, that they were cheated out of one half of that. They were also many times entirely neglected from day to day, and received no provision at all. They were also frequently imposed upon in regard to the quality, as well as quantity of their provision, especially in the necessary article of bread, of which they often received such rotten, and moldy stuff as was entirely unfit for use. There was indeed pretentions of accommodations [hospitals] *for the sick and a large number of the most feeble were removed down to the Quaker Meeting House in Queen Street, where many hundreds of them perished, in a much more miserable situation than the dumb beasts, while those whose particular business it was to provide them relief, paid very little or no attention to their unparalleled sufferings. This house I understand was under the superintendence of one Doctor Debuke, who was European born, but had dwelt many years in America, and had been (at least), once convicted of stealing, in consequence of which (not finding the country very agreeable for his profession) he with many other of like character had fled here for protection. It was said that this fellow often made application of his cane among the sick, instead of other medicines. Nor was there any more solemnity or ceremony bestowed on those miserable sufferers, after they were dead, than while living, for their bodies were thrown out on the ground, where they lay almost naked, exposed to the weather (though never so stormy, etc.). Indeed it was said that some of them were exposed to the unnatural devouring of swine and other greedy animals, in a most inhuman and ridiculous manner. However this might be, they were most of them buried, although it was in a manner very uncommon for the interment of human bodies, many of them being thrown into the ground in a heap, almost naked, where they were slightly covered over with earth. Although this beastly treatment of those senseless corpses, does not affect their persons, yet when considered in connection with their usage of the living, it shows the unnatural, the savage and inhuman disposition of the enemy into whose hands we are fallen, and whose character (notwithstanding all their boasts of lenity and humanity) will bear a just comparison to those whose tender mercies are cruelty. When we attempted to visit the prisoners at the churches, in their miserable situation, we were frequently repulsed and denied admittance by the guard, who often treated us with the greatest insolence, driving us back with their bayonets, swords or canes. Indeed I have often been in danger of being stabbed for attempting to speak with a prisoner in the yard.[1]*

According to his diary, the first thing Fitch did after receiving his liberty to walk the city on November 20, 1776, was to visit his colonel, Joel Clark, at Mrs. Lesley's house where the other field officers captured on Long Island were living. He found Colonel Clark in much worse condition than he expected, and he stayed to visit with him for a while. Leaving Mrs. Lesley's, he went off to see other friends in the city and was treated with a good supper. Having been deprived of an adequate diet for almost two months, Fitch's daily diary entries provide an ongoing commentary on what was becoming an obsession with food and how to obtain it.

---

[1] *Fitch*, pp. 148-149.

On Thursday the 21st, Fitch received word from Ensign Higgins that Captain Abijah Rowley had died, but he did not provide the circumstances of his death. Rowley had been captain of the 6th Company in Huntington's 8th Connecticut Regiment during 1775. In the afternoon Fitch made his first visit to the churches from which we derived the above description from his "Narrative." In the evening Fitch visited Colonel Clark again, obviously much concerned with the progress of his commanding officer's unspecified illness.

There are no further updates on the condition of any of the soldiers confined in the churches until the 25th, when Fitch reported that he had gone to "the churches" to visit the men, and found Sergeant Rufus Tracy and Private Elisha Miller, both of Capt. Jewett's Company, in very poor condition. Two days later Fitch took a dish of soup to Sergeant Tracy and some of the other sick prisoners at the "Dutch Church." Fitch then learned that Elisha Miller had died the day before, and that Sergeant Tracy was worse still.

On November 28, Colonel Ethan Allen came to Hampden Hall for the first time, having just arrived in New York, and told his fellow officers the long story of his captivity. Then, at mid-day, Fitch went back to "the Dutch Church" to visit with Sergeant Tracy and the sick prisoners, who were "in a very pitiful situation, both on account of sickness and accommodation." In the afternoon Fitch went to the "Burying Ground" and watched four of the prisoners being buried in one grave. However, about 3 o'clock, he "took a very good dinner with the Frenchmen," after which he went to a Mr. Giles' where he had "an agreeable conference with him and his wife." He also "drank a dish of tea with them." Obviously, the deplorable condition of the privates had not spoiled Fitch's own appetite or inclination to socialize.

After what were becoming routine morning ramblings, on Sunday, Dec 1st, Fitch went home by way of "the Burying Ground" where he saw "our people burying three men in a grave, who died the last night, at the Quaker Meeting House." He did not identify the bodies. Immediately afterwards, Fitch went on to the "Frenchmens" where he sat some time and had a very good dinner of roast beef. The following is a typical diary entry made by Fitch during this period of time, and it further illustrates the contrast between the way the American officers were being treated and the ghastly situation in the churches:

Wednesday, December 4, 1776: Was a rainy morning, our breakfast was late on account of the want of bread.

About 11 o'clock I went with Lt. Gillet down to Mr. Archer's where we drank some small beer, which was very agreeable. We then went up to the churches and made the poor prisoners a visit, found them in a very pitiful situation, etc. We parted here, and I took a walk through the burnt part of the city and then home, where I found Ensign Higgins alone. At about 2, I went down to the Frenchmen, whom I understood to be two of Governor Tryon's domestics. About sunset I went over to Mr. Sunderland's, where I set a little while with Colonel Moulton [Colonel Stephen Moulton, the father of private Salmon Moulton and Sergeant Howard Moulton of Huntington's Regiment]. *Mrs. Sunderland also gave me some spermaceti, which I took as I was going to bed, and found great advantage thereby on account of my rest.*

The following Friday, December 6th, Fitch took an old pair of pants he had been given down to "the Dutch Church" for Private Jaspar Griffin of Jewett's Company. Clearly, Fitch felt a sense of responsibility for the soldiers of his company, and provided for their needs in any way he could. Fitch's resources were very limited, however, as he was dependent on the sympathetic dispositions of the minority Whig citizenry of the town for his own support. Much of Fitch's time was taken up with endless rounds of visiting, in the hope that his hosts would feed him while he was in their company.

On the 9th, Fitch visited the Dutch Church again, but following that he did not mention visiting the prisoners for several days. On Thursday, December 12, Fitch went to Mrs. Lesley's again to visit with Lt.-Colonel Clark, whom he indicated was "dangerously sick." The next day he resumed his visits to the Dutch Church to see the prisoners, where he found Sergeant Graves in extremely poor condition and not likely to survive much longer. Fitch was growing increasingly concerned with Joel Clark's condition, and he went with Corporal George Gordon to sit with the colonel again in the evening, observing that Clark remained "very poor." Lt.-Colonel Clark must have received special permission from the British for Corporal Gordon to attend to him. Fitch also made note this day that:

It is twelve months this night since I arrived at my own house, from the campaign of 1775, since which I have passed through a variety of fatiguing adventures, of which my present captivity hath been by far, the greatest, and most tedious on many accounts.

On Monday, December 16, 1776, Lieutenant-Colonel Joel Clark, who had assumed command of the 17th Continental Regiment at the Battle of Long Island during the illness of Colonel Huntington, died. Lt. Fitch made note of the sad fact in his diary entry for the day, saying:

About 1 o'clock this morning, Lt. Col. Clark of our regiment died, having been sick of an unusual disorder for a considerable time. At about 4 o'clock ensign Lyman came home from watching and acquainted us of the Colonel's death.

Lt.-Colonel Clark's funeral was held at 4 o'clock that afternoon. In his Narrative, Fitch added the details that Clark's body was "decently interred" during the evening in the Brick Church Yard (in the area bounded by today's Beekman St., Nassau St. and Park Row), attended by a large number of the officers who had been taken on Long Island. Fitch was not able to identify the cause of death other than it had been a "lingering disorder" from which he had suffered since the *Mentor* had landed.[1] Clark had finally received the field command that he had petitioned Governor Trumbull for at the beginning of the war, and it had cost him his life. Had he survived a few weeks longer, he likely would have been exchanged and, as a regimental commander, asked to provide his testimony regarding his regiment's participation in the Battle of Long Island. In the process he might have secured for himself and the other men in his regiment the well-deserved honor and gratitude of succeeding generations of his countrymen.

As it was, an unfortunate and unintended epitaph for Lieutenant-Colonel Clark was published by the New York loyalist, James Rivington, in the form of a satirical play at the expense of the American officers present at the Battle of Long Island. The play, entitled "The Battle of Brooklyn," was coincidentally published on the very same day as the death of Clark. Although intended to poke fun at American officers, the play may have inadvertently confirmed some of the historical details provided by Fitch that happened just prior to the battle. In the play, Clark, along with two other colonels, Lasher and Remsen, are portrayed as profiteers, more interested in

---

[1] *Fitch*, p. 152

cattle rustling than combat. Clark is introduced to the audience as a retailer of rum from Connecticut. What follows is a sample of an imagined dialogue between Clark and Lord Stirling at the commencement of hostilities:

> *Stirling: Now will I endeavour to get button'd up and my gaiters tied. (enter Clark) O Colonel Clark ! from whence- from whence are you?*
>
> *Clark: From where our out sentries are attacked. I see you are getting ready, my Lord.*
>
> *Stirling: But where are they attacked? Where is the enemy? Are there many of them- are they coming forward- is anybody killed, say dear Will* [possibly a nickname for Joel]?
>
> *Clark: I cannot tell you half of what you have already asked me; but I will tell you all I know. They sent a Captain to relieve me: I would not be relieved by a Captain, so I went to sleep at one Bergen's, from whence the out sentries were relieved. This Bergen awakened me awhile ago, and said there was shooting in his field.*
>
> *Stirling: God bless me ! shooting in his field ! was it near the house?*
>
> *Clark: Very near…I have lost the cattle that were in Bergen's orchard (Aside).* [farther along, Clark says] *O what a scrape those cattle have brought me into. I am afraid I shall be obliged to fight at last.*[1]

Lt. Fitch did not record any reaction to this character assassination of his commanding officer, but the American officers on parole in the city must have known of the publication of Rivington's play. If it had come at any other time, the play might not have created much of a stir among the officers, but the irony of its publication on the day of Clark's death would not have been understood as a coincidence, and surely must have enraged them.

Although the dialogue between Clark and Stirling is certainly contrived, there may be some truth behind the fiction. Lt. Fitch's account regarding the home of Simon Bergen being used as

---

[1] *The Battle of Brooklyn, a farce in two acts; as it was performed on Long-Island, on Tuesday the 27ᵗʰ day of August, 1776. By the representatives of the tyrants of America, assembled at Philadelphia* (New York: printed for J. Rivington, 1776), partial transcription in *The New York Diary of Lt. Jabez Fitch*, p. 88.

headquarters for the sentries is confirmed in the play. The dialogue also claims that fighting began in the immediate vicinity of Bergen's farm, quite possibly in his fields, which has been previously discussed. Perhaps this dialogue was based on some information extracted from Clark by the British regarding his role in the battle. If so, then Clark himself may have provided some of the details mentioned in the dialogue. Perhaps Clark remained at Bergen's farm with General Parsons after his men had returned from picket duty the day before, and personally rode to Brooklyn to notify Lord Stirling that fighting had broken out near the Red Lion on the morning of August 27.

On Tuesday, the 17th of December, Fitch went down to visit the prisoners at the Dutch Church, but an insolent Hessian guard refused to allow Fitch to speak with the men through the fence. The next day, Fitch went to the Dutch Church again and:

> *...visited the poor prisoners, whom I found in a very miserable condition, 4 of em lay dead in the yard, and several others died in the house. Sergeant Graves appears to have but little time to live, as well as several others of our regiment, and indeed the whole of em appear complete objects of pity, and although they may be deprived of that favor, from the powers of earth and hell, it is to be hoped that a superior power may soon interpose in their favor, heaven grant the happy period may be hastened.*

On the 19th, Fitch learned that one of his roommates, a Doctor "Kyes," was likely infected with smallpox. Fitch had never been inoculated, so in fear of coming down with the disease, he left Hampden Hall and obtained lodging with the "Frenchmen." He identified the Frenchmen as the "Laperees," but the editor of Fitch's Diary was never able to determine with any certainty anyone by this name. Fitch also did not make clear whether or not he had to obtain permission from the British authorities to move out of Hampden Hall, but he must have. Ensign Bradford remained at Hampden Hall and noted that Dr. Keyes (as he spelled the name) was removed to the hospital on the 20th.

On December 21, Fitch visited "the churches" again and found that long-suffering Sergeant Roswell Graves had died, "with great composure of mind." The tradition in the family was that "he was found with a piece of brick in his mouth." He left a wife and five children.[1] Fitch also reported that "200 of the prisoners had been sent off this day to the southward." This must be a reference to a prisoner exchange, which allowed that number of American prisoners to be sent home to the southern states. The same day, Capt. Ebenezer Fitch Bissell and Captain Jonathan Brewster were allowed to go home to Connecticut on exchange. Fitch's diary is full of rumors of exchanges during this time, but this is the first mention by Fitch that any of the officers of the 17th had actually been sent home. Fitch was encouraged by this development to ask Commissary Loring two days later of the chances of his soon going home, but Loring could offer him no hope of an early repatriation.

On the 24th, Fitch received a letter from Lieutenant John Harris of the 17th, not captured on Long Island, with information that Fitch's son was well. Also included was some clothing, sorely needed as winter had now set in. The items for Fitch had likely been given to him by Major Wells, whose mission of mercy to obtain money and supplies from Connecticut for the prisoners had been successful. Ensign Bradford noted in his diary that Wells had returned the day before with "cash and baggage for the prisoners." Lt. Fitch went to Wells' house later and received an unspecified sum of money and more letters from his family. A number of letters for some of the other men of Fitch's company were also received, which Fitch immediately went off to personally deliver.

To his great surprise, Fitch found that the surviving men of the 17th had left their prison and been marched to the Albany Pier, which was located on the lower east side of Manhattan, nearly opposite the end of Broad St. From there they were loaded aboard ship and made ready to sail for Connecticut. Fitch found Sergeant Tracy among the men on board and delivered the letters and money to him.

Ensign Bradford had spent a great part of the day helping the poor debilitated prisoners from the church down to the Albany Pier. At least one of the men was completely unable to walk, and Bradford had to carry him down into the ship with the assistance of Sergeant Moses Smith, also of Capt. Trowbridge's Company.

Lt. Fitch went down again to Albany Pier on Christmas Day, Wednesday, and found the vessel, with its pathetic human cargo, still docked there. He was there informed that at least 21 prisoners, at

[1] *John Graves, 1635 Settler of Concord, MA*, family #128.

various locations in the city, had died the night before. Two of them had come from the ship docked at the Albany Pier. The relief Major Wells had obtained from Connecticut had come too late to be of any assistance to those men.

The same day, Ensign Bradford returned to the "church," and found that two of the men from his regiment, "Turner and one Jennings," had been left behind the day before, no doubt because they were completely incapacitated, and both were now dead. Listed among the missing from the Battle of Long Island were Private William Turner of Capt. Trowbridge's Company, and Corporal Oliver Jennings of Capt. Tyler's Company. Another man who had been left behind was still alive, and identified by Bradford as "one Fisher." There were none with this surname listed as missing from Huntington's Regiment, but it might have been Private John Fletcher of Capt. E. F. Bissell's Company. With the help of Quartermaster Thomas Fanning they were able to get "Fisher" down to the Albany Pier to join his fellow prisoners. The rest of the afternoon, Bradford, probably with the help of Fanning, gathered supplies for the prisoners.

On the 26th, Bradford wrote that a nor'easter was blowing with snow, rain and hail. The prisoners aboard ship at the Albany Pier were not well, and 50 men had died in the two nights since they had left the church. The next day, the 27th, the wind was favorable, and the vessel finally sailed off with the surviving prisoners at about 7 a.m.

Both the Americans and the British blamed each other for the length of time that it took to affect an exchange of prisoners, but historians tend to agree that the prisoners in New York languished in captivity far longer than necessary. The frustration expressed by Fitch, Gillet, Allen, and other officers, at the inability to address the needs of the soldiers in the churches, led to an action on their part that had likely resulted in the exchange of the prisoners which began on Christmas Eve. We need to return to the flowery narrative of Colonel Ethan Allen at this point, to learn about the efforts of the officers to secure the release of their private soldiers:

The officers on parole were most of them zealous, if possible, to afford the miserable soldiery relief, and often consulted with one another on the subject, but to no effect, being destitute of the means of subsistence, which they needed; nor could the officers project any measure, which they thought would alter their fate or so much as be a means of getting them out of those filthy places to the privilege of fresh air. Some projected that all the officers should go in procession to General Howe, and plead the cause of the perishing soldiers; but this proposal was negatived for the following reasons, viz: because that general Howe must needs be well acquainted, and have a thorough knowledge of the state and condition of the prisoners in every of their wretched apartments, and that much more particular and exact than any officer on parole could be supposed to have, as the general had a return of the circumstances of the prisoners, by his own officers, every morning, of the number which were alive, as also the number which died every twenty-four hours; and consequently the bill of mortality, as collected from the daily returns, lay before him with all the material situations and circumstances of the prisoners; and provided the officers should go in procession to general Howe, according to the projection, it would give him the greatest affront, and that he would either retort upon them, that it was no part of their parole to instruct him in his conduct to prisoners; that they were mutining against his authority, and by affronting him, had forfeited their parole; or that, more probably, instead of saying one word to them, would order them all into as wretched confinement as the soldiers whom they sought to relieve; for, at that time, the British, from the general to the private sentinel, were in full confidence, nor did they so much as hesitate, but that they should conquer the country. Thus the consultation of the officers was confounded and broken to pieces, in consequence of the dread, which at that time lay on their minds, of offending Gen. Howe; for they conceived so murderous a tyrant would not be too good to destroy even the officers, on the least pretence of an affront, as they were equally in his power with the soldiers; and as Gen Howe perfectly understood the condition of the private soldiers, it was argued that it was exactly such as he and his council had devised, and as he meant to destroy them, it would be to no purpose for them to try to dissuade him from it, as they were helpless and liable to the same fate, on giving the least affront; indeed anxious apprehensions disturbed them in their then circumstances.

Mean time mortality raged to such an intolerable degree among the prisoners, that the very school boys in the streets knew the mental design of it in some measure; at least, they knew that they were starved to death. Some poor women contributed to their necessity, till their children were almost starved, and all persons of common understanding knew that they were devoted to the cruelest and worst of deaths. It was also proposed by some to make a written representation of the condition of the soldiery, and the officers to sign it, and that it should be couched in such terms, as though they were apprehensive that the General was imposed upon by his officers, in their daily returns to him of the state and condition of the prisoners; and that therefore the officers, moved with compassion, were constrained to communicate to him the facts relative to them, nothing doubting but that they would meet with a speedy redress; but this proposal was most generally negatived also, and for much the same reason offered in the other case; for it was conjectured that Gen. Howe's indignation would be moved against such officers as should attempt to whip him over his officers' backs; that he would discern that himself was really struck at, and not the officers who made the daily returns; and therefore self-preservation deterred the officers from either petitioning or remonstrating to Gen. Howe, either verbally or in writing; as also the consideration that no valuable purpose to the distressed would be obtained.

I made several rough drafts on the subject, one of which I exhibited to the colonels Magaw, Miles and Atlee, and they said that they would consider the matter; soon after I called on them, and some of the gentlemen informed me that they had written to the general on the subject, and I concluded that the gentlemen thought it best that they should write without me, as there was such spirited aversion subsisting between the British and me.[1]

Colonel Allen went on to theorize that the release of the prisoners was motivated by the victories that General Washington had over the British at Trenton and Princeton. Allen supposed that the two victories by Washington had awakened General Howe to a sense of his own vulnerability and a renewed sense of conscience over the treatment of prisoners of war, the most immediate effect of which was to bring about an instant release of the soldiers held in New York. However, the facts on the ground don't quite jibe with this proposition. Fitch personally witnessed the prisoners being taken

[1] De Puy, *Ethan Allen and the Green Mountain Heroes of '76*, pp. 256-258.

aboard ship on the 24th of December, but the first of Washington's great victories did not come until a day later. Obviously Howe, on the 24th, would not have anticipated the surprise attack and American victory at Trenton, or the later attack on Princeton.

More likely, the petition referred to by Colonel Ethan Allen had the desired impact on General Howe. Captain Alexander Graydon, captured at the fall of Fort Washington, was assigned to deliver this petition, which was prepared and signed by Colonels Magaw, Miles, and Atlee. Capt. Graydon, in his memoirs, later wrote that:

The representation which had been submitted to General Howe in behalf of the suffering prisoners was more successful than had been expected. The propositions had been considered by Sir William Howe, and he was disposed to accede to them. These were that the men should be sent within our lines, where they should be receipted for, and an equal number of the prisoners in our hands returned in exchange. Our men, no longer soldiers (their terms for which they had enlisted having expired) and too debilitated for service, gave a claim to sound men, immediately fit to take the field, and there was moreover great danger that if they remained in New York the disease with which they were infected might be spread throughout the city. At any rate hope was admitted into the mansions of despair, the prison doors were thrown open, and the soldiers who were yet alive and capable of being moved were conveyed to our nearest posts, under the care of our regimental surgeons, to them a fortunate circumstance, since it enabled them to exchange the land of bondage for that of liberty.[1]

It is quite possible that the 200 prisoners sent south, referred to by Fitch in his entry of December 21, contained some of Graydon's own Pennsylvania troops, captured during the fall of Fort Washington. The embarkation of the prisoners that occurred on December 24th was the release of about 225 surviving privates and non-commissioned officers from New England who were taken at the battles on Long Island, Fort Washington, and other places. At Albany Pier they boarded the British transport that we will later learn was named the *Glasgow*, bound for Connecticut. All, except for perhaps a few, of the

---

[1] Dandridge, *American Prisoners of the Revolution*, p. 31.

remaining soldiers of Huntington's Regiment were in this group. The officers of the regiment had not endured the hardships of the rank-and-file, and were not among these exchanged prisoners. Many of them would not be repatriated for many months.

To sum up this sad chapter in the story of the captivity of the American Prisoners taken on Long Island, Danske Dandridge, the author of *American Prisoners of the Revolution* in 1910, wrote:

> *Of all the places of torment provided for these poor men the churches seem to have been the worst, and they were probably the scenes of the most brutal cruelty that was inflicted upon these unfortunate beings by the wicked and heartless men, in whose power they found themselves. Whether it was because the knowledge that they were thus desecrating buildings dedicated to the worship of God and instruction in the Christian duties of mercy and charity, had a peculiarly hardening effect upon the jailers and guards employed by the British, or whether it was merely because of their unfitness for human habitation, the men confined in these buildings perished fast and miserably. We cannot assert that no prisoners shut up in the churches in New York lived to tell the awful tale of their sufferings, but we do assert that in all our researches we have never yet happened upon any record of a single instance of a survivor living to reach his home.[1]*

Had Dandridge in 1910 had the benefits of the research aids and historical material easily available today, he might have found that, indeed, some prisoners did make it home, but not many. Various writers have estimated that 1,500 to 2,000 out of the 4,000 prisoners taken on Long Island and at Fort Washington died in the churches, sugarhouses, and prison ships of New York. It is not within the scope of this work to determine a better overall estimate, but research has revealed that some of the men from Huntington's Regiment did survive the captivity and returned home.

But we have digressed from the ongoing odyssey of the men of the 17th, now placed aboard the *Glasgow*, bound for home and freedom in Connecticut. Fitch wrote in his *Narrative* that "...a large number were embarked on board a ship in order to be sent to New

---

[1] Dandridge, *American Prisoners of the Revolution*, p. 16.

England. What privates of the 17th Regiment remained living were included in this number, but about one half of them had already perished in the churches of New York."[1] We should feel hopeful for the ultimate survival of these men after all they had endured, but the trip on the *Glasgow* was not to be the joyful, short cruise across Long Island Sound to freedom these poor afflicted wretches must have expected, and certainly deserved.

However, before we go on to the next chapter in the saga of the men of the 17th, there is an epilogue to the sordid tale of the imprisonment of the American soldiers in New York during the fall of 1776. The following story is provided to offer solace to the reader who might wish that justice had been meted out to the British commissaries of prisoners, jailers, and guards responsible for the gross mistreatment and the massive death toll of the men in their custody. The Middle Dutch Church, soon after January 1, 1777, and now emptied of its inmates, was:

> *...turned into a riding school for training dragoon horses. The floor was taken up and the area covered with tan bark. A pole ran across the middle of the church for the horses to leap over. The glass was taken from the windows, and the shutters unhung. The fence around the church was torn down, and the private* [burial] *vaults were ruthlessly opened and lifeless bodies of strangers and soldiers cast in, thus adding insult to injury.*[2]

> *...the riding-school was opened for the first time on the Sabbath, as if in defiance of the Lord of the Sabbath, or as if in contempt of the pious souls who worshiped their Maker in that house of prayer. The day was hot. In the forenoon a vessel arrived from England, with powder, balls and other munitions of war. She anchored in the East River opposite the city. About 4 P.M. a cloud, black dark, and threatening was seen from the summit of Snake Hill, in the Jerseys. It crossed the Hudson and hovered over the city. A crash was heard which shook the world. A red-hot shot from the battery of heaven entered the magazine; the ship was blown into oblivion. The good Whigs in town and*

---

[1] *Fitch*, p. 149.
[2] "Desecration of the Dutch Churches in New York During the Revolutionary War," Onderdonk, *Long Island and New York in Olden Times*.

county exclaimed: The eye of Omnipotence directed that thunderbolt.[1]

Our pious, Puritan forefathers would not have doubted for a minute that divine justice had come to bear that day. It took the form of a lightening bolt that blew up a British munitions ship in retaliation for the desecration of the Middle Dutch Church. We, today, find some comfort at the possibility of divine retribution as well.

The Middle Dutch Church was left in a ruined condition for some years after the war. It wasn't until 1790, that the church was fully restored and rededicated by one of its former pastors, the Reverend Doctor Livingston. In 1839, the 50th anniversary of Washington's inauguration was celebrated at the church, presided over by John Quincy Adams. However, the building would function as a church for only a few more years until August 11, 1844, when the last service was conducted there.

The Middle Dutch Church building was next leased by the U. S. Government, and on January 28, 1845, opened as the New York Post Office. It continued in this capacity for about 30 years before the Post Office found newer quarters, and the old building found its final purpose: this time for commercial shops. What was left of the Middle Dutch Church was finally torn down in 1882 to make room for the Mutual Life Insurance Company building. Most recently, the original site of the Middle Dutch Church was entombed by the 60-story, 813-foot aluminum and glass tower of the Chase Manhattan Bank headquarters, built in 1961.

Somehow, two inscribed, red sandstone tablets from the Middle Dutch Church, possibly removed during the renovations for the Post Office in 1844, came into the possession of Civil War General George H. Sharpe. He presented them to the Old Dutch Church of Kingston, New York, where he was a member, in 1876. The two tablets were inlaid in the exterior wall of the Kingston church and to this day occupy an honored position on either side of the main entrance facing Main Street.

The tablets were possibly the original dedicatory plaques for the Middle Dutch Church, made when that church was dedicated in 1729.

---

[1] Grant Thorburn, "Tales of the Prison Sugarhouse in Liberty Street, New York, or Anecdotes of the Revolution," *The Hartford Daily Courant*, Jan. 23, 1854, p. 2, http://proquest.umi.com/

Both are in Dutch, with separate marble plaques beneath them inscribed with the English translations. On the left is a quote from Psalm 26:8: "I have loved the habitation of thy house," with the date, "1729." On the right side, from Isaiah 56:7: "My house shall be called a house of prayer," also with the date, "1729." It is probably no coincidence that General Sharpe presented these special memorial gifts to the Kingston church in 1876, exactly one-hundred years after the American prisoners of war had been interned in the Middle Dutch Church in New York City.[1]

The other relic that survived the demise of the Middle Dutch Church was its bell. It had originally been ordered from Amsterdam by Abraham De Peyster, former chief justice of the Province of New York, shortly before his death in 1728. It was delivered and installed in the church in 1731. The bell has since become known as New York's Liberty Bell because it was rung upon the arrival of the news of the signing of the Declaration of Independence in New York on July 9, 1776. When the British invaded the City two months later, it was removed and hidden by the descendants of Abraham De Peyster for the duration of the war.

The bell was returned to its steeple after the British evacuated New York in 1783, and was rung out when President Washington was inaugurated, and for the inauguration and death of every president since. It was removed from the Middle Dutch Church once and for all, when the building was converted to the New York Post Office. The bell was reinstalled in the church which was built to replace the Middle Dutch Church at a different location, and then in two succeeding church structures. It is now in everyday use in the belfry of what is known as the Middle Collegiate Church, located at 2nd Avenue and 7th Street, where it was installed in 1949.[2] It is somewhat ironic that the bell that became known as New York's Liberty Bell came from a building that had been used as the instrument of destruction of so many young lives. But at least it had not been present and rung while the British had been using the Middle Dutch Church for that purpose.

---

[1] Donna M. Light, unpublished notes for the *One Third Millennium Celebration,* (Old Dutch Church of Kingston, NY: 1992).
[2] http://middlechurch.org

The Middle Dutch Church and Sugar House in the foreground
(courtesy New York Public Library)

9. Hardship, Ill Usage, Hunger and Cold

If the estimate is correct that nearly half of all the American prisoners held in New York during the fall of 1776 perished, then it is likely that no more than 80 to 100 men from Huntington's 17th Continental Regiment were still alive to board the *Glasgow* on December 24. It was reported that there were 225 on board in all: the rest of the men were other prisoners from New England who had been taken at Long Island, Fort Washington, and other battles during the retreat of the army from New York.

The *Glasgow* was a British man-of-war of twenty guns and a complement of 150 sailors. It had been on this side of the Atlantic for some time, and had already seen significant action off Rhode Island in the spring of 1776. One of the 225 prisoners on board the *Glasgow* was Thomas Catlin, a resident of Litchfield, Connecticut, who was taken by the British at New York on September 15, 1776. He reported that:

> *...about the 25th of December, 1776, he and about two hundred and twenty-five others were put on board the* Glasgow *at New York to be carried to Connecticut for exchange. They were on board eleven days, and kept on black, coarse broken bread, and less pork than before. Twenty-eight died during these eleven days! They were treated with great cruelty, and had no fire for sick or well. They were crowded between decks, and many died through hardship, ill usage, hunger and cold.[1]*

How would it have been possible for a voyage from New York City to Connecticut to have taken eleven days, a distance of no more than 50 miles? Lieutenant Oliver Babcock of the 10th Continental

---

[1] Payne Kenyon Kilbourne, *Sketches and Chronicles of the Town of Litchfield* (Hartford: Case, Lockwood & Co., 1859), p. 102, http://persi.heritagequestonline.com/...

(Connecticut) Regiment was taken prisoner at the fall of Fort
Washington, and brought to Hampden Hall to be housed with the
other American officers on November 19.   Somehow, perhaps
because he too was ill or wounded, he was exchanged at the same
time as the privates and was on board the *Glasgow*. Babcock kept an
abbreviated, daily log during the voyage that explained the length of
time the prisoners were kept on board, and provided significant details
regarding the trip:

> *December 24: Drew provision & was exchanged by Mr. Loring.*
>   *25: went on board the ship glasco, James Craig,*
>   *master- dined with Mrs. Cassander in Company*
>   *Lieut. Stratten*
>   *26: Get one dozen wine for the sick- Rainy icey*
>   *weather- wind N. East. Bot bread & spilt it in the*
>   *dark*
>   *27: Set sail from N. York & came up to Blackwell's*
>   *Point, dropt anchor, went Longsland* [Long Island]
>   *shore & buried 7 men.*
>   *28: Went up to Hallets Cove- went on shore and buried*
>   *2 dead*
>   *29, 30, 31: Lay at Hallets Cove, wind NE- went on*
>   *shore- buried the dead-bought 1 sheep*
> *January   3: Landed our poor sick men at Milford &c*
>   *7: Was admitted to Both houses of Assembly and*
>   *Related the sufferings of my poor fellow prisoners at*
>   *New York.*[1]

Based on a combination of the information provided by Fitch, Catlin,
and Babcock, it is possible to reconstruct the voyage of the *Glasgow*
to Connecticut. Oliver Babcock was an officer and as such was
apparently allowed to go on shore on the evening of December 25 to
dine with Mrs. Cassander and Lt. Stratton, neither of whom has been
identified. Stratton is mentioned later on in Fitch's diary, and,
therefore, must have remained in New York. For three days the
Glasgow did not move. It remained docked at the pier waiting for
favorable wind and weather to sail.

---

[1] *Fitch,* note, p. 94.

After leaving the Albany Pier on December 27, the *Glasgow* sailed north up the East River past the southern tip of Blackwell's Island, which Babcock refers to as "Blackwell's Point." Blackwell's Island is known today as Roosevelt Island. The seven men buried on the shore of Long Island opposite Blackwell's Island were the first to die after setting sail. Their bodies may have been accumulating over the previous three days while the ship sat in harbor at the Albany Pier. On the 28th, the *Glasgow* continued its voyage north and anchored in Hallet's Cove in Queens, just south of the entrance to Hell's Gate. Prisoners, probably escorted by the crew, went ashore there and buried two more men that had died that day.

The *Glasgow* would have required a southerly or westerly wind to navigate the difficult passage through Hell's Gate. Another northeast wind forced them to stay at anchor for three more days. While there, they buried more dead. Babcock does not indicate what happened on January 1st or 2nd, but the *Glasgow* must have been slowly negotiating Hell's Gate and sailing east up Long Island Sound towards Milford, where they landed on January 3.

Although Babcock survived the trip long enough to describe the horrors of captivity in New York to the Connecticut General Assembly on January 7, he did not live much longer. He succumbed to smallpox, a disease that he had likely acquired at Hampden Hall, or on board the *Glasgow*, and died on January 24. Two of his children died of smallpox soon after; the impact of the disease now extending to the innocent families of the prisoners.

What happened when the *Glasgow* disgorged its woeful cargo onto the Connecticut shore at Milford was well documented later on by local historians:

Late in the afternoon of January 1, 1777, some of Milford's residents sighted a British man-of-war, flying a flag of truce, putting into harbor in the vicinity of Fort Trumbull. A heavy fog and waning light soon obscured the vessel from view, and it was never seen again. That same evening Captain Isaac Miles, who lived near the shore, heard the sound of tramping feet and many voices. He found his front yard filled with ragged, shivering men, most of them desperately ill. They were prisoners of war who had been set ashore from the man-of-war when it was discovered that they were sick with small-pox. With no thought for his own or his neighbors' safety, Captain Miles made hasty arrangements to shelter the men from the intense cold, and to give them such medical care as was then available. The two-hundred were housed in private residences until the town hall could be converted into an emergency hospital. Captain Stephen Stow, a resident, knowing full well that he was endangering his own life, offered to nurse these sick men. Dr. Elias Carrington volunteered his services as physician. Captain Stow made a will, put his affairs in order, bade farewell to his family and friends, and began his task of mercy. Within a month he and forty-six of his patients had succumbed to the dread disease. The full extent of Captain Stow's heroism can be appreciated only when it is considered that in 1777 little was known about fighting this plague, and its death toll was appalling.[1]

From the *History of the Colony of New Haven*, we have another account, which provides further details of the landing of the *Glasgow*:

On Wednesday, the 1st of January, 1777, a flag of truce vessel arrived at Milford, from New York, having on board 200 American prisoners. They had been for some time confined in a prison ship. More than half of them were sick at the time they were landed, and many of these but just alive. Twenty had died on the passage from New York. The town made comfortable provision for them, but before the first of February, 46 of those who were landed alive had died. These soldiers were all buried in a line near the south corner of the grave yard.[2]

The reader may have noticed that there is a discrepancy between the date of landing of the *Glasgow* reported by Lt. Babcock and that claimed by the two local histories. The date offered by Lt. Babcock in his diary, as well as the eleven days for the journey reported by Thomas Catlin (calculated from December 24th, the date Fitch claimed the men boarded the *Glasgow*), is probably the correct date. Both Babcock and Catlin were on board the Glasgow and should be considered reliable witnesses. The two quoted histories were written

---

[1] Omar W. Platt, *History of Milford, Connecticut, 1639-1939* (Bridgeport, CT: Press of Braunworth & Co., 1939), pp. 62-63, http://persi.heritagequestonline.com/...
[2] Edward R. Lambert, *History of the Colony of New Haven* (New Haven: Hitchcock & Stafford, 1838), p. 136, http://persi.heritagequestonline.com/...

some decades after the fact, therefore January 3 was the more likely landing date, rather than January 1.

At the southwest corner of the old Milford cemetery, a monument was erected in memory of Captain Stephen Stow who ministered to the prisoners of the *Glasgow*, and the 46 men who died after reaching Milford. The names of the men are listed in *Historical Sketches of the Town of Milford*.[1] Among them are several whose names match the names of those missing from Huntington's Regiment after the Battle of Long Island. However, some of the names are common, and their military units are not identified, so we can't be absolutely certain those are men from the 17th, but it is likely that they are. From the list of the 46, the home towns or states of residence of the men were given, and those names are provided on the left side of the table below. On the right are the probable matches with the names of the missing from Huntington's Regiment:

DIED AT MILFORD	HUNTINGTON'S REGIMENT
John Smith, Chatham:	John Smith, Capt. Tyler's Co.
Samuel Fuller, Norwich:	Samuel Fuller, Capt. Brewster's Co.
John White, Mass.:	John White, Capt. E. F. Bissell's Co.
Joseph Arnold, Chatham:	Joseph Arnold, Capt. Tyler's Co.
Abel Hart, Farmington:	Abel Hart, Capt. Percival's Co.
Sergt. Smith, Mass.:	Sgt. Moses Smith, Capt. Trowbridge's Co.
Daniel Farnham, Windham:	Sgt. Daniel Farnam, Capt. Trowbridge's Co.
Sergt. Wright, Bolton:	Sgt. Ebenezer Wright, Capt. O. Bissell's Co.

The identities of most of the men from this list have been determined with some degree of certainty from other records, and that information will be provided below; unfortunately, John Smith, John White, Samuel Fuller, and Daniel Farnam have such common names that it was difficult to differentiate between them and other men of the same name.

☞ **Joseph Arnold** was perhaps the son of Simon and Hannah Arnold, who was born at Haddam, Connecticut, on August 2, 1738. He was a private in Capt. Tyler's Company. According to Milford vital records, "he was taken dead from a British ship, Jan. [ ], 1777."

---

[1] George Hare Ford, *Historical Sketches of the Town of Milford* (New Haven: Tuttle, Morehouse & Taylor Co., 1914), p. 24.

This would have made him one of the last to perish aboard the *Glasgow* before it landed at Milford.

☞   **Abel Hart**, of Farmington was a private in Capt. Percival's Company. He was the son of Thomas Hart of Farmington, born September 5, 1756.[1]

☞   **Sgt. Smith** was likely Sgt. Moses Smith, of Captain Trowbridge's Company, who had helped Ensign Bradford carry his helpless shipmates aboard the *Glasgow* just two weeks before. He was probably the Moses Smith who was baptized at Athol, Worcester County, Massachusetts, on July 14, 1751, the son of Aaron and Abigail Smith. He married Elizabeth Lombard, April 29, 1773, at Athol. They had one child born December 12, 1774, and a second was born November 19, 1776, while Moses was imprisoned in New York. This Moses Smith's death was recorded by the town of Athol for December 6, 1776, as he was "upon his way from the Army at York."[2] If the identification is correct, the date of death was likely an error, and he died at Milford shortly after January 3, 1777.

☞   **Sergt. Wright** of Bolton, Connecticut, was Sergeant Ebenezer Wright of Captain Ozias Bissell's Company in Huntington's Regiment. He was among those from Bolton who were listed as exempt from the payment of certain taxes to the State for service during 1775.[3]   He was captured at the Battle of Long Island on August 27, 1776. Lt. Fitch described in his diary for that day's events how he had found Wright with a broken leg and carried him down the hill to place him in the shade of a tree in the aftermath of the fight on Battle Hill. Lt. Fitch also reported in his diary entry of October 13, 1776, how Sergeant Wright had lost his leg, but was expected to recover. Since he had been seriously injured during the battle, Wright had probably been kept at the hospital at New Utrecht on Long Island for a time before being sent to be housed with the rest of the prisoners.

The son of an Ebenezer Wright later claimed in 1854, that his father was Sgt. Ebenezer Wright of Huntington's Regiment, but also claimed his father had a Connecticut militia service as Lt. Ebenezer Wright during the same time that Sgt. Wright was a prisoner in New

---

[1] CT State Library, *Barbour Collection.*
[2] *Massachusetts Vital Records, 1600's-1800's,* Family Tree Maker, CD #220; *Marriage Index: Massachusetts, 1633-1850,* Family Tree Maker, CD #231.
[3] *Lists and Returns of Connecticut Men in the Revolution.* p.1.

York.[1] He also said that his father had been from Wethersfield, Connecticut, before the war. However, the definitive identity of Sgt. Ebenezer Wright was established by the record that Sergeant Wright, of Bolton, perished of smallpox at Milford in January 1777, having been one of those on board the disease breeding *Glasgow*.[2] That record is reinforced by the church records of Bolton, Connecticut, which provide that Ebenezer Wright died January 8, 1777, in the army, at 26 years of age. This would have made his date of birth about 1751. Unfortunately, neither Connecticut vital records nor church records have a birth record for an Ebenezer Wright born at that time, but he was likely a member of one of three Wright families that, according to Bolton church records, were living at Bolton at the time.

A second list of men who must have been aboard the *Glasgow* is found in the *Record of Service of Connecticut Men in the War of the Revolution*.[3] The list is prefaced by the statement, "Two hundred prisoners from New York arrived at Milford, Jan. 1, '77, of whom, twenty died on the passage and twenty within a week after landing. The following were from Connecticut:" This statement is rather ambiguous, and leaves us to decide whether the names on this list were survivors, or a list of the dead. However, some of the men on the list are determined to have survived by other records, and some were found to have died. The only safe conclusion to make is that the following list is an incomplete list of the names of some of the men from Connecticut who were on board the *Glasgow*; either survivors, or dead. Again, the names given here are a part of the list for which we can find corresponding names from the list of men missing from Huntington's Regiment after the Battle of Long Island:

ARRIVED AT MILFORD	HUNTINGTON'S REGIMENT
John Atwood, Wethersfield:	John Atwood, Capt. E. F. Bissells's Co.
Elijah Boardman:	Cpl. Elisha Boardman, Capt. E.F.Bissells' Co.
Aaron Drake, East Windsor:	Aaron Drake, Capt. Hubbard's Co.
Jacob Sterling, Lyme:	Jacob Sterling, Capt. Jewett's Co.
Erastus Humphry, Simsbury:	Erastus Humphrey, Capt. E. F. Bissell's Co.
Samuel Fuller, Norwich:	Samuel Fuller, Capt. Brewster's Co.

---

[1] NARA, Series M805, Roll 891,Revolutionary War Pension Application, X866.
[2] Ford, *Historical Sketches of the Town of Milford*, p. 24.
[3] *Record of Service of Connecticut Men in the War of the Revolution*, p. 120.

Peleg Edwards, Norwich:	Cpl. Peleg Edwards, Capt. Jewett's Co.
Thomas Maddison, New London:	Thomas Matterson, Capt. Brewster's Co.
Benjamin Hills, Glastonbury:	Benjamin Hills, Capt. Hubbard's Co.
Levi Loveland, Glastonbury:	Levi Loveland, Capt. Hubbard's Co.
Nathan Whitney, Chatham:	Nathan Whiting, Capt. Hubbard's Co.
George Foster, Killingly:	George Foster, Capt. Trowbridge's Co.
Ebenezar Keys, Killingly:	Ebenezer Keyes, Capt. Trowbridge's Co.
Daniel Fotham, Windham:	Sgt. Daniel Farnam, Capt. Trowbridge's Co.
Daniel Yearington, Preston:	David Yerrington, Capt. Jewett's Co.

Samuel Fuller, of Norwich, was probably Private Samuel Fuller of Capt. Brewster's Company who was reported missing after the Battle of Long Island. His name appears on both the previous lists, but his presence on the first list confirms his death at Milford. Daniel "Fotham" on the second list, was most likely **Sgt. Daniel Farnam** (or Farnham), of Windham, from Capt. Trowbridge's Company who was reported missing after the Battle of Long Island and was also reported on the first list to have died at Milford. Other than the fact that both these men died at Milford, no other information has been found.

John Atwood, the first name on the second list, was the son of Oliver and Dorothy (Curtis) Atwood, baptized April 20, 1755. He was on the Lexington Alarm list for Wethersfield in April 1775. He next enlisted on July 9, 1775, in Captain Abraham Filer's (Tyler's) Company in Huntington's 8th Connecticut Regiment. In 1776 he enlisted in Capt. E. F. Bissell's Company in Huntington's 17th Continental Regiment, and was reported missing at the Battle of Long Island. According to the *Families of Ancient Wethersfield*, he "was a Revol[utionary]. soldier and d[ied] soon after his disch[arge] from confinement in the Sugar House Prison in N. Y. City."[1] We can conclude John Atwood was another victim of the New York prisons and the *Glasgow*, although he may have survived long enough to reach home.

Elijah Boardman is probably the Corporal Elisha Boardman on the return of the missing from Huntington's Regiment. However, the complete roll of Capt. E. F. Bissell's Company taken before the Battle of Long Island, contains the name Corporal Elijah Bordman. These are undoubtedly the same man. From the *History of Ancient*

---

[1] Henry R. Stiles, *Families of Ancient Wethersfield* (New York: 1904; Electronic edition, Family Tree Maker, CD #515), Vol. II, p. 39.

Wethersfield we find the following information: "Boardman, Ilijah, b. 1756; was in Lexington. Alarm Co., 1775; served at the siege of Boston, and was taken prisoner at New York; Sgt. in Capt. Watson's Co., Col. S. B. Webb's Additional Regiment, enlisted for the war, April 22, 1777; promoted Sgt., November 20, 1777; cr. to Continental Army, August 1778; Ensign, 4th Co., 1st Militia Rgt. from Wethersfield, January 1780; later removed to Harford, where he became keeper of the jail."

Although the above information would seem to be firm evidence as to the identity of Elijah Boardman, the writer believes that the information combines the record of two separate individuals by the same name. Revolutionary War pension files contain two Elijah Boardmans from Wethersfield, Connecticut, that might fit the profile: W10433 and W15754. The two applications were made by the widows of the men, both of whom had died some years before. Both women had only sketchy memories when it came to the actual revolutionary war service of their husbands, so no certain, firm identification could be made based on the pension files.

The roll of names in Captain Joel Clark's Company in Huntington's 8th Connecticut Regiment in 1775 lists the names "Elijah Bordman 1st", and "Elijah Bordman 2nd".[1] This is understood by one writer to mean that there were two men by that name, one was older, and the other younger, but they were not Senior and Junior. After the former period of service, the records of the two men diverge, but both continued to serve after 1776. The only thing certain, as it relates to our story, is that both Elijah Boardmans survived the war, and did not die as a result of captivity in New York. However, that said, this writer believes that the Elijah Boardman, W10433, whose widow was Mercy, is the man of Huntington's Regiment who survived the prisons of New York and the voyage on the *Glasgow*. The widow of the other Elijah (W15754) makes a strong claim for a conflicting record of service for her husband in Canada in 1776, rather than in New York during the same time period.

"Our" Elijah Boardman was most likely the son of Elnathan and Jerusha (Goffe) Boardman of Rocky Hill, then a section of Wethersfield, Connecticut. He married Mercy Nott, the daughter of Abraham and Mercy (Dimmock) Nott, on September 16, 1781. He reenlisted on April 22, 1777, in Colonel S. B. Webb's "additional

---

[1] *Record of Service of Connecticut Men in the War of the Revolution*, p. 87.

regiment," Connecticut Line, and ultimately was discharged June 9, 1783, due to poor health. He went on to become keeper of the Hartford jail, and a landlord of the City Hall Tavern, both in the same building. He and his wife had six children. Elijah died September 4, 1808, and his wife, Mercy, died February 23, 1848. Both are buried at Rocky Hill, Connecticut.[1]

👉 **Aaron Drake** died on January 16, 1777. The death is recorded in the vital records of Windsor, Connecticut, where he probably died, two weeks after the *Glasgow* landed. He was born April 13, 1751, in Windsor, the son of Josiah and Hannah (Wilson) Drake. He had first enlisted in Captain Charles Ellsworth's 5th Company in Huntington's 8th Connecticut Regiment, on July 16, 1775, and then in Captain Elizur Hubbard's Company in Huntington's 17th Regiment in 1776.

👉 **Jacob Sterling**, from Lyme, was Private Jacob Sterling, of Capt Jewett's Company, whom we met in Chapter 2. Jacob was one of the survivors of the *Glasgow*, as he deposed in his pension application in 1818. We will relate the rest of his story later.

👉 **Erastus Humphrey** was a private in Capt. E. F. Bissell's Company. According to the Humphreys genealogy, he died in 1776, after being reported missing at the Battle of Long Island. Since his name appears on the list above, he must have died before reaching home, but after the landing of the *Glasgow*. He was born February 12, 1753, the son of Oliver and Sarah (Garrett) Humphreys of Simsbury, Connecticut. The couple lost two sons in 1776; the other son, Oliver, died at the Battle of Harlem Heights during the American Army's retreat from New York.[2]

👉 **Corporal Peleg Edwards** of Captain Joseph Jewett's Company was from Preston (next to Norwich), Connecticut. He was the son of William and Mary Edwards, born March 5, 1755, in Preston.[3] According to DAR Volume 13, page 17, he was reported missing after the Battle of Long Island and "was among the exchanged prisoners, scourged with smallpox, who were left without food and shelter at Milford that winter night, Jan. 1, 1777."

👉 The name **Thomas Maddison** closely corresponds to the name Thomas Matterson who was reported missing from Captain

[1] Stiles, *Families of Ancient Wethersfield*, Vol. II, pp. 117, 119, 120.
[2] *The Humphreys Family in America*, pp. 300, 301, 314.
[3] CT State Library, *Barbour Collection*.

Brewster's Company after the Battle of Long Island. Milford vital records give the name Thomas Madison, of New London, who died Jan. [ ], 1777. The three spellings must have been for the same man, and he was another casualty of the *Glasgow*.

☛ **Benjamin Hills** of Glastonbury was listed as missing after the Battle of Long Island from Captain Hubbard's Company. According to the *Barbour Collection,* Benjamin Hills was born in Glastonbury, Connecticut, on December 14, 1754, the son of Benjamin and Martha (Damon) Hills. No other reference in Connecticut vital records was found, but the Damon genealogy says that he died on January 12, 1777, in Durham, Connecticut.[1] If that is so, Benjamin got as far as Durham, where he probably died of smallpox while on his way home to Glastonbury.

☛ **Private Levi Loveland** of Glastonbury, was from Capt. Elizur Hubbard's Company. He was captured at the Battle of Long Island, and kept a prisoner until he was exchanged at Milford, Connecticut in January 1777. His widow applied for his pension benefits in 1845, stating that her husband died in 1830, therefore, we may conclude that Levi Loveland survived his experience as a prisoner.[2]

☛ The name **Nathan Whitney**, of Chatham, most closely corresponds to the name Nathan Whiting of Capt. Hubbard's Company who was reported missing after the Battle of Long Island. No further information based on either spelling has been found.

☛ **George Foster** was a private in Captain Caleb Trowbridge's Company. According to his father, Josiah Foster, of Killingly, Connecticut, George and "many others were landed at Milford, where he lay sick with the smallpox until the 1st day of the next March from whence he was removed to Killingly and there lay in a languishing condition until the 28th day of April, and there died."[3]

☛ **Ebenezar Keys** (or Keyes, Key, Keis) was reported missing from Capt. Trowbridge's Company after the Battle of Long Island. He may have been the Ebenezer Key, born May 1751 in Killingly, Connecticut. If this identification is correct, he was a survivor and later married Anna Harris on December 20, 1787, in Plainfield.[4]

---

[1] Richard A. Damon, *The Damon Family of Reading, Mass.* (Amherst, MA: R. A. Damon, 1999).
[2] NARA, Series M805, Roll 539, Revolutionary War Pension Application, W9145.
[3] CT State Library, *Connecticut Archives*; Rev. War Ser. I, Vol. XIII; 391, 392.
[4] CT State Library, *Church Records Slip Index.*

☞   **Daniel Yearington** was a survivor whose identity was
definitively established by the pension file of Daniel Yarrington of
Preston, Connecticut.[1] He testified that he was a private in Capt.
Joseph Jewett's Company at the Battle of Long Island, and was taken
prisoner. He is probably the "David" Yerrington whose name appears
among the missing from Jewett's Company after the Battle of Long
Island. Daniel later reenlisted at New Milford, Connecticut, in the
regiment of Colonel Heman Swift in 1777 for the term of three years.
He was in the Battle of Monmouth in 1778, and discharged at
Springfield, New Jersey, in 1780. In 1818, he was living in the town
of Sidney, Delaware County, New York. No family information was
provided by the pension file.

☞   Although his name is not on the two lists above, **Jesse Swaddle**
of Chatham, Connecticut, was named in the East Hampton Church
Records as having died returning from captivity, December 1776.[2]
Perhaps he was one of the men reported by Lt. Babcock as having
been buried on Long Island during the voyage of the *Glasgow*, and his
death reported by survivors. Jesse Swaddle was a corporal in Capt.
Abraham Tyler's Company, and listed as missing after the Battle of
Long Island. Jesse was born January 30, 1739/40, the son of John and
Susannah (Welmut) Swaddle.[3]

Although not saying so specifically in their Revolutionary War
Pension Records, several men made statements that indicate they
survived the hell-ship voyage of the *Glasgow* too. Sergeant
Theophilus Huntington of Captain Jonathan Brewster's Company
deposed in his pension application that:

> ...*many of the prisoners died in consequence of the barbarous
> treatment received from the enemy, that he with the surviving ones
> were released by exchange or otherwise, on or about the first of
> January, 1777* [at Milford, Connecticut, as stated on a separate
> document in his pension file]. *That he was sick for some time
> before he was released by the enemy, and for a long time
> afterwards particularly with the smallpox, which disease he
> believes was designedly spread among the American prisoners by*

[1] NARA, Series M805, Roll 894, Revolutionary War Pension Application, S45478.
[2] CT State Library, *Church Records Slip Index.*
[3] CT State Library, *Barbour Collection.*

the enemy. That his constitution was so much impaired by the diseases contracted in the army, that he has not since enjoyed a sound state of health.[1]

Unfortunately for Sgt. Huntington, the Connecticut General Assembly would not grant him compensation for the medical expenses he incurred during his illness, stating that he did not contract smallpox until after he had returned home.[2]

Private Peter Way, of Capt. Joseph Jewett's Company, also deposed in his pension record that:

...on the 27th day of August, 1776 he was taken a prisoner by the common enemy while in the line of his duty and that he remained a prisoner more than four months or until some time in January, 1777, when he was exchanged & landed at Milford in the State of Connecticut.[3]

Private Elijah Stanton of Capt. Timothy Percival's Company testified in his pension application that he was in the Battle of Long Island and that he was:

...wounded and taken prisoner at the battle and carried on board the prison ship and from there into New York where he was kept a prisoner for about five months before they were discharged. They were put on board a sloop at New York and kept there eleven days, and there a man brought on board sick of the smallpox and almost all the prisoners took it and died. Applicant had it. He thinks it was the object of the British to kill them by this maneuver. They were then set on shore, and applicant got home and the second day after he got home, he broke out of the smallpox. Got home 9th day of January, 1777. He suffered much of the time from his wound and for a long time was unable to do hard duty as a soldier.[4]

---

[1] NARA, Series M805, Roll 457, Revolutionary War Pension Application, S44960.
[2] CT State Library, *Connecticut Archives*, Rev. War Ser. I, Vol. XVI, #866.
[3] NARA, Series M805, Roll 844, Revolutionary War Pension Application, W18228.
[4] NARA, Series M805, Roll 766, Revolutionary War Pension Application, S14623.

☞   **Private John Vandeusen**, of Captain Jonathan Brewster's Company, later petitioned the General Assembly of Connecticut for wages that he had not received while captive of the British from August 27, 1776, when he was taken prisoner, until "the 3ʳᵈ day of January, 1777, when he was released at Milford, about 80 miles from Norwich, the place of his abode." The General Assembly granted his petition, and ordered the Committee of the Pay Table to give him his back wages in May 1780.[1] This must have been the same John Vandeusen who reenlisted almost immediately, on February 20, 1777, in Colonel Jedediah Huntington's 1ˢᵗ Regiment/Connecticut Line, and served until discharged on February 29, 1780.[2] Although *Connecticut Men in the War of the Revolution* provided his place of residence as Danbury, he was claimed by Norwich for service during those years.[3]

Among those who wrote about their captivity in their pension applications were those who provided an approximate date of release that corresponds to the voyage of the *Glasgow*. By 1818, when most of them applied for their pensions, they were old men, and specific dates might have been difficult to recall. But, based on the dates of release as they remembered them late in life, it can be reasonably concluded that they too were on board the *Glasgow*.

☞   **Private Zadock Pratt**, of Capt. Joseph Jewett's Company, was one of those who said that he was "taken a prisoner at the Battle at Flatbush on Long Island and in the State of New York and remained a prisoner with the British on board the *Whitby* and at the City of New York until about the first of January, 1777, when he was exchanged at New York and returned home."[4]

☞   **Sergeant Cornelius Russell**, of Captain Ebenezer Fitch Bissell's Company, deposed in his pension application that, "he was taken prisoner by the British on Long Island and continued prisoner about four months being reduced to great distress. That in the latter part of December 1776 he was exchanged... ."

☞   **Private Salmon Moulton** deposed in his pension application that after being taken aboard the *Whitby*, he "remained there he should think a month or more and was taken on shore to the hospital

---

[1] CT State Library, *Connecticut Archives*, Rev. War Ser. I, Vol. XVIII, #282-83.
[2] *Record of Service of Connecticut Men in the War of the Revolution*, p. 154.
[3] *Lists and Returns of Connecticut Men in the Revolution*, p. 74.
[4] NARA, Series M805, Roll 665, Revolutionary War Pension Application, S44263.

[at New Utrecht?] a short time and a few days before Fort Washington was taken, he was removed to New York and kept and confined in a meeting house for a time, and was kept there until he with others were suffered to go home on parole, and he returned directly to Stafford, Connecticut, where he arrived he thinks in the month of February 1777. That he thinks it was about a week [from] the time they were discharged at New York before he arrived home...."[1] Moulton was uncertain about his date of discharge from confinement. It was likely not February, but January, as the others recalled.

☞ **Private Seth Turner**, of Captain Elizur Hubbard's Company, stated in his pension application "That he was in the Battle of Flatbush on Long Island on the 27th of Aug, 1776 and was there wounded but never asked a pension [until the time of the writing of this document], and on the same day taken prisoner and was confined in prison ships and in New York till February 1777, when he was released on parole... ."[2] He too was probably aboard the *Glasgow*.

☞ We have already mentioned **Private Daniel Thomas**, who claimed in his pension application that he was held aboard the *Whitby* "on the whole for the period of five months."[3] He did not provide any of the details regarding his release, but the period of five months imprisonment more or less corresponds with the length of time the others said they were held.

☞ The *Historical Sketches* of the town of Windsor, Connecticut, provides the names of two other Windsor men besides Hezekiah Hayden who were reported to have died in captivity in New York after the Battle of Long Island: the first was **Nathaniel Lamberton**, and the second was **William Parsons**. Nathaniel Lamberton was not listed on the return of the missing after the Battle of Long Island, but was on the complete return of Capt. Ebenezer Fitch Bissell's Company before the battle. There is no explanation for Lamberton's absence from the list of the missing. He was the son of Obed and Elizabeth (Taylor) Lamberton, born October 14, 1749, in Windsor.[4] William Parsons was listed as missing from Captain Elizur Hubbard's Company. Both were said by *Historical Sketches* to have been "thrust

---

[1] NARA, Series M805, Roll 603, Revolutionary War Pension Application, S23810.
[2] NARA, Series M805, Roll 816, Revolutionary War Pension Application, S35365.
[3] NARA, Series M805, Roll 797, Revolutionary War Pension Application, S11536.
[4] CT State Library, *Barbour Collection*.

into the old *Jersey* prison ship, which was anchored at the Wallabouts, now Brooklyn, where they died of starvation."[1] This is a common piece of misinformation. For lack of precise information regarding the captivity of prisoners in New York, later writers often said that the prisoners died in the "sugarhouse," or "prison ships," The *Jersey* prison ship was not used to house prisoners until some time after the surviving prisoners of the Battle of Long Island had returned home. The *Memorial History of Hartford County* adds that both Lamberton and Parsons died on November 9, 1776.[2]

☞ The Center Church Cemetery in Clinton, Connecticut, contains the grave of **Corporal Samuel Boardman** of Captain Ebenezer Fitch Bissell's Company, "who in 11 days after his Captivity in New York departed this life Jan. 12th, 1777, aged 20 years."[3] He too must have come ashore at Milford, only to succumb to smallpox after returning home. The vital records of Middletown, Connecticut, provide that Corporal Samuel Boardman was the son of Samuel and Hannah Boardman, born January 11, 1757. He died one day after his 20th birthday.

☞ **Private Jasper Griffing** (spelled "Griffin" in *Connecticut Men in the War of the Revolution*) of Capt. Joseph Jewett's Company, "returned home to Lyme with the smallpox, of which he died 19 Jany., 1777, aged 23 years;"[4] no doubt another victim of the *Glasgow*. He was the son of Jasper and Eunice Griffing, born February 28, 1754, in Lyme, Connecticut.[5]

☞ **Private Roger Filer**, of Captain Ebenezer Fitch Bissell's Company, notable in the letter written by Lt. Jonathan Gillet for having lost a leg after being wounded in the Battle of Long Island, died two weeks after he returned home to Windsor, Connecticut, of smallpox.[6] According to Bloomfield, Connecticut, church records,

---

[1] Jabez H. Hayden, *Historical Sketches* (Windsor Locks, CT: The Windsor Locks Journal, 1900), p. 112, http://persi.heritagequestonline.com/...
[2] Trumbull, *Memorial History of Hartford County*, Vol. II, p. 513.
[3] Clinton Town History, www.freepages.genealogy.rootsweb.com
[4] Clara J. Stone, *Genealogy of the Descendants of Jasper Griffing* (New York (?): N.D., 1881), p. 44, http://persi.heritagequestonline.com/...
[5] CT State Library, *Barbour Collection*.
[6] Stiles, *The History and Genealogies of Ancient Windsor*, Vol. II, p. 276; DAR Lineage Books, Vol. 35, p. 103.

Roger Filer died January 18, 1777, at 34 years of age, no doubt another delayed victim of the *Glasgow*.[1]

☞ **Private John Kingsbury** of Plainfield, Connecticut, was 18 years old when he enlisted for service in the Revolutionary War. The Kingsbury genealogy states that he was "taken prisoner at the Battle of Long Island; kept on the prison ship at New York, and died in 1777." A similar account was provided by the Plainfield church records, saying that John Kingsbury died a prisoner early in 1777, "New Yorkward." John's clothes were sent home to his friends, and in one of his pockets was found a description of his food and sufferings, written in the form of a poem.[2] Unfortunately, the poem itself was not given. Had he died in New York, he would probably have been buried in his clothes, or they would have been disbursed to those in need. It is more likely that he died aboard the *Glasgow*, and friends saved his clothes and property to return to his family.

☞ **Private Carmi Higley,** of Captain Ebenezer Fitch Bissell's Company, was captured at the Battle of Long Island. The family genealogy recorded that he "was for some time confined in one of the New York churches, which was used as a prison; but his lot finally fell with the large number- more than twelve thousand men- who were placed in the wretched hulks of British prison-ships moored near the site of where the United States Navy Yard at Brooklyn, N. Y., now is, and were starved to death." The first part of this statement is no doubt accurate, but the second part is probably confused with the voyage of the *Glasgow*." At any rate, he was another casualty of the New York prisons, who probably died aboard the *Glasgow*, at the end of December 1776. Hester Higley settled the estate of her husband, presenting an inventory in court, on March 2, 1779. She died in 1790.[3]

☞ Although not specifically connected with either Milford or the *Glasgow*, DAR records provide that **Private Abner Fuller**[4] of Capt. E. F. Bissell's Company, and **Corporal Levi Farnum**[5] of Capt. Trowbridge's Company both died on the "prison ship." "Prison ship," is, again, likely a generic term for any place the prisoners died during

---

[1] CT State Library, *Church Records Slip Index.*
[2] Kingsbury, *The Genealogy of the Descendants of Henry Kings*bury, p. 123.
[3] Johnson, *The Higleys and Their Ancestry*, pp. 409-410.
[4] DAR Lineage Books, Vol. 59, p. 325.
[5] DAR Lineage Books, Vol. 31, p. 88.

their captivity in New York, but these two probably were among those who also died aboard the *Glasgow*. Abner Fuller enlisted first from Wethersfield, Connecticut, in 1775, and married Mary Hilyard Crowfoot, July 16, 1767.[1] Abner was the half brother of Private Lemuel Fuller[2] of Captain Ebenezer Fitch Bissell's Company, who is not to be confused with the Private Lemuel Fuller of Captain Joseph Jewett's Company, who was not captured at the Battle of Long Island. Both Abner Fuller and Lemuel Fuller of E.F. Bissell's Company were listed among the missing after the Battle of Long Island.

Corporal Levi Farnum was born August 13, 1748, the son of Zebediah and Mary (Fuller) Farnum in Windham, Connecticut. The date of death of Levi was recorded at Windham, Connecticut, for Christmas Day, December 25, 1776, the day after the men had been put aboard the *Glasgow*. Levi was the brother of **Sergeant Daniel Farnum**, also of Trowbridge's Company, who was born in Windham, July 19, 1752, and who died at Milford just two weeks later on January 9, 1777; his date of death is also recorded at Windham.[3]

We have noted that Lt. Fitch wrote in his diary that **Corporal Nathan Raymond**, Captain Jewett's nephew, had been personally assaulted by Hessian General De Heister during the aftermath of the Battle of Long Island. It is quite possible that Nathan had been directly involved in the incident that resulted in the death of his uncle, but we cannot know for sure. The Jewett genealogy provides only that Nathan died January 16, 1777, of smallpox, "soon after his release and his return home."[4] He had probably been on board the *Glasgow*, with the others. He had never married.

One year after the *Glasgow* landed at Milford, one of the selectmen of Preston, Connecticut, petitioned the Connecticut Assembly for reimbursement of medical expenses incurred in caring for one "Matthew" Button, who had been a soldier in Captain Jonathan Brewster's Company. According to the petition, Button was taken prisoner at the Battle of Long Island, and after captivity in New York was sent out aboard a flag-of-truce ship which landed at Milford, Connecticut. On January 13, 1777, Button arrived at Preston, and was promptly taken ill with smallpox and died. As Button had no

[1] CT State Library, *Barbour Collection*.
[2] http://www.angelfire.com/ok3/comehere/aqwn10.htm
[3] CT State Library, *Barbour Collection*.
[4] Jewett, *History and Genealogy of the Jewetts of America*, p. 193.

resources of his own, the selectmen of the town were compelled to arrange care for him. The name Matthew is apparently an error, as the man in Brewster's Company was **Corporal William Button**, another victim of the smallpox time-bomb planted on the *Glasgow*.[1] William was the son of Matthias and Mary (Safford) Button, of Preston, born January 26, 1753.[2]

☞ By far the most colorful and romantic- albeit tragic- story concerns **Sergeant Elisha Benton** of Captain Abraham Tyler's Company. Both he and his brother, **Azariah,** were listed as missing from Huntington's Regiment after the battle. A genealogy of the Benton family states that Azariah "died in prison ship, Long Island Sound, December 29, 1776."[3] Although the *Glasgow* was a man-of-war, and not strictly a prison ship, this record apparently identifies Azariah as a casualty aboard that vessel on the voyage to Milford. This information was probably passed on to the family by his brother, Elisha, who survived the voyage to return home.

The family home where the Benton brothers lived is still standing, and is owned and operated as a museum by the Tolland Historical Society. The Elisha Benton story probably contributed to the interest in preserving the house, which was built in 1720 by Daniel Benton, the grandfather of Elisha and Azariah.

As we learned in the second chapter, just prior to the Revolutionary War Elisha had fallen in love with a very young local girl named Jemima Barrows. The relationship was condemned by the family, perhaps because she was only fifteen, while Elisha was twelve years her senior.

When Elisha returned from captivity shortly after the *Glasgow* landed, he was already infected with smallpox and extremely ill. Since none of the rest of the family had had the disease, it would have been understood that Elisha's presence endangered them all. They must have been relieved when Jemima Barrows volunteered to nurse her future husband. The two were isolated in what was known as "the dying and borning room," next to the keeping room in the old homestead. All Jemima's efforts were for naught, however, for on January 21, 1777, Elisha died. Reportedly, in order to prevent

---

[1] *Public Records of the State of CT, Oct. 1776 to Feb. 1778*, p. 556.
[2] CT State Library, *Barbour Collection*.
[3] John Hogan Benton, *David Benton, Jr., and Sarah Bingham, their Ancestors and Descendants* (Boston: David Clapp & Son, 1906), p. 9, http://persi.heritagequestonline.com/...

infecting the rest of the house, Elisha's body was lowered through the window of the room and buried only a few yards away, next to the carriage road. An unmarked stone was placed on his grave which remains there to this day.

Further misfortune awaited Jemima, as she had received a fatal dose of smallpox while caring for her intended. She survived him by only five weeks, and passed away on February 28, 1777, just short of her eighteenth birthday. Because she had never married Elisha, by custom she could not be buried next to him. The family relented to a certain degree because of her heroic sacrifice, and allowed Jemima to be buried on the opposite side of the carriage road from Elisha's grave. She too has an unmarked stone erected over her grave, perhaps thirty feet away from the man she had intended to marry.[1]

The death of Elisha Benton is recorded in Tolland Cemetery Records, which states that Elisha Benton was "captivated on Long Island the 27th August, 1776, and exchanged Jan. the 3rd, 1777, and died the 21st with the smallpox in the 29th year of his age."

It was a common belief among those who survived the prisons of New York in 1776, that the British had intentionally infected them with smallpox, so that, not only would the American soldiers themselves suffer and die, but some of them would live long enough to reach home and infect their families and neighbors as well. Whether or not it was intentional, the spread of the disease did, in fact, follow that course. We have seen this happen in at least three cases: that of our poor Jemima Barrows; Captain Stephen Stow of Milford, the hero who nursed the 46 who perished there; and Lt. Oliver Babcock, who left the little diary of the voyage of the *Glasgow*.

Many families must have never discovered the fate of their loved ones, learning only that they were taken prisoner at the Battle of Long Island, and never returned to their families. **Corporal Oliver Jennings**, who wrote the two wonderful little letters to his wife from Roxbury during the siege of Boston, was one of these. To his family, he simply vanished, and his date of death was considered to be August 1776. Thanks to Ensign Anthony Bradford's diary, we know that Jennings was left behind when the prisoners evacuated the

---

[1] David E. Philips, *Legendary Connecticut* (Willimantic, CT: Curbstone Press, 1992).

Middle Dutch Church on December 24, 1776. He was found there dead by Bradford the next day. Jennings left his wife, Joanne, and three children without a father. His two sons were sent to live with "different families," while his daughter continued to live with her mother. Joanne married, second, Jerod Foote, and this couple was later living at Stewart's Corner, Cayuga County, New York, where she died on May 17, 1823.[1]

☞   **Private Elijah Hammond** of Captain Jonathan Brewster's Company was reported missing at the Battle of Long Island and never returned home. He was born in Bolton, Connecticut, August 16, 1753, the son of Elijah and Mary (Kingsbury) Hammond. Before serving in the 17th Regiment, Elijah had enlisted for the first time in Colonel Parson's Regiment on May 9, 1775, and served until December 1775. He never married.[2]

☞   **Private Daniel Moses** was not captured at the Battle of Long Island. His name appears in military records only on the ammunition return for Captain Bissell's Company at New York, May 15, 1776. He may have been wounded during the battle, however, for just twelve days later, on September 8, 1776, he died at Harlem Heights.[3] At the time, General Washington had placed his army in a series of positions from the southern tip of Manhattan, north to Kings Bridge, with the bulk of his army at Harlem Heights. Daniel Moses died just a few days before the battle by that name. He left a wife with eight children.

☞   Private **Robert Newcomb**, the young drummer from Truro, Massachusetts in Captain Ebenezer Fitch Bissell's Company at the Battle of Long Island "was taken prisoner and never heard from afterwards; he was unmarried and perhaps died while a prisoner."[4]

These and many other soldiers of the 17th Regiment were now free from their earthly woes, but most of the officers of the regiment continued as prisoners in New York. Although the officers were

---

[1] Jennings, *A Genealogy of a Jennings Family,* pp. 8-16.
[2] Frederick Stam Hammond, *Histories and Genealogies of the Hammond Families in America* (Oneida, NY: Ryan & Burkhart, Printers, 1902), pp. 272,273, 287,288, http://persi.heritagequestonline.com/...
[3] Moses, *Historical Sketches of John Moses of Plymouth,* pp. 147-148.
[4] Newcomb, *Andrew Newcomb, 1618-1686, and His Descendants,* p. 58.

living in far more acceptable conditions, they paid a price in extended captivity.

10. Artful, Mean and Pitiful Pretences

Evidence from Lt. Fitch's diary may contradict the popular theory that the British intentionally infected American prisoners of war in New York with smallpox. Fitch mentioned that one officer died of smallpox at Hampden Hall when the American officers were still quartered there, but he also noted that smallpox was not confined to the prisoner population, and was spreading among the civilian population of the city. Fitch had not had the disease, which is why he had fled to other quarters when smallpox broke out at Hampden Hall. Inoculation was made available to the American officers, but Fitch had been in poor health and decided not to undergo what was then a very risky procedure; at least for the time being. It is reasonable to assume that the British would not have made inoculation available to the American officers if they had planned to exterminate them via the disease.

Lt. Fitch had good reason to be apprehensive regarding smallpox inoculation, if Ensign Bradford's experience is any indication what he might have expected. On Sunday, December 29, Bradford, "received the infection of the smallpox by Dr. Spalding. Took a gill [1/4 pint] of mercury in the evening." On the 30th, "Took another gill…Joined messing chamber with Capt. Percival, Lieut. Gove, Ens. Higgins, Sergt. Coit, Lieut. Orcutt & Ens. Chapman." Although Bradford did not say so, these men may also have received inoculation. On the 31st, Bradford continued, "Took a gill of mercury this evening." On January 1, 1777, "The jallup taken this morning makes me sick enough." On Sunday, January 5, "Had the infection put in again this morning." On the 8th, "Had the infection renewed." On the 10th, "Had the matter put in again this morning." On Sunday, the 12th, "Took physick and had a very sick day." On the 13th, "This afternoon began to have a violent pain in my head and back." On the 14th, "Pain continues. Had a very restless day." On the 15th, "Pain abated. Several pocks appear on my arm." On the 17th, "Pocks come out & fill very well, though not [?]." On January 21, "Pock begins to turn." Sunday, January 26, "Took my last portion of physic. The smallpox left me very well, except a pain in my shoulder." The lengthy process had lasted nearly a month, but there is no telling what the long-term impact of the "gills" of mercury were on Bradford's health.

Except for the inoculation process, life was becoming rather boring for Lt. Fitch and the other American officers still confined in New York. Fortunately, at least some funds were now being provided by the various states for their support. But now that food and housing were more available, there was a daily monotony setting in with nothing of real meaning to do. They were removed from participation in the war and left with the nagging sadness of missing family and friends. For the lack of anything better to do, the favorite pastime of the officers seems to have been fueling the rumor mill over the status of the American Army: its victories, retreats, and defeats. The on-going British propaganda machine represented the American Army as close to complete collapse, but the officers occasionally received the American version of events from new prisoners as they were brought into the city.

Other rumors surrounded the anticipated releases and exchanges of prisoners. It had been a nearly daily prediction that an exchange of the American officers for British officers held captive by the various colonies was imminent. For some of the field officers and generals, that proved to be true, but for most of the lower ranking officers, the New Year came and went with no immediate hope of exchange. Even so, the trickle of exchanges that did occur kept those left behind in a constant state of expectation.

Adjutant Elisha Hopkins may have been exchanged on the 12th of January, for Fitch wrote in his diary that he sealed a letter on the 11th for his brother, Elisha Fitch, in Norwich, to be delivered by Hopkins who was going out of the city the next morning. Bradford recorded that Hopkins had been released by the 14th. On the 23rd of January, Connecticut Governor Trumbull, in a letter to George Washington, mentioned that Lt. Hopkins was out on parole, but had to secure the release of a British officer of equal rank from the Americans, if he were to remain on parole, and not return to New York.[1] In spite of a flurry of letters between Trumbull and Washington on the subject of

---

[1] *Collections of the Massachusetts Historical Society*, Vol. X., p. 29.

the prisoners in New York, the exchange of the officers taken at the Battle of Long Island was a slow and tedious process, taking many months before all would be released.

On January 17 Fitch wrote that he had spoken with Corporal George Gordon, who had been living with the officers. Gordon told him he was being exchanged the next day. On the 21st, Gordon was still in New York and spoke to Fitch, but continued to be in expectation of exchange. Fitch gave Corporal Gordon a letter to deliver to his wife. There is no further mention of him in Fitch's diary, so Gordon may have been exchanged on or about the 22nd of January, which is not inconsistent with the testimony given in Gordon's pension application.

On January 20 Fitch and the other officers on parole were informed that they were going to be moved over to Long Island to board with some of the local residents there. The move was delayed for two days, and it wasn't until the 22nd that Fitch boarded the ferry to cross the East River for the first time since the previous August. Captain Ozias Bissell and Lt. Fitch were sent to billet with the family of George Rapelye, whose farm was located about ½ mile east of New Lots; a small cluster of houses just east of Flatbush. Rapelye was a descendant of Huguenot settlers, but other officers were billeted with Dutch farmers in the area. Ensign Bradford recorded in his diary that "20 of us" moved over to New Lots on the 30th, several days after the others; this group was probably still recovering from their inoculation ordeal.

Because of the considerable number of American officers transferring from parole in New York, they had to be spread out through the towns of Gravesend, New Utrecht, Flatlands, and Flatbush, billeted two or three to a house. The officers were given freedom to roam through their respective towns during the day without guard, but were bound by the conditions of their parole not to travel to other towns.[1]

New Lots was so named because it had been purchased from the Indians as an extension of the already settled town of Flatbush towards the east. The main street in the village extended about 1 ½ miles from west to east, with about twelve farmhouses and a few taverns and shops spread out along the way. Part of this street had

---

[1] *Fitch*, p. 156.

been the highway used by William Howe to accomplish his flanking maneuver the night before the Battle of Long Island.

Daily responsibility for the American prisoners fell to an elderly justice-of-the-peace, Nicholas Wyckoff, to whom the prisoners reported and from whom they received orders from the British Commissary in New York. Wyckoff's home became known as "headquarters" to the American officers and was located about ½ mile to the west of the Rapelye farm.

Although initially apprehensive about their transfer from New York, the men found that the new quarters on Long Island were more agreeable than their previous accommodations. They could freely visit each other, and were even allowed to frequent the neighborhood taverns. Their hosts were provided with $2 a week for each of their tenants, to be paid by the Continental Congress; at that point not an altogether reliable source. Nevertheless, the officers seemed to have been well provided for in the arrangement. Life settled into a familiar pattern of socialization among the American officers and their Dutch neighbors. Card playing became the primary diversion, much to the chagrin of Lt. Fitch.

Two events of note occurred during the early part of the officers' sojourn on Long Island. Fitch noted in his diary entry of February 23, 1777, that Simon Bergen, the same man who had hosted the officers of the 17th Regiment at his farm on the Gowanus Road just prior to the Battle of Long Island, had died. The report Fitch received indicated Bergen had been shot by a British sailor.[1] Fitch gratefully remembered Bergen's hospitality and generosity. On Friday the 28th, Fitch noted that William Howard, the tavern keeper, had also died. It was Howard whom Lord Howe had forced to guide his flanking force to the Jamaica Road the night before the battle. Howard was a victim of smallpox.

Besides Capt. Ozias Bissell, who was also billeted at George Rapalye's farm, Fitch made note that Captain Timothy Percival, Captain Caleb Trowbridge, Lieutenant Solomon Orcutt, Ensign Joseph Chapman, Ensign Elihu Lyman, Ensign Anthony Bradford, Ensign John Kinsman, Quartermaster Thomas Fanning, and Ensign Cornelius Higgins, all of Huntington's Regiment, were billeted with

---

[1] The stories as told in Stiles' *History of the City of Brooklyn*, Vol. I, p. 54, as well as other sources, vary in one important respect: that Bergen bled to death when he was *accidentally* shot in the leg by a sailor while in the process of purchasing a musket from him.

the various families at New Lots. Colonel Ethan Allen was also transferred to Long Island to be among this group.

Ensign Bradford noted that he and Ensign Chapman were billeted with the "Widow Vandeveer." On February 9, 1777, Bradford wrote that "Friday last, Peter, a free negro, broke out with smallpox at this house." So, smallpox was now spreading on Long Island as well. If smallpox weren't enough to deal with, at the end of March, Ensign Bradford came down with the measles, and was very sick and uncomfortable for the next week.

The next release of officers from the 17th was noted by Fitch in his entry of April 5, 1777, when Ensigns Higgins, Kinsman, and Chapman were sent to New York for exchange. By the 2nd of May, Capt. [Ozias] Bissell, Capt. Trowbridge, Capt. Percival, Lt. Orcutt, Lt. Gove, Lt. Fanning, Lt. Fitch, Lt. Gillet, Ensign Bradford, and Ensign Lyman were still on Long Island when their names were taken, along with other officers from Connecticut held on Long Island, in order to petition the Connecticut General Assembly for back wages from the time they were captured. The British allowed Lt.-Col. Selah Heart (or Hart), another Connecticut officer held prisoner, to take the list back to Connecticut on parole to secure the compensation.

The General Assembly acted quickly, on May 20 providing 496 pounds in back wages for all the Connecticut officers on Long Island.[1] Selah Heart's petition for back wages coincided with another petition signed by 32 friends and relatives of the Connecticut parolees on Long Island calling for the support of the prisoners, who were "suffering under the insults of the enemy, & destitute of necessary cloathing or money to purchase the necessaries of life."[2] According to Ensign Bradford, Selah Heart returned to Long Island on May 31 with the money for the Connecticut officers. All the officers from Connecticut signed receipts for their back wages between June 2, and June 16, 1777. The money was distributed evenly, with each officer receiving eight pounds as partial compensation for back wages.[3]

Ensign Bradford noted on May 13, while Lt.-Col. Heart was away, that smallpox was spreading among the blacks in the neighborhood, and that other residents were being inoculated. Lt.

---

[1] CT State Library, *Connecticut Archives*; Rev. War Ser. I, Vol. XI, 139a, 139b.
[2] CT State Library, *Connecticut Archives*; Rev. War Ser. I, Vol. VII, 224.
[3] CT State Library, *Connecticut Archives*; Rev. War Ser. I, Vol. XII, 130-183.

Fitch finally relented and received inoculation along with Capt. Ozias Bissell.

Another noteworthy event recorded in Fitch's diary during this time was an apparent tryst between Captain Ozias Bissell and his former landlady in New York: Mrs. Jenkins. The evidence confirming the nature of the relationship is carefully and thoroughly explored by the editor of Fitch's diary, W. H. W. Sabine. Though circumspect, Fitch made several allusions to the relationship in his diary (one can picture his raised eyebrows), noting that Mrs. Jenkins came from New York to pay Bissell a visit on Thursday, February 13, with several other ladies from Bushwick, Long Island. Due to his parole restriction to New Lots, Bissell would not have been allowed to visit New York, so Mrs. Jenkins must have left New York to take up residence in Bushwick. Fitch went on to make particular note of the nights when Bissell did not return to his quarters at farmer Rapelye's. During one period of time, Fitch wrote that he slept alone for eight successive nights. Bissell's absence would have been a parole violation for him.

It was also about this time that Fitch wrote his *Narrative of the Treatment with which the American Prisoners were Used who were taken by the British & Hessian Troops on Long Island, York Island, etc*. It must have been written surreptitiously, for Fitch never directly spoke of the *Narrative* in his diary. However, he did mention in various daily entries spending considerable time in writing, far more than would have been necessary for his abbreviated diary. The *Narrative* was a more detailed and extensive essay on his captivity, in which he was far more descriptive and much more inflammatory, with a significant bent towards anti-British propaganda. It was dated at New Lots on April 2, 1777, and addressed to his brother Elisha Fitch at Norwich. The volume must have been sent out with an officer on exchange; quite probably with one of the ensigns who were exchanged on the 5th. In the diary entry for that day Fitch noted the exchange of the three ensigns, and mentioned that he gave a letter for his wife to Ensign Kinsman. He may have also given Kinsman the *Narrative* to deliver to his brother in the hope that it would receive wider dissemination and perhaps be published.

While the two were still captive together in New York, Fitch had struck up a friendship with Colonel Ethan Allen, but on Long Island the relationship seems to have blossomed. No doubt Fitch was taken with the larger-than-life conqueror of Fort Ticonderoga, and with him

Fitch had "considerable entertaining discourse." Fitch mentioned sharing certain stories with Allen over which they had a good laugh. It is possible that Allen collaborated with Fitch in the writing of Fitch's *Narrative*. If not, Fitch certainly benefited from Allen's expressiveness and story-telling ability, to say nothing of Allen's vitriolic animosity towards the British. After the war, Allen wrote his own, but much better known story, coincidentally (?), also entitled the *Narrative* of his captivity, never mentioning Fitch. Allen's book was published soon after his release in 1779, but perhaps because Fitch was not a popular hero, his *Narrative* was not published until 1871, several decades after his death.

It was perhaps inevitable, considering the idleness of the American prisoners, that those who were the least able to contain themselves would find a way to get into trouble. Although Fitch did not directly link the two incidents, Colonel Ethan Allen was arrested on August 25, and Captain Ozias Bissell was arrested the next day. Both were returned to New York and placed in close confinement in the infamous Provost Jail. Fitch found out about the arrests on September 1st, and made note of them in that day's diary entry. According to Fitch, Bissell had gotten into some kind of a "scrape," perhaps associated with his relationship with Mrs. Jenkins. Ethan Allen was no more forthcoming about the details of the incident that resulted in his own re-imprisonment when he wrote:

The 25th day of August I was apprehended, and under pretext of artful, mean and pitiful pretences, that I had infringed on my parole, taken from a tavern where there were more than a dozen officers present, and, in the very place where those officers and myself were directed to be quartered, put under a strong guard and taken to New York, where I expected to make my defence before the commanding officer; but, contrary to my expectations, and without the least solid pretence of justice or trial, was again encircled with a strong guard with fixed bayonets, and conducted to the provost-gaol in a lonely apartment, next above the dungeon, and was denied all manner of subsistence either by purchase or allowance.[1]

---

[1] DePuy, *Ethan Allen and the Green Mountain Heroes of '76*, p. 266.

Fortunately for us, Henry Onderdonk clarified the circumstances of the incident resulting in Allen's arrest, stating that "Allen was billeted at Daniel Rapalje's. On hearing the news of the battle of Bennington, he mounted on the roof of Howard's Inn, and gave three cheers, which so exasperated the British officers present, that he was thrown in the Provost [jail]."[1]

Although infinitely amusing today, this episode resulted in serious discomfort for Allen, who went on to describe the conditions in the jail and the fact that all food was withheld from him for three days. Onderdonk also related that Captain Ozias Bissell and Major Levi Wells were taken under similar false pretenses (again without describing the specific incidents leading to their arrest) and confined in the Provost Jail, where they continued to be incarcerated until their release five months later.

Bissell may have been arrested because he violated his parole by not staying in the house to which he was assigned, while probably in the quarters and bed of Mrs. Jenkins. Ensign Bradford noted in his diary entry of August 28, that Bissell was arrested in Bushwick, probably where Mrs. Jenkins was living, a clear violation of his parole. Bradford added that Allen was arrested in New Lots, and both he and Bissell were detained, "Tis said for breach of parole and a suspicion of having a design to set fire to York." The accusation that Allen and Bissell were plotting to burn New York may have been a trumped up charge by the British, or perhaps just another rumor circulated among the American officers.

The parole of the officers remaining on Long Island was interrupted abruptly on November 28, 1777. The day before, a force of 1,400 American troops from New Jersey had made an abortive raid on a British encampment on Long Island. The Americans quickly withdrew when they learned the camp had been moved. However, when the British received further intelligence that another raid was planned- this time to free the American prisoners on Long Island- they took the prudent measure of moving the prisoners.

According to Fitch, the American officers were rounded up and brought with all their baggage in wagons to Howard's Tavern. From there, they were driven to King's Ferry, the Brooklyn ferry landing,

---

[1] Onderdonk, *Revolutionary Incidents of Suffolk and Kings Counties*, Sec. 840, p. 178.

and loaded aboard flat-bottom boats. They then sailed around the tip of Manhattan and up the west side to a dock near Trinity Church, where they were put aboard a transport ship of the British line named the *Judith*. Fitch reported that the accommodations were similar to those on the *Mentor* the year before: besides the crew, it was packed with 140 prisoners. They were stuffed again into dark, dirty and cold quarters between decks. Most of the men had no beds, blankets, or warm coats. As on the *Mentor*, they had to compete for space on the ship's planks for room to sleep. An ever-aspiring poet, Fitch wrote the following verse the next day, November 29:

> *The meals which to our lot this day do fall*
> *Are few and course or rather none at all.*
> *In gloomy darkness, crowded here we sit*
> *Scourged with excessive hunger, cold and wet.*
> *This hard and disagreeable adventure*
> *Resembles that on board the Mentor.*

Fitch mentioned that they were docked near several other ships also containing American prisoners: among them were the *Myrtle* and the *Centurion*. Ensign Bradford recorded that he, Captain Percival, Major Wells, Lt. Gove, and Ensign Lyman were on board the *Myrtle*. Despite the poor sleeping arrangements, two days later the prisoners were provided with some food and allowed to go on shore to supplement their mess. Blankets were also provided by the commissary for those who were lacking them. On board the *Myrtle*, Bradford wrote on December 5 that Capt. VanZandt and Lt. Priestly fought a duel on the quarterdeck. VanZandt's pistol misfired and no damage was done by Priestly. Bradford offered no further explanation of the event or further identification of the men involved.

Fortunately for Lt. Fitch and Captain Trowbridge, their time on the *Judith* was brief. On December 9, they were informed they were to finally be exchanged and permitted to go home. Fitch and Trowbridge were immediately allowed to go ashore, where they made the rounds of those who had befriended them during their captivity in New York the previous fall, to say their farewells. The next day, they and several others from Connecticut, boarded the sloop *Charming Polly* to sail up through Hell Gate to New Haven, Connecticut. At long last, after three days aboard the *Charming Polly*, Fitch and Trowbridge landed at New Haven on Friday, December 12, 1777.

They had spent 13 ½ months in captivity. They were not the last to be exchanged. Some of the other American officers captured at the Battle of Long Island were held months longer.

If Ethan Allen's report was correct, that Capt. Ozias Bissell was held in the Provost Jail for five months, then it wasn't until the end of January before Bissell was released. According to Bissell's pension file, he re-enlisted as a captain in the First Connecticut Battalion on March 12, 1778.[1] So, between the end of January and the beginning of March he must have been exchanged and returned to Connecticut. Considering that he would have needed some time to recover from his ordeal in the Provost, the time of the exchange would seem to have been closer to the former time than the latter.

According to Ensign Bradford, the remaining officers from the Battle of Long Island were transferred back to their former quarters on Long Island on December 10, 1777, after again signing articles of parole. Bradford wrote that several officers escaped while the ship was at anchor close to shore and before they signed their paroles: among them was Captain VanZandt, of dueling fame, who was captured farther out on Long Island on the 14th. By his escape and capture, VanZandt is shown to have been an American and not a British officer.

Ensign Anthony Bradford's final diary entry was made on April 5, 1778, when he wrote that between 50 and 60 American officers received word that they were to be exchanged, and would soon set out for home. Among them were all the remaining prisoners from the Battle of Long Island and the retreat from New York. The long exile of the officers of Huntington's 17th Continental Regiment on parole on Long Island had finally come to an end.

---

[1] NARA, Series M805, Roll 90, Revolutionary War Pension Application, S37764.

11. Devoted Wholly, Lord, To Thee

Despite Danske Dandridge's inability to find evidence that any of the prisoners of the Battle of Long Island survived to reach home, some of the men from Huntington's Regiment did. The pension records that have been referred to are the most significant proof of that. The officers of the regiment came off very well: only Lt.-Col. Clark, Captain Joseph Jewett, and Lieutenant Solomon Makepeace perished, but the mortality rate among the soldiers held prisoner on the *Whitby* or in the churches of New York was extreme.

According to *Connecticut Men in the War of the Revolution*, 185 soldiers- not including officers- from Huntington's Regiment were taken prisoner at the Battle of Long Island. We have estimated that only about 80 to 100 men from the regiment survived the four-months' captivity in New York to be loaded onto the *Glasgow* on December 24, 1776. Of those men, at least 24 perished on the *Glasgow* after disembarking at Milford, or shortly after returning home. That leaves between 56 and 76 men who may have lived for any length of time afterwards.

There is reasonably clear evidence that the following officers and men from Huntington's Regiment survived the ordeal of 1776 to return home. There were probably a few more, but no information has yet been found that can identify who they were with any degree of certainty. The lives of the soldiers who survived from the group in the second chapter will be followed here, as well as a few others for whom we had no biographical information prior to the Revolution. Again, the following names are listed alphabetically according to rank:

Due to illness, **Colonel Jedediah Huntington** was in New York at the time of the Battle of Long Island, and not in command of his regiment or taken prisoner. He had returned to the command of his regiment by October 3, when his name appeared on a return of that date.[1] The few soldiers of his regiment who remained after the battle joined the main army in New York, and moved north when the city was evacuated. They later participated in the Battle of White Plains. The regiment, as well as the rest of the Continental Army, was disbanded on December 31, 1776, the one-year term of enlistment of the men having expired. Shortly after that date, Colonel Huntington was given command of the new 1st Regiment of the "Connecticut Line" (the new national army was referred to as the "Continental Establishment"), again primarily men from the New London and Norwich, Connecticut, area. The term of enlistment for the new Continental Establishment, of which the 1st Regiment was a part, was three years "or the war." Huntington's new regiment was ordered to rendezvous at Norwich, Connecticut, on April 14, 1777, and then marched to Peekskill, New York. Colonel Huntington was among those officers in command of a mostly militia force who attacked Tryon's forces during the raid on Danbury, April 25-28, 1777, Huntington's own regiment probably not arriving at Peekskill until after Tryon's raid. After marching to Peekskill, the 1st Regiment remained there until ordered to join Washington's Army in Pennsylvania in September.

Jedediah Huntington was promoted to the rank of Brigadier-General of the 2nd Brigade on May 12, 1777. Lt.-Col. Samuel Prentice was promoted to colonel and commanding officer of the 1st Regiment, which was then attached to Huntington's 2nd Brigade. The regiment fought at the Battle of Germantown, Pennsylvania, in October 1777, and wintered over with Washington at Valley Forge during the winter of 1777-78.

In the spring of 1778, Huntington returned home where he married his second wife, Ann, the daughter of Thomas Moore of New York City, on April 9, 1778.[2] They would eventually have seven children together. After his marriage, General Huntington returned to his command. When the British evacuated Philadelphia in June 1778, Huntington's Brigade participated in the Battle of Monmouth, when the American Army attacked the rear-guard of the British on their retreat through New Jersey.[3] General Huntington was on General Charles Lee's court martial for misconduct during the Battle of

---

[1] NARA, Series M246, *Rev. War Rolls, 1775-1783*, "Continental Troops, 17th Regt., 1776."
[2] CT State Library, *Barbour Collection.*
[3] *Record of Service of Connecticut Men in the War of the Revolution*, p. 145.

Monmouth in July 1778, and was later a member of the court of inquiry that investigated British Major John Andre's part in the treason of Benedict Arnold in 1780.

By December of that year, Huntington's Brigade was the only Connecticut brigade in service, and Huntington remained with his brigade until the close of the war in 1783. In May 1783, he was part of a committee of four that drafted the plan of organization for officers of the Revolutionary War called the Society of the Cincinnati, and became its vice-president. By June, with the war winding down, the Continental Army had only four brigadiers left; all serving as part of the command of the garrison at West Point. General Huntington was one of the four. At the close of the war, Huntington was brevetted major-general.

When the war ended, Jedediah Huntington returned to private business in Norwich, Connecticut. He later held public office as sheriff of the county, judge of probate, first alderman of the City of Norwich, a Representative in the State Legislature, treasurer of the State, and a delegate to the state convention that ratified the Constitution of the United States. In 1789, his personal friend, President George Washington, appointed him the collector of customs at New London, Connecticut, a position he held through four successive presidential administrations. Jedediah was a man of faith, active in his church throughout his life and one of the original members of the American Board of Commissioners for Foreign Missions, an organization that was instrumental in the great Protestant foreign missions movement of the 19th century.

Jedediah Huntington died September 25, 1818, having been an important officer during the Revolutionary War, a preeminent member of his community, and a man of great service to his church and new nation.[1]

There is some ambiguity in the records relating to **Major Elihu Humphreys**. He was not listed as missing after the Battle of Long Island in the *Record of Service of Connecticut Men in the War of The Revolution*. Lt. Jabez Fitch mentioned in his diary entry of August 25, 1776, just two days before the Battle of Long Island, that he had dined with Major Humphreys. That was the last time that Fitch mentioned him in his diary, despite at least some mention of every other officer

[1] Caulkins, *History of Norwich*, pp. 417-18; *The Huntington Family in America,* pp. 448-450.

from the 17th who was taken prisoner. However, in the "Return of Prisoners Taken on Long Island," submitted by British Commissary Loring right after the Battle, one major from the 17th Continental Regiment is listed.[1] Only the number of missing and their ranks were provided, so this major was not named. On all of the returns submitted for the surviving portion of the 17th Regiment after the Battle of Long Island until the regiment disbanded in December 1776, no major is listed.[2]

Both the Humphreys genealogy and the *Memorial History of Hartford County* state that Major Humphreys was wounded at the Battle of Long Island, taken prisoner, and confined in the Old Sugarhouse by the British, and so barbarously treated that when he was released and returned to Simsbury, he died soon after.[3] Even though he could not have been confined in the Sugarhouse, which was probably not used for prisoners until some time after the Battle of Long Island, and was never used for officers, it is difficult to dismiss the rest of this information. His family would certainly have known and passed on the fact that he was wounded and that he died of a combination of his wounds and the treatment he received at the hands of the British.

The editor of Fitch's diary believed that Humphreys was not taken prisoner, but soon after the Battle of Long Island was taken ill and returned to Simsbury where he died.[4] Perhaps there are other possibilities: that Humphreys was indeed wounded during the Battle, taken prisoner, confined briefly in one of the hospitals on Long Island (probably at Flatbush, since Fitch did not mention his being with the prisoners near Gowanus), and soon after exchanged due to the seriousness of his wounds; or, he was wounded, but able to escape and return to the lines before being captured. Either scenario would account for the fact that Fitch did not mention that Humphreys was ill two days prior to the Battle, and that Humphreys did not appear on a return of the regiment on September 27th. Nor was Humphreys listed among the missing when Huntington submitted his return of the missing from the Battle of Long Island in November.

---

[1] Force, *American Archives*, 5th Series, Vol. I, p. 1258.
[2] NARA, Series M246; *Rev. War Rolls, 1775-1783*, "Continental Troops, 17th Regt.,1776."
[3] Trumbull, *The Memorial History of Hartford County*, p. 362.
[4] *Fitch*, p. 29.

Whatever the circumstances, Major Humphreys died on February 25, 1777, and was buried at Hop Meadow Burying Ground in Simsbury, Connecticut. He was 38 years old. Daniel Barber, a private in Humphreys' company in 1775, wrote that Elihu, "dying about the close of the year 1776, left, as a legacy to his family, a name, whose reputation will not be forgotten during many generations. I knew him- I revered him- and I loved him." Elihu Humphreys' will was dated, August 8, 1776, and must have been written at New York City just prior to the Battle of Long Island. In his will he mentioned three daughters: Asenath, Ophelia and Rowena; and three sons, Elihu, Sterling and Young. His wife, Asenath, died just a little over a year after her husband, on April 11, 1779. She was just 33 years old.[1]

☞ **Chaplain John Ellis** was not listed as missing after the Battle of Long Island. Considering Lt. Fitch's remarks prior to the battle, Ellis probably remained within the fortifications at Brooklyn during the battle. Upon the termination of his period of enlistment in 1776, Ellis reenlisted on January 1, 1777, and served as brigade chaplain in Brigadier-General Jedediah Huntington's 2nd Connecticut Brigade. He continued to serve as a chaplain in the Continental Army throughout the War, perhaps the only Revolutionary War chaplain to do so; this, in spite of Lt. Fitch's implication just prior to the Battle of Long Island that Ellis lacked courage under fire.[2] It was later written of Rev. John Ellis that:

> *...honorable mention should be made of the self-sacrificing patriotism of Mr. Ellis. He took a lively interest in the welfare of the country, and cheerfully shared with his people the burdens of war. In 1775 he relinquished one hundred pounds of his salary, in consideration, as he says in a letter still preserved, of the burdens which had come upon his people in aiding to fit out the expedition to Crown Point. In the Revolution also, Mr. Ellis warmly espoused the cause of independence, and entered the army as a chaplain in 1775. In this office he served until the*

---

[1] *The Humphreys Family in America*, pp. 136-138; Barber, *Connecticut Historical Collections*, p. 103.
[2] *Record of Service of Connecticut Men in the War of the Revolution*, p. 144.

conclusion of the war. Two of his sons also went into the army with him[1]

Rev. Ellis' son, Joseph, served in Capt. Jonathan Brewster's Company in Huntington's Regiment and was reported missing at the Battle of Long Island. Due to his prolonged absence during the war, Rev. Ellis was dismissed from the pastorate of the Franklin Congregational Church when he returned home. He next served the church at Rehoboth, Massachusetts, where he was installed on March 30, 1785. Ellis preached at Rehoboth until 1796, when he retired and returned to Norwich, Connecticut. He died there on October 20, 1805, age 79. His widow, Bethiah, died January 30, 1814, age 84, also at Norwich.[2]

☞ **Adjutant Elisha Hopkins** was taken prisoner at the Battle of Long Island and, according to Lt. Fitch, was exchanged on or about January 12, 1777. In his letter to George Washington on January 23, 1777, Governor Trumbull wrote that Lt. Hopkins was out on parole. Effective January 1, 1777, Hopkins was made lieutenant and adjutant in Col. Samuel B. Webb's additional or 9th Regiment, Connecticut Line. He was captured a second time during the raid on Long Island on December 10, 1777, and held for three more years, until December 17, 1780. Ensign Bradford made note of the second capture of Hopkins in his diary entry of December 10, 1777, and further wrote that Hopkins was again sent on parole to New Lots on Long Island. While he was still a prisoner, on October 10, 1778, Hopkins was promoted to Captain in Webb's Regiment. After his second release from captivity, he served for the remainder of the war. When most of the Continental Regiments were disbanded in June 1783, Hopkins continued in service in Colonel Heman Swift's "Final Formation" of the Connecticut Line until December 1783. This regiment remained in the Hudson Highlands until the British evacuation of New York. Hopkins' Company was then part of Col. Hull's Light Battalion that led American troops into New York City upon the evacuation by the enemy on November 25, 1783. Later that year, Elisha became an

---

[1] *The Celebration of the 150th Anniversary of the Primitive Organization of the Congregational Church and Society in Franklin, Connecticut* (New Haven: Tuttle, Morehouse & Taylor, 1869), pp. 102-103, http://persi.heritagequestonline.com/...
[2] Wheeler, *History of Brunswick, Topsham, and Harpswell, Maine*, p. 833; CT State Library, *Barbour Collection*, and *Church Records Slip Index*.

original member of the Society of the Cincinnati, and was at that time living in Hartford.[1]

According to the pension application of a Frederick Hopkins, Captain Hopkins was identified as his brother, Elisha B. Hopkins, and also Frederick's guardian after the death of their father. Frederick enlisted during the war in the spring of 1781 at the age of 13 in his brother's company, and served for the rest of the war.[2] Captain Elisha Hopkins was married at Christ Church, in Philadelphia, June 15, 1796, to his cousin, the widow Sarah (Hopkins) Sims. She returned to Hartford in 1848. When she was admitted to the church there, she was referred to in church records as the "w. of Elisha" but there is no mention of Elisha himself. As there are no church records indicating the arrival of Elisha in Hartford, it is possible he died before his wife returned to Connecticut. There were two children of record, but both died young. Elisha's wife, Sarah Hopkins, died at Hartford, July 1854.[3]

☞ **Surgeon's Mate Silas Holmes** was taken prisoner at the Battle of Long Island and, according to his Revolutionary War pension application, was exchanged, and returned home on December 24, 1776. That date coincides with the date the privates were loaded on board the *Glasgow* in New York. Quite probably Holmes was sent with them to care for the men of his regiment. He survived the ordeal, for on May 10, 1777, Silas Holmes was appointed Surgeon's Mate in the Military Hospital of the Eastern Department, in New London, Connecticut, and was later promoted to Junior Surgeon in the same hospital on October 14, 1777. He served at least until April 20, 1780.[4]

The *Windham Herald* reported on Saturday, August 20, 1791, that "On Tuesday of last week, as Doct. Silas Holmes of Stonington, was returning home, from Block Island, in a small boat, with two men belonging to Block Island, named Condrey and Clark- a flaw of wind upset the boat near Watch hill point, and she immediately sunk, when they were all drowned. Doct. Holmes was much esteemed for his abilities in his profession and was a valuable member of society; he

[1] *Record of Service of Connecticut Men in the War of the Revolution*, pp. 245, 246, 332, 367, 368, 374.
[2] NARA, Series M805, Roll 441, Revolutionary War Pension Application, R5215/BLWT45961-160-55
[3] Hopkins, *John Hopkins of Cambridge, Mass., 1634*, pp. 202-204.
[4] NARA, Series M805, Roll 438, Revolutionary War Pension File, W8282

has left a widow and several children. Condrey, it is said, has left a widow and nine or ten children. Clark was a young single man. Their bodies have been found in different places, and interred."[1] Stonington church records confirm Holmes' date of death as August 3, 1791, and the cause of death as drowning. In 1806, his widow Louisa married, second, Elijah Palmer, a surveyor from Stonington. She made application for a pension based on Silas' service record on June 5, 1837. Louisa died only six months later, on December 26, 1837. At that time, only two of her six children by Dr. Holmes were still alive: Dr. Jabez Holmes of Bristol, Rhode Island, and Silas Holmes of New York City.

Captain Ebenezer Fitch Bissell was among the missing after the Battle of Long Island. According to *The History of Ancient Windsor*, he "was captured and imprisoned in one of the old churches in N.Y. city; several of his men died of starvation, and Capt. B. himself fared little better than they. His family, hearing of his pitiable condition, made great sacrifices to procure silver money (then only current in the British lines), and sent it, but it never reached him." Capt. Bissell's wife, the sister of 2nd Lt. Thomas Hayden, was persistent in her efforts to provide relief for her husband, even succeeding in visiting him once during his captivity.[2] The only mention of him in Fitch's diary was that "Capt. F. Bissil" was sent out of town on exchange on December 21, 1776. Perhaps Bissell's wife, Esther, had been able to influence his release somehow.

In 1778, Capt. Ebenezer Fitch Bissell was assigned to guard the mass of British and Hessian prisoners taken at the Battle of Saratoga, known as the Convention Army, as they were marched through Connecticut on their way from Massachusetts to Virginia.[3] Except for this, Bissell had no other record of service in the War after his captivity. Capt. Bissell and his family resided in the Ebenezer Hayden homestead in Windsor, Connecticut, that his father had purchased when he moved to Windsor. Capt. Bissell was a stage-house and tavern keeper. He and his wife, Esther, had six children, all born before the Revolution. According to Windsor vital records, his wife, Esther, died March 15, 1806, at the age of 61. Strangely, Capt.

---

[1] www.geocities.com/Heartland/Fields/4791/windhamheraldaug1791.html
[2] Stiles, *History and Genealogies of Ancient Windsor*, Vol. II, p. 83.
[3] *Rolls and Lists of Connecticut Men in the Revolution*, p. 188; *Record of Service of Connecticut Men in the War of the Revolution*, p. 631.

Bissell's death was recorded in the Norwich church records, which stated that he died in 1818, at Windsor, several towns away.

☞ By March 1778, **Captain Ozias Bissell** had been released from the Provost Jail in New York, for he had enlisted March 12 as a captain in the First Connecticut Battalion, and had served nine months. In June 1779 he was commissioned captain in Colonel Ebenezer Huntington's (Jedediah's brother) Regiment, serving until March 20, 1780. On that date he was appointed captain in Colonel Levi Wells' Connecticut Militia Regiment. Wells' regiment was tasked with guarding the Connecticut coastline. Bissell was serving with this regiment when he was taken prisoner again with Colonel Wells at Horse Neck (now Greenwich, Connecticut) on December 10, 1780, and confined in New York a second time. Bissell was held until June 1781, when he was discharged for the final time. No diarist recorded his last stint as a prisoner in New York, so we do not know if he renewed his "acquaintance" with Mrs. Jenkins. He served a total of 5 years and 8 months during the War, was in three general actions, seven skirmishes, and was wounded three times, once severely.

Ozias Bissell was a resident of Vernon, Tolland County, Connecticut in 1818, when he made application for a pension for his service in the Revolutionary War. His wife, Mabel, had already died on October 31, 1803, at the age of 76. In 1818, Ozias was eighty-seven years old. The genealogy of the Bissell family admits to a discrepancy in the name and age of his second wife. Ozias' pension application does not give a name for this wife, but states that she was 58 in 1820. The genealogy says his second wife was named Sarah Hoffman, and that she died August 26, 1828 or 29, at the age of 73. This would have made her several years older than the age suggested by his pension application. Ozias' occupation at the time of his pension application was "farmer," but he said he was unable to work. His property was valued at $192. Ozias Bissell died, according to his pension file, on November 16, 1822, but Vernon vital records say the date was November 30, 1822, at the age of 92.[1]

☞ **Captain Jonathan Brewster** was taken prisoner at the Battle of Long Island, and from Lt. Fitch's diary we know that Brewster was exchanged and returned to Connecticut on December 21, 1776, along

---

[1] Jessop, *General Daniel Bissell,* pp. 31-35; NARA, Series M805, Roll 90, Revolutionary War Pension Application, S37764; CT State Library, *Barbour Collection.*

with Captain Ebenezer Fitch Bissell. Lt. Fitch, on November 28, 1777, the first night aboard the *Judith*, dreamed in his unhappy situation that, "Imagination kindly aided me home to Connecticut, where I see several of my old friends, one of whom was Captain Jonathan Brewster." Old friend indeed, for although the first name is not given, Jabez Fitch first mentioned "Corporal" Brewster, and on a later occasion, "Sergeant" Brewster, in that part of his diary which was kept during the French and Indian War. On November 8, 1757, Fitch was visited in his tent by Corporal Brewster, while they were stationed at Roger's Island near Fort Edward. They spoke of home. Two days later, in his capacity as clerk, Fitch wrote out the sergeant's warrant (promotion) for Brewster.[1]

There is no record of service in the Revolutionary War for Capt. Brewster after his release from captivity in New York. Apparently Brewster kept a company orderly book prior to the Battle of Long Island, for his son, Jonathan Brewster, submitted a copy of a muster roll from that book in support of Jacob Hazen's pension application in 1832. This is the same roll of Brewster's Company that appears on pages 101 and 102 of the *Record of Service of Connecticut Men in the War of the Revolution.*[2] Jonathan Brewster and his wife, Mary, lived at Preston, Connecticut, after the War, where they had four children. He died March 2, 1805.

☛ **Captain Elizur (Elihu in *Connecticut Men*) Hubbard** was not taken prisoner at the Battle of Long Island. Although he is not listed as present on a return for the regiment on September 27, his absence is accounted for on October 5 when he was listed as absent due to sickness. His first name is also provided on the return of October 5 as "Eliezar", a spelling variant of Elizur- yet further proof of his identity. By the return submitted November 1, Elizur had returned to active duty.[3] After the 17th disbanded on December 31, 1776, Elizur returned to service as a captain in the Connecticut state militia in 1778 and 1779. During the latter period of service, he was a militia captain whose company turned out to repel Tryon's invasion of New Haven,

---

[1] *The Mayflower Descendant* (Boston: MA Society of Mayflower Descendants, 1899), Vol. VII, p. 245; Vol. VIII, p. 44.
[2] NARA, Series M246, *Rev. War Rolls, 1775-1783*, "Continental Troops, 17th Regt., 1776," folder 93, p. 1, www.footnote.com/image18395507
[3] NARA, Series M246, *Rev. War Rolls, 1775-1783*, "Continental Troops, 17th Regt., 1776," folder 93, p. 10, www.footnote.com/image18395586

Connecticut, on July 5.[1] Captain Hubbard's first wife, Lois, died September 14, 1794, in Glastonbury, Connecticut. They had six children. Captain Hubbard married second, Huldah Brainerd, a widow, on December 7, 1795. Huldah died April 26, 1807. Captain Elizur Hubbard followed her on September 14, 1818, at the age of 82.[2]

☞ **Captain Timothy Percival** was captured by the British at the Battle of Long Island. There are numerous references to him in Fitch's diary, the most notable in regard to the death of his son, Private Timothy Percival, at the hospital in New Utrecht on September 10, 1776, near the beginning of their captivity. Captain Percival was held with the other officers of the 17th Regiment during their parole in New York and on Long Island. Fitch reported Percival was still on Long Island on the 27th of November, 1777, the day before the officers were all herded aboard the *Judith*. On a receipt for back wages due him for the time he was a prisoner of the British, Percival stated he had been held until May 15, 1778.[3] By order of the Connecticut state treasurer, he received 190 pounds in back wages.

By July 1778, Percival had again enlisted, and was serving as a captain in the Connecticut militia at New London, and also under General Spencer in Rhode Island. In January 1779, Captain Percival was a selectman in the Town of Chatham, now East Hampton, Connecticut. He and his wife, Mary, had seven children. In 1793, they relocated, along with his father-in-law, to Freehold, Albany County, New York. From there they moved to Ohio, and then in 1801, to Boone County, Kentucky. He died January 15, 1815, and his wife died March 12, 1819: both in Boone County, Kentucky.[4]

☞ **Captain Caleb Trowbridge** returned to Connecticut from captivity in New York on December 12, 1777, as recorded in Fitch's diary. He had been held for a total of 15½ months in New York and

---

[1] *Rolls and Lists of Connecticut Men in the Revolution*, pp. 222 & 208; *Record of Service of Connecticut Men in the War of the Revolution*, p. 547.
[2] Eastbury Cemetery Records, Glastonbury, CT, http://ftp.rootsweb.com/pub/usgenweb/ct/hartford/towns/glastonbury/cemetery/eastbury.txt
[3] CT State Library, *Connecticut Archives*, Rev. War Ser. I, Vol. XII, #193.
[4] *A Roster of Revolutionary Ancestors of the Indiana Daughters of the American Revolution* (Commemoration of the Unites States of America Bicentennial, July 4, 1776), Vol. I, p. 504, http://persi.heritagequestonline.com/...; *Record of Service of Connecticut Men in the War of the Revolution*, p. 614.

then on Long Island. The Trowbridge genealogy stated that "It was his unwillingness to yield to the wishes of his captors that caused him to be detained so long a prisoner, as an officer of equal rank was frequently offered in exchange. The British demanded that he should not again take up arms against them, a consideration to which he would not agree. On the contrary, he told them that as soon as he should get his liberty, he would be at them again."[1] It is probable that Trowbridge's opinion was not unique among the officers, and that it was a general consensus that they would not acquiesce to British demands that they not serve again in the American Army. The Trowbridge genealogy went on to say that his captivity would have been much more difficult if his wife had not sold her silver and forwarded the money to her husband on Long Island. In May 1778, Trowbridge petitioned the State of Connecticut for compensation for the loss of property at the hands of the British after being taken prisoner on Long Island, in the amount of 78 pounds, 11 shillings, and 5 pence. The articles for which he claimed compensation were left in camp in New York prior to the Battle of Long Island, and included $180 in cash, a watch, bed and blankets, and a variety of other items necessary for camp living.[2]

After he returned to New Haven, Caleb Trowbridge hoped to receive a promotion to major, but when that was not forthcoming, he returned to sea aboard a privateer. A group of citizens from New Haven raised the hull of a ship burned and sunk by the British, refitted it, and turned it over to Trowbridge as its captain. It was named, appropriately, *The Fire Brand*, was well armed, and with Trowbridge in command, took several enemy ships as prizes. When the British captured New Haven, they sacked Trowbridge's house and destroyed his furniture. It was said that when the house was repaired, bullets were found in the ceiling. Caleb and his wife Mary had eight children between 1770 and 1790. Caleb Trowbridge died at New Haven on December 15, 1799, aged 54.[3]

👉 **Captain Abraham Tyler** was not taken prisoner at the Battle of Long Island. Due to Capt. Hubbard's illness, Tyler remained the only captain fit for duty in the remnants of the 17th Regiment for the entire period of time between the Battle of Long Island and the time when

---

[1] Chapman, *The Trowbridge Family*, p. 54.
[2] CT State Library, *Connecticut Archives*, Vol. X, 372, 373.
[3] CT State Library, *Church Records Slip Index*.

the regiment was disbanded on December 31. He was promoted to major in Colonel McLellan's Regiment of Connecticut State Militia raised in March 1778 and served in Rhode Island during August and September. In October 1779, he was promoted to Lieutenant-Colonel in Colonel Andrew Ward's 7th Regiment of Connecticut State Militia, composed of men from Saybrook, Guilford, Killingworth, and Haddam. Abraham Tyler served as state representative from the Town of Haddam in 1783. He and his wife, Jedidah, had 10 children. He died November 13, 1804, age 71, in Haddam.[1]

First Lieutenant Jabez Fitch, without whose diary this work would have been greatly impaired, was released from captivity on December 15, 1777, and returned to Norwich, Connecticut. A month later, on January 18, 1778, he petitioned the Connecticut General Assembly for compensation for money spent for his support while a prisoner of war.[2] In May 1779, Fitch received an appointment as a lieutenant in a regiment of militia intended for the defense of Connecticut, and was promoted to captain in July. Ozias Bissell was a captain in the same regiment. It proved difficult to raise the money necessary for recruiting and Fitch's company was never completed. Because of this, Fitch resigned his commission on June 25, 1780, and never served again during the War.

In May 1781 Fitch was made a Justice of the Peace for New London County and was annually reappointed for some years. Also in 1781, he became, with several others from Norwich, one of the proprietors of a new township in Vermont, to which he relocated in 1788. For many Revolutionary War veterans, the new State of Vermont was the land of opportunity after the war, and they relocated there by the droves to seek their fortunes. Fitch's new home was named Hyde Park after Jedediah Hyde, another Norwich man, and one of the proprietors. For many years, Fitch served as the Town Clerk of Hyde Park. He was a constable and a frequent moderator of the town meetings. His occupation was farming.

Lt. Fitch and his wife, Hannah, had five sons and three daughters. Three of their sons relocated to Hyde Park, Vermont, with their father. Hannah followed with one daughter in 1791, and a year later

---

[1] *Roster of Revolutionary Ancestors of the Indiana DAR*, p. 322; CT State Library, *Church Records Slip Index*; *Record of Service of Connecticut Men in the War of the Revolution*, pp. 434, 543.
[2] CT State Library, *Connecticut Archives*, Rev. War, Ser. I, Vol. X, 10.

the other two daughters followed them. Jabez Fitch maintained his lifelong diary until five days before his death. He complained throughout his life that his health had been seriously impaired from the effects of ill treatment during his time as a prisoner in New York. But Fitch had lived a hard and very physical life from the time of his service during the French and Indian War through the Revolution, and his later life pioneering in Vermont. His wife, Hannah died at Hyde Park August 13, 1808, aged 74. Lt. Jabez Fitch died on February 29, 1812. His obituary, published in the Danville, Vermont, *North Star* on May 30, 1812, read as follows:

Departed this life February 29, 1812, Jabez Fitch, Esq., of Hyde Park, aged 75, much respected and lamented. The deceased was a revolutionary officer. He was captured on Long Island, on the 27th of August, 1776, and suffered the severities of British barbarity on board their prison-ships, at New York, the effect of which embittered and rendered almost insupportable more than 30 years of his life. He entered the military service when but a youth; was in three campaigns in the old French war, and a firm opposer of the unjust restrictions and oppressive demands of the British government, when those states were ripening for independence, and was with the first who drew the sword in defence of their country's rights, and to avenge the blood of their fellow-citizens. He was early engaged, also, in the abolition of the Africa slavery, and a zealous advocate of religious and civil liberty, which principles he retained till his death. With universal satisfaction he filled the offices of deputy sheriff in New London, Ct., and justice of the peace, and captain in Gen. Washington's army. The last twenty years of his life were spent in retirement, being unable to labor by means of a scorbutic complaint, contracted while a prisoner. This portion of time was devoted to reading and writing, and the latter part of it particularly to the study of his favorite book, the Bible. By minutes [his diary] which he left it appears he read it through in course, 47 times during the last 7 years of his life. An extract from the minutes above mentioned states:

'Feb. 26, 1807, arrived to 70 years of age- having during my 70th year, read the Bible through in course 8 times, and the

New Testament the 9ᵗʰ time, on which occasion I formed the following-

> *Illuminate my mind, O Lord,*
> *While I peruse thy holy Word,*
> *Teach me to understand aright*
> *Those glorious truths in their just light.*
>
> *Thus may the scriptures make me wise,*
> *To thy salvation may I rise,*
> *Through faith, which is in Christ alone,*
> *And thus approach thy glorious throne.*
>
> *There may I sweet acceptance find,*
> *To thy blest will complete resign'd*
> *Dispos'd to love and serve the Lord*
> *As here directed by the word.*
>
> *May thy good spirit yet impart*
> *Thy love to purify my heart*
> *That my remaining days may be*
> *Devoted wholly, Lord, to thee.*[1]

☞ **First Lieutenant Jonathan Gillet**, was captured at the Battle of Long Island, and kept with the other officers, first aboard the troop ships, and then at Hampden Hall in New York City. Very early in the captivity, Lt. Gillet was granted the freedom to go live with a Masonic brother, John Archer, and his wife, in New York City. As the sad tale of abuse detailed in the letter smuggled out to his wife on December 2, 1776, explained, he suffered greatly in captivity before being allowed to live with the Archers, and continued to suffer from dysentery for some time afterward.

According to the *History and Genealogies of Ancient Windsor*, Lt. Gillet remained a prisoner on parole at the Archer's home until the fall of 1779, when he was released and allowed to return home. He died a few weeks later, on December 9, 1779, due to persistent ill health that resulted from his abuse at the hands of the British.[2] The

---

[1] *Fitch*, pp. 258-261; Jones, *The Brewster Genealogy*, pp. 112-113; *Record of Service of Connecticut Men in the War of the Revolution*, p. 615.
[2] Stiles, *History and Genealogies of Ancient Windsor*, Vol. II, p. 298.

former date of release from captivity cannot be correct, however, for in May 1778, Gillet petitioned the State of Connecticut for compensation for the property he had lost after being captured by the British on Long Island and held prisoner for eighteen months.[1] This would have made his date of release about February 1778, allowing enough time for Gillet to have had a subsequent war record, as told below.

G. G. Gillet, a grandson of Lt. Jonathan, reported in 1862 that, "On being released [Lt. Gillet] reentered the service of the Republic, was a captain of marines on board a man-of-war and was victorious in a naval action in which the sailing captain was killed and fell in Gillette's arms. Lt. Gillette was offered repeatedly the command of another vessel, but he was prostrated by the severity of his service and died at the early age of 42."[2] Lt. Gillet and his wife Elizabeth had eight children, six of whom survived to adulthood and lived to old age.

On his death bed, Lt. Gillet reportedly told his son, who was eighteen at the time and soon to enlist as a soldier in the Revolution, that if he found himself a prisoner of the British in New York, to look up John Archer for assistance. As unlikely as it may seem, the son, Jonathan, was later captured at Horse Neck by British Col. De Lancey's Light Horse, and taken as a prisoner to the Liberty Street sugarhouse, adjacent to the Middle Dutch Church, in New York City. He was able to get word to John Archer, who provided him with substantial aid during his captivity, as he had his father.[3]

First Lieutenant Nathaniel Gove was captured at the Battle of Long Island, and after first being held aboard one of the troop ships, was kept at Hampden Hall in New York City with the other officers. We learned from Fitch's diary that he was likely a shoemaker by trade, when Fitch reported that Gove made a pair of shoes for Ensign Cornelius Higgins. According to the Gove genealogy, "He was one of the many who were poisoned while in prison and escaped death, though at the expense of being a cripple ever after from its effects."[4]

---

[1] Hoadly, *Public Records of the State of Connecticut, May 1778 to April 1780*, pp. 59-60.

[2] Vivian Lyon Moore, *Michigan Bible Records and Other Genealogical Notes* (N.D.: For the Burton Historical Collection, 1931), p. 89, http://persi.heritagequestonline.com/...

[3] Stiles, *History and Genealogies of Ancient Windsor*, Vol. II, p. 298.

[4] Gove, *The Gove Book*, p. 68.

He returned to Preston, Connecticut after he was released, but was permanently incapacitated from the injuries he sustained during captivity, and saw no further service during the war. It isn't known how he sustained the injuries he described, whether from wounds during battle, or disease while in captivity. On February 15, 1779, he conveyed to Patrick Pemberton of Preston four acres of land with a house, tan-yard, bark mill and other buildings, for four hundred pounds. The tan-yard and bark mill were facilities that would have been associated with the tanning of hides and, ultimately, shoemaking. After the sale of his property, Gove moved, first to Bennington, Vermont, and then Rutland, Vermont. He was one of the organizing members of the Masonic Grand Lodge of Rutland, Vermont, in 1794.

Lt. Gove built a house at Rutland at 26 South Main St. He became a tavern-keeper, and at various times operated several establishments in and around Rutland. The county courthouse was built on his land, and provided to the county rent-free. The only condition was that the entry to the courthouse not face the street, but towards Gove's tavern, which was connected by a boardwalk! He and his wife, Esther, had eight children, seven of whom survived to adulthood. Esther died at Rutland on September 16, 1784, and Lt. Gove died at Rutland on September 9, 1813, during an epidemic in that year. His term as a prisoner of war impaired his speech and crippled him for life, forcing him to walk with two canes, only able to shuffle a few inches at each step.[1]

First Lieutenant Simeon Huntington was not captured at the Battle of Long Island, and remained with his regiment until it disbanded on December 31, 1776. He married Freelove Chester in Norwich, Connecticut, on January 27, 1777.[2] At some point, Simeon was made a captain of local militia, a title which he used for the remainder of his life. In July 1782, he was a member of the Association against Illicit Trade, an anti-smuggling coalition from Norwich. Other members of the same organization were former soldiers of the 17th Regiment, including Jabez Fitch, and Thomas Fanning.[3] Simeon was one of the Common Council of the City of Norwich in 1785, while his cousin and former commanding officer of

[1] www.vtfreemasons.org
[2] CT State Library, *Barbour Collection*.
[3] Caulkins, *History of Norwich*, p. 398.

the 17th Regiment, Jedediah Huntington, was senior alderman. Simeon and his wife, Freelove, had six children, three of whom survived to adulthood. Freelove (Chester) Huntington died June 16, 1787, and Simeon married second, Patience Keene at Wethersfield, Connecticut on January 15, 1788. Lt. Simeon Huntington died August 10, 1817. His second wife, Patience, survived him until September 11, 1820.

☞ **First Lieutenant Solomon Orcutt** was captured in the Battle of Long Island. Jabez Fitch reported in his diary entry of October 19, 1776, that Orcutt had nursed him in his illness by making beef broth for him. Fitch also mentioned that Lt. Orcutt received housing in New Lots on Long Island, along with the other paroled officers of the 17th Regiment. According to his pension application, Lt. Orcutt remained a captive for one year and nine months, which would have made his date of release approximately May 1778. He later helped to build a fort at New London, Connecticut. At the time of his pension application in 1818, he was living in Randolph, Vermont.[1] His wife, Mary, died October 1, 1811, and was buried in the Randolph Center Cemetery. Lt. Solomon Orcutt died February 25, 1826, aged 96, and was also buried in the Randolph Center Cemetery. His gravestone inscription stated his rank as captain, which may have come as a result of later militia service in Vermont since his Connecticut pension was based on his rank as a lieutenant during the war.[2]

☞ **First Lieutenant Abraham Wright** was not taken prisoner at the Battle of Long Island, although, according to his pension application, he was present at the battle. He, along with the few other surviving members of Huntington's 17th Continental Regiment, fought again at the Battle of White Plains. He was discharged at Peekskill, New York, in March 1777. According to his wife, Rebeccah, at the time she applied for her husband's pension benefits, Lt. Wright served again in the war, was taken prisoner and spent the winter of 1779-80, ironically, in the Old Sugarhouse next to the Middle Dutch Church, on Liberty Street in New York.[3] Abraham and Rebeccah Wright had three children. They lived in Berlin, Connecticut, where, in addition to being a tinsmith, he operated a

---

[1] NARA, Series M805, Roll 623, Revolutionary War Pension Application, S41037.
[2] Randolph Center Cemetery records,
usgennet.org/usa/vt/county/orange/Randolph/cems
[3] NARA, Series M805, Roll 891, Revolutionary War Pension Application, W22699.

tavern for several years out of their home.[1] Lt. Abraham Wright died September 10, 1825.

☞   **Second Lieutenant/Quartermaster Thomas Fanning** was captured at the Battle of Long Island and mentioned several times in Fitch's diary. He apparently continued to fulfill the responsibilities of a quartermaster while the officers were confined at Hampden House in New York. After his release from captivity, he served again during the Revolutionary War as a quartermaster and assistant commissary general appointed by the State of Connecticut. After the resignation of Commissary General Hubbard in November 1780, Fanning was appointed to succeed him on January 12, 1781. Although appointed by the State, Connecticut commissaries also assisted the quarter-master-general of the Continental Army.[2]

Thomas Fanning married Lydia Tracy, the daughter of Samuel and Sibyl (Lathrop) Tracy on November 4, 1779. They had three daughters before Lydia died at the age of 32 on December 19, 1787. Thomas married, second, Lydia Coit, the daughter of William and Sarah (Lathrop) Coit, on June 11, 1789. She died less than six months later on Nov. 1, 1789, age 23. Thomas married, third, Lucy Coit, the daughter of Wheeler and Mehitable (Lester) Coit. She bore Thomas two sons.[3]

After the war, Thomas Fanning was a merchant in Norwich, Connecticut, and was active in the civic and political affairs of that town. He was one of the signers of the Association against Illicit Trade in 1782, and was one of those who donated the Chelsea Parade Ground in Norwich for a town park in 1791. After Norwich experienced terrible property losses resulting from a disastrous fire in 1794, the Norwich Mutual Assurance Company was formed to provide insurance for local property owners. Thomas Fanning was one of the officers of the new company. Two of Jedediah Huntington's brothers, Ebenezer and Joshua, were also officers of the company.[4] In May 1794, Norwich merchants convened a meeting to draft a resolution to Congress complaining of British depredations, and to urge immediate retaliatory action. Thomas Fanning was the

---

[1] North, *History of Berlin, Connecticut*, p. 231.
[2] *Record of Service of Connecticut Men in the War of the Revolution*, p. 431.
[3] www.homepage.mac.com/jcrossley
[4] Marshall, *A Modern History of New London County*, pp. 170, 171, 459, 460.

clerk who drafted the resolution. Thomas Fanning died May 24, 1812.[1]

☞ **Second Lieutenant Thomas Hayden** was not captured at the Battle of Long Island. On October 20, 1776, he was made adjutant of the remnants of Huntington's 17th Continental Regiment. When that regiment was disbanded in January 1777, Hayden was promoted to 1st Lieutenant in Col. Wyllys' 3rd Regiment, Connecticut Line. On April 8, 1777, he was made adjutant to Col. Zebulon Butler, in command of the Connecticut troops at Danbury. Hayden was discharged April 25, 1778, and returned to his home in Windsor, where his family was suffering economically due to his three years' absence in service to his country.

On June 20, 1782, Thomas Hayden again enlisted in the Continental service as a 1st lieutenant in Captain John Francis' Company, 1st Regiment, Connecticut Line, Lt.-Col. Hezekiah Sabin, Jr., commanding, and remained in service until the close of the War. Daniel Barber, a private in the same company in Huntington's 8th regiment in 1775, wrote of Lt. Hayden that "Hayden was, no doubt, a military man; but I should guess no soldier ever admired him for his pleasant airs."[2] It was said by other, more flattering neighbors that Lt. Hayden "was a tall man and fine looking; but his wife was small in stature and weight, with a sweet face and most lovely disposition. She was always spoken of as an excellent wife, a kind neighbor, and in every way an estimable woman." Thomas and Abigail had eleven children, only six of whom survived to maturity. Lt. Thomas Hayden died November 28, 1817, aged 72. His wife, Abigail, died just two weeks later, on December 14, 1817.[3]

☞ **Ensign Anthony Bradford** was taken prisoner at the Battle of Long Island, was moved into Hampden Hall with the other officers, and was later paroled to New Lots on Long Island. He remained there until on, or after, April 5, 1778, according to his diary, and did not serve again during the War. He married March 22, 1781, Olive Douglas, who was born in Plainfield, Connecticut, on Feb. 28, 1758, the daughter of Brig.-Gen. John and Susannah Douglas. Anthony Bradford remained in Plainfield where he became a justice of the

---

[1] Caulkins, *History of Norwich*, p. 480.
[2] Barber, *Connecticut Historical Collections*, p. 103.
[3] Stiles, *History and Genealogies of Ancient Windsor*, Vol. II, p. 372-373; *Record of Service of Connecticut Men in the War of the Revolution*, pp. 169, 586.

peace, and served for several years as a state representative. He was one of the organizers of the Plainfield Union Manufacturing Company, a producer of cotton goods. Anthony and Olive Bradford had one child, Henry, born in 1782. Anthony died July 16, 1819, and his wife, Olive, died in 1830.[1]

☞ **Ensign Elisha Brewster** was not captured at the Battle of Long Island. Upon the formation of Colonel Jedediah Huntington's 1st Regiment, Connecticut Line, in January 1777, Brewster was promoted to 2nd lieutenant. He served until August 1, 1777, when he resigned his commission.[2] Elisha Brewster married April 16, 1777, Margaret, the daughter of Samuel and Lois (Belding) Curtis of Wethersfield, born March 5, 1752. They had four children, all born at Middletown. According to the Brewster Genealogy, Elisha became a sea captain, but he and all his crew and vessel were lost at sea in 1798.[3]

☞ **Ensign Joseph Chapman** was taken prisoner at the Battle of Long Island. He may have been wounded or otherwise injured during the Battle, for on September 10, 1776, Lt. Fitch reported in his diary that "Ensign Chapman grows more harty [sic]." At the time, Chapman was on board the *Mentor* with Fitch. On October 13, Fitch sold the deceased Captain Jewett's hat to Ensign Chapman. Lt. Fitch later made mention that Ensign Chapman was assigned a billet with the widow Vandeveer in New Lots on Long Island, in January 1777. Chapman was exchanged on or about April 5, 1777, along with Ensigns Higgins and Kinsman. According to his pension application, Chapman reenlisted almost immediately as a lieutenant in Captain Stephen Brown's Company, Colonel John Durkee's 4th Regiment, Connecticut Line. During this period of service, he saw action at the Battles of Germantown, Fort Mifflin, and at Monmouth. This record is confirmed in *Connecticut Men in the War of the Revolution*: Chapman was commissioned 2nd lieutenant, May 12, 1777, and 1st lieutenant, January 20, 1778; appointed quartermaster September 13,

[1] *Plainfield Bicentennial, A Souvenir Volume* (Plainfield, CT: Pub. by the Bicentennial Committee, 1899), pp. 92, 97, 112, http://persi.heritagequestonline.com/...; Douglas, *Douglas or Allied to Families of that Name*, pp. 108, 109, 204; Richard M. Bayles, *History of Windham County,Connecticut* (New York: W. W. Preston & Co., 1889), p. 439, http://persi.heritagequestonline.com/...
[2] *Record of Service of Connecticut Men in the War of the Revolution*, p. 146.
[3] Jones, *The Brewster Genealogy*, p. 151.

1778, and captain/lieutenant, October 26, 1780; also acted as adjutant; and "retired by consolidation," January 1, 1781.[1]

In August 1820, Ensign Chapman deposed in his pension application that he was a resident of Wilkes Barre, Pennsylvania, age 72 years. He had formerly been a farmer, but due to advanced age, he was no longer able to work. His wife had predeceased him, and he had been living with his grown children for the past seven or eight years.[2] According to Norwich vital records, by Joseph's first wife, Lois, he had one child, and seven by his second wife, Elizabeth.[3] Five of the children were born between 1768 and 1776, and three more after Joseph was released from captivity. Two of them died in infancy. Joseph Chapman died August 9, 1822, in Berwick, Pennsylvania.

☞   **Ensign Joel Gillet** was captured by the British at the Battle of Long Island. The only mention of him in Lt. Fitch's diary was on the day of the Battle: after Fitch was taken prisoner, he was marched to a barn on the Gowanus Road where he found a number of other officers, including Ensign Gillet. In his Revolutionary War pension application, Gillet stated that he remained a prisoner about four months until he was exchanged in January 1777 at Milford, a statement that undoubtedly placed him aboard the *Glasgow*. The fact that he was never mentioned again in Fitch's diary may indicate he was not held with the other officers at Hampden Hall, and was certainly not at New Lots on Long Island as evidenced by his early exchange date.

Gillet's statement that he was exchanged at Milford may mean that he was held with the common soldiers in the Middle Dutch Church until he was exchanged and sent home on the *Glasgow*. Upon exchange, he returned to Harwinton, Connecticut. According to Harwinton, Connecticut, vital records, Joel Gillett married Rhoda Hinsdale just two months later, on March 13, 1777. They had a daughter, Almira, born a year later. Gillet's pension application mentioned another twelve-month period of Revolutionary War service as a captain in 1778, but provided no other details. This record is clarified somewhat by *Connecticut Men in the War of the Revolution*,

---

[1] *Record of Service of Connecticut Men in the War of the Revolution*, p. 182, 183.
[2] NARA, Series M805, Roll 177, Revolutionary War Pension Application, S40821/BLWT377-200.
[3] See also, Walworth, *The Hyde Genealogy*, p. 148.

that provides that he was a captain in command of a company in Colonel Enos' Regiment of Connecticut Militia stationed on the Hudson River for three months in 1778. In 1818, he was 72 years old and suffering from poor health due to an unspecified long-term, severe disability that he said was due to his treatment while a prisoner in New York. His wife was still alive, but not able to work. He had been a laborer, but he was no longer able to work and subsisted from the small produce of his farm. Joel Gillet, referred to in cemetery records as "Captain" Gillet, died February 11, 1823, age 77 years, at Harwinton. His wife, Rhoda, died October 10, 1834, age 86 years.[1]

Ensign Cornelius Higgins was captured by the British at the Battle of Long Island. We learned from Lt. Fitch that Higgins was housed with the other officers at Hampden Hall in New York City, and was then granted parole to New Lots on Long Island. It was for Ensign Higgins that Lt. Gove had made a pair of shoes on October 31, 1776. Higgins had been without shoes for over two months since the battle, after which he had been stripped and robbed by Hessian soldiers. Lt. Fitch also noted in his diary that Higgins was exchanged and released from parole on Long Island on or about April 5, 1777.[2] Higgins later deposed that he had been held in New York until he could pay for his room and board on Long Island, and was not exchanged until April 13. He received eleven pounds and ten shillings from the Connecticut Assembly in February 1778 as compensation for his room and board and the loss of his watch and property at the hands of the British after his capture at the Battle of Long Island.[3]

Almost immediately upon returning home to Haddam, Connecticut, Ensign Higgins reenlisted with a promotion to 2nd lieutenant in Captain Eli Catlin's Company, Colonel Philip Burr Bradley's 5th Regiment, Connecticut Line. His commission was dated January 1, 1777. Ensign Higgins married his second wife, Esther, later that year on September 24, 1777, at Haddam, Connecticut. Higgins continued to serve in Bradley's Regiment, and on March 17, 1778, was promoted to 1st lieutenant. He fought at the Battle of Monmouth on June 28, 1778, serving until August 15, 1779, when he

---

[1] NARA, Series M805, Roll 358, Revolutionary War Pension Application, S36540; *Record of Service of Connecticut Men in the War of the Revolution*, pp. 537, 541; CT State Library, *Hale Collection*, South Cemetery, Harwinton, CT.

[2] *Fitch*, p. 159.

[3] CT State Library, *Connecticut Archives*; Rev. War Ser. I, Vol. X, p. 146: Hoadly, *Public Records of the State of Connecticut, Oct. 1776-May 1778*, p. 555.

was discharged. In 1820, Cornelius and his wife, Esther, had their daughter, Esther, and their grandchild, Peter Page, living with them.[1] Cornelius Higgins died November 25, 1834, aged 90 years, and his wife, Esther, died December 28, 1836, aged 84.[2]

Ensign John Kinsman was taken prisoner at the Battle of Long Island, and went with the other officers during their captivity to Hampden Hall, and then to New Lots on Long Island. According to Fitch, Kinsman was released at the same time as Ensign Higgins, on or about April 5, 1777. His later claim for compensation for personal expenses incurred as a result of his captivity was denied by the Connecticut Assembly.[3] While on parole in New York during 1776, he learned the hatting trade. After he was released, he returned to Lisbon, Connecticut, where he immediately set up shop and began to produce hats for the American Army. According to his biographer, Kinsman's health was forever impaired from his time as a captive in New York, and he saw no further service during the War. Whatever his handicap, he was still able to farm and run a business.

On October 4, 1792, John Kinsman married Rebecca Perkins, of Lisbon, Connecticut, who was born Sept. 29, 1773, the daughter of Simon and May Olive (Douglas) Perkins. For three years, beginning in 1797, John Kinsman was elected to the State Legislature from Lisbon. While serving in this capacity, he became involved with the Connecticut Land Company that was selling land in, and organizing the settlement of, the Western Reserve in Ohio. In 1799, Kinsman made his first trip to the Western Reserve, and aided in the survey of the town that was to later bear his name: Kinsman, Trumbull County, Ohio. He became the one and only proprietor of the town.

After spending three years in preparation, in 1804, John Kinsman moved his family from Lisbon, Connecticut, to the new town of Kinsman. The move required one two-horse wagon carrying the family, two four-horse wagons for all the household goods and supplies, one four-ox wagon, and two riding horses. Several employees with their families also made the journey with the Kinsmans. The caravan traveled by way of Fishkill, New York, Lancaster, Pennsylvania, and Beaver and Youngstown, Ohio.

---

[1] NARA, Series M805, Roll 425, Revolutionary War Pension Application, W21325; *Record of Service of Connecticut Men in the War of the Revolution*, p. 194.
[2] Old Cemetery, Haddam,
http://freepages.genealogy.rootsweb.com/~jdevlin/source_files/haddam_cem.htm
[3] CT State Library, *Connecticut Archives*, Rev. War Ser. I, Vol. VII, #446.

It was said of John Kinsman that, "His age, experience, enterprise, wealth, and more than all, perhaps, his practical sound judgment, gave him an influence in the affairs of the town which no other individual could pretend to exert." Once established in Ohio, he went on to become a justice of the peace and an associate county judge; he helped to organize the county government; he held the office of postmaster; he assisted in establishing the Western Reserve Bank, of which he was the principal stockholder; he was a land speculator; and he became a wealthy businessman who built mills, ran a store, and improved a large farm. His wife, Rebecca, was "a woman of decided and devoted Christian character, of strong mind, and a large heart. She was active in promoting the religious culture of the place, both in word and deed." By the time John and Rebecca Kinsman left Connecticut, they had produced four children. Two more were born after the move to Ohio. John Kinsman died August 13, 1813, aged sixty years, and Rebecca Kinsman died May 27, 1854, aged 80 years.[1]

☞ **Ensign Elihu Lyman** was taken prisoner at the Battle of Long Island, and went with the other officers to live at Hampden House, and later to Long Island. The references to him are numerous in Fitch's diary. On the list of Connecticut officers held by the British on Long Island on May 2, 1777, Lyman listed his place of residence as Middlebury, Connecticut.[2] He was not exchanged until May 10, 1778, and never reenlisted in the service. In the same month, he petitioned the General Assembly of Connecticut for compensation for his losses, stating that, "he was wounded and taken prisoner in the action with the enemy upon Long Island the 27th day of August in said year [1776], and continued a prisoner until he was exchanged a few days past, and that he was stripped naked by the enemy who took from him sundry articles of cloathing [sic], arms &c."[3] He became a member of the Society of the Cincinnati in 1786, at the time a resident of Southington, Connecticut.[4] If this "Elihu" is the man referred to in the Lyman Genealogy, there is very little information related to him. It was said only that he was "a physician and d. at the south; left 2 children, Alfred and Maria."[5] Neither the *Barbour Collection* of state

---

[1] *History of Trumbull and Mahoning Counties*, Vol. II, pp. 296-297.
[2] CT State Library, *Connecticut Archives*, Rev. War Ser. I, Vol. XI, 139.
[3] Hoadly, *Public Records of the State of Connecticut, May 1778-April 1780*, p.51.
[4] *Record of Service of Connecticut Men in the War of the Revolution*, p. 376.
[5] Coleman, *Genealogy of the Lyman Family*, p. 210.

vital records nor the *Church Records Slip Index* has any information related to him.

☞ **Ensign Joshua Tracy** was not taken prisoner at the Battle of Long Island. When Colonel Jedediah Huntington formed the 1st Regiment, Connecticut Line, in the spring of 1777, Joshua Tracy was promoted to 2nd lieutenant. He died of smallpox almost immediately, on March 26, 1777. He left a wife, Naomi, and three sons.[1] On April 3, 1777, Hezekiah Tracy, Joshua's brother, was appointed 2nd lieutenant to take his brother's place in Huntington's 1st Regiment, Connecticut Line.[2]

☞ **Sergeant Elisha Benton** barely survived long enough to return home, where, as we have seen, he died of smallpox contracted while on board the *Glasgow*. His betrothed, Jemima Barrows, became a delayed victim as well. The family homestead where he died survives as the oldest standing house in Tolland, Connecticut, and is preserved by the Tolland Historical Society. The house is an outstanding example of a circa 1720 cape and is in a wonderful state of preservation. It is open to the public, and has recently undergone a complete restoration. After the death of Elisha in January 1777, the cellar was used to house 24 Hessian prisoners taken at the Battle of Saratoga later on in the same year. Although it might seem that the cellar of the Benton homestead would be a dark, damp, and dismal place of confinement, it was said that the Hessians were not averse to the accommodations or their treatment. They became trustees, of a sort, and were allowed to hire out as farmhands in the area. Graffiti carved into the beams in the cellar by the Hessians can still be seen. It was said that the prisoners became so enamored of this country (and the women) that many of them deserted and remained here after the War.[3]

☞ **Sergeant Roger Coit** was taken prisoner by the British at the Battle of Long Island. Thanks to Lt. Jabez Fitch, we know that Sgt. Coit, along with two other sergeants of the 17th, was allowed by British Commissary of Prisoners, Loring, on October 12, 1776, to go live with the officers at Hampden Hall. This fact no doubt saved Coit from the fate of the soldiers who continued to suffer in the Middle Dutch Church. No other mention of Coit is found in Fitch's diary, and

[1] Walworth, *Genealogy of the Family of Lt. Thomas Tracy*, p. 45.
[2] Hoadly, *Public Records of the State of CT*, Oct.11, 1776-May 6, 1778, p. 202.
[3] Tolland Historical Society, http://pages.cthome.net/tollandhistorical/Benton.htm

we do not know when Coit was released. But he was home by September 28, 1780, when he married Olive, the daughter of Simon and Anne Brewster of Norwich, Connecticut. At the time, Roger Coit was a resident of the Town of Preston. They had three children.[1]

☞ **Sergeant Theophilus Huntington** was captured by the British at the Battle of Long Island. Many of the details of his capture and internment have been provided elsewhere, including his exchange with the other soldiers of Huntington's Regiment at Milford, Connecticut, on January 3, 1777. He contracted smallpox while either a prisoner in New York or on board the *Glasgow,* before being set ashore at Milford. He believed that he, along with the others, had been intentionally infected with the disease by the British. At the time of his pension application in 1818, he claimed that the effects of the disease had impaired his health for the rest of his life. He did not serve again during the Revolutionary War.

Sergeant Huntington returned to Bozrah, Connecticut, where a child was born to him and his wife, Ruth, in December 1778. By 1783, the family had moved north and a child was born in Lebanon, New Hampshire, that year. Theophilus' wife, Ruth, died at Chelsea, Vermont, February 10, 1793, and he married second, Phebe, the daughter of Capt. James Hall, at Lebanon, New Hampshire. According to the Huntington genealogy, Theophilus had eleven children by his first wife, and three by his second.[2] The history of Chelsea, Vermont, provided that Theophilus Huntington was the treasurer of the town during 1805-1806, and a Selectman from 1789-91, and 1797-1803. He also served as the Chelsea representative to the state General Assembly in the years 1791, 1792, 1799, 1800, 1802, and 1805. His impaired health obviously did not keep him out of public service, and he became an esteemed member of the community while living at Chelsea.[3]

By 1818, when he made application for his pension, Theophilus Huntington was living in the Town of Clarence, Niagara County, New York. He had moved there some time between 1814, when he first applied to Congress for relief while a resident of Vermont, and the time of his successful application in 1818. At Clarence, Theophilus

[1] Jones, *The Brewster Genealogy*, p. 91; CT State Library, *Barbour Collection.*
[2] *The Huntington Family in America*, p. 99.
[3] John Moore Comstock, *Chelsea, The Origin of Chelsea, Vermont* (location and publisher unknown, 1944), pp. 44 & 51, http://persi.heritagequestonline.com/...

was living on about 80 acres of land that he had acquired from the Holland Land Company by a financial agreement which had since expired. Apparently, he had purchased the land for $430, but had only been able to pay eight dollars of that amount at the time of purchase. However, he was still living on the land and had improved 12 acres and built a log cabin. Theophilus' second wife, Phebe, died October 10, 1823, and he died at Clarence, New York, on July 11, 1830.[1]

☞   **Sergeant Stephen Otis,** of Captain Joseph Jewett's Company, was taken prisoner at the Battle of Long Island and survived captivity to return home to Connecticut. He later served a period in the state militia in 1781 during the time of the burning of New London and the taking of Fort Griswold by the British under the command of the traitor, Benedict Arnold. According to the Otis genealogy, Stephen was a farmer and a shoe-maker. After returning from captivity, the Otises had four more children in addition to the eight born previous to the start of the war. Stephen and his wife, Lucy, later moved to Shelburne, Massachusetts, and then Halifax, Vermont, where he died on December 7, 1831, age 93. Lucy died March 4, 1837, age 98.[2]

☞   **Sergeant Cornelius Russell** was taken prisoner at the Battle of Long Island, and likely held in the Middle Dutch Church in New York City until the latter part of December 1776, when he was exchanged, according to his pension application. He was probably aboard the *Glasgow* and sent to Milford, Connecticut, with the others. In spite of "being reduced to great distress" while in captivity, he immediately reenlisted in Captain Ezekiel Sanford's Company in Colonel Philip B. Bradley's 5th Regiment in the Connecticut Line. He was made an ensign by a commission that was dated January 1, 1777. On December 15, 1777, he was promoted to 2nd lieutenant in the same company and regiment. On March 16, 1779, he was again promoted, this time to 1st lieutenant. While Russell was assigned to Bradley's Regiment, he fought in the Battle of Germantown in Oct. 1777; was at Valley Forge during the winter of 1777-1778; and fought at the Battle of Monmouth in June 1778. The regiment was at Redding 1778-1789; Morristown Huts 1779-1780; Connecticut Village 1780-1781; Peekskill, NY, June 1781; and Phillipsburg, NY, July 1781. In 1781 Russell was transferred to Captain Thaddeus Weed's Company in

[1] *The Huntington Family in America*, p. 99.
[2] Otis, *The Otis Family in America*, pp. 111-119.

Colonel Heman Swift's 2nd Regiment, Connecticut Line. In August 1781, he was detached to serve in Col. Alexander Hamilton's Light Battalion, in General Lafayette's Light Division. This battalion was famous for the storming of Redoubt 10 during the seige of Yorktown, Virginia. Cornelius remained in service until the close of the war, and was one of the original members of the Society of the Cincinnati.[1]

Cornelius Russell married Huldah Pember in November 1784, in Windsor, Connecticut. The Pember genealogy lists five probable children born to this couple, and says that the family moved to Randolph, Vermont, where a deed was registered on the land records for Cornelius Russell in 1794. They were following Huldah's brothers, Samuel and Thomas Pember, who had settled on land purchased by their father in Randolph as early as 1778. Thomas Pember was scalped by Indians in a raid near Randolph on October 16, 1781. His brother, Samuel, was taken captive to Canada in the same raid but returned to Randolph the next spring. Cornelius Russell lived the remainder of his life in Randolph where he died on August 3, 1823, aged 73. He was buried in Randolph Center Cemetery. His wife, Huldah, died in Randolph on August 4, 1829, aged 75.[2]

Corporal George Gordon, of Captain Caleb Trowbridge's Company, stated in his pension application that he was in the Battle of Long Island on the 27th day of August, 1776, and "he was made a prisoner in that Battle and carried on board the prison ship *Mentor* with his hands tied behind him where he remained a prisoner he believes several months [illegible] the precise time when he was transferred to the City of New York, from which place he returned home on parole."[3] A summary document within the same file written in 1930, explained that Gordon, "returned home on parole about the end of the year, 1776." Jabez Fitch's diary mentioned him as one of the soldiers who was allowed by the British to remain with the officers at Hampden Hall during their captivity. Gordon probably

---

[1] NARA, Series M805, Roll 710, Revolutionary War Pension Application, S41112/BLWT248-200; *Record of Service of Connecticut Men in the War of the Revolution*, pp. 194, 327, 355, 373.
[2] Celeste Pember Hazen, *John Pember: The History of the Pember Family in America* (Springfield, VT: N.D., 1939), pp. 87-88, http://persi.heritagequestonline.com/...; Randolph Center Cemetery Records, Randolph,Vermont,
www.usgennet.org/usa/vt/county/orange/randolph/cems/rand/pierce-sanford.htm
[3] NARA, Series M805, Roll 366, Revolutionary War Pension Application, S39599.

owes his survival to this fact. According to Fitch, Gordon was exchanged and returned home about January 22, 1777. He did not serve again during the Revolutionary War. In 1818, when he applied for his pension, Gordon was a resident of Norwich, Connecticut, but by 1820, he had moved to Ohio County, Virginia. His occupation was as a farmer, but he was no longer able to work. George Gordon died September 1, 1823. Unfortunately, his pension file contains no family information.[1]

☞ **Private Lemuel Fuller**, of Captain Joseph Jewett's Company, was not captured during the Battle of Long Island. In his pension application, he testified that Jewett's Company was badly cut up during the Battle, but did not state that he was present during the Battle. Because of his specific knowledge that only 14 men from his company survived the battle, it may be safe to conclude that he was, indeed, present. He did say that he remained with the remnants of Huntington's Regiment until January 1777, when he was discharged at Peekskill, New York. Lemuel provided no other details regarding his war service, and claimed no further service during the Revolution.

Lemuel Fuller married an Elana or Eleanor, last name unknown, and date and place of marriage unknown. Lemuel was living in Grafton County, New Hampshire, when he made application for his pension in 1828. He had moved to New Hampshire about 1786 when he had received a deed for land in Piermont, New Hampshire. Lemuel's first wife died on December 6, 1816, and he married second, June 14, 1817, the widow, Polly Davis, in Corinth, Vermont. The births of ten children are recorded in Bradford, Vermont. The eighth child, Elana, was born December 5, 1803, named for Lemuel's first wife. The birth may have resulted in his wife, Elana's, death, which was recorded the next day. The last two children of Lemuel, by his second wife, Polly, born in 1819 and 1821, were living with Lemuel and Polly in 1828, when he filed for his pension. In his pension papers, Lemuel provided that his occupation was that of a farmer. When Polly applied for her deceased husband's pension benefits in 1853, she stated that her husband, Lemuel Fuller, had died on September 26, 1840. When she applied for Revolutionary War Bounty Lands two years later, she stated her age as 75.[2]

---

[1] NARA, Series M805, Roll 366, Revolutionary War Pension Application, S39599.
[2] NARA, Series M805, Roll 343, Revolutionary War Pension Application, W648/BLWT26490-160-55.

☞ **Private Samuel Gibbs**, of Captain Joseph Jewett's Company, was not listed among the missing from Huntington's Regiment after the Battle of Long Island. We might not have known he was a soldier in Huntington's Regiment but for the mention of him in Lemuel Fuller's pension application as a survivor of Jewett's Company. Gibbs' own pension application provided that he was in the Battle of Long Island, and therefore among the few from Jewett's Company who were not taken prisoner in the battle. No other details of the battle were given by Gibbs.   He first enlisted during the Revolutionary War in Huntington's 17th Continental Regiment in December 1775, at Lyme, Connecticut. He stayed with the remainder of his regiment after the Battle of Long Island until he was discharged at Peekskill, New York, in January 1777. He claimed no other period of service during the War.

When he first applied for his pension in 1818, Samuel Gibbs was 60 years old, a farmer living in Becket, Berkshire County, Massachusetts. His wife's name was Caty, and she was then 49 years old. Her maiden name was Caty Johnson, and their marriage was recorded at Sheffield, Massachusetts on June 26, 1805. According to family records, Samuel was married three times: first to a Lucy who died June 23, 1788, at Granville, Hampden County, Massachusetts; second, to Charlotte Tourgee; and third to Caty Johnson. By his three wives Samuel had nine children.[1] He died July 14, 1829, at Becket, Massachusetts. Caty Gibbs died June 6, 1855, in Tolland, Massachusetts.[2]

☞ For an unknown reason, **Private Solomon Ingham** was in New York during the Battle of Long Island, and therefore not taken prisoner. During the retreat from New York, he was at Newark, New Jersey, where he was "employed for some time in the hospital and in burying the dead from it." After that, he briefly served at Hackensack, and "various other places." Towards the end of December 1776, due to illness, he was sent to Stamford, Connecticut, to a hospital where he was shortly pronounced unfit for further duty and discharged. He did not serve again during the war, and later

---

[1] www.usgennet.org/usa/ny/county/niagara/webbs/surnames/index.cgi?read=104.
[2] NARA, Series M805, Roll 354, Revolutionary War Pension Application, W689/BLWT29731-160-55; *Marriage Index: Massachusetts, 1633-1850*, Family Tree Maker CD 231; *Massachusetts Vital Records, 1600's-1800's*, Family Tree Maker CD 220.

received a pension based on eighteen months' total service. In 1780, he removed to Middlefield, Hampshire County, Massachusetts, which was just being settled at the time. He married Molly Wright of Murrayfield in May 1781. The marriage was recorded at Chester on March 19, 1783. Solomon Ingham was the first town clerk of Middlefield, a selectman for several years, and a farmer. The history of Middlefield records that, "He was a home man, had strong intellectual powers, plain in person and manners, well informed, strong in argument and positive in his religious and political opinions. He made no profession of religion until near middle life after which he became well read in theology and strong religious literature of the past." It was also said that he was often "preoccupied or absent-minded," and as an example of this his son, Alexander, told the story that as a boy:

he once put his father to a psychological test on the point. Milking time having come, his father sent him to fetch the milk pail, but he returned with a market basket which he casually handed his father as he sat down to milk. Mr. Ingham proceeded as usual, not noticing that the milk was streaming down his legs, while the boy rolled upon the ground, overcome with uncontrollable laughter. 'Alec, Alec, what are you laughing at?' questioned his father, and he had to repeat the query several times before the boy was able to control his shouts long enough to point out the absurdity of what his father was doing.

Solomon Ingham and his wife, Molly, had seven children, six of whom lived to maturity. Solomon died on November 9, 1837, at the home of his son-in-law, Abner Wing, in Hinsdale, Massachusetts.[1]

Private John Lewis, of Captain Brewster's Company, was captured at the Battle of Long Island. He died before Congress voted pension benefits to Revolutionary War soldiers, and therefore left no pension file. As a result, we do not know the circumstances of his internment or his release. However, a John Lewis enlisted in Colonel Jedediah Huntington's 1st Regiment, "Connecticut Line," on June 2,

---

[1] NARA, Series M805, Roll 462, Revolutionary War Pension Application, W13527; Edward Church Smith and Philip Mack Smith, *A History of the Town of Middlefield, Massachusetts* (N.D.: privately printed, 1924), pp. 312 & 506-507, http://persi.heritagequestonline.com/...

1777. He served for 8 months and was discharged January 12, 1778. During that time, the regiment fought at the Battle of Germantown, and afterwards went into winter quarters at Valley Forge.[1] Shortly after John first enlisted in 1775, his wife and children relocated to the town of Washington, Massachusetts, near Pittsfield, where several other members of an extended family of parents, aunts, uncles, and cousins were living at the time. By 1782, John Lewis was living at Sunderland, Vermont, where he signed as witness to the sale of his father's farm in Washington, Massachusetts. John Lewis also served a period in the Vermont state troops in the campaign of 1781, according to a payroll issued at Sunderland. By 1790, he had moved north, and was living at Weybridge, Vermont. John Lewis and wife, Sarah, had at least seven children. He likely married second, Eleanor, by whom John had at least one more child, a son, John, Jr., born in 1780. John Lewis, Sr., died January 22, 1802, in Weybridge, Vermont, at the age of 79. Eleanor Lewis died on November 11, 1835, in Middlebury, VT.[2]

Private Levi Loveland, of Captain Elizur Hubbard's Company, was taken prisoner at the battle of Long Island and survived the voyage of the *Glasgow* to return home to Glastonbury, Connecticut. His wife, Esther, applied for widow's pension benefits in 1845, at about the age of 90. As she was applying for benefits at an advanced age, there aren't many details that she was able to provide about her husband's war service. She did not state specifically that Levi was captured at the Battle of Long Island. She did say, however, that he had served in Captain Hubbard's Company. She also said that Levi went into the service the next year after they were married, or in 1776, and served between one and two years. Also, according to Esther Loveland, her husband served a later period of service as a teamster in Captain Isaac Goodrich's Company from March 17, 1777, to January 1, 1780. If so, then he reenlisted just two months after he came home from captivity. Connecticut records provide a period of service for Levi Loveland beginning February 21, 1778, for "the War," in Colonel Wyllys' 3rd Regiment, Connecticut Line.

After the war, Levi and Esther remained at Glastonbury for some years, where they had a total of ten children. His occupation was that of a farmer. About 1800, the family moved to Partridgfield,

---

[1] *Record of Service of Connecticut Men in the War of the Revolution*, p. 151.

[2] Lewis, *John Lewis of Berkshire, Vermont*, pp. 46-52.

Berkshire County, Massachusetts, and then, a few years later, moved
to Madison, Geauga County, Ohio. Levi died there, November 17,
1830. Esther died at Amherst, Lorain County, Ohio, on July 16,
1847.[1]

☞ **Private Salmon Moulton** was captured at the Battle of Long
Island, and the account of his captivity has been provided elsewhere.
His brother, **Sergeant Howard Moulton**, also of Captain Ozias
Bissell's company, was captured as well, and was reported in
Salmon's pension application to have survived and was later living at
Troy, New York. In May 1780, Salmon Moulton reenlisted as a
quartermaster in Major Abiel Pease's Connecticut Militia for six
weeks at New London, and enlisted for the third time as a
quartermaster for six months in Colonel Levi Wells' Connecticut
Militia Regiment at New London.

Salmon Moulton married Susanna Johnson, the daughter of Seth
and Mary (Edson) Johnson, on February 15, 1780. They had seven
children. About 1802, Salmon Moulton and his family removed to the
new community of Floyd, Oneida County, New York, along with
several of his brothers with their families. Their father, Colonel
Stephen Moulton, had explored the country west to the Ohio several
years before, and he also settled at Floyd. Salmon Moulton was a
farmer, who later achieved the rank of major in the local militia.
Known locally as the "Moulton Boys" the descendants of Colonel
Stephen Moulton, including Salmon, became well-respected leaders
in their community.[2]

Salmon's wife, Susan, died December 27, 1831. Salmon must
have married second, Elizabeth (last name not provided), for both she
and Susan are named as Salmon's "consort," on their respective
tombstones. Both are buried next to Salmon in the Moulton Family
Cemetery in Floyd, New York. Elizabeth died May 2, 1852, age 65
years. Salmon lived only a few weeks more, and died June 22, 1852,
age 93 years.

---

[1] NARA, Series M805, Roll Revolutionary War Pension Application, W9145;
Loveland, *Genealogy of the Loveland Family*, p. 198; *Record of Service of
Connecticut Men in the War of the Revolution*, p. 176.
[2] NARA, Series M805, Roll 603, Revolutionary War Pension Application, S23810;
Carroll Andrew Edson, *Edson Family History and Genealogy* (Ann Arbor, MI:
Edwards Bros., 1969?), pp. 87-88, http://persi.heritagequestonline.com/...; CT State
Library, *Barbour Collection*; www.rootsweb.com/~nyoneida/towns/floyd

☞ **Private Zadock Pratt** has already been mentioned as having been captured at the Battle of Long Island. He was first interned aboard the *Whitby*, and then transferred to the Middle Dutch Church. He returned with the others to Milford on board the *Glasgow* at the beginning of January 1777. A story, unconfirmed by military records, says that after his release Zadock served again as a soldier and took part in the storming of the fort at Stony Point in 1779.[1] Zadock married Hannah Pickett, the daughter of Benjamin and Eunice Pickett of New Milford, Connecticut, on November 1, 1781. About 1790, Zadock removed with his family to Stephentown, Rensselaer County, New York, and in 1802 moved again to Windham (now Jewett), Greene County, New York. He operated a small tannery there, but his son, Zadock, Jr., later became wealthy at the trade, and went on to serve as a U. S. congressman. Zadock Pratt, Sr., died at Jewett, Greene County, New York, on July 27, 1828.[2]

☞ **Private Elijah Stanton** was wounded in the Battle of Long Island, was aboard the *Glasgow*, and came down with smallpox two days after he returned home on January 9, 1777. For over a year he suffered from the effects of his wound and disease, and was unable to serve again as a soldier until April 1778. In that month, he went to Tiverton, Rhode Island, and was appointed one of General Cornell's guards for one year under the overall command of General Sullivan. He went home after he was discharged from this period of service, and then enlisted a third time in April 1779, at Springfield, Massachusetts: this time for three years.

During his three-year enlistment, Stanton was in a Connecticut company commanded by Captain Ebenezer Fitch Bissell, and then in the 9th Massachusetts regiment of Colonel Henry Jackson. The regiment marched to West Point where Stanton remained for most of his term of enlistment. He was in no general action, but was called out to march south to the lines near New York, and was involved in skirmishes there. When the American Army marched south to engage Cornwallis at Yorktown, Stanton's company remained behind at White Plains as part of two or three regiments in garrison there. While at White Plains they established and maintained the illusion of a large encampment to deceive the British into believing that the

---

[1] Cutter, *New England Families, Genealogical and Memorial*, Vol. III, p. 1280.
[2] Chapman, *The Chapman Family*, p. 262; CT State Library, *Church Records Slip Index*.

American army was still there in position to attack New York. After the Battle of Yorktown, where Cornwallis surrendered, Stanton's regiment returned to West Point to winter over. In March 1782, Elijah Stanton was discharged the final time. A few years after the war, he removed to Fairfield, Herkimer County, New York, where he was living when he applied for his pension in 1832.[1]

On January 5, 1915, the Rochester, New York, *Democrat and Chronicle*, reported that Mrs. Samantha (Stanton) Nellis of Naples, New York, was celebrating her 105th birthday. The article stated that she was born at Fairfield, Herkimer County, New York, January 5, 1810, the daughter of Elijah Stanton. She was the ninth of ten children, but the article did not provide the name of her mother. Mrs. Nellis reported that her father, Elijah Stanton, had served in the Revolutionary War as one of George Washington's bodyguard, and was a personal friend of General Washington. She also claimed that after the War, General Washington had visited their home. Elijah Stanton did not claim to have been one of Washington's bodyguards in his pension application, but he did make a point of saying he served under General Washington. Given the fact that Elijah served as long as he did at West Point, there may be some truth to the claim made by his daughter, Samantha.[2]

Private Jacob Sterling survived the passage of the *Glasgow* to return to Lyme, Connecticut; however, two of his daughters died two months later, in March 1777. One of them was the second child by the name of Abigail, the first daughter named Abigail having died in 1775 while Jacob was with his regiment in Roxbury. The Sterling genealogy does not state specifically whether or not Jacob contracted smallpox while on the voyage of the *Glasgow*, but merely wrote that "Jacob fortunately escaped fatal disease and returned to Lyme." Although he survived, it is likely that Jacob brought smallpox home with him from the *Glasgow*, which proved to be the cause of the demise of his two daughters just a few weeks later. At any rate, the disease was not confined to Jacob's immediate family, for his older brother, Stephen, also died of smallpox on March 1, 1777, "during an epidemic of that disease." Jacob and Edey later had two more daughters to replace the two who died: one in 1778, and the other in 1782. Jacob claimed no other service during the Revolution, and he

---

[1] NARA, Series M805, Roll 766, Revolutionary War Pension Application, S14623.
[2] www.usgennet.org/usa/ny/county/ontario/Newsitems/newstown/newsnaples1900

and his wife lived the rest of their lives at Lyme. He died at Lyme shortly after he made application for his pension, on October 9, 1818. His wife, Edey, survived him until she passed away on February 11, 1834. Both are buried at the old cemetery at Sterling City, a section of Lyme.[1]

☞ **Private Daniel Thomas** of Captain Ozias Bissell's Company was taken prisoner by the Hessians at the Battle of Long Island, and it was he who claimed to have remained aboard the prisonship, *Whitby*, until his release about five months later. According to his pension application, he was 75 years of age in 1832, born in Preston, Connecticut. He first enlisted during the Revolution in April 1775, in a company commanded by Captain Edward Mott, Benjamin Throop, Lieutenant, and Jeremiah Halsey, Ensign, and marched through Hartford, Albany, and Lake George to Fort Ticonderoga. His term of enlistment was one year, although he was sick for part of the time. In 1776, he enlisted at Norwich in Captain Ozias Bissell's Company, in Huntington's Regiment, and soon after, marched to New York with the rest of the regiment.

Just three months after he was released from captivity, Private Thomas enlisted again on April 23, 1777, for the term of three years in Captain Beriah Bill's Company, Colonel John Durkee's 4th Regiment, Connecticut Line, in the 1st Connecticut Brigade. According to his pension application he was promoted to corporal during this period of service, and was discharged in New Jersey on April 13, 1780, with a written discharge signed by Colonel R. J. Meigs. Part or all of this regiment saw action at the battles of Germantown, Fort Mifflin, Monmouth, and Stony Point. Daniel Thomas stated in his pension application that he served several other brief periods of enlistment, the most notable of which was for six months beginning in September 1780 in North Kingston, Rhode Island, when he served with the French troops under General Rochambeau. In 1792, he moved to Groton, Connecticut, where he was living at the time of his pension application in 1818. In 1829, he had a wife, unnamed, age 72, and eight children: four sons, and four daughters. All of his children were living independently in various locations with families of their own. Thomas' sister-in-law, age 84, was the only other member of his family, besides his wife, who was

---

[1] CT State Library, *Barbour Collection*; NARA, Series M805, Roll 767, Rev. War Pension Application, S36797; Sterling, *The Sterling Genealogy*, pp. 324-325.

living with him.   His pension file contains no other family information.[1]

👉   **Private Seth Turner**, whose pension application helped to determine the identity of his company commander, Captain Elizur Hubbard, joined that company in November or December 1775, at Middletown, Connecticut. He deposed in his pension application that they marched to Boston, and that his was the first company to take possession of Dorchester Heights in March 1776. He later marched with his regiment to New York, and was wounded and taken prisoner at the Battle of Long Island. He said that he was first confined in a prison-ship and then at New York until February 1777 (the month is probably a failure of memory, and he too was discharged at Milford in January). Turner indicated that he served at the rank of corporal, however, he is listed as a private among those missing after the Battle of Long Island. At the time of his pension application in 1818, he was living in New Haven, Connecticut, and was 61 years of age. Turner listed his occupation as physician, and he had a wife named Sarah. According to the Driggs family genealogy, "Dr." Seth Turner was married to Sarah Hall. They had at least one child, Sarah, born at Hartford, Connecticut, July 9, 1785, who married Spencer Driggs in 1801, at Hudson, New York.[2]

👉   **Private Calvin Waterman**, of Captain Jonathan Brewster's Company, was captured at the Battle of Long Island. He testified in his pension application, "that he was taken at the Battle of Long Island by the British and remained a prisoner until after the year expired and until the Spring of the year 1777, when he was sent to New London in Connecticut and exchanged and discharged." In another document within the same file, he clarified that it was May or June 1777, before he was exchanged. Because of his specificity regarding the date and place of exchange, he must have been released later than the others who were aboard the Glasgow, but the reason and the circumstances are not explained; of course, as an old man when he applied for his pension, the date and place of his release may no longer have been clear in his memory.

[1] NARA, Series M805, Roll 797, Revolutionary War Pension Application, S11536; *Record of Service of Connecticut Men in the War of the Revolution*, p. 190.
[2] NARA, Series M805, Revolutionary War Pension Application, S35365; Lewis Lynne Driggs and Harry Stoddard Driggs, *The Driggs Family in America* (Phoenix, AZ: Driggs Family Assoc., 1971), p. 30.

Calvin Waterman first enlisted in the fall of 1775, and joined Huntington's 8th Connecticut Regiment at Roxbury. He reenlisted with Huntington's new 17th Continental Regiment and marched with that regiment to New York. After his release from internment, he served again during the Revolution when he enlisted in Captain Charles Miels' Company, Brig.-Gen David Waterbury's Connecticut State Brigade, on April 23, 1781, for one year. This brigade, consisting of just two battalions drafted from state militia, was first assigned to guard the coastline from Horseneck to New Haven. In July of that year, the brigade joined Washington's encampment at Phillipsburg, New York, and later took up duty guarding Westchester County. Calvin was living at Camillus, Onondaga County, New York, by 1807, when his name appeared on a list of residents eligible to vote in the Van Buren section of the Town of Camillus. He was living on Lot 29, along with an Eleazer Waterman, Elijah Waterman, and Thomas Waterman: no relationship determined. Calvin and Priscilla (last name not given) Waterman were married on March 27, 1820, at Camillus.In 1827, he was 72 years old, with his wife, Priscilla, who was 60, and a thirteen-year-old illegitimate granddaughter living with them. He was a farmer and a shoemaker. Calvin Waterman died at Van Buren on October 16, 1840.[1]

Private Peter Way was taken prisoner at the Battle of Long Island, and was dumped ashore at Milford along with the other surviving prisoners from the *Glasgow* on January 3, 1777. He returned to Lyme, Connecticut, and, according to his pension application, enlisted and served again during the year 1779. In that year, he served as a member of the garrison at New London and assisted in caring for wounded and sick soldiers for several months. He married Lucy Brockway, also of Lyme, at New London on October 1, 1779. Lucy may have been the Lucy Brockway born at Lyme, March 5, 1757, the daughter of Jedediah and Sarah (Fox) Brockway. Peter Way was discharged from his second period of service at New London on October 28, 1779, and he and Lucy returned to Lyme. When the British, under the command of the traitor Benedict Arnold, attacked New London on September 4, 1781,

---

[1] NARA, Series M805, Roll 842, Revolutionary War Pension Application, W8985/BLWT26934-160-55; *Record of Service of Connecticut Men in the War of the Revolution*, p. 571; Dwight H. Bruce, (ed.),*Onondaga's Centennial* (N.D.: The Boston History Co., 1896), pp. 163, 718 & 733, http://persi.heritagequestonline.com/...

Peter joined a local company and marched off to the relief of that town and served three or four days. Peter died at Lyme on June 17, 1826, and his widow applied for his pension benefits in 1838 from Lyme.[1]

The foregoing is a substantial sampling of the biographies, albeit brief, of the few soldiers from the 17th Continental Regiment who survived the catastrophic events of 1776. It must have taken remarkable courage and strength- or perhaps an overwhelming desire for revenge- for any of the survivors to enlist again in the service, yet some of them did. A few served for even the remaining six years of the war. Other men's bodies were so broken or otherwise impaired that they could not reenter the service, and suffered the ill effects of the battle and subsequent imprisonment for the rest of their lives.

In beginning this work, we were apprehensive that, like Danske Dandridge, we would find "...that in all our researches we have never yet happened upon any record of a single instance of a survivor living to reach his home." It has been with some relief that we found that the 17th Continental Regiment was not completely destroyed by the Battle of Long Island or its depressing aftermath, and that, despite their ordeal, some of the men from the regiment did reach home and went on to live rewarding and productive lives. Perhaps in the crucible of the dismal dungeons of New York, the survivors were forged into the kind of men who could then make significant and lasting contributions to their families, their churches, their communities, and their new nation. Connecticut became renowned for the enormous amount of food, material and arms contributed to the Revolutionary War effort, but perhaps it made no greater contribution- or sacrifice- than its brave citizen-soldiers who enlisted in Colonel Jedediah Huntington's 17th Continental Regiment in 1776.

---

[1] Francis E. Brockway, *The Brockway Family* (Owego,NY: Leon L. Brockway's Power Print, 1890), pp. 21-22, http://persi.heritagequestonline.com/...; NARA, Series M805, Roll 844, Revolutionary War Pension Application, W18228.

Appendix

COLONEL HUNTINGTON'S REGIMENT—1776.

17th CONTINENTAL.

[Huntington's regiment of 1775, as reorganized for service in the Continental army for the year 1776. After the siege of Boston, it marched under Washington to New York (by way of New London and the Sound in schooners), and remained in that vicinity from April to the close of the year. Assisted in fortifying the City; ordered Aug. 24 to the Brooklyn front; engaged in the Battle of Long Island Aug. 27, in and near Greenwood Cemetery; was surrounded by the enemy and lost heavily in prisoners; moved with the main army until after Battle of White Plains; disbanded under General Heath, near Peekskill, Dec. 31, 1776. Rolls incomplete.]

FIELD AND STAFF.

Colonel:	Jedidiah Huntington,	Norwich,	Served through the year (absent, sick in Aug.); re-ent. Cont. Service in '77.
Lieut.-Colonel:	Joel Clark,	Farmington,	Taken pris. Battle of L. I. Aug. 27; died at N. Y. Dec. 19, '76.
Major:	Elihu Humphreys,	Simsbury,	
Surgeon:	John Waldo,	Colchester,	
Surgeon's Mate:	Silas Holmes,		Taken pris. Battle of L. I. Aug. 27; exchanged early in '77.
Chaplain:	Rev. John Ellis,	Franklin,	Served in Cont. army in '77, etc.
Adjutant:	William Peck,	Lyme,	Appt. A. D. C. to General Spencer. See Genl. Staff.
"	Elisha Hopkins,	Hartford,	Appt. from Serj., Brewster's Co.; Pris. Battle of L. I. Aug. 27.
Quartermaster:	Thomas Fanning,	Norwich,	Taken pris. Battle of L. I. Aug. 27.
Paymaster:	Gardner Carpenter,	Norwich,	Appt. Sept. 9, '76.

[From Page 101, *Connecticut Men In the War of the Revolution*]

CAPTAINS.

Names.	Residence.	Remarks.
Abram Tyler,	Haddam,	
Caleb Trowbridge,	New Haven,	Pris. Bat. of L. I. Aug. 27.
Joseph Jewett,	Lyme,	Mortally wd. and pris. Battle of L. I. Aug. 27; died Aug. 29, '76.
Jonathan Brewster,	Preston,	Pris. Bat. of L. I. Aug. 27.
Ozias Bissell,	Hartford,	Pris. Bat. of L. I. Aug. 27.
Elihu Hubbard,	[Middletown],	
Timothy Percival,	Chatham,	Pris. Bat. of L. I. Aug. 27.
Ebenezer Fitch Bissell	Windsor,	Pris. Bat. of L. I. Aug. 27.

FIRST LIEUTENANTS.

Names.	Residence.	Remarks.
Solomon Orcutt,	Windham Co.,	Pris. Bat. of L. I. Aug. 27.
Zebediah Farnum,		In naval service, 1780.
Jabez Fitch, Jr.,	Norwich,	Pris. Bat. of L. I. Aug. 27.
Simeon Huntington,	Norwich,	
Abraham Wright,		
Jonathan Gillet,	[Lyme],	Pris. Bat. of L. I. Aug. 27.
Nathaniel Gove,	Preston,	Pris. Bat. of L. I. Aug. 27.
William Peck,	Lyme,	See Adjutant above.

SECOND LIEUTENANTS.

Names.	Residence.	Remarks.
Aaron Hale,	Haddam,	
Thomas Fanning,	Norwich,	See Quartermaster, above.
John Harris,		
Ebenezer Perkins,	Norwich,	Re-ent. Cont. service in '77.
Solomon Makepeace,		Pris. Bat. of L. I. Aug. 27.
Thomas Hayden,	Windsor,	Re-ent. Cont. service in '77.
Simeon Newell,	Southington,	
Jonathan Humphreys	Simsbury,	

ENSIGNS.

Names.	Residence.	Remarks.
Cornelius Higgins,	Haddam,	
Anthony Bradford,	Plainfield,	Pris. Bat. of L. I. Aug. 27.
John Kinsman,		Pris. Bat. of L. I. Aug. 27.
Joshua Tracy,	[Preston],	Pris. Bat. of L. I. Aug. 27.
Joseph Chapman,	Norwich,	
Elihu Lyman,	Middletown,	Pris. Bat. of L. I. Aug. 27. Wounded and pris. Bat. of L. I. Aug. 27. Exch. May, '78.
Joel Gillet,	[Lyme?],	
Moses Goodman,	[Hartford?]	
Elisha Brewster,	Preston,	Pris. Bat. of L. I. Aug. 27.

(101)

[From Page 101, *Connecticut Men In the War of the Revolution*]

CONNECTICUT IN THE REVOLUTION.

CASUALTIES IN COL. HUNTINGTON'S REGIMENT, BATTLE OF LONG ISLAND, AUG. 27, 1776.

CAPTAIN TYLER'S CO.

Serjeants.
Bartlett Lewis, Missing.
Elisha Benton, "

Corporals.
Reuben Bates, Missing.
Olive Jennings, "
Joseph White, "
Jesse Swaddle, "

Privates.
Joseph Arnold, Missing.
Joel Ballard, "
Azariah Benton, "
Lemuel Lewis, "
Seth Rider, "
John Smith, "
Jeremiah Sparks, "
Jonathan Witherd, "
Josiah Benton, "
Luke Kimball, "
Jonathan Barnard, "
James Lindsey, "

CAPTAIN JEWETT'S CO.

Serjeants.
Stephen Ottis, Missing.
Rufus Tracy, "
Roswel Graves, "

Corporals.
Nathan Raymond, Missing.
Peleg Edwards, "

Privates.
Joshua Blake, Missing.
Billa Dyer, "
Theophilus Emerson, "
Jaspar Griffin, "
Elisha Miller, "
Adam Mitchel, "
Charles Phelps, "
Silas Phelps, "
Oliver Rude, "
Ebenezer Smith, "
Jacob Sterling, "
Timothy Tiffany, "
Peter Way, "
Lebbeus Wheeler, "
Nathan Wood, "
David Yerrington, "
Duroy Whittlesey, "
William Eluther, "
Zadock Pratt, "
Eliphalet Reynolds, "
Rufus Cone, "

CAPT. TROWBRIDGE'S CO.

Serjeants.
Daniel Ingalls, Missing.
Daniel Farnam, "
Moses Smith, "

Corporals.
George Gordon, Missing.
Levi Farnham, "

Drum-Major.
Silas Bottom, Missing.

Privates.
William Bedlock, Missing.
Alexander Brine, "
Joseph Clarke, "
John Colegrove, "
Luke Durfee, "
George Foster, "
Caleb Green, "
John Gardner, "
Ebenezer Keyes, "
John Kingsbury, "
Robert Lithgow, "
Benjamin Lownsbury "
Ishmael Moffit, "
Joseph Mursur, "
Daniel Malone, "
Solomon Mears, "
John Pollard, "
Stephen Potter, "
Joseph Russell, "
Allen Richards, "
Monday Smith, "
David Saunders, "
John Talmage, "
William Turner, "
John Thomas, "
Samuel White, "
John Winter, "

CAPT. OZIAS BISSELL'S CO.

Serjeants.
Ebenezer Wright, Missing.
Howard Moulton, "

Privates.
Freegrace Billings, Missing.
Nathan Barney, "
Abner Belding, "
Seth Belding, "
Daniel Church, "
Lemuel Dening, "
George Edwards, "
Thomas Green, "
Jesse Judson, "
David Lindsey, "
Michael Mitchel, "
Samuel Moulton, "
Joseph A. Minot, "
Giles Nott, "

[From Page 102, *Connecticut Men In the War of the Revolution*]

CONNECTICUT IN THE REVOLUTION.

CASUALTIES IN COL. HUNTINGTON'S REGIMENT, BATTLE OF LONG ISLAND, AUG. 27, 1776.

James Price, Missing.
Jonathan Price, "
Benjamin Ripnor, "
Timothy Risley, "
Joel Skinner, "
Daniel Thomas, "
Robert Wallas, "

CAPT. BREWSTER'S CO.

Serjeant.
Theophilus Huntington, Missing

Corporals.
Jabez Avery, Missing.
William Button, "

Privates.
Simon Armstrong, Missing.
Jesse Barnett, "
Joseph Ellis, "
Asa Fox, "
Samuel Fuller, "
Elijah Hammond, "
Solomon Huntley, "
Sanford Herrick, "
Luther Japhet, "
John Lewis, "
Thomas Matterson, "
Rufus Parke, "
Amasa Pride, "
Jehiel Pettis, "
Roger Packard, "
Samuel Tallman, "
John Vandeusen, "
Calvin Waterman, "
John Williams, "

CAPT. PERCIVAL'S CO.

Serjeants.
Roger Coit, Missing.
Uriah Hungerford, "
Rous Bly, Killed.

Privates.
Samuel Agard, Missing.
Daniel Bartholomew "
Silas Bates, "
John Bray, "
Solomon Carrington, "
John Curtis, "
John Dutton, "
Daniel Freeman, "
Gad Fuller, "
Abel Hart, "
Jason Hart, "
Timothy Isham, "
Azariah Lothrop, "
John Moody, "
Timothy Percival, "
Isaac Potter, "

Elijah Rose, Missing.
Elijah Stanton, "
Benjamin Tubbs, "
Abraham Yarrington "
Jesse Roberts, "

CAPT. FITCH BISSELL'S CO.

Serjeants.
Cornelius Russel, Missing.
Eleazer House, "
Hezekiah Haydon, "

Corporals.
Samuel Boardman, Missing.
Aaron Porter, "
Elisha Boardman, "

Drummer.
Robert Newcomb, Missing.

Privates.
John Atwood, Missing.
Orias Atwood, "
William Craddock, "
Ira Clark, "
Roderick Clark, "
Lemuel Fuller, "
Abner Fuller, "
Roger Tyler, "
Carmi Higley, "
Erastus Humphrey, "
Jonathan Halladay, "
John Willson, "
John White, "
John Fletcher, "

CAPT. HUBBARD'S CO.

Serjeants.
William Talmage, Missing.
Samuel Skinner, "
William Parsons, "
Ebenezer Coe, "

Privates.
Eleazer Brooks, Missing.
Samuel Buck, Jr., "
Cornelius Coverling, "
Aaron Drake, "
Benjamin Hills, "
Alexander Ingham, "
Elias Leet, "
Levi Loveland, "
Elijah Roberts, "
Reuben Shipman, "
Samuel Strictland, "
Seth Turner, "
Nathan Whiting, "
Job Wetmore, "

[From Page 102, *Connecticut Men In the War of the Revolution*]

ROLL OF CAPT. JONATHAN BREWSTER'S COMPANY, HUNTINGTON'S REGIMENT, 1776.

Rev. Rolls, Pension Bureau.

Captain Jonathan Brewster,
Lieut. Simeon Huntington,
Lieut. Ebenezer Perkins,
Ensign Joshua Tracy,
Sergt. Frederick Williams,
" Theophilus Huntington,
" Henry Denison,

Sergt. Elisha Hopkins,
Corpl. Jabez Avery,
" Paul Kinyon,
" William Butten,
" Nathan Tyler,
Drum' Thomas Ryan,
Fifer Frederick Park.

Privates.

Abiel Pettis,
Rufus Parke,
David Parke,
Isaac Prince,
George Reed,
Samuel Raiment,

David Sanger,
William Smith,
Oliver Story,
Robert Swift,
Abel Spicer,
Nathan Stoddard,
Andrew Simons.

John Lewis,
David Kellogg,
Elijah Jones,
Luther Japhet,
Elisha Fanning,
Maher Tupper,
Miceal Torry,
Dudley Tracy,
Samuel Tolman,
John Vendusen,
Simon Armstrong,
Mathias Butler,
Elisha Burchard,
James Allen.

Jesse Barnet (?),
Eliakim Brown,
Asa Brewster,
Everet Eames,
Joseph Ellis,
Samuel Fuller,
David Fanning,
Hezekiah Fitch,
Benjamin Fuller,
Edmund Huntley,
Solomon Huntley,
Thomas Huntington,
Hiram Huntington,
Sanford Herrick.

Benajah Havens,
Elijah Hammond,
Alexander McDaniel,
Thomas Mattesons,
Robert Newcomb,
Chandler Wattles,
Benjamin Williams,
Calvin Waterman,
John Williams,
Elijah Whipple,
Abel Washunks,
John Quame,
Amos Avery,
Stephen Johnson.

Amasa Pride,
Jacob Hazen,
Elisha Murdock,
Asa Fox,
Phineas Knight,
Jehiel Pettis,
Uriah Edgerton,
Eben' Armstrong,
Roger Packard,
Nathaniel Farnsworth,
Kingsbury Sanford,
John Wight.

PRIVATES IN COL. HUNTINGTON'S REGT., SICK IN HOSPITAL AT STAMFORD, DISCHARGED IN NOV., 1776.

Stephen Ranson,
John Ferrein,
Ludwick Hotchkiss,
Joseph Boardman,
Abel Washings,
Ebenezer Armstrong,

Dunas Warner,
Hezekiah Brunson,
John Warner,
Belcher Starkweather,
David Mitchell,
Robert Clark,

David Fanning,
Samuel Fuller,
Solomon Inghan,
Elisha Messenger,
Joseph Lines,
Aaron Carpenter,

Eliphalet Abbey,
Elisha Case,
Jacob Bennet,
Eleazer Scott,
Nathaniel Martin.

Private John Eames, Capt. Percival's Co., and Private John Gardner, Capt. Trowbridge's Co. in Col. Huntington's Regt. at N. Y., 1776. Also Privates Moses Lockwood and Josiah Hubbard.

[From Pages 102-103, *Connecticut Men In War of the Revolution*]

CONTINENTAL REGIMENTS-1776

SEVENTEENTH REGIMENT—COL. HUNTINGTON

[See Record of Connecticut Men in the Revolution, page 101.]

CAPT. BISSELL'S COMPANY.

An Ammunition Return of Cap⁺ Ebenezer Fitch Bissells Company y⁺ 17ᵗʰ Reg⁺ New York May yᵉ 15ᵗʰ 1776
Mens names that have Got Guns and other Ammunition

Serj⁺ Cornelius Russell
Serj⁺ John Roundey
Serj⁺ Eleazer House
Serj⁺ Hezek⁺ Haydon
Corp¹ Sam¹¹ Bordman
Corp¹ Aaron Porter
Corp¹ Sam¹¹ Hall
Corp¹ Elijah Bordman
John Atwood
Will⁺ Andruss
Ozias Atwell
Will⁺ Arvin
Ephriem Alderman
Joshua Burgess
Shubell Cook
Will⁺ Cradock
Elisha Case
Jedidiah Case
Ira Clark
John Chambers
Abner Fuller
Lemuel Fuller
Benjamin Fuller
Hezekiah Filley
Roger Filer
Reuben Flowers
Daniel Gilburt
Carmi Higley
Obed Higley
Erastus Humphrey
Joel Humphrey
John Humphrey
Jesse Halley
Jonath⁺ Holaday
Jareth Ingraham
Henry Edwards

Phinihas Kellogg
Henery Kirkam
Samuel Kirkam
Nath¹¹ Lamberton
Elijah Loomis
Sam¹¹ Landers
George Lewardy
Elijah Lusk
James Lawrance
Isaac Merrell
Increas Mather
Alpheus Munsell
Daniel Moses
John Miller
Daniel Munsell
Frances Merrey
Isaac Mix
Elisha Messenger
Loammi Nearing
John Newbury
Daniel Olmsted
James Powers
Lewis Standley
John Smith
W⁺ Shephard
Joseph Sedgwick
Alex⁺ Thomson
Roswell Warner
Abner Warner
John Wilson
John White
John Whiting
Daniel Waller
Rhoderick Clark
Augustus Miller
John Flether

[Connecticut Historical Society.]

[From, *Rolls and Lists of Connecticut Men In the Revolution*]

Bibliography

Books

A Roster of Revolutionary Ancestors of the Indiana Daughters of the American Revolution. Evansville, IN : Unigraphic, 1976. http://persi.heritagequestonline.com/hqoweb/library/do/books/ [hereafter, heritagequestonline.com]

A Roster of Revolutionary Ancestors of the Indiana Daughters of the American Revolution. Vol. I. N.D.: Commemoration of the United States of America Bicentennial, July 4, 1776. heritagequestonline.com

Adjutants-General, *Record of Service of Connecticut Men in the War of the Revolution.* Hartford: Case, Lockwood & Brainard Co., 1889.

Baker, Eleanor Johnson. *A Genealogy of the Descendants of William Johnson of Charlestown, MA.* Newburyport, MA: Newburyport Press, Inc., 1969. heritagequestonline.com

Barber, John Warner. *Connecticut Historical Collections.* New Haven: by the author, 1836.

Bayles, Richard M. *The History of Middlesex County [CT] 1635-1885.* New York: J. H. Beers & Co., 1884.

Bayles, Richard M. *History of Windham County,Connecticut.* New York: W. W. Preston & Co., 1889. heritagequestonline.com

Benton, John Hogan. *David Benton, Jr., and Sarah Bingham, their Ancestors and Descendants.* Boston: David Clapp & Son, 1906. heritagequestonline.com

Brainard, Lucy Abigail. *The Genealogy of the Brainerd-Brainard Family in America 1649-1908.* Vol. II, Part VI. Hartford: Case, Lockwood & Brainard Co., 1908. heritagequestonline.com

Brooklyn Trust Company and Walton Advertising and Printing Co. *Rambles about Historic Brooklyn.* Brooklyn, NY: Printed for the Brooklyn Trust Company, 1916.

Caulkins, Francis Manwaring. *The History of Norwich.* Hartford: Case, Lockwood & Brainard, 1873. heritagequestonline.com

Chapman, F. W. *The Chapman Family.* Hartford: Case, Tiffany and Co., 1854. heritagequestonline.com

Chapman, F. W. *The Trowbridge Family.* New Haven: Punderson, Crisand & Co., 1872. heritagequestonline.com

Cleaveland, Nehemiah. *Green-Wood Cemetery: A History of the Institution from 1838-1864*. New York: Anderson & Archer, 1866. heritagequestonline.com

Coleman, Lyman. *Genealogy of the Lyman Family*. Albany: J. Munsell, 1872. heritagequestonline.com

Collections of the Connecticut Historical Society. Vol. XX. Hartford: Published by the Society, 1923.

Collections of the Connecticut Historical Society. Vol. VII. Hartford: Published by the Society, 1899.

Collections of the Massachusetts Historical Society. 5th Series, Vol. IX. Boston: Published by the Society, 1885.

Commager , Henry Steele and Morris, Richard B. (eds.) *The Spirit of 'Seventy-Six*. New York: Harper Collins, 1958, 1967. Reprint, Castle Books, 2002.

Crawford, Mary Caroline. *Old Boston Days & Ways*. Boston: Little, Brown, and Co., 1909. [excerpts from Lt. Jabez Fitch's diary, Jan.-April 1776]

Cutter, William Richard. *New England Families, Genealogical and Memorial*. New York: Lewis Historical Publishing Co., 1913. Electronic edition, Family Tree Maker, CD515.

Damon, Richard A. *The Damon Family of Reading, Mass.* Amherst, MA: published by the author, 1999.

Dandridge, Danske. *American Prisoners of the Revolution*. Charlottesville, Virginia: N.D., 1911. www.gutenberg.org/ebooks/7829

Depuy, Henry W. *Ethan Allen and the Green-Mountain Heroes of '76*. New York: Phinney, Blakeman, & Mason, 1861. Facsimile reprint, Heritage Books, 1994.

Douglas, Charles Henry James. *Douglas or Allied Families of that Name*. Providence: E. L. Freeman & Co., 1879. heritagequestonline.com

Duncan, Lt.-Col. Louis C. *Medical Men in the American Revolution*. Carlisle Barracks, PA: By direction of the Secretary of War, 1931.

Force, Peter. *American Archives*. 5th Series, Vol. I. Published under the authority of an act of Congress passed on March 2, 1833, and March 3, 1843. Washington, D.C.: N.D., 1848-1853.

Ford, George Hare. *Historical Sketches of the Town of Milford*. New Haven: Tuttle, Morehouse & Taylor Co., 1914.

Fraser, Georgia. *The Stone House at Gowanus*. New York: Witter and Kintner, 1909. heritagequestonline.com

Fuller, William Hyslop. *Some of the Descendants of Matthew Fuller.* Vol. III. Palmer, MA: by the author, 1914. heritagequestonline.com

Furman, Gabriel. *Notes, Geographical and Historical Relating to the Town of Brooklyn.* Brooklyn, NY: A. Spooner, 1824. heritagequestonline.com

Gallagher, John J. *The Battle of Brooklyn.* New York: De Capo Press, 1995. Reprint, Castle Books, 2002.

Gilman, Daniel Coit. *A Historical Discourse delivered in Norwich, Connecticut, September 7, 1859.* Boston: G. C. Rand and Avery, 1859. heritagequestonline.com

Goodwin, Nathaniel. *Genealogical Notes or Contributions to the Family History of some of the First Settlers of Connecticut and Massachusetts.* Hartford: N.D., 1856. Electronic edition, Family Tree Maker, CD515.

Gove, William Henry. *The Gove Book.* Salem, MA: Sidney Perley, 1922. heritagequestonline.com

Graves, Kenneth Vance. *John Graves, 1635 Settler of Concord, MA.* Wrentham, MA: pub. by the author, 2002.

Hall, Charles S. *Hall Ancestry.* New York: G. P. Putnam, 1896.

Hall, Charles S. *Life and Letters of Samuel Holden Parsons.* Binghamton, NY: Otseningo Pub. Co., 1905.

Halsey, Jacob Lafayette and Halsey, Edmund Drake. *Thomas Halsey of Hertfordshire, England, and Southampton, Long Island 1591-1679.* Morristown, NJ: by the authors, 1895. heritagequestonline.com

Hammond, Frederick Stam. *Histories and Genealogies of the Hammond Families in America.* Oneida, NY: Ryan & Burkhart, Printers, 1902. heritagequestonline.com

Hayden, Jabez H. *Historical Sketches.* Windsor Locks, CT: The Windsor Locks Journal, 1900. heritagequestonline.com

Hinman, Royal R. *Historical Collection from Official Records, Files, etc., of the Part Sustained by Connecticut During the War of the Revolution.* Hartford: E. Gleason, 1842.

History of Trumbull and Mahoning Counties. Vol. II. Cleveland: H. Z. Williams & Bro., 1882. heritagequestonline.com

Hoadly, Charles H. *The Public Records of the State of Connecticut, Oct., 1776-Feb., 1778.* Hartford: Case, Lockwood & Brainard Co., 1894.

Hopkins, Timothy. *John Hopkins of Cambridge, Mass., 1634.* N.D.: N.D., 1932. http://persi.heritagequestonline.com/...

Humphreys, Frederick. *The Humphreys Family in America.* New York: Humphreys Print., 1883. heritagequestonline.com

Index of the Rolls of honor (ancestor's index) in the Lineage Books of the National Society of the Daughters of the American Revolution. Volumes 1-160. N.D.: Press of Pierpont, Siviter, 1916-40.

Huntington, Rev. E. B. *A Genealogical Memoir of the Huntington Family In America,* Stamford, CT: pub. by the author, 1863.

Ingham, Arthur B. *The Ingham Family.* Pebble Beach, CA: pub. by the author, 1968.

Jennings, Frank Lamont. *A Genealogy of a Jennings Family and Allied Families of Lamont-Aldrich and Germond.* Greenwood, IN: published by the author, 1972. heritagequestonline.com

Jessop, Edith Newbold. *General Daniel Bissell, His Ancestors and Descendants.* New York: N. D., 1927. heritagequestonline.com

Jewett, Frederic Clarke. *History and Genealogy of the Jewetts of America.* Vol. I. Rowley, MA: The Jewett Family in America, 1908. heritagequestonline.com

Johnson, Mary Coffin. *The Higleys and Their Ancestry.* New York: D. Appleton & Co., 1896. heritagequestonline.com

Johnston, Henry P. *The Campaign of 1776 Around New York and Brooklyn.* N.D.: N.D., 1878. Reprint, Scholar's Bookshelf, Cranbury, NJ, 2005.

Jones, Emma C. Brewster. *The Brewster Genealogy, 1566-1907.* New York: Grafton Press, 1908. heritagequestonline.com

Kilbourne, Payne Kenyon. *Sketches and Chronicles of the Town of Litchfield.* Hartford: Case, Lockwood & Co., 1859. heritagequestonline.com

Kingsbury, Frederick John. *The Genealogy of the Descendants of Henry Kingsbury.* Hartford: Case, Lockwood & Brainard Co., 1905. heritagequestonline.com

Lambert, Edward R. *History of the Colony of New* Haven. New Haven: Hitchcock & Stafford, 1838. heritagequestonline.com

Lauber, Almon W. (ed.) *Orderly Books of the Fourth New York Regiment, 1778-1780, the Second New York Regiment, 1780-1783.* Albany: University of the State of New York, 1932. heritagequestonline.com

Leach, F. Phelps. *Additions and Corrections for Thomas Hungerford.* East Highgate, VT: published by the author, 1932. heritagequestonline.com

Lewis, Charles H. *John Lewis of Berkshire, Vermont.* Westminster, MD: Heritage Books, Inc., 2004.

Lists and Returns of Connecticut Men in the Revolution, 1775-1783. Hartford: CT Historical Society, 1909. Electronic edition, Heritage Books, Inc., CD1360.

Lossing, Benson J. *Pictorial Field Book of the Revolution.* New York: Harper & Brothers, 1860. Electronic edition, Heritage Books, Inc., CD3261.

Loveland , J. B. and Loveland , George. *Genealogy of the Loveland Family.* Fremont, Ohio: I. M. Keeler & Son, 1892. heritagequestonline.com

Marshall, Benjamin Tinkham (ed.). *A Modern History of New London County Connecticut.* New York: Lewis Historical Publishing Co., 1922. heritagequestonline.com

Martin, Joseph Plumb. *Memoir of a Revolutionary Soldier/ The Narrative of Joseph Plumb Martin.* New York: Dover Publications, Inc., 2006.

Metz, Herman A. *Colonial Highways of Greater New York.* New York: Bureau for the Examination of Claims, Dept. of Finance, 1908. heritagequestonline.com

Moody, Herbert A. *Historical Notes Concerning the Moody Family.* Turners Falls, MA: N.D., 1947. heritagequestonline.com

Moore, Vivian Lyon. *Michigan Bible Records and Other Genealogical Notes.* N.D.: For the Burton Historical Collection, 1931. heritagequestonline.com

Moses, Zebina. *Historical Sketches of John Moses, of Plymouth.* Hartford: Case, Lockwood & Brainard, 1890. heritagequestonline.com

Newcomb, Bethuel Merritt. *Andrew Newcomb, 1618-1686, and His Descendants.* New Haven: The Tuttle, Morehouse & Taylor Co., 1923. heritagequestonline.com

North, Catharine Melinda. *History of Berlin, Connecticut.* New Haven: Tuttle, Morehouse & Taylor Co. heritagequestonline.com

Onderdonk, Henry, Jr. *Revolutionary Incidents of Suffolk and Kings Counties, With and Account of the Battle of Long Island.* New York: Leavitt & Co., 1849. Reprint by Higginson Book Co., Salem, MA, 2007.

Otis, William A. *The Otis Family in America*. Chicago: published by the author, 1924. heritagequestonline.com

Patterson, Samuel White. *Famous Men and Places in the History of New York City*. New York: Noble and Noble, 1923. heritagequestonline.com

Pennsylvania Archives. Second Series, Vol. I. Harrisburg: Lane S. Hart, 1879. www.footnote.com

Pennsylvania Archives. Fifth Series, Vol. VIII. Harrisburg: Harrisburg Pub. Co., State printer, 1906. www.footnote.com

Perkins, Mary E. *Old Houses of the Antient [sic] Town of Norwich 1660-1800*. Norwich, CT: The Bulletin Co., 1895. heritagequestonline.com

Philips, David E. *Legendary Connecticut*. Willimantic, CT: Curbstone Press, 1992.

Phillips, Daniel L. *Griswold- A History*. New Haven: Tuttle, Morehouse & Taylor Co., 1929. heritagequestonline.com

Plainfield Bicentennial, A Souvenir Volume. Plainfield, CT?:Pub. by the Bicentennial Committee, 1899. heritagequestonline.com

Platt, Omar W. *History of Milford, Connecticut, 1639-1939*. Bridgeport, CT: Press of Braunworth & Co., 1939. heritagequestonline.com

Rolls and Lists of Connecticut Men in the Revolution 1775-1783. Hartford: CT Historical Society, 1901. Electronic edition, Heritage Books, Inc., CD1360.

Rolls of Connecticut Men in the French and Indian War, 1755-1762. Hartford: Connecticut Historical Society, 1903. Electronic edition, Heritage Books, Inc., CD1360.

Russell, George Ely. *The Descendants of William Russell of Salem, Mass.,1674*. Middletown, MD: Catoctin Press, 1989.

Sabine, W. H. W. (ed.). *The New-York Diary of Lieutenant Jabez Fitch*. New York: pub. by the editor, 1954.

Sterling, Albert Mack. *The Sterling Genealogy*. New York: The Grafton Press, 1909. heritagequestonline.com

Stiles, Henry R. *Families of Ancient Wethersfield*. Vol. II. New York: N.D., 1904. Electronic edition, Family Tree Maker, CD515.

Stiles, Henry R. *The Civil, Political, Professional and Ecclesiastical History and Commercial and Industrial Record of the County of Kings and the City of Brooklyn, NY*. New York: W. W. Munsell & Co., 1884. heritagequestonline.com

Stiles, Henry R. *The History and Genealogies of Ancient Windsor, Connecticut.* Vol. II. Hartford: Case, Lockwood, & Brainard Co., 1892. Electronic edition, Family Tree Maker CD515, Disc 2.

Stiles, Henry Reed. *A History of the City of Brooklyn.* Vol. I. Brooklyn: published by subscription, 1867.

Stone, Clara J. *Genealogy of the Descendants of Jasper Griffing.* New York (?): N.D., 1881. heritagequestonline.com

Stone, William L. *History of New York City.* New York: Virtue & Yorston, 1872. heritagequestonline.com

Strong, Thomas M. *The History of the Town of Flatbush in Kings County on Long Island.* Brooklyn: Loeser & Co., 1908. heritagequestonline.com

The Celebration of the 150th Anniversary of the Primitive Organization of the Congregational Church and Society in Franklin, Connecticut. New Haven: Tuttle, Morehouse & Taylor, 1869. heritagequestonline.com

The Huntington Family in America. Hartford: The Huntington Family Association, 1915.

The Jewett Family of America Yearbook of 1912-1913. Rowley, MA: The Jewett Family of America, 1913. heritagequestonline.com

The Mayflower Descendant. Vol. VII, & Vol. VIII. Boston: MA Society of Mayflower Descendants, 1899.

The Public Records of the Colony of Connecticut, April 1636-October 1776. Hartford: Brown & Parsons, 1850-1890. www.colonialct.uconn.edu

Timlow, Heman R. *Ecclesiastical and other Sketches of Southington, Conn.* Hartford: Case, Lockwood and Brainard Co., 1875. heritagequestonline.com

Todd, Charles B. *A Brief History of the City of New York*, New York: American Book Company, N.D. heritagequestonline.com

Todd, Charles Burr. *The Story of The City of New York*, New York and London: G. P. Putnam's Sons, 1907. heritagequestonline.com

Trumbull, J. Hammond (ed.), *Memorial History of Hartford County.* Boston: Edward Osgood Pub., 1886. heritagequestonline.com

Vital Records of Norwich, 1659-1848. Vol. I. Hartford: Society of Colonial Wars in the State of Connecticut, 1913.

Waldo, Loren P. *The Early History of Tolland [CT].* Hartford: Case, Lockwood & Co., 1861. heritagequestonline.com

Walworth, Reuben H. *Genealogy of the Family of Lt. Thomas Tracy of Norwich, Connecticut.* Milwaukee: D. S. Harkness Co., 1889. heritagequestonline.com

Walworth, Reuben H. *The Hyde Genealogy.* Albany, NY: J. Munsell, 1864. heritagequestonline.com

Watson, John F. *Annals and Occurrences of New York City and State in the Olden Times.* Philadelphia: Henry F. Anners, 1846. heritagequestonline.com

Wheeler , George Augustus and Wheeler , Henry Warren. *History of Brunswick, Topsham, and Harpswell, Maine.* Boston: Alfred Mudge & Son, 1878. heritagequestonline.com

Whittelsey, Charles Barney. *Genealogy of the Whittlesey-Whittelsey Family.* 2nd edition. New York: McGraw-Hill Book Co., 1941. heritagequestonline.com

Whittemore, Henry. *The Heroes of the American Revolution and their Descendants, Battle of Long Island.* Brooklyn: Heroes of the Revolution Pub. Co., 1897. heritagequestonline.com

Zlatich, Marko and Copeland, Peter F. *General Washington's Army 1: 1775-1778.* Men-At-Arms Series 273. Oxford, UK: Osprey Pub., 1994.

Archives and Collections

Connecticut State Library: *Barbour Collection of State Vital Records*; *Church Records Slip Index*; *Connecticut Archives/ Revolutionary War, 1763-1789,* Series I.

Library of Congress, Manuscript Division: *George Washington Papers.* http://memory.loc.gov/ammem/gwhtml/gwseries.html

Marriage Index: Massachusetts, 1633-1850, Family Tree Maker, CD231.

Massachusetts Vital Records, 1600's-1800's, Family Tree Maker, CD220.

National Archives and Records Administration: Series M805, *Revolutionary War Pension and Bounty Land Warrant Application Files.* http://persi.heritagequestonline.com and www.footnote.com; Series M246, *Revolutionary War Rolls, 1775-1783, Continental Troops, 17th Regiment-Col. Jedediah Huntington, 1776.* www.footnote.com.

Newspapers and Periodicals

Article 3-No Title, *The Connecticut Courant and Hartford Weekly Intelligencer*, July 15, 1776. http://proquest.umi.com/

Beam, Larry. "Moments in Time," *The Steeple-News and Current Events of the First Congregational Church of Griswold,* Vol. VIII, No. 5, May 2005. www.firstchurchgriswold.org/steeples%20PDF/May%20steeples%202005.pdf

Chadwick, John W. "The Battle of Long Island," *Harper's New Monthly Magazine*, Vol. LIII, Aug. 1876. New York: Harper & Brothers, 1876.

Classified Ad 2. "Deserted from Capt. Perceval's company," *The Connecticut Courant and Hartford Weekly Intelligencer*, April 29, 1776. http://proquest.umi.com/

"Extract of a letter from Princetown, dated the 10th inst.," *The Connecticut Courant and Hartford Weekly Intelligencer*, July 22, 1776. http://proquest.umi.com/

"Hezekiah Hayden, to his parents, camp New York, July 4, 1776," *Hartford Daily Courant*, Dec. 21, 1841. http://proquest.umi.com/

"New York, August 29," *The Connecticut Courant and Hartford Weekly Intelligencer*, Sept. 2, 1776. http://proquest.umi.com/

"One Hundred Years Ago-Some Old Letters-The Battle of Long Island-The Connecticut Participants," *The Hartford Daily Courant*, November 29, 1878. http://proquest.umi.com/

Thorburn, Grant. "Tales of the Prison Sugarhouse in Liberty Street, New York, or Anecdotes of the Revolution," *The Hartford Daily Courant*, Jan. 23, 1854. http://proquest.umi.com/

Weber, David. "No Glory for Israel Bissell," *Republican-American* (Waterbury, CT), April 19, 2007

Windham Herald, August 20, 1791. www.geocities.com/Heartland/Fields/4791/windhamheraldaug1791.html

Unpublished Material

Banworth, Linda. "History of the Simon DeHart Home, Brooklyn, NY."
http://homepages.rootsweb.com/~am1/deharthome_brooklyn.html

Bradford, Anthony. *Diary, 1775-1778.* Unpublished Manuscript, Connecticut Historical Society Manuscripts Collection: transcribed by S.F. Bradford, 1886. (Handwritten.)

Braisted, Todd W. "Prince of Wales' American Regiment." Lecture, April 1998. www.rootsweb.com/~canmil/uel/pwar.htm

"Brief History of the Brick Church: Presbyterian Church In Manhattan."
http://thehistorybox.com/ny_city/ny_city_worship_history_brick_church_article00539.htm

"Historical Footnotes: Stonington in Rebellion." The Stonington Historical Society. www.stoningtonhistory.org/archiv5.htm

"Independent Companies (Hierlihy's) Memorial." The On-Line Institute for Advanced Loyalist Studies.
www.royalprovincial.com/military/rhist/indp_co_hierlihy/ichmem1.htm

"New York City Regional Geology."
http://3dparks.wr.usgs.gov/nyc/morraines/nycquaternary.htm

Light, Donna M. *The One Third Millennium Celebration.* Unpublished notes: Old Dutch Church of Kingston, NY, 1992.

Onderdonk, Henry, Jr., (ed.) "Desecration of the Dutch Churches in New York During the Revolutionary War," *Long Island and New York in Olden Times.* Jamaica, LI: unpublished collection of newspaper extracts and historical sketches, 1851. heritagequestonline.com

"The Prison Ship Martyrs Monument." www.fortgreeenepark.org/pages/prisonships.htm

Wert, Randall. *Samuel Wirth: Historical Information.* Unpublished research, n. d. www.user.fast.net/~rtwert/nti00108.htm

Index

(The principal biographical information is indicated
by bold page numbers)

10th Continental Regiment 77

1st Brigade 55

1st Connecticut Brigade 259

1st Connecticut Regiment 21, 23, 24, 36, 46

1st Regiment, Connecticut Line 242, 243, 248

20th Regiment of Connecticut Militia 8

2nd Brigade 55, 70, 224

2nd Connecticut Brigade 227

2nd Connecticut Regiment 19, 25, 42, 45, 49, 53

2nd Regiment, Connecticut Line 251

3rd Regiment, Connecticut Line 242, 255

4th Brigade 55

4th Connecticut Regiment 19, 24, 28

4th New York Regiment 42

4th Regiment, Connecticut Line 243, 259

6th Connecticut Regiment 52, 70

7th Connecticut Regiment 46

8th Connecticut Regiment 10, 12, 20, 21, 22, 24, 25, 26, 28, 33, 37, 41

Abel, Anne (Bachus) 37

Abel, Capt. Joshua 37

Adams, John 94, 103

Adams, John Quincy 188

Agnew, General James 125

Albany Pier 181, 182, 185, 193

Allen, Colonel Ethan 24, 166, 169, 176, 182, 185, 217, 218, 219, 222

Amherst, OH 256

Amsterdam 189

Andre, Major John 225

Andrus, Private William 132

Archer, John 154, 177, 237, 238

Arndt, Capt. John 107

Arnold, Benedict 28, 29, 225, 250, 261

Ashford 36, 48

Association Against Illicit Trade 239, 241

Atlee, Colonel Samuel 89, 91, 92, 94, 95, 97, 98, 101, 103, 104, 107, 112, 113, 114, 115, 116, 117, 124, 126, 129, 133, 134, 139, 146, 184, 185

Avery, Corporal Jabez 171, 172

Backus, Benjamin 67

Bailey, Dr. Richard 144, 151, 173

Baldwin, Capt. John 25

Baldwin, Colonel Loammi 59

Barber, Private Daniel 11, 227, 242

Barber, Rev. Daniel 24

Barker, Capt. Joshua 41

Barnard, Capt. Edward 23

Barney, Private Nathan 170

Barrows, Jemima 39, 209, 210, 248

Batt 1, 2, 4

Battle Hill 101, 103, 104, 105, 106, 107, 112, 113, 114, 115, 116, 117, 123, 124, 130, 131, 133, 134, 142, 152, 196

Battle of Bennington 220
Battle of Brooklyn 178
Battle of Bunker Hill 9, 21, 50, 86
Battle of Germantown 224, 250, 255
Battle of Lake George 145
Battle of Monmouth 202, 224, 225, 243, 245, 250, 259
Battle of Saratoga 230, 248
Battle of White Plains 224, 240
Battle Pass 77
Bear Market 149
Beaver, OH 246
Becket, MA 253
Bedford, Long Island 62, 76, 77, 80, 81, 85, 86, 88, 107, 108
Beekman St. 155, 178
Beers, Landlord 165
Benjamin, Captain 165
Bennet, Wynant 92, 126
Bennet's Cove 95
Bennington, Vermont 239
Benton, Daniel 39, 45
Benton, Mary (Wheeler) 39, 45
Benton, Private Azariah 39, **45**
Benton, Sergeant Elisha **39, 248**
Bergen, Simon 81, 82, 90, 97, 179, 216
Berks County, Pennsylvania 89
Berlin 33, 240
Berwick, PA 244
Betts, Landlord 165
Bill, Capt. Beriah 259
Bingham, Jonathan 38
Bingham, Mary (Abbey) 38
Birchard, Jane (Hyde) 36
Birchard, John 36

Bissell, Capt. Ebenezer Fitch 18, **23**, 24, 34, 41, 42, 46, 47, 50, 51, 129, 130, 131, 132, 164, 172, 181, 204, 205, 206, 207, 208, 211, **230**, 232, 257
Bissell, Capt. Ozias **24**, 33, 35, 37, 50, 51, 117, 124, 129, 131, 145, 146, 151, 156, 171, 196, 215, 216, 218, 219, 220, 222, **231**, 235, 256, 259
Bissell, Daniel, Jr. 23
Bissell, Esther 230
Bissell, Hannah (Denslow) 24
Bissell, Israel 8
Bissell, Jerusha (Fitch) 23
Bissell, John 24
Bissell, Mabel 231
Bissell, Mabel (Robarts) 24
Bissell, Sarah (Hoffman) 231
Black facings 67
Block Island 229
Blockje's Bergh 91, 92, 95, 105
Bloomfield 46, 206
Bly, Sergeant Rous **132**
Bolton 24, 41, 47, 195, 196, 197, 211
Boone Co., Kentucky 233
Bost 4, 5
Boston 8, 13, 14, 15, 17, 18, 21, 24, 27, 29, 32, 34, 35, 40, 43, 45, 46, 49, 51, 52, 53, 57, 61, 67, 70, 141, 199, 210, 260
Box, Daniel 63
Bozrah 41, 48, 49, 249
Bradford, Ensign Anthony **35**, 75, 128, 142, 143, 146, 148, 150, 169, 170, 173, 180,

181, 182, 196, 210, 213,
215, 216, 217, 220, 221,
222, 228, **242**

Bradford, Henry   243
Bradford, James   35
Bradford, Jerusha (Thomas) 35
Bradford, Olive (Douglas) 242
Bradley, Colonel Philip Burr
                              245, 250
Brewster, Anne   249
Brewster, Capt. Ebenezer   52
Brewster, Capt. Jonathan   18,
   25, 33, 37, 39, 41, 45, 49,
   51, 56, 128, 130, 131, 146,
   149, 151, 172, 181, 197,
   198, 202, 204, 208, 211,
   228, **231**, 232, 260
Brewster, Dorothy (Witter) 25
Brewster, Elisha, Sr.   35
Brewster, Ensign Elisha **35**, 36,
   243
Brewster, Jonathan, Jr.   232
Brewster, Joseph   25
Brewster, Lucy (Yeomans) 35
Brewster, Margaret (Curtis)
                                    243
Brewster, Mary   232
Brewster, Mary (Williams   25
Brewster, Simon   249
Brick Church   155, 160, 172,
   178
Broad St.   181
Broadway   149, 150, 170
Brockway, Jedediah   261
Brockway, Sarah (Fox)   261
Brodhead, Lt.-Col. Daniel 108
Broo   1, 2, 3, 4
Brooklyn 8, 56, 62, 63, 75, 76,
   77, 78, 79, 80, 81, 82, 85,
   86, 88, 89, 90, 91, 92, 101,

104, 105, 108, 109, 110,
111, 112, 115, 117, 123,
137, 138, 144, 145, 156,
180, 206, 207, 220, 227

Brooklyn Naval Yards   157
Brooklyn, Connecticut   8
Brown, Capt. Stephen   243
Brown, Major   139
Browne, Governor Montfort
                              153, 154
Burd, Major Edward   89
Burg   2
Bushwick, Long Island   218,
   220
Butler County, Ohio   53
Butler, Capt. Zebulon   41, 242
Cambridge, Massachusetts 22
Camillus, NY   261
Canada   18
Canton   47
Cape Ann, Massachusetts   51
Cape Breton Island   17, 69
Case, Josiah   47
Case, Thomas   47
Catlin, Capt. Eli   245
Champion, Colonel   20
Chapman, Elizabeth   244
Chapman, Elizabeth (Abel) 37
Chapman, Ensign Joseph   **36**,
   37, 51, 81, 82, 145, 146,
   147, 216, 217, **243**, 244
Chapman, Lois   244
Chapman, Lois (Birchard)   36
Chapman, Mary   36
Chapman, Thomas   36
Char   5
Charlestown, SC   71
Chase Manhattan Bank   188
Chatham   28, 195, 198, 201,
   202, 233

Chelsea Parade Ground 241
Chelsea, Vermont 249
Cheney, Capt. Timothy 24
Chester, Colonel John 42, 85, 108
Chester, MA 254
chevaux-de-frise 56, 63
Clarence, Niagara Co., NY 249
Clark, Dinah (Bishop) 19
Clark, Eunice (Cook) 19
Clark, Lois 19
Clark, Lt.-Col. 142
Clark, Lt.-Col. Joel **18**, 19, 20, 33, 37, 70, 77, 81, 82, 91, 94, 97, 115, 130, 141, 142, 143, 146, 147, 151, 170, 175, 176, 177, 178, 179, 199, 223
Clark, Moses 19
Clark, Mr. 229
Clark, Silas 19
Clinton, Sir Henry 88
Coe, Sergeant Ebenezer 151
Coit, Abigail (Billings) 39
Coit, Benjamin 39
Coit, Lt.-Col. Samuel 49
Coit, Mehitable (Lester) 241
Coit, Olive (Brewster) 249
Coit, Sarah (Lathrop) 241
Coit, Sergeant Roger **39**, 151, **248**, 249
Coit, Wheeler 241
Coit, William 241
Colchester 14, 15, 41, 56, 165
Condrey, Mr. 229
Cone, Capt. 28
Cone, Esther (Stewart) 45
Cone, Grace 45
Cone, James 45
Cone, Private Rufus **45**, 171

Conn 5
Connecticut General Assembly 12, 20, 128, 193, 203, 217, 235
Connecticut Land Company 246
Connecticut Village 250
Cont 5
Continental Army 12, 26, 65, 199, 224, 225, 227, 241
Continental Congress 7, 12, 55, 65, 148, 216
Continental Establishment 224
Convention Army 230
Corlear's Hook 72
Cornell, Lt.-Col. 110, 257
Cornwallis, Gen. Charles, Lord 81, 88, 106, 107, 110, 111, 112, 257, 258
Cortelyou House 110
Council of Safety 165
Court of Common Pleas 21
Cross, John 48
Cross, Patience (Fuller) 48
Crown Point 24, 30, 227
Curtis, Lois (Belding) 243
Curtis, Samuel 243
Danbury 154, 204, 224, 242
Dandridge, Danske 157, 186, 223, 262
Danville, Vermont 236
Davis, Captain 144
Day, Sergeant 150
De Peyster, Abraham 189
Debuke, Doctor 174
Declaration of Independence 58, 189
DeHeister, General 86, 128, 208
DeLancey, Colonel 238

Delaware 90, 99, 106, 134, 202

Dimock, Capt. Samuel   28

Dorc   4

Dorchester Heights 13, 40, 44, 52, 260

Doughty, Mrs.   151

Douglas, Capt. John   42, 43

Douglas, General John   242

Douglas, Lt.-Col. John   27

Douglas, Susannah   242

Dowdswell, Lt.   141

Driggs, Daniel   40

Driggs, Elizabeth (Strickland)   40

Driggs, Spencer   260

Duane St.   170

Dunn, Captain   142

Durham   34, 38, 201

Durkee, Colonel John   41, 49, 71, 243, 259

Dutton, Private John   130

Duxbury, Massachusetts   41

East   3, 4

East Haddam   28, 40, 45, 53

East Hampton   202, 233

East Hartford   49

East River 56, 62, 63, 77, 137, 156, 187, 193, 215

Eastbury   27

Ellis, Bethiah   228

Ellis, Bethiah (Palmer)   22

Ellis, Caleb   22

Ellis, Private Joseph   228

Ellis, Rev. John   **22**, 79, **227**, 228

Ellsworth, Capt. Charles   35, 200

Elmore, Capt. Samuel   41

Ely, Capt. Christopher   51

Emerson, Private Theophilus   171

Enos, Colonel Roger   50, 245

Fairfield, NY   258

Fanning, Anne (Reynolds)   34

Fanning, Lt. Thomas   **34**, 125, 143, 146, 182, 216, 239, **241**, 242

Fanning, Lucy (Coit)   241

Fanning, Lydia (Coit)   241

Fanning, Lydia (Tracy)   241

Fanning, Thomas, Sr.   34

Farmington   37, 195, 196

Filer, Allyn   46

Filer, Asa   46

Filer, Capt. Abraham *See* Tyler, Capt. Abraham

Filer, Jeremiah   46

Filer, Jerusha   46

Filer, Jerusha (Kelsey)   46

Filer, Private Roger   **46**, 164, 206, 207

Filer, Roger, Jr.   46

Filer, Roxy   46

Filer, Tryphena (Wolcott) Allyn   46

Fire Brand   234

Fishkill, NY   246

Fitch Hannah (Perkins)   30

Fitch, Ann (Knowlton)   30

Fitch, Capt. Adonijah   30, 41

Fitch, Colonel Eleazer   49

Fitch, Cordilla   150

Fitch, Elisha   214, 218

Fitch, Hannah   235

Fitch, Jabez   30

Fitch, Lt. Jabez **30**, 35, 55, 56, 67, 77, 78, 79, 81, 82, 90, 94, 97, 103, 112, 115, 117, 124, 125, 126, 138, 139,

146, 148, 150, 154, 158,
  171, 178, 179, 181, 196,
  208, 213, 214, 215, 216,
  217, 218, 221, 225, 227,
  228, 231, 232, **235**, 236,
  239, 240, 243, 244, 245,
  248, 251
Flatbush 75, 76, 77, 78, 79, 80,
  81, 85, 86, 88, 97, 106, 107,
  109, 110, 116, 117, 127,
  128, 141, 142, 143, 144,
  146, 155, 162, 204, 205,
  215, 226
Flatbush Pass   76, 78, 109
Flatlands   75, 76, 82, 88, 215
Fletcher, Private John   182
Floyd, NY   256
Foreign Missions   225
Fort Box   63
Fort Edward   30, 232
Fort Greene Park   157
Fort Independence   56
Fort Mifflin   243, 259
Fort Putnam   63, 137, 157
Fort Ticonderoga 13, 166, 218,
  259
Fort Washington157, 158, 162,
  164, 173, 185, 186, 191,
  192, 205
Fort William Henry   30
Fox, Ezekiel   22
Fox, Mehitabel   22
Francis, Capt. John   242
Franklin   228
Franklin, Connecticut   22
Franklin, Henry   157
Freehold, Albany Co., New
  York   233
French   18

French and Indian War 18, 19,
  23, 24, 25, 27, 28, 29, 30,
  31, 41, 46, 47, 79, 132, 152,
  232, 236
Frenchmen   176, 177, 180
Fuller, Abigail (Wentworth) 46
Fuller, Elana   252
Fuller, Judah   46
Fuller, Polly Davis   252
Fuller, Private Abner   57
Fuller, Private Gad   130
Fuller, Private Lemuel **46**, 130,
  208, **252**, 253
Fulton St.   170
Garden St.   155
Gardner, Private John   57
Gate   2
Gibbs, Caty (Johnson)   253
Gibbs, Charlotte (Tourgee) 253
Gibbs, Lucy   253
Gibbs, Private Samuel   **253**
Giles, Mr.   176
Gillet, Almira   244
Gillet, Elizabeth   238
Gillet, Elizabeth (Steele)   31
Gillet, Ensign Joel   **37**, 125,
  130, **244**, 245
Gillet, Jonathan, Jr.   238
Gillet, Lt. Jonathan**31**, 82, 124,
  146, 150, 154, 162, 164,
  171, 177, 206, 217, **237**, 238
Gillet, Rhoda (Hinsdale)   244
Gillet, Zachariah   37
Gist, Major Mordecai   91
Glastonbury   25, 26, 42, 49,
  198, 201, 233, 255
Goodrich, Capt. Isaac   255
Gordon, Corporal George   **43**,
  151, 177, 215, **251**, 252
Gordon, George, Sr.   43

Gordon, Jennet (Gibson)   43
Gove, Elizabeth   31
Gove, Esther   239
Gove, Esther (Tyler)   31
Gove, Lt. Nathaniel   **31**, 146, 150, 170, 217, 221, **238**, 239, 245
Gove, Nathaniel, Sr.   31
Governor's Island   56, 63
Gowanus 62, 63, 75, 76, 77, 80, 81, 85, 86, 89, 90, 91, 94, 95, 101, 104, 105, 106, 110, 111, 112, 113, 114, 117, 123, 125, 126, 127, 138, 148, 216, 226, 244
Grafton County, NH   252
Grand Street   55
Grant, Capt. Noah   24
Grant, General James   86, 88, 95, 97, 98, 110, 126, 139
Grant, Lt.-Col. James   98, 100, 103, 104, 105, 106, 107
Granville, MA   253
Graves, Benjamin   40
Graves, Elizabeth (Driggs)   40
Graves, Mary (Jones)   40
Graves, Sergeant Roswell   **40**, 126, 127, 140, 152, 177, 180
Gravesend   75, 76, 140, 142, 143, 215
Graydon, Capt. Alexander   60, 166, 185
Great Awakening   17
Green, Borrodil (Bennet)   170
Green, Mr. Francis   32
Green, Private Caleb   **169**
Green, Winter   169
Greene, General Nathanael   62, 63, 64, 70
Greeneville   15

Greenwich   231
Green-Wood Cemetery   76, 92, 101
Greenwood Hills   76, 91, 92, 94, 112, 117
Griffing, Private Jaspar   177
Griswold   169, 250
Griswold, Lieutenant Governor   11
Groton   259
H.M.S. Argo   148
H.M.S. Centurion   221
H.M.S. Charming Polly   221
H.M.S. Glasgow 185, 186, 187, 191, 192, 193, 194, 195, 196, 197, 198, 199, 200, 201, 202, 204, 205, 206, 207, 208, 209, 210, 223, 229, 244, 248, 249, 250, 255, 257, 258, 260, 261
H.M.S. Judith   221, 232, 233
H.M.S. Lord Rochford   142, 143, 147, 148
H.M.S. Mentor   143, 144, 145, 146, 147, 148, 149, 178, 221, 243, 251
H.M.S. Myrtle   221
H.M.S. Pacific   140, 142, 146
H.M.S. Rose   11
H.M.S. Whitby   145, 146, 148, 156, 157, 160, 165, 204, 205, 223, 257, 259
Hackensack, NJ   253
Haddam 28, 29, 37, 40, 45, 53, 195, 235, 245
Halifax   64
Halifax, Vermont   250
Hall, Capt. James   249
Halsey, Ensign Jeremiah   259

Hamilton, Colonel Alexander 251

Hampden Hall 149, 150, 151, 153, 154, 158, 170, 171, 173, 176, 180, 192, 193, 213, 237, 238, 241, 242, 244, 245, 246, 247, 248, 251

Hand, Colonel Edward 60, 75, 77, 78, 89

Harlem 147, 161, 200, 211

Harney, Lt. 99

Harris, Lt. John 143, 181

Hartford 14, 21, 22, 24, 27, 51, 164, 165, 200, 206, 226, 229, 259, 260

Harwinton 37, 244

Haslet, Colonel John 90, 91, 92, 99, 111

Havana 21, 24, 46, 49

Hayden, Abigail 242

Hayden, Abigail (Parsons) 34

Hayden, Capt. Nathaniel 34

Hayden, Daniel 23, 34

Hayden, Ebenezer 230

Hayden, Elizabeth (Mather) 40

Hayden, Esther 23

Hayden, Esther (Moore) 23, 34

Hayden, Lt. Thomas **34**, 40, 230, **242**

Hayden, Naomi (Gaylord) 40

Hayden, Nathaniel 40

Hayden, Sergeant Hezekiah **40**, 73, 74, 172, 205

Hazen, Private Jacob 56, 131, 232

Heart, Lt.-Col. Selah 217

Heath, General William 55, 62

Hebron 47, 48, 132

Hell Gate 221

Henshaw, Lt.-Col. 110

Hessians 72, 78, 80, 81, 92, 107, 109, 110, 113, 116, 117, 123, 124, 125, 126, 127, 128, 129, 156, 248, 259

Hickey, Thomas 57

Hierlihey, Capt. Timothy 49

Hierlihy, Major Timothy 152, 153

Hierlihy, Timothy, Jr. 152

Higgins, Cornelius, Sr. 37

Higgins, Eleanor (Hazelton) 37

Higgins, Ensign Cornelius **37**, 38, 128, 146, 170, 171, 176, 177, 216, 238, **245**, 246

Higgins, Esther 245

Higgins, Esther (Kelsey) 38

Higgins, Peter Page 246

Higgins, Sarah (Hawes) 37

Highlanders 116, 117

Higley, Apphia (Humphreys) 47

Higley, Hester 47

Higley, Hester (Case) 47

Higley, John 47

Higley, Private Carmi **47**

Higley, Private Obed 129, 131

Hills, Ebenezer 49

Hinman, Colonel Benjamin 24

Hinman, Royal R. 133

Hinsdale, MA 254

Hitchcock, Amos 129

Hitchcock, Colonel Daniel 85, 109, 110

Holcomb, Capt. Nathaniel 21, 23

Holland Land Company 250

Holmes, Hannah (Halsey) 22

Holmes, Jabez 230

Holmes, John 22

Holmes, Louisa 230

Holmes, Louisa (Fox)   22
Holmes, Silas, Jr.   230
Holmes, Surgeon's Mate Silas
   22, 144, 146, 151, 155, 171,
   173, **229**
Holy Ground   170
Hop Meadow Burying Ground
   227
Hopkins, Adjutant Elisha   **22**,
   146, **228**
Hopkins, Elisha   22
Hopkins, Elisha B.   229
Hopkins, Ensign Elisha   214,
   229
Hopkins, Frederick   23, 229
Hopkins, Martha
   (Buckingham)   23
Hopkins, Sarah (Hopkins)
   Sims   229
Horn, Doctor   139
Horse Neck   231, 238
Horseneck   261
Howard, William   88, 216
Howard's Tavern   220
Howe, Admiral Lord Richard
   64
Howe, General William 64, 76,
   85, 86, 88, 105, 133, 141,
   183, 184, 185, 216
Hubbard, Capt. David, Jr.   27
Hubbard, Capt. Elizur   **25**, 26,
   27, 31, 34, 38, 42, 47, 48,
   50, 56, 128, 131, 132, 151,
   172, 197, 198, 200, 201,
   205, **232**, 233, 234, 255, 260
Hubbard, Commissary General
   241
Hubbard, David   26
Hubbard, Huldah Brainerd 233
Hubbard, Lois   233

Hubbard, Lois (Wright)   26
Hubbard, Private Elihu   25
Hubbard, Prudence (Goodrich)
   26
Hubbell, Capt. William C.   45
Hudson Highlands   228
Hudson River   18, 56
Hudson, NY   260
Huguenot   215
Hull, Colonel   228
Humphreys, Asenath   21, 227
Humphreys, Capt. Noah   21
Humphreys, Col. Jonathan   21
Humphreys, Desire (Owen)   21
Humphreys, Elihu, Jr.   227
Humphreys, Esq. John   21
Humphreys, Lydia (Reed)   21
Humphreys, Major Elihu   **21**,
   81, **225**, 226, 227
Humphreys, Ophelia   227
Humphreys, Private Joel   131
Humphreys, Rowena   227
Humphreys, Sterling   227
Humphreys, Young   227
Hungerford, Sergeant Uriah
   171
Hunt   5
Huntington, Ann (Moore)   224
Huntington, Colonel Jedediah
   7, 8, 10, 17, 19, 23, 26, 33,
   35, 37, 38, 39, 41, 46, 48,
   49, 123, 129, 135, 204, **223**,
   224, 225, 227, 240, 241,
   243, 248, 254, 262
Huntington, Ebenezer   7, 231,
   241
Huntington, Faith (Trumbull)7,
   10
Huntington, Freelove (Chester)
   239

Huntington, Jabez   7, 26
Huntington, Joshua   7, 19, 241
Huntington, Lois (Hyde)   41
Huntington, Lt. Simeon **32**, 33, **239**, 240
Huntington, Patience (Keene)
       240
Huntington, Peter   32
Huntington, Phebe (Hall)   249
Huntington, Private Thomas
       131
Huntington, Ruth   249
Huntington, Ruth (Edgerton)32
Huntington, Ruth (Talcott)   41
Huntington, Samuel   7
Huntington, Sergeant
    Theophilus   **41**, 128, 171, 172, 202, **249**
Huntington, Sergeant Uriah130
Huntington, Theophilus, Sr. 41
Huntington's 8th Connecticut
    Regiment 11, 22, 23, 25, 27, 28, 29, 31, 33, 34, 35, 39, 42, 43, 48, 49, 51, 176, 198, 199, 200, 261
Huntington's Brigade 224, 225
Hyde Park, Vermont   235, 236
Hyde, Jedediah   235
Ingham, Alexander   254
Ingham, Catherine (Noble)   47
Ingham, Daniel   48
Ingham, Dr. Samuel   47
Ingham, Mahitabel (Phelps) 48
Ingham, Molly (Wright)   254
Ingham, Private Alexander **47**, **132**
Ingham, Private Solomon   10, 14, 26, **48**, 56, 64, 67, 131, 132, **253**, 254
Ingham, Ruth   47

Ingham, Thomas   47
Jackson, Colonel Henry   257
Jamaica Pass   76, 80, 86, 88, 107
Jamaica Road   76, 77, 86, 88, 107, 108, 109, 110, 216
Jamaica, Long Island   48
Jenkins, Mrs.   218, 219, 220, 231
Jennings, Corporal Oliver   **43**, 44, 45, 182, 210
Jennings, David   43
Jennings, Joanne (Clerk)   43
Jennings, Sarah (Turner)   43
Jewett, Capt. Joseph **27**, 28, 31, 38, 40, 41, 45, 46, 47, 52, 53, 56, 78, 124, 125, 126, 128, 130, 131, 132, 138, 139, 141, 147, 148, 152, 171, 176, 197, 198, 200, 202, 203, 204, 206, 208, 223, 243, 250, 252, 253
Jewett, Deborah (Lord)   27
Jewett, Lucretia (Rogers)   27
Jewett, Nathan   27
Jewett, NY   257
Johnson, Mary (Edson)   256
Johnson, Seth   256
Johnston, Colonel Philip   85, 109
Johnston, Henry P.   109, 139
Jones' Hill   55
Kellogg, Private Phineas   131
Kichlein, Lt.-Col. Peter 89, 91, 92, 94, 100, 104, 105, 106, 107, 112, 129, 147
Killingly   170, 198, 201
Killingworth   235
King George's War   17
King's Bridge   56, 62, 64, 72

Kings Bridge 145, 211
King's Ferry 220
Kingsbury, Private John **48**
Kingsbury, Sarah (Spalding)48
Kingsbury, Stephen 48
Kingston, New York 188, 189
Kinsman, Ensign John **38**, 146, 150, 216, 218, **246**, 247
Kinsman, Jeremiah 38
Kinsman, Rebecca (Perkins) 246
Kinsman, Sarah (Thomas) 38
Kinsman, Trumbull Co., OH 246
Kips Bay 147
Kyes, Doctor 180
Lafayette, General 251, 274
Laidlie, Rev. Archibald 160
Lake Champlain 18
Lake George 18, 24, 60, 259
Lambert, Captain 142
Lancaster, PA 246
Lasher, Colonel 161, 178
Lasley, Mrs. S. 150
Lawrence, Private James 132
Lebanon 7, 15, 31
Lebanon, NH 249
Ledlie, Capt. Hugh 25
Lee, 5
Lee, General Charles 62, 71, 224
Lefferts, Judge 78
Lesley, Mrs. 175, 177
Lewis, Bathsheba (Swift) 172
Lewis, Eleanor 255
Lewis, George 172
Lewis, John, Jr. 255
Lewis, Martha (Mills) Denton 48

Lewis, Private John 45, **48**, 49, 172, **254**, 255
Lewis, Private Lemuel **172**
Lewis, Reuben 49
Lewis, Sarah 255
Lewis, Sarah (Cross) 48
Lewis, Sergeant Bartlett 171, **172**
Lexington Alarm List 28, 29, 30, 31, 33, 35, 39, 40, 41, 42, 43, 45, 46
Lexington and Concord 8, 9, 24, 27, 34
Liberty St. 238, 240, 280
Light Dragoons 36, 69
Lisbon 246
Little, Colonel Moses 85, 109
Livingston, General William 133
Livingston, Rev. 188
Londers, Samuel 57
Long Island Sound 15, 46, 153, 187, 193, 209
Loring, Joshua 141, 142, 171, 181, 192, 226, 248
Loring, Mrs. 141
Louisbourg 17, 18, 19, 69
Loveland, Elisha 49
Loveland, Esther 255
Loveland, Esther (Hills) 49
Loveland, Hannah (Hills) 49
Loveland, Private Levi **49**, **255**
Lower East Side 55
Loyalist 57, 141, 153
Lutz, Colonel 77, 89
Lyman, Alfred 247
Lyman, Colonel Phineas 21, 30, 31, 46, 47, 49

Lyman, Ensign Elihu **38**, 82, 145, 146, 152, 153, 178, 216, 217, 221, **247**

Lyman, General Phineas 27

Lyman, Hope (Hawley) 38

Lyman, John 38

Lyman, Maria 247

Lyme11, 27, 37, 41, 51, 52, 53, 197, 200, 206, 253, 258, 261

MacDonough, Major Thomas 91

Madison, OH 256

Magaw, Colonel Robert 60, 184, 185

Makepeace, Gershom 34

Makepeace, Jane (Elyot) 34

Makepeace, Lt. Solomon **34**, 51, 146, 151, 152, 223

Manh 4, 5

Manhattan Island 55, 63, 145, 147, 148

Manning, Diah 32

Mansfield 28, 48

Martense Lane 76, 81, 85, 89, 95

Martin, Colonel Ephraim 79

Maryland 85, 90, 92, 106, 107, 111, 134

Masonic Grand Lodge 239

Mather, Capt. Timothy 41

Mather, Nathaniel 40

Mather, Private Increase 132

Maxfield, John 57

McLellan, Colonel 235

Meigs, Colonel R.J. 259

Mentgis, Lt. Francis 100

Mercein, Andrew 162

Middle Collegiate Church 189

Middle Dutch Church155, 157, 158, 160, 161, 162, 171,

187, 188, 189, 211, 238, 240, 244, 248, 250, 257

Middlebury 247

Middlebury, Vermont 255

Middlefield 38

Middlefield, MA 254

Middletown 25, 35, 36, 38, 152, 153, 172, 206, 243, 260

Middletown, Connecticut 25

Miels, Capt. Charles 261

Mifflin, Commissary-General Thomas 15

Miles, Colonel Samuel 77, 86, 88, 107, 108, 143, 170, 184, 185

Milford 16, 192, 193, 194, 195, 196, 197, 198, 200, 201, 202, 203, 204, 206, 207, 208, 209, 210, 223, 244, 249, 250, 257, 260, 261

Miller, Private Elisha 176

Mini 4

Ministerial Troops 16

Mitchel, Private Adam 171

Moffat, Private Ishmael **170**

Moffatt, Elizabeth (Bennit) 170

Moffatt, John 170

Monckton, Lt.-Col. 114

Montreal 21, 166

Montresor's Island 161

Montville 41, 45

Moody, Private John 164

Moody, Samuel 164

Moore, Thomas 224

Morristown Huts 250

Moses, Caleb 50

Moses, Hannah (Beaman) 50

Moses, Mary (Wilcox) 50

Moses, Private Daniel **50**

Mott, Capt. Edward 259

Moulton, Colonel Stephen 177, 256
Moulton, Eleanor (Converse)   50
Moulton, Elizabeth   256
Moulton, Howard   50
Moulton, Private Salmon **50**, 129, 142, 145, 177, 204, **256**
Moulton, Sergeant Howard   177, 256
Moulton, Stephen   50
Moulton, Susanna (Johnson)   256
Mount Prospect Range 75, 76
Murdock, Private Elisha 132
Murray St.   148
Murrayfield, MA   254
Mutual Life Insurance Company   188
Myer, Adolph   161
Naples, NY   258
Narrows 72, 75, 76, 85, 89
Nassau St.   155, 178
Nellis, Samantha (Stanton) 258
New   3, 5
New Concord   48
New Dutch Church *See* Middle Dutch Church
New England Militia 17, 18
New Haven 18, 28, 33, 165, 194, 221, 232, 234, 260, 261, 272
New Jersey 56, 64, 72, 79, 85, 109, 110, 202, 220, 253, 259
New London 10, 14, 15, 40, 45, 48, 52, 53, 198, 201, 224, 225, 229, 233, 235, 236, 240, 250, 256, 260, 261

New Lots 82, 215, 217, 218, 220, 228, 240, 242, 243, 244, 245, 246
New Milford   257
New Providence, Bahamas 153
New Utrecht 75, 76, 142, 144, 145, 151, 155, 171, 173, 196, 205, 215, 233
New York   14, 17
New York Post Office   188
New York's Liberty Bell   189
Newcomb, Mary (Young) 51
Newcomb, Private Robert **51**
Newcomb, Robert, Sr.   51
Nort   2
North Dutch Church 155, 157, 158, 160
North Kingston, RI   259
North Lyme   27
North River   56, 72
North Stonington   22
Northern Army   16
Northern Department   29
Norwich 7, 8, 9, 12, 14, 15, 19, 22, 25, 30, 32, 33, 34, 36, 37, 38, 41, 46, 48, 49, 51, 67, 150, 195, 197, 198, 200, 204, 214, 218, 224, 225, 228, 231, 235, 239, 241, 244, 249, 252, 259
Norwich Mutual Assurance Company   241
Nova   4
Nova Scotia   17, 64, 154
Ohio County, VA   252
Old Dutch Church 155, 160, 188
Olmstead, Private Daniel 132
Onderdonk, Henry   220

Orcutt, Lt. Solomon **33**, 98, 113, 128, 146, 150, 154, 216, 217, **240**
Orcutt, Mary (Rockwell) 33
Orcutt, Sarah 33
Orcutt, William 33
Otis, James 41
Otis, Lucy 250
Otis, Lucy (Chandler) 41
Otis, Sarah (Tudor) 41
Otis, Sergeant Stephen **41**, 143, **250**
Palmer, Elijah 230
Park Row 178
Parry, Lt.-Col. 98, 99, 103, 134
Parsons, General Samuel H. 40, 51, 52, 70, 71, 89, 90, 91, 94, 95, 97, 103, 104, 107, 112, 113, 114, 115, 116, 117, 129, 133, 134, 135, 145, 180, 205, 206, 211
Partridgefield, MA 255
Paulus Hook 56, 72
Payson, Colonel Nathan 31
Pearl St. 155
Pease, Major Abiel 256
Peekskill, New York 224, 240, 250, 252, 253
Pember, Samuel 251
Pember, Thomas 251
Pemberton, Patrick 239
Pennsylvania Rifle Regiment 77, 86, 89, 143, 147
Pennsylvania riflemen 75, 77, 94, 104, 105, 107, 129
Percival, Capt. Timothy 14, **28**, 31, 40, 52, 66, 125, 128, 130, 131, 132, 143, 145, 150, 151, 164, 169, 171,

195, 196, 203, 213, 216, 217, 221, **233**
Percival, Hannah (Whitmore) 28
Percival, John 28
Percival, Mary 233
Percival, Mary (Fuller) 28
Percival, Private Timothy 143, 145, 233
Percy, Hugh, Earl 88
Perkins, Jabez 30
Perkins, May Olive (Douglas) 246
Perkins, Simon 246
Phelps, Capt. Ichabod 47
Philadelphia 8, 12, 94, 224, 229
Phillipsburg, NY 250, 261
Pickett, Benjamin 257
Pickett, Eunice 257
Piermont, NH 252
Pintard, John 161
Pintard, Lewis 161
Piper, Colonel 147
Pitkin, Capt. George 24
Pitkin, Lt.-Col. John 24
Plainfield 35, 48, 201, 207, 242
Plainfield Union Manufacturing Co. 243
Pomfret 8, 10
Poquetanuck 25
Port Road 92, 106, 109, 110
Portland 172
Potter, Private Isaac 130
Powers, Private James 132
Pratt, Hannah (Picket) 257
Pratt, Private Zadock **51**, 145, 158, 204, **257**
Pratt, Zadock, Jr. 257
Pratt, Zephaniah 51
Pratt, Abigail 51

Prentice, Lt.-Col. Samuel 224
Presbyterian Church 151, 155
Preston 25, 31, 35, 36, 39, 49, 52, 132, 198, 200, 202, 208, 232, 239, 249, 259
Priestly, Lt. 221
Prince of Wales American Regiment 153
Princeton, New Jersey 184
Prison Ship Martyrs 157
Prospect Hills 75
Prospect Park 77, 78, 117
Protestant Reformation 18
Providence, Rhode Island 9, 14
Provost 59, 219, 220, 222, 231
Punderson, Ebenezer 150
Putnam, Colonel Rufus 61, 63
Putnam, General Israel 20, 62, 79, 80, 90
Quaker Church 155, 160, 172, 174, 176
Queen St. 174
Queens County 144
Randolph, Vermont 240, 251
Rapalje, Daniel 220
Rapelye, George 215
Raymond, Corporal Nathan **45**, 128
Raymond, Joshua 45
Raymond, Lucy (Jewett) 45
Reading, Massachusetts 48
Red Hook 56, 63, 77, 80, 86, 161
Red Lion Tavern76, 85, 89, 90, 91, 107, 180
Reed, Colonel Joseph 133
Rehoboth, Massachusetts 228
Remsen, Colonel 178
Remsen's Mill 156

Rhode Island85, 132, 191, 230, 233, 235, 259
Ridge St 55
Ripley, Capt. John 23
Rivington, James 178
Robinson, Capt. Elijah 42
Robinson, Lt. Elijah 50
Rochambeau, General 259
Rochester, NY 258
Rockwell, Margaret 33
Rockwell, Samuel 33
Rogers, Elizabeth (Hyde) 27
Rogers, Theophilus 27
Root, Representative 20
Rose, Private Elijah **169**, 170
Rose, Sarah (Harris) 170
Rose, Thomas 170
Rowley, Capt. Abijah 10, 31, 35, 48, 176
Roxb 5
Roxbury 8, 9, 10, 11, 19, 34, 40, 42, 43, 44, 45, 48, 49, 50, 52, 53, 70, 210, 258, 261
Royal Highlanders 101
Russell, Huldah (Pember) 251
Russell, Mareitje (or Mary) (Hoff) 42
Russell, Samuel 42
Russell, Sergeant Cornelius **42**, **250**
Rutland, Vermont 239
Sabin, Lt.-Co. Hezekiah, Jr. 242
Sabine, W.H.W. 150, 218
Sandy Hook 64
Sanford, Capt. Ezekiel 250
Saybrook 53, 235
Setauket (Brookhaven), Long Island 42
Seven Years War 18

Sharpe, Gen. George H.   188
Sheffield, MA   253
Shelburne, MA   250
Sheldon, Colonel   36
Sherman, James   28
Shetucket River   15
Sill, Capt. David Fithian   52
Simsbury 11, 21, 50, 197, 200,
    226, 227
Skinner, Nathaniel, Jr.   56
Skinner, Sergeant Samuel   **56**
Slade, William   157
smallpox   23, 180, 193, 197,
    200, 201, 202, 203, 206,
    208, 209, 210, 213, 216,
    217, 248, 249, 257, 258
Smallwood, Colonel William
    90, 91, 92, 111, 112, 133
Smith, Sergeant Moses   181,
    195, 196
Snake Hill, New Jersey   187
Society of the Cincinnati   225,
    247, 251
Sons of Liberty 7, 30, 32, 149
Southington   19, 37, 130, 247
Spalding, Doctor   213
Sparks, Private Jeremiah   45
Spen   5
Spence, Mister   141
Spencer, General Joseph   14,
    20, 41, 42, 45, 49, 52, 53,
    55, 62, 70, 233
Spencer's redoubt   55
Springfield, MA   257
St. Johns, Newfoundland   154
Stafford   33, 34, 50, 151, 205
Stamford   253
Stanton, Dinah   52
Stanton, Private Daniel   52

Stanton, Private Elijah **52**, 128,
    203, **257**, 258
Staten Island 56, 64, 71, 72, 75,
    142
Stedman, Capt.   99
Stephentown, NY   257
Sterling City   259
Sterling, Abigail   52, 258
Sterling, Edey   258
Sterling, Edey (Tucker)   52
Sterling, Jane (Ransom)   52
Sterling, John   52
Sterling, Private Jacob **52**, 197,
    200, **258**
Sterling, Stephen   258
Stewart, James   45
Stewart, Keziah   45
Stewart, Lt.   99
Stiles, Henry   105, 129
Stirling, Gen. William
    Alexander, Lord   55, 80, 81,
    90, 91, 94, 95, 98, 100, 110,
    113, 153, 179, 180
Stonington   22, 229
Stonington Point   11
Stony Point   257, 259
Stratford   28, 165
Strong, Corp. John   14
Suffield   34
Suffolk County   144
Sugarhouse 206, 226, 238, 240
Sullivan, General John 46, 62,
    70, 71, 77, 78, 79, 85, 88,
    97, 106, 107, 109, 110, 257
Sunderland, Mr.   177
Sunderland, Vermont   255
Swift, Colonel Heman   202,
    228, 251
Talmage, Benjamin   42, 172
Talmage, Samuel   42, 172

Talmage, Sergeant William **42**, 172

Talmage, Susannah (Smith) 42

Talman, Private Samuel 127

Thomas, General John 38

Thomas, Private Daniel 124, 128, 145, 156, 205, **259**

Throop, Lt. Benjamin 259

Throop, Lt. Robert 147

Ticonderoga 24

Tiverton, RI 257

Tolland 33, 39, 45, 48, 49, 209, 210, 231, 248, 253

Tracy, Ensign Joshua **38**, 39, **248**

Tracy, John 38

Tracy, Lt. Hezekiah 248

Tracy, Margaret (Hyde) 38

Tracy, Naomi 248

Tracy, Naomi (Bingham) 38

Tracy, Private Dudley 132

Tracy, Samuel 241

Tracy, Sergeant Rufus 143, 176, 181

Tracy, Sibyl (Lathrop) 241

Trenton, New Jersey 184

Trinity Church 221

Trowbridge, Anna (Sherman) 28

Trowbridge, Capt. Caleb **28**, 29, 35, 43, 48, 57, 125, 131, 145, 147, 150, 151, 152, 169, 170, 181, 182, 195, 198, 201, 207, 216, 217, 221, **233**, 234, 251

Trowbridge, Joseph 28

Trowbridge, Mary 234

Trowbridge, Mary (Woodward) 28

Troy, NY 256

Trumbull, Benjamin 78

Trumbull, Governor Jonathan 7, 8, 15, 19, 33, 58, 178, 214, 228

Trumbull, John 9

Truro, Massachusetts 51, 211

Tryon, Governor William 154, 177, 224, 232

Tubbs, Benjamin 14

Turner, Private Seth 26, 128, 205, **260**

Turner, Private William 182

Turner, Sarah (Hall) 260

Tyler, Capt. Abraham **29**, 33, 38, 39, 43, 44, 57, 131, 154, 171, 172, 182, 195, 202, 209, **234**, 235

Tyler, Capt. John 40

Tyler, Capt. Moses 31

Tyler, Col. Abraham 29

Tyler, Colonel John 71, 77, 78

Tyler, Eunice (Arnold) 29

Tyler, Jedidah 235

Tyler, Jedidah (Thomas) 29

Valley Forge 224, 250, 255

Van Buren, NY 261

Vanderbilt, Mr. Rem 142

Vandervoort, Mr. 67

Vandeveer, Widow 217, 243

VanZandt, Capt. 221, 222

Vernon 231

Vesey St. 149

Virginia 71, 230, 252

Voluntown 43

Wadsworth, Colonel 20

Waldo, Surgeon John 70

Wall St. 155

Wallabout 62, 63, 156

Wallace, Captain James 11

Ward, Colonel Andrew 235

Ward, Colonel Artemus   20
Warren St.   149
Warren, Massachusetts   34
Wash   3, 5
Washington, General George
     12, 13, 14, 15, 16, 26, 42,
     56, 59, 65, 79, 80, 94, 111,
     112, 129, 133, 134, 137,
     153, 184, 211, 214, 225,
     228, 258
Washington, MA   255
Watch Hill Point   229
Waterbury, Colonel   20
Waterbury, General David 261
Waterman, Eleazer   261
Waterman, Elijah   261
Waterman, Priscilla   261
Waterman, Private Calvin **260**
Waterman, Thomas   261
Watson, John   162
Way, Lucy (Brockway)   261
Way, Private Peter   **53, 261**
Webb, Colonel Charles   45
Webb, Colonel Samuel B. 228
Weed, Capt. Thaddeus   250
Wells, Capt.   28
Wells, Capt. Edmund   47
Wells, Colonel Levi   231, 256
Wells, Major Levi   164, 165,
     170, 181, 182, 220, 221
Wert, Lt. George   170
West Hartford   31, 164
West Point   225, 257, 258
Westchester County   155, 261
Western Reserve   246, 247
Wethersfield 16, 42, 197, 198,
     199, 208, 240, 243
Weybridge, Vermont   255
Wheeler, Private Libeus   142
White Plains   23, 257

White, Corporal Joseph   154,
     169
Whiting, Colonel Nathan   47,
     198, 201
Whiting, Private John   132
Whittlesey, Abigail (Chapman)
     53
Whittlesey, Joseph   53
Whittlesey, Private Duroy   **53,**
     171
Wilcox, Azariah   50
Wilkes Barre, PA   244
Willes, Capt. Solomon   45, 49
Willes, Lt.-Col. Solomon   85
William Howard's Tavern   88
William St.   155
Williams, Joseph   25
Willington   33, 43, 44
Windham   32, 38, 195, 198,
     208, 229
Windham, NY   257
Windsor 8, 23, 34, 40, 42, 173,
     197, 200, 205, 206, 230,
     237, 242, 251
Wing, Abner   254
Winter Hill   46
Woburn, Massachusetts   59
Wolcott, Abigail (Colley)   46
Wolcott, Colonel   50
Wolcott, Henry   46
Woodhull, General Nathaniel
     86, 144, 145, 151
Wooster, Colonel David   29
Wooster, General   20
Worcester   8
Wrentham, MA   8
Wright, James   26
Wright, Lois (Loomis)   26
Wright, Lt. Abraham   **33, 240**
Wright, Rebeccah   240

Wright, Rebeckah (Norton) 33
Wright, Sergeant Ebenezer115,
  117, 152, 195, 196, 197
Wyckoff, Nicholas　　　　216
Wykoff's Hill　　92, 95, 105

Wyllys, Colonel Samuel70, 85,
  108, 142, 164, 242, 255
Wyllys, Hezekiah　　　　165
Yorktown　　　　　251, 257
Youngstown, OH　　　　246
Zedwitz, Lt.-Col.　　　　90

ABOUT THE AUTHOR

CHARLES H. LEWIS is a retired manager with the Connecticut State Department of Correction, and former 1st Selectman (Chief Elected Official) of the Town of Canaan (Falls Village), Connecticut. In retirement he has become an avid historian and genealogist, and is the author of *John Lewis of Berkshire, Vermont, and Other Descendants of William Lewis (Who Came to Boston on the Ship "The Lion" in 1632) through His Grandson James Lewis of Jamaica, Long Island* (Heritage Books, 2004). He also assisted with the editing and posthumous publication of the memoirs of his missionary and diplomat grandfather, Robert E. Lewis, entitled, *Search of Far Horizons* (Brian K. Lewis, Ph.D., ed.; Infinity Publishing, 2004).

34627728R00178

Made in the USA
Middletown, DE
28 August 2016